Accustomed to Obedience?

Accustomed to Obedience?

Classical Ionia and the Aegean World, 480–294 BCE

❦

Joshua P. Nudell

University of Michigan Press

Ann Arbor

For questions or permissions, please contact um.press.perms@umich.edu

Published in the United States of America by the
University of Michigan Press
Manufactured in the United States of America
Printed on acid-free paper
First published March 2023

A CIP catalog record for this book is available from the British Library.

Library of Congress Cataloging-in-Publication data has been applied for.

ISBN 978-0-472-13337-6 (hardcover : alk. paper)
ISBN 978-0-472-90387-0 (OA)
DOI: https://doi.org/10.3998/mpub.12067181

The University of Michigan Press's open access publishing program is made
possible thanks to additional funding from the University of Michigan Office of
the Provost and the generous support of contributing libraries.

For my grandmothers,
Charlotte Nudell and Charlotte Spaulding

Contents

Digital materials related to this title can be found on
the Fulcrum platform via the following citable URL:
https://doi.org/10.3998/mpub.12067181

Maps

A Note to the Reader

The transliteration of Greek names into English is a chronic problem. I have anglicized names and terms except where common usage dictates otherwise. Translations of ancient sources are identified in the notes; all unattributed translations are my own. All dates are BCE unless otherwise indicated. Journal titles are abbreviated as in *L'Année Philologique*.

Abbreviations

Ager	Sheila L. Ager. *Interstate Arbitrations in the Greek World, 337–90 B.C.* Berkeley: University of California Press, 1996.
BNJ	*Brill's New Jacoby.* Edited by Ian Worthington. Leiden: Brill, 2007–.
FGrH	Felix Jacoby, et al. *Die Fragmente der griechischen Historiker.* Leiden: Brill, 1923–.
I.Didyma	Albert Rehm. *Didyma.* Part 2, *Die Inschriften.* Berlin: de Gruyter, 1958.
I.Eph.	Hermann Wankel and Reinhold Merkelbach. *Die Inschriften von Ephesos.* 7 vols. Bonn: Rudolf Habelt, 1979–81.
I.Ery.	Hermann Engelmann and Reinhold Merkelbach. *Die Inschriften von Erythrai und Klazomenai.* 2 vols. Bonn: Rudolf Habelt, 1972–73.
IG	*Inscriptiones Graecae.* Berlin: De Gruyter, 1873–.
I.Priene	Friedrich Hiller von Gaertringen. *Inschriften von Priene.* Berlin: de Gruyter, 1906.
I.Priene²	Wolfgang Blümel and Reinhold Merkelbach, in collaboration with Frank Rumscheid. *Die Inschriften von Priene.* 2 vols. Bonn: Rudolf Habelt, 2014.
McCabe, Miletos	Donald F. McCabe. *Miletos Inscriptions: Texts and List.* Princeton, NJ: IAS, 1985.
McCabe, Didyma	Donald F. McCabe. *Didyma Inscriptions: Text and List.* Princeton, NJ: IAS, 1985.
McCabe, Kolophon	Donald F. McCabe. *Kolophon Inscriptions: Text and List.* Princeton, NJ: IAS, 1985.
McCabe, Priene	Donald F. McCabe. *Priene Inscriptions: Texts and List.* Princeton, NJ: IAS, 1987.

Milet I   Theodor Wiegend. *Milet: Ergebnisse der Ausgrabungen
                 und Untersuchungen seit dem Jahr 1899.* Part 1. 9 vols.
                 Berlin: Reimer for Königliche Museen, 1906–28.
Milet VI   Peter Herrmann, Wolfgang Günther, and Norbert
                 Ehrhardt. *Milet: Ergebnisse der Ausgrabungen und
                 Untersuchungen seit dem Jahr 1899.* Part 6, *Inschriften
                 von Milet.* 3 vols. Berlin: de Gruyter, 1997–2006.
ML   Russell Meiggs and David M. Lewis. *Greek Historical
                 Inscriptions to the End of the Fifth Century BC.* Oxford:
                 Oxford University Press, 1969.
OGIS   Wilhelm Dittenberger. *Orientis Graeci Inscriptiones
                 Selectae.* 2 vols. Leipzig: Hirzel, 1903–5.
RC   C. B. Welles. *Royal Correspondence in the Hellenistic
                 Period.* London: Ares, 1934.
RO   P. J. Rhodes and Robin Osborne. *Greek Historical
                 Inscriptions, 404–323 BC* and *Greek Historical
                 Inscriptions, 478–404 BC.* Oxford: Oxford University
                 Press, 2007, 2017.
SEG   *Supplementum Epigraphicum Graecum.* Leiden: Brill,
                 1923–.
SIG³   Wilhelm Dittenberger. *Sylloge Inscriptionum Graecarum.*
                 3rd edition. Leipzig: Hirzel, 1915–24.
Tod   M. N. Tod. *Greek Historical Inscriptions.* 2 vols. Oxford:
                 Oxford University Press, 1985.

Acknowledgments

This book began as my dissertation project at the University of Missouri. I had already gone through several possible ideas when my adviser, Ian Worthington, asked if I was interested in writing a book on Caria. He had been talking with an editor who asked him the same question about his next book. Ian was not interested, but he knew a graduate student then casting about for a topic.

I had no particular interest in Caria, but I set about doing my due diligence with a review of the current literature. In that process, my attention drifted to other regions in Asia Minor before settling on Ionia. There was no lack of scholarship, but it seemed overwhelmingly focused on the Archaic period, when Ionia was one of the epicenters of Greek culture, or the Hellenistic period, when the region once again flourished. Between those two periods of cultural prominence, Ionia was treated as having gone through a long fallow period during which the region was subjected to the demands of a succession of imperial powers. The result was that Ionia usually appeared in conjunction with other, external developments.

What, I thought, would a history of Greece centered on Ionia look like?

That simple question drove the research that became my dissertation, but the first draft of these ideas looked quite a bit different from the version in this book. They were shaggier, more repetitive, and included false starts. But the core idea was there. On the day that I defended the dissertation, my committee of Ian Worthington, Anatole Mori, Jeff Stevens, Mark Smith, and Ted Tarkow wanted to know what the book version of the project would look like. This is very nearly the book I pitched.

Getting here was easier said than done. Where I had modest research support at the University of Missouri, including a dissertation writing fellowship in my penultimate year, most of the revisions took place while I worked at a succession of part-time, contingent faculty jobs, teaching as many as six classes a semester—on top of the disruption caused by the Covid-19 pandemic.

These circumstances make me even more grateful for the people whose support both directly and indirectly made this book possible. Some offered guidance and support during years of tenuous academic employment, some gave feedback on parts of this project, and others provided opportunities to develop underproofed ideas. Prominent among them are Ian Worthington, Yossi Roisman, Anatole Mori, Jeanne Reames, Jeff Stevens, Aaron Hershkowitz, Matt Simonton, Joel Christensen, Dan Leon, Aggelos Kappelos, and Christine Plastow. To these and many more: thank you.

I also need to thank Ellen Bauerle for taking a chance on my first book and championing it through the chaos of a global pandemic, as well as the production team at the University of Michigan Press and the anonymous reviewers whose careful and generous feedback improved the book in a myriad of ways. The maps were created by Beehive Cartographers and made possible with support from Truman State University.

Lastly, several close friends and family deserve special recognition. My parents and Bubbie have been unfailingly supportive of my academic journey, even at its most quixotic. Josh Klindienst and Hana Akselrod have been a constant source of encouragement, and Hana once took time away from saving lives to translate an article for me from Russian. I also owe my deepest gratitude to my partner Elizabeth, who was there from the beginning of this project, watched it through its ups and downs, and was very glad when it was done.

Joshua P. Nudell
Kirksville, MO

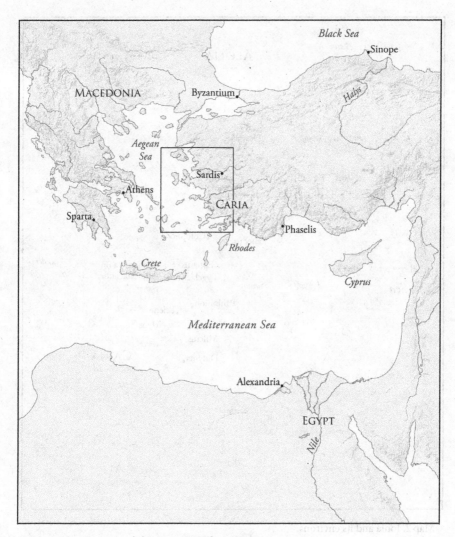

Map 1. The Aegean and the eastern Mediterranean

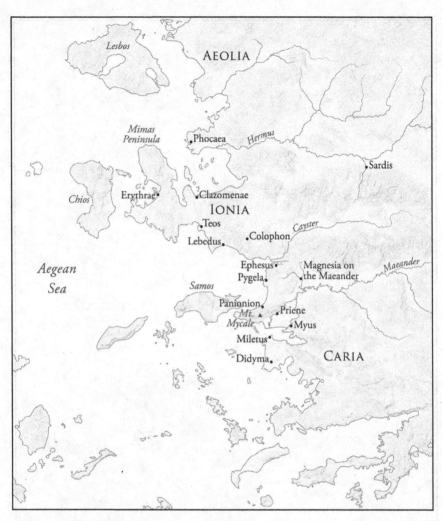

Map 2. Ionia and its environs

CHAPTER 1

❧

Prologue

The Land of Ionia

Introduction

The first decade of the second century BCE saw a showdown between the Seleucid king Antiochus III, so called Antiochus *Megas*, and a Roman Republic fresh off its victory in the Second Punic War. The Romans defeated Antiochus in battle after battle, all the while echoing generations of Hellenistic warlords and kings in declaring that their armies in the Aegean were the guarantors of Greek liberty (Livy 34.57). Thus, they stipulated, Antiochus had to accept the freedom and autonomy of all Greek poleis as a condition for peace. Rome had won the war and Antiochus had little leverage, but the negotiations leading up to the Treaty of Apamea in 188 stretched out anyway. At one point, the historian Appian tells us, Antiochus relented, announcing to the Romans that he would relinquish his claim over the European Greeks, as well as the Rhodians, Byzantines, Cyzicaeans, and all the other Greeks, "but he would not release the Aeolians and the Ionians, since they had long been accustomed to obey the barbarian kings of Asia" (*Syr.* 12.1).[1]

This is a curious passage. Antiochus sets himself as the heir to the non-Greek kings in an ill-fated gambit to preserve part of his realm, but his explanation for wanting to keep control over Ionia—that the region's history meant that it forfeited the right to autonomy—provides an insight into the consensus opinion about Ionia.

In some ways, Antiochus' assessment is astute. Ionia had become subject to "the barbarian kings of Asia" at least by the early sixth century BCE, and that subordinate relationship had continued throughout the Classical and early Hel-

---

1. Αἰολέας δὲ καὶ Ἴωνας οὐ συνεχώρει ὡς ἐκ πολλοῦ καὶ τοῖς βαρβάροις βασιλεῦσι τῆς Ἀσίας εἰθισμένους ὑπακούειν.

lenistic periods, regardless of formal declarations of autonomy. However, there are also two significant problems with Antiochus' statement. First, Ionia was subordinate not only to barbarian kings, but also to Greek poleis and Macedonian kings. Second, although Antiochus referred to the Ionians as accustomed to obedience, they were anything but.

Histories of Classical Greece tend to follow well-trod paths. A series of political and military events like the Persian and Peloponnesian Wars mark the trail and point out a standard set of sights. Athens is well represented, for reasons of evidence as much as anything, and puncturing the Spartan mirage has done little to blunt popular fascination, while Thebes and Macedonia make grand appearances in the fourth century. And yet, if one were to complete this metaphor, most of Greek history takes place elsewhere in the forest and only obliquely intersects with the usual paths.

That is, the story of ancient Greece is *not* the history of Athens or Sparta or Macedonia, but the history of more than a thousand independent poleis scattered across the breadth of the Mediterranean and Black Seas bound by language, culture, genealogy, and Panhellenic institutions that together created an imagined community of "Greeks."[2] Recent scholarship has begun to reflect this reality. The recent wave of regional histories,[3] polis histories,[4] and studies that either evaluate the Greek world at the intersection of poleis or set Greek history in light of its interactions with non-Greeks[5] has dramatically enriched

2. The Copenhagen Polis Center, directed by Mogens Herman Hansen and Thomas Heine Nielsen, identified 1,035 communities as "poleis" between c.800 and 323 BCE. I have borrowed the term "imagined communities" from Benedict Anderson, *Imagined Communities: Reflections on the Origins and Spread of Nationalism* (New York: Verso Books, 1983).

3. To name a few, Jeremy McInerney, *The Folds of Parnassos: Land and Ethnicity in Ancient Phocis* (Austin: University of Texas Press, 1999); Christy Constantakopoulou, *The Dance of the Islands: Insularity, Networks, the Athenian Empire, and the Aegean World* (Oxford: Oxford University Press, 2007); Brian Rutishauser, *Athens and the Cyclades: Economic Strategies, 510–314 BC* (Oxford: Oxford University Press, 2012); Jeremy LaBuff, *Polis Expansion and Elite Power in Hellenistic Caria* (Lanham, MD: Lexington Books, 2015); Aneurin Ellis-Evans, *The Kingdom of Priam: Lesbos and the Troad* (Oxford: Oxford University Press, 2019); Alan M. Greaves, *The Land of Ionia: Society and Economy in the Archaic Period* (Hoboken, NJ: Wiley-Blackwell, 2010).

4. Miletus: Vanessa B. Gorman, *Miletos, the Ornament of Ionia* (Ann Arbor: University of Michigan Press, 2001) and Alan M. Greaves, *Miletos: A History* (New York: Routledge, 2002); Samos: Graham Shipley, *A History of Samos, 800–188 BC* (Oxford: Oxford University Press, 1987); Hellenistic Ephesus: Guy Maclean Rogers, *The Mysteries of Artemis of Ephesos: Cult, Polis, and Change in the Graeco-Roman World* (New Haven, CT: Yale University Press, 2012); Elis: Graeme Bourke, *Elis: Internal Politics and External Policy in Ancient Greece* (New York: Routledge, 2017); Thebes: Nicholas Rockwell, *Thebes: A History* (New York: Routledge, 2019).

5. E.g., John Hyland, *Persian Interventions: The Achaemenid Empire, Athens, and Sparta, 450–386 BCE* (Baltimore, MD: Johns Hopkins University Press, 2018); Rebecca Futo Kennedy, *Immigrant Women in Athens: Gender, Ethnicity, and Citizenship in the Classical City* (New York: Routledge, 2014); Kostas Vlassopoulos, *Greeks and Barbarians* (Cambridge: Cambridge University Press, 2013); Kostas Vlassopoulos, *Unthinking the Greek Polis: Ancient Greek History beyond Eurocentrism* (Cambridge: Cambridge University Press, 2007), 166–67, makes a compelling case

our understanding of ancient Greece. To date, though, there has not been a dedicated study of Classical Ionia.

My aim in this book is to use Ionia to offer a new perspective on Classical Greece. Consisting of twelve poleis on and immediately off the coast of Asia Minor, Ionia straddled the border between the spheres claimed by Athens and Persia, which made it central to the imperial conflicts of the period. It is tempting to present the Ionian poleis as the prizes of imperial competition,[6] but closer inspection reveals that this characterization is deeply misleading. The Ionians were active partners in the imperial endeavor, even as imperial competition constrained local decision-making and exacerbated local and regional tensions.

The remainder of this chapter offers an introduction to Ionia before sketching its early history down to the revolt of 499–494 BCE. Scholarship on Archaic Ionia has long used the Persian suppression of this revolt as the lens through which to interpret the region's history.[7] Certainly, the revolt marked a traumatic rupture in the history of Ionia, but this approach both overrates Ionia's importance in the earlier developments of Greek history and underrates its continued importance through the Classical period. The Ionian revolt did not conclude a story so much as turn over a new page.

The Geography of Ionia

"Ionia" and "Ionian" are terms with multifarious definitions. *Yauna*—Ionian— was what much of the world called Greeks in antiquity, and common meanings range from ethnic terminology, a linguistic dialect, and an architectural style to a general label for Greeks who lived on the coast of Asia Minor between Sinope in the north and Phaselis in the south. However, Ionia also had a concrete referent from the sixth century: the region inhabited by citizens of poleis that belonged to the Panionion and whose ancestors had participated in the Ionian Migration at some point in the distant past (Hdt. 1.142; see below, "The Poleis of Ionia").[8]

---

that the polis ought not be the fundamental unit of analysis Greek history and offers examining the intersection of the polis and the region as one profitable direction of inquiry.

6. Kai Brodersen, "Aegean Greece," in *A Companion to the Classical World*, ed. Konrad H. Kinzl (Hoboken, NJ: Wiley-Blackwell, 2006), 103 on Miletus: "Rather than enjoying its former independence, it remained a prize in the conflicts between Athens, Sparta and Persia."

7. Dina Guth, "The 'Rise and Fall' of Archaic Miletus," *Historia* 66, no. 1 (2017): 2–20, makes this argument about interpretations of Archaic Miletus, but I believe it also applies to our interpretations of the Classical period.

8. In earlier periods this region was known as Asia (e.g., Homer *Il.* 2.461), perhaps connected

Herodotus claimed that Ionia was the best land in Asia, but it makes little sense as a discrete region.[9] Two mountainous horst ridges bisect Ionia from east to west, forming peninsulas that jut into the sea in the form of Mount Mimas (modern Çeşme) in the north and Mount Mycale (modern Samsun Dağı or Dilek Dağları) in the south.[10] Large rivers snaked through the valleys between the ridges, carrying alluvium from far inland Anatolia that led to rapid silting of Ionian harbors even while creating fertile farmland and fishing grounds.[11] In the south, the Maeander River (modern Büyük Menderes), from which we get the English word "meander," emptied into the Aegean Sea near Miletus, Myus, and Priene, while, on the other side of Mount Mycale, the Cayster River (modern Küçük Menderes) passed near Ephesus.[12] Beyond Mount Mimas to the north, the Hermus River (modern Gediz) by Smyrna ostensibly marked the divide between Ionia and Aeolis.[13]

These ridges facilitated east-west communication by allowing people to move along the peaks, but they interrupted north-south movement.[14] Herodotus' description of Ionia clearly reflects this fragmentation (1.142.3-4):

> They do not regularly use the same tongue but have four dialects. Miletus lies furthest to the south, and afterward Myus and Priene. These reside adjacent to Caria with their own dialect, while those adjacent Lydia, Ephesus, Colophon, Lebedus, Teos, Clazomenae, and Phocaea, those poleis share a dialect among them that is distinct from the former one.

---

to the Hittite Assuwa, but the word "Ionian" underwent a transformation in the sixth century BCE as Asia came to refer to the whole continent. See Naoíse Mac Sweeney, "Separating Fact from Fiction in the Ionian Migration," *Hesperia* 86, no. 3 (2017): 384–86, with n. 19 and n. 25, in particular.

9. For a more comprehensive discussion of Ionian geography, see Greaves, *Land of Ionia*, 45–68, and Peter Thonemann, *The Maeander Valley: A Historical Geography* (Cambridge: Cambridge University Press, 2011).

10. Greaves, *Land of Ionia*, 47–50.

11. The Gulf of Latmus provides the most striking example of the pace of silting. In the period of this study, Miletus lay at the end of a peninsula looking out into the wide expanse of the Gulf of Latmus. By the start of the Byzantine period, it was landlocked. See Helmut Brückner, "Delta Evolution and Culture—Aspects of Geoarchaeological Research in Miletos and Priene," in *Troia and the Troad: Scientific Approaches*, ed. Günther A. Wagner, Ernst Pernicka, and Hans-Peter Uerpmann (Berlin: Springer, 2003), 121–42; Greaves, *Land of Ionia*, 59; Alexander Herda et al., "From the Gulf of Latmos to Lake Bafa: On the History, Geoarchaeology, and Palynology of the Lower Maeander Valley at the Foot of the Latmos Mountains," *Hesperia* 88, no. 1 (2019): 1–86.

12. The two river systems are geologically distinct, but the modern Turkish names, which translate to the "Big" and "Little" Maeander, indicate a conceptual link that Thonemann, *Maeander Valley*, 21–22, suggests emerged from the territorial claims of the first Turkish emirate in southwest Anatolia since the rivers bounded its territory. Cf. Greaves, *Land of Ionia*, 47–50.

13. In truth, Ionian Phocaea lay to the north of the Hermus river.

14. As Greaves, *Land of Ionia*, 49.

γλῶσσαν δὲ οὐ τὴν αὐτὴν οὗτοι νενομίκασι, ἀλλὰ τρόπους τέσσερας παραγωγέων. Μίλητος μὲν αὐτέων πρώτη κέεται πόλις πρὸς μεσαμβρίην, μετὰ δὲ Μυοῦς τε καὶ Πριήνη. αὗται μὲν ἐν τῇ Καρίῃ κατοίκηνται κατὰ ταὐτὰ διαλεγόμεναι σφίσι, αἵδε δὲ ἐν τῇ Λυδίῃ, Ἔφεσος Κολοφὼν Λέβεδος Τέως Κλαζομεναὶ Φώκαια· αὗται δὲ αἱ πόλιες τῇσι πρότερον λεχθείσῃσι ὁμολογέουσι κατὰ γλῶσσαν οὐδέν, σφισι δὲ ὁμοφωνέουσι.

Herodotus goes on to say that Erythrae shared a language with the large island polis of Chios, while the Samos had a unique dialect. In addition to these divisions, there were numerous smaller islands such as Milesian Leros, Halonnesus in the territory of Erythrae, and the polis Clazomenae that has since been joined to the mainland.

These distinctions lead the archaeologist Alan Greaves to characterize the sea that surrounded, separated, and connected the poleis as the medium that allowed Ionia to be considered a single region.[15] But the sea around Ionia was dangerous. Strong currents run through the region, particularly in the straights between the islands and the peninsulas, and rocky coasts created dangers not only from Aegean storms, but also from the pirates.[16] And yet most Ionian poleis consisted of a patchwork of noncontiguous territories, scattered across the mountains, islands, and valleys, that contributed to political fragmentation.[17] Even the two large island poleis, Samos and Chios, had *peraeae*, or holdings on the Anatolian mainland. By the same token, the sea held Ionia together and contributed to its prosperity since it was exactly here that one of the principal north-south maritime routes turned west to cross the Aegean.[18]

The Poleis of Ionia

"To think of Ionia is to think of cities," writes Alan Greaves.[19] He goes on to explain that he means *cities* in the modern sense of an urban center (the Greek

---

15. Greaves, *Land of Ionia*, 55–57, 65–68.
16. Piracy was endemic in the Mediterranean; see particularly Philip de Souza, *Piracy in the Greco-Roman World* (Cambridge: Cambridge University Press, 1999), 15–30; Clifford R. Backman, "Piracy," in *A Companion to Mediterranean History*, ed. Peregrine Horden and Sharon Kinoshita (Malden, MA: Wiley, 2014), 170–83. Cf. Peter B. Campbell and George Koutsouflakis, "Aegean Navigation and the Shipwrecks of Fourni: The archipelago in Context," in *Under the Mediterranean I*, ed. Stella Demesticha and Lucy Blue (Leiden: Sidestone Press, 2021), 279–98.
17. Colophon, which had an acropolis situated some fifteen kilometers inland from the sea, is the exception that proves the rule about the centrality of the sea, but the frequent conflicts over the status of the port Notium demonstrate that it was not exempt; see Chapter 3.
18. Recent maritime excavations off Fourni, a small island that in antiquity belonged to Samos, have revealed more than fifty shipwrecks; see Campbell and Koutsouflakis, "Aegean Navigation."
19. Greaves, *Land of Ionia*, 124.

ἄστυ) rather than πόλις. The latter term is often glossed as "city," but was inclusive of its citizens (*demos*), the urban center, and the territory (*chora*). While Greaves is correct that it is impossible to think of Ephesus without drawing to mind the spectacular facade of the Library of Celsus, it is not those urban centers, but the twelve member poleis of the Panionion, that sit at the center of this study.[20]

The membership rolls of the Panionion did not remain entirely stable, but Herodotus provides the canonical list from north to south: Phocaea, Clazomenae, Erythrae, Chios, Teos, Lebedus, Colophon, Ephesus, Samos, Priene, Myus, and Miletus (1.142). A thirteenth polis, Smyrna, requested membership in the Archaic period but likely only received admission in the Hellenistic.[21] These poleis lay scattered across the geographical landscape but maintained a sense of collective identity through participation in the Panionion on Mount Mycale, which was established after a common war against Melie.[22] However, this memory of cooperation did little to blunt the rivalries. In fact, Naoíse Mac Sweeney characterizes the Panionion as a "fight club" because "inter-Ionian competition became not just a sideshow—it was the fundamental principle underlying the Ionian League."[23]

These twelve poleis ostensibly traced their lineage back to the Ionian Migration. Many ancient accounts claimed that there was a wide-scale migration of people from the northern Peloponnese and led by Athenian settlers across the Aegean (e.g., Hdt. 1.142–50; Paus. 7.2–5; Plato *Ion* 542d). However, there is little to suggest that these stories represent historical fact. Mac Sweeney has recently demonstrated that only roughly half of the foundation stories mention the Ionian Migration and many of those that do frame it as one of several possible origin myths.[24] Moreover, the archaeological remains from Ionia show not

---

20. On the development of these nucleated centers, see Michael Kerschner, "The Spatial Development of Ephesos from ca. 1000–ca. 670 BC against the Background of Other Early Iron Age Settlements in Ionia," in *Regional Stories: Towards a New Perception of the Early Greek World*, ed. Alexander Marikakis Ainian, Alexandra Alexandridou, and Xenia Charalambidou (Volos: University of Thessaly Press, 2017), 487–503.

21. Herodotus characterizes Smyrna as a colony from Colophon (τὴν ἀπὸ Κολοφῶνος κτισθεῖσαν, 1.16), but the evidence for this is slim. Lene Rubinstein, "Ionia," in *An Inventory of Archaic and Classical Poleis*, ed. Mogens Herman Hansen and Thomas Heine Nielsen (Oxford: Oxford University Press, 2004), 1099, suggests that Herodotus' mention of Smyrna's application but silence on admission indicates a rejection at that time. Smyrna eventually received membership based on alleged kinship with Ephesus (Strabo 14.1.4); see Nicholas Cross, "The Panionia: The Ritual Context for Identity Construction in Archaic Ionia," *Mediterranean Studies* 28, no. 1 (2020): 7–8. Greaves, *Land of Ionia*, 96–107, provides the best survey of each site.

22. On the creation of Ionian regional identity, see Naoíse Mac Sweeney, "Regional Identities in the Greek World: Myth and *Koinon* in Ionia," *Historia* 70, no. 3 (2021): 268–314; cf. Appendix 1.

23. Naoíse Mac Sweeney, *Foundation Myths and Politics in Ancient Ionia* (Cambridge: Cambridge University Press, 2013), 196–97.

24. Mac Sweeney, "Separating Fact from Fiction." Cf. Mac Sweeney, *Foundation Myths*, where she evaluates competition between these early foundation myths and Ferdinando Ferraioli, "Tra-

only that these sites were occupied from an early date, but also that there was significant cultural continuity.[25] Mac Sweeney concludes that it was only in the early sixth century when the standard term for this region shifted from "Asia" to "Ionia" and the first traces of collective activity at the Panionion can be identified. Thus, she suggests, these stories about common descent developed to set these communities apart from their neighbors.[26]

I evaluate the history of the Classical period principally in light of the happenings of this narrow set of poleis, and focus unevenly on them even then, but the story of Ionia would be incomplete without considering the other people who lived in the region. There were numerous small communities scattered throughout Ionia that existed in the shadow of their more famous neighbors. Just as the members of the dodecapolis negotiated their position between imperial powers, so, too, was a parallel dance taking place within Ionia, where Teos, Colophon, Ephesus, and others sought to dominate their small neighbors like Cyrbissus, Notium, and Pygela. Borders in and around Ionia were contested spaces,[27] and the relationships between these communities were disputed in terms of legal status and identity, which created the conditions for a fluid political environment.[28]

Archaic Ionia

The Archaic period is generally regarded as the high point of Ionian history, and with good reason. As early as the eighth century, intrepid settlers from Ionia had begun to found colonies on the shores of the Bosporus and around

---

dizioni sull'autoctonia nelle città ioniche d'Asia," *Erga-Logoi* 5, no. 2 (2017): 113–22, who evaluates the emergence of foundation myths that claimed autochthony for Miletus, Ephesus, Samos, Chios, and Smyrna.

25. Cf. David Hill, "Conceptualising Interregional Relations in Ionia and Central-West Anatolia from the Archaic to the Hellenistic Period," in *Bordered Places, Bounded Times: Cross-Disciplinary Perspectives on Turkey*, ed. Emma L. Baysal and Leonidas Karakatsanis (Ankara: British Institute at Ankara, 2017), 85–96; John Michael Kearns, "Greek and Lydian Evidence of Diversity, Erasure, and Convergence in Western Asia Minor," *Syllecta Classica* 14 (2003): 23–36; Jana Mokrišová, "On the Move: Mobility in Southwest Anatolia and the Southeast Aegean during the Late Bronze to Early Iron Age Transition" (PhD diss. University of Michigan, 2017), 230–67, 284–87.

26. Mac Sweeney, "Separating Fact from Fiction," 284, with n. 19. This was also roughly the same time when the "Hellas" transformed from designating a narrow geographical area to a broader meaning; see Jonathan Hall, *Hellenicity: Between Ethnicity and Culture* (Chicago: University of Chicago Press, 2002), 129–34. On invention of these identities, cf. Emily Sarah Wilson, "What's in a Name? Trade, Sanctuaries, Diversity, and Identity in Archaic Ionia" (PhD. diss., University of Chicago, 2018), 22–51.

27. As Hill, "Conceptualising Interregional Relations."

28. See Appendix 2.

the Black Sea.[29] Miletus alone was said to have founded more than ninety settlements (Pliny *H.N.* 5.122), while Phocaea established colonies as far away
as Massilia in southern France.[30] Ionian merchants also helped establish the
emporia Naucratis in Egypt and Posideion in Syria.[31] These overseas connections led many Ionians to seek fortune abroad. Graffiti at Abu Simbel listing
the names of men from Teos and Colophon testify to the Ionian mercenaries in
the pay of Egyptian pharaohs, and an inscription records the gifts given from
Pharaoh Psammetichus I (r. 664–620) to one Pedon of Priene (*SEG* 37, 994).[32]

This interaction with the wider eastern Mediterranean world also contributed to the development of Ionia as an epicenter of Archaic Greek culture.
Mary Bachvarova has argued that Hittite religious festivals created a poetic ferment out of which developed Greek epic.[33] It should not be a surprise that no
fewer than three Ionian poleis, Chios, Colophon, and Smyrna, claimed Homer
as their own (Strabo 14.1.35; *Suda* omicron 251). Other stories linked Homer

---

29. Christian Marek, *In the Land of a Thousand Gods: A History of Asia Minor in the Ancient World*, in collaboration with Peter Frei, trans. Steven Rendall (Princeton, NJ: Princeton University Press, 2016), 128–30. Any explanation for this wave of settlements remains speculative, but it coincided with a wider colonizing movement throughout the Aegean world that likely coincided with a growing population; see Walter Scheidel, "The Greek Demographic Expansion: Models and Comparisons," *JHS* 123 (2003): 120–40, if not the explosive growth sometimes imagined. Joseph Manning, *The Open Sea: The Economic Life of the Ancient Mediterranean World from the Iron Age to the Rise of Rome* (Princeton, NJ: Princeton University Press, 2018), 52, suggests that most Greek colonies settling in fertile agricultural regions indicates the need to support larger populations.

30. The Milesian colonies are typically identified in that they shared government structures and religious calendar with their mother city, but Alan M. Greaves, in "Milesians in the Black Sea: Trade: Settlement, and Religion," in *The Black Sea in Antiquity*, ed. Vincent Gabrielsen and John Lund (Aarhus: Aarhus University Press, 2007), 9–21, and in *Land of Ionia*, 134, argues that rather than being foundations composed of Milesians, they were colonies sanctioned by the oracle at Didyma.

31. Greek distinguishes between two types of colonies, *apoikia* (new settlements) and *emporia* (trading posts), though Greaves, *Land of Ionia*, 123–27, notes the challenges of distinguishing between the two in the archaeological remains. For Naucratis and Posideion, one key characteristic was collaborative foundation.

32. Wilson, "What's in a Name?," 95–100, offers the best survey of Ionian mercenaries in the eastern Aegean, but cf. Greaves, *Land of Ionia*, 166–68. Assyrian records indicate a battle between Sargon and the Yamnāiu/Yaunāiu (certainly Greeks, possibly Ionians) in the late eighth century; see Giovanni B. Lanfranchi, "The Ideological and Political Impact of the Assyrian Imperial Expansion on the Greek World in the 8th and 7th Centuries BC," in *The Heirs of Assyria*, ed. Sanna Aro and R. M. Whiting (Helsinki: The Neo-Assyrian Text Corpus Project, 2000), 13–21, with n. 20 on the identification of Yamnāiu/Yaunāiu.

33. Mary Bachvarova, *From Hittite to Homer: The Anatolian Background of Greek Epic* (Cambridge: Cambridge University Press: 2016). On court of Polycrates on Samos generating the Homeric Hymns to Apollo, see Antonio Aloni, "The Politics of Composition and Performance of the Homeric 'Hymn to Apollo,'" in *Apolline Politics and Poetics*, ed. Lucia Athanassaki, Richard P. Martin, and John F. Miller (Athens: Hellenic Ministry of Culture, 2009), 55–65; Walter Burkert, "Kynaithos, Polycrates, and the Homeric Hymn to Apollo," in *Arktouros*, ed. Glen W. Bowersock, Walter Burkhert, and Michael C. J. Putnam (Berlin: de Gruyter, 1979), 53–62; M. L. West, "The Invention of Homer," *CQ*[2] 49, no. 2 (1999): 364–82.

with Creophylus of Samos, who claimed to have hosted him, but was variously said to have been Homer's teacher or emulated him (Strabo 14.1.18). This same ferment produced an unusual concentration of philosophical and scientific luminaries, including Bias of Priene (Strabo 14.1.12), Pythagoras of Samos (Strabo 14.1.16), Anaximenes and Thales of Miletus (Strabo 14.1.7; *Suda* theta 17), and Heraclitus of Ephesus (Strabo 14.1.25). Thales was said to have been a Phoenician by descent if not birth (Hdt. 1.170.3). Lyric poetry also found fertile ground in the aristocratic culture of Archaic Ionia, much as it did in Aeolis to the north.[34] Nor were the fruits of Ionian engagement with Western Asia limited to literary culture. These interactions both shaped material culture in the region and likely accelerated the development of monumental architecture, particularly in the temples that began to appear during this period.[35]

However, it is a mistake to identify Ionian autonomy as the cause of these achievements. From the mid-seventh century, the Mermnad dynasty had consolidated and strengthened the Lydian kingdom centered at Sardis.[36] The growth of Lydian power led to conflict with the nearby Ionian poleis. The lyric poet Mimnermus composed verses about battles between the Lydian king Gyges and the people of Smyrna in the 660s (*BNJ* 578 F 5), and Herodotus says he attacked Miletus and captured Colophon (1.15).[37] Herodotus' subsequent chapters paint a picture of continued conflict between Lydia and Ionia. The

34. There are poets attested through fragments or testimony from Miletus (on Phocylides, see M. L. West, "Phocylides," *JHS* 98 [1978]: 164–67), Ephesus (Callinus and Hipponax, Strabo 14.1.25), Teos (Anacreon, Strabo 14.1.30; *Suda* alpha 1916), and Colophon (Xenophanes and Mimnermus, Strabo 14.1.28), with at least one of those, Mimnermus, possibly hailing from Smyrna. West, "Phocylides," describes Phocylides' gnomic verses as "wisdom of the east," while Walter Burkert, *The Orientalizing Revolution: Near Eastern Influences on Greek Culture in the Early Archaic Period*, trans. Margaret E. Pinder and Walter Burkert (Cambridge, MA: Harvard University Press, 1992) posited that Greek culture owed a significant debt to engagement with the eastern Mediterranean.

35. Wilson, "What's in a Name?," 155–64, makes the case that Ionian sacred architecture diverged from its Anatolian neighbors over the course of the sixth century, both as a product of these maritime connections and as a way of staking out a distinct Ionian identity; cf. Chapter 9. On the Lydian influence on material culture, see Michael Kerschner, "Die Lyder und das Artemision von Ephesos," in *Die Archäologie der ephischen Artemis: Gestalt und Ritual eines Heiligtums*, ed. Ulrike Muss (Vienna: Phoibos, 2008), 223–33.

36. On the growth of Lydian power, see Christopher H. Roosevelt, *The Archaeology of Lydia, From Gyges to Alexander* (Cambridge: Cambridge University Press, 2009), 22–26. Cf. Mait Kõiv, "Greek Rulers and Imperial Powers in Western Anatolia (8th–6th Centuries BC)," *Studia Antiqua et Archaeologica* 27, no. 2 (2021): 357–73, on the interaction between Ionian and Lydian elites.

37. The sources for these early Lydian campaigns make it difficult to reconstruct the chronology, which is why I have chosen to largely follow Herodotus. Polyaenus credits Alyattes, rather than Gyges, with capturing Colophon (7.2). J. M. Cook, "On the Date of Alyattes' Sack of Smyrna," *ABSA* 80 (1980): 25–28, offers evidence for the sack taking place c.600. On other chronological issues, see Hans Kaletsch, "Zur lydischen Chronologie," *Historia* 7, no. 1 (1958): 1–47; Mario Lombardo, "Osservazioni cronologiche e storiche sul regno di Sadiatte," *ASNP* 10, no. 2 (1980): 307–62; Robert W. Wallace, "Redating Croesus: Herodotean Chronologies, and the Dates of the Earliest Coinages," *JHS* 136 (2016): 168–81.

second Mermnad king, Ardys, raided Miletus again and captured Priene (1.16). Herodotus passes over the reign of the third king, Sadyattes, but subsequently credits him with beginning a war against Miletus that raged for twelve years and only ended when a fire started by the Lydians burned a temple of Athena of Assesos (1.17–19). According to Herodotus' tale, Alyattes would only recover when he had rebuilt the temple, so the king ended up suing for peace—helped in no small part by a scheme concocted by the tyrant Thrasybulus that tricked Alyattes into not recognizing how desperate things had become in Miletus (1.20–22).[38] Throughout this period, Alyattes had also raided Clazomenae and captured Smyrna, and his son Croesus followed in his footsteps by raiding Ephesus and other Ionian poleis (Hdt. 1.26).[39]

Unsurprisingly, these attacks prompted a wave of construction on defensive fortifications, but, while the Mermnad kings of Lydia posed a common threat to Ionia, the region nevertheless remained fractured.[40] The only attested example of one polis offering aid to another was Chios to Miletus, and then only because the Milesians had extended aid in an earlier war against Erythrae (Hdt. 1.18.3). Once Croesus had captured the mainland Ionians, Herodotus says, he began to prepare for a naval campaign against the large island poleis, only to be dissuaded by Bias of Priene or Pittacus of Mytilene (1.27). What developed from these campaigns was a hegemonic relationship that is striking for its similarity to the relationship between Ionia and the imperial actors of the Classical period. The Ionians paid tribute (Hdt. 1.6.1, 1.27.1) but were left to govern themselves while the Lydian kings made conspicuous dedications at Ionian sanctuaries and employed Ionian craftsmen (Hdt. 1.22, 92; cf. Nikolaos of Damascus *BNJ* 90 F 65).[41]

38. Alyattes also engaged in other diplomatic endeavors. One of his wives was an Ionian woman, the son of whom was enough of a threat to the throne that Croesus, whose mother was Carian, had him executed when he took the throne (Hdt. 1.92.2–4). These relationships were not unusual. The tyrants of Ephesus traced their descent back to Gyges through Alyattes (Aelian *VH* 3.26), while Nikolaos of Damascus records that "Miletos" was both descended from Melas, the brother-in-law of Gyges, and married to the sister of Sadyattes (*BNJ* 90 F 63).

39. On Alyattes' capture of Smyrna, see Nikolaos of Damascus *BNJ* 90 F 64. Kevin Leloux, "The Campaign of Croesus against Ephesus: Historical and Archaeological Considerations," *Polemos* 21, no. 2 (2018): 47–63, recently reevaluated the archaeological evidence to suggest that Ephesus surrendered to Croesus without a siege.

40. On the dating of Archaic walls, see Rune Fredericksen, *Archaic City Walls of the Archaic Period, 900–480 BCE* (Oxford: Oxford University Press, 2011), particularly 50–69; Greaves, *Land of Ionia*, 156–63. Greaves suggests that the Ionian fortifications were built not just as protection against incursions, but also in emulation of Lydian fortifications. Even after the Ionian revolt, Artaphernes required the Ionians to make treaties with each other (Hdt. 6.42), though Cross, "Panionia," 15, regards this as a suppression of the Ionian League, but see Appendix 1.

41. Walter Burkert, "Gyges to Croesus: Historiography between Herodotus and Cuneiform,"

When Cyrus toppled the Mermnad dynasty in 545–543, the Ionians were on the losing side.[42] According to Herodotus, Cyrus tried to divide Croesus' army by persuading the Ionians to defect (1.76.3).[43] He offers no explanation for why the Ionians chose to stay with Croesus, but they adamantly held out even after the fall of Sardis. Where the Lydian conquest had taken place piecemeal, the Persians were methodical in subjugating Ionia. Cyrus' general Harpagus systematically besieged the Ionian cities excepting only Miletus, which had made an earlier treaty with Cyrus (Hdt. 1.162–69).

Herodotus characterizes this turn as the second time that the Ionians had been enslaved (οὕτω δὴ τὸ δεύτερον Ἰωνίη ἐδεδούλωτο, 1.169.2), but it is worth asking what had actually changed.[44] The Persian imperial state that Cyrus introduced to western Asia Minor came with traditions of centralized control inherited from the Medes, who themselves had adopted them from Assyria.[45] However, early Persian rule in Ionia was no more immediate than Lydian rule had been. The Ionians owed tribute and were required to supply men and ships to Persian campaigns such as Cambyses' invasion of Egypt in 525 (Hdt. 3.1.1),[46] but their location on the imperial frontier gave considerable leeway to local actors. On Samos, Polycrates seized control of the state and not only maintained open relationships with both the Persian king Cambyses and the Egyptian Amasis (Hdt. 2.192; 3.39–44; Diod. 1.95), but also waged war on Miletus (Hdt. 3.39) and, ultimately, contributed ships to Cambyses' invasion of Egypt—even if he also allegedly used the expedition to eliminate potential rivals by requesting Cambyses not send them home (Hdt. 3.44).[47] Jack Balcer

in *Schools of Oriental Studies and the Development of Modern Historiography*, ed. Antonio Panaino, Andrea Piras, and Gian Pietro Basello (Milan: Mimesis, 2004), 48, suggests that Lydia offered another avenue for Ionian trade to Western Asia.

42. For a narrative of the Persian conquest, see Jack Martin Balcer, *Sparda by the Bitter Sea: Imperial Interaction in Western Anatolia* (Providence, RI: Brown University Press, 1984), 95–109.

43. Roosevelt, *Archaeology of Lydia*, 26, characterizes these Ionian soldiers as mercenaries, but it is better to interpret their service as an obligation to the Lydian empire, as the Ionians would later provide to Persia.

44. Herodotus modifies his language, referring to the first as a καταστροφή (1.91.6), which marks a subjugation or ruin, but not quite slavery.

45. Balcer, *Sparda*, 118–19; but see Pierre Briant, *From Cyrus to Alexander: A History of the Persian Empire*, trans. Peter T. Daniels (Winona Lake, IN: Eisenbrauns, 2002), 13–28, on the disjunctions in this interpretation. Reza Zarghamee, *Discovering Cyrus: The Persian Conqueror Astride the Ancient World* (Washington, DC: Mage Publishers, 2013), 251–92, describes Achaemenid royal ideology as a subversion of Assyrian and Babylonian practice in its tolerance of local customs.

46. Balcer, *Sparda*, 107, argues that Cyrus' tribute demands were less regular than Croesus', based on Herodotus' description of the subjects owing "gifts" (3.89.3). Herodotus marks the change to fixed tribute as a sign of Darius' miserliness, but Cyrus' demands had likely placed greater emphasis on symbolic submission.

47. Shipley, *Samos*, 97, observes that in this version of the story, Polycrates volunteered his

explained the last action as a clear sign of "Samos' vassalage status within the Persian Empire," but this description does not entirely square with the portrait of Polycrates negotiating his position in the eastern Aegean.[48] When necessary, he acknowledged his subordinate position toward the king; where possible, he flaunted demands from the king's representatives and flagrantly raided the king's subjects. Indeed, it was this very activity that forced Miletus to bind itself closer to Persia in return for protection.[49]

The structure of the Achaemenid empire changed in 522 after the accession of the third Persian king, Darius. In some ways a second founder of the Persian Empire, Darius' path to the throne was not straightforward. Both his imperial propaganda and historical sources suggest widespread opposition to this upstart related to Cyrus only through marriage (e.g., Hdt. 3.88, 133). The Persian succession crisis and Darius' measures to secure his empire are beyond the scope of this study, but it is worth noting that although Oroetes, the satrap of Sparda (which included Ionia), was one of Darius' opponents (Hdt. 3.127), his rebellion does not appear to have drawn the Ionian poleis into the conflict.[50]

Once Darius secured his throne, he set about overhauling the loose administrative structures he inherited. In practical terms, this meant two changes: creating twenty satrapies and regularizing the assessed tribute that subjects owed to the Persian throne (Hdt. 3.89). Under this new organization, Darius grouped the Ionians with the Magnesians, Aeolians, Carians, Lycians, Milyans, and Pamphylians, who, together, owed four hundred talents of silver (Hdt. 3.90). Darius also conscripted labor from around the empire for his ambitious building projects. Evidence from Susa and Persepolis reveals the presence of Ionian artisans on the Iranian plateau.[51] Likewise, Classical sources attest to

---

ships to Cambyses. The gambit backfired when the dissidents Polycrates failed to kill fled to Sparta, leading to a Spartan expedition and siege (Hdt. 3.45–49, 54–59).

48. Balcer, *Sparda*, 108.

49. As Guth, "Rise and Fall," convincingly argues.

50. On the rebellions at the outset of Darius' reign, see Balcer, *Sparda*, 123–43; Briant, *From Cyrus to Alexander*, 107–22. Darius recorded his victory in an inscription at Behistun. The monument includes Lydia and the Greeks among the subject people but does not include them among the rebellions.

51. See Briant, *From Cyrus to Alexander*, 429–39, for the lives of these craftsmen, with 422–25 on the nature of the evidence. The foundation inscription at Susa (DSf) proudly lists the Ionians as stonecutters working on the project; see Pierre Lecoq, *Les Inscriptions de la Perse achéménide* (Paris: Gallimard, 1997), 237. The Persepolis Fortification Tablets (PFT) reveal mothers (1224), grain handlers (1942, 1965), and other Ionians (1224, 1798, 1800, 1810, 2072) in this labor force. Persian accounting did not distinguish between the Yauna of Ionia and those of other Greek poleis, but it is likely that a significant portion of these workers came from Ionia proper. Carl Nylander, *Ionians in Pasargadae: Studies in Old Persian Architecture* (Uppsala: Acta Universitatis Upsaliensis, 1970), remains the classic study of Ionian building techniques at the Persian palaces and is broadly accepted by Margaret Cool Root, *The King and Kingship in Achaemenid Art: Essays on the Creation of an Iconography of Empire* (Leiden: Brill, 1979), 9–14, with the caveat that these styles were in the

the presence of Ionian artists and engineers in Persian employ, including Tele-phanes, an artist from Phocaea (Pliny *H.N.* 34.68), and the Samian engineer Mandrocles, who built the bridge across the Bosporus for Darius' first expedi-tion to Europe (Hdt. 4.87–89).

Darius' administrative changes connected Ionia more closely to the impe-rial center, but their effect on the political life in the region was mixed. Darius conquered Samos at the behest of Polycrates' brother Syloson, who, Herodotus says, he owed a favor stemming from his generosity during Cambyses' cam-paign in Egypt (Hdt. 1.139). When the Samians resisted the installation of this client ruler, the Persian general Otanes ordered his soldiers to take no prison-ers and handed the island devoid of men over to Syloson (Hdt. 3.146–49).[52] This portrait of a desolate island is likely exaggerated but reflects the historical reality that the Persians brooked no opposition and reserved the right to relo-cate their subjects. Nor was Syloson the only tyrant that the Persians installed. During Darius' campaign in 513, the Scythians tried to persuade the Greeks to destroy the bridge across the Danube and strand the Persian king, but Histiaeus of Miletus persuaded the Greeks present, including Strattis of Chios, Aeaces of Samos (Syloson's son, Hdt. 6.13), and Laodamas of Phocaea, not to follow this advice on the grounds that it was through Persian power that each of them held power—without Darius, he said, their people would choose democracy (Hdt. 4.137). Beneath this rubric of Persian-backed tyrants, local politics continued abreast until the eruption of the Ionian revolt in 499.[53]

A Region in Revolt: Ionia 499–494

By the year 500, Ionia had been subordinated to more powerful neighbors for generations. That year, exiles from Naxos and Paros approached Aristagoras, Histiaeus' cousin and the new client ruler of Miletus,[54] asking that he restore

---

service of an "Achaemenid programmatic vision" where Greeks were just one part; but cf. Alan M. Greaves, John Brendan Knight, and Françoise Rutland, "Milesian Élite Responses to Persia: The Ionian Revolt in Context," *Hermathena* 204–5 (2020): 87–89, who argue that there are few Ionian artistic influences in Achaemenid art. The workers may have stayed only for a short time before returning home, but Richard T. Hallock, *Persepolis Fortification Tablets* (Chicago: University of Chicago Press, 1969), 6, suggests that the ration texts indicate that most travelers to Persepolis remained there.

52. On Syloson as a client ruler, see Briant, *From Cyrus to Alexander*, 140; Shipley, *Samos*, 103–6.

53. For instance, the Milesian *aesymnetes* list (*Milet* I.3 no. 122), inscribed in the 330s, records a plausible list of eponymous executives that begins in this period and Teos was refounded during this same period; see Chapter 2.

54. Histiaeus had been detained at Darius' court since 511/0 (Hdt. 5.24).

them to power (Hdt. 5.29–30). Aristagoras lacked the resources to carry out the plan but brought the proposal to the Persian satrap Artaphernes, who agreed to provide him a fleet with which to capture the Cyclades (Hdt. 5.30–32). The following spring, Aristagoras and the Persian general Megabates sailed for Naxos at the head of a large fleet that included a significant number of Ionian ships and soldiers levied by Persia (Hdt. 5.32–44). Far from an easy conquest, the siege dragged on for four months, sapping the allotted funds and much of Aristagoras' own money (Hdt. 5.34).[55] According to Herodotus, Aristagoras began to doubt his ability to deliver on his promise and feared that the consequence of his failure would be the loss of Miletus (5.35.1–2).

About the same time, he allegedly received a secret message from Histiaeus tattooed on the head of an enslaved man and hidden beneath his hair, instructing him to foment revolt (Hdt. 5.35.3–4). Aristagoras, Herodotus says, then gave up his tyranny and seized the other tyrants and handed them back to their cities (5.37–38) before sailing to Sparta and Athens in search of allies (5.38–55, 97–99).[56] Naturally, most of the deposed tyrants fled to Persia.

Such was the genesis of the Ionian revolt, an event that has traditionally been treated as the final punctuation mark on Archaic Ionia. Of course, Herodotus does not ask the same questions as modern historians and thus does not offer satisfactory answers. The result has been a lack of consensus on the actual cause of the revolt. The two most common proposals are both unsatisfactory. In the one, the Persian conquest gradually eroded Ionian prosperity, whether through excessive tribute demands or preferential treatment for Phoenician merchants, which, in turn, caused resentment of Persian rule. And yet the Persian economic system did not favor Phoenician merchants and, as Pericles Georges points out, the Ionians had already lived within a tributary regime for at least a half century.[57] In the other proposal, the Ionian

55. Arthur Keaveney, "The Attack on Naxos: A 'Forgotten Cause' of the Ionian Revolt," CQ^2 38, no. 1 (1988): 76–81, reads hostility between the Greek and Persian leaders that he believes led to Megabates sabotaging the expedition as described by Herodotus; cf. Pericles Georges, "Persian Ionia under Darius: The Revolt Reconsidered," Historia 49, no. 1 (2000): 17–18.

56. Although Herodotus makes it clear that Aristagoras formally handed back power to the Milesians and dissolved other tyrannies in the eastern Aegean, he presents Aristagoras a demagogue who manipulated his audiences, both in Miletus (5.36.1–2) and abroad (e.g., 5.97.2) with misleading words that appealed to what they wanted to hear.

57. Georges, "Persian Ionia," 22; Briant, From Cyrus to Alexander, 149–50. The economic thesis is most prominent in George L. Cawkwell, The Greek Wars: The Failure of Persia (Oxford: Oxford University Press, 2005), 71–74; Peter Green, The Greco-Persian Wars, reprint ed. (Berkeley: University of California Press, 1996), 45–47; O. Murray, "The Ionian Revolt," in Cambridge Ancient History², vol. 4, ed. John Boardman, N. G. L. Hammond, David M. Lewis, and Martin Ostwald (Cambridge: Cambridge University Press, 1988), 475–76; H. T. Wallinga, "The Ionian Revolt," Mnemosyne⁴ 37, nos. 3–4 (1984): 401–37. Green specifically blames Darius' "short-sighted avarice." Recently Marek, Land of a Thousand Gods, 142, suggested that the Ionians might have believed that Persian expansion might interfere with their prosperity irrespective of whether it actually did.

revolt erupted because of a developing sense of "nationalism."[58] However, interpreting the Ionian revolt as a general anti-Persian conflict is misleading even when eschewing the anachronistic term "nationalism."[59] Recent scholarship has begun to consider how the local political conditions in the Ionian poleis might have caused the revolt, looking at popular opposition to the tyrannies and how the obligations these tyrants owed to the Persian king changed their relationship with the people they ruled.[60] This interpretation thus brings Aristagoras back to the fore as a proto-demagogue who was able to turn a wave of underlying resentment toward his own ends.

But what is meant by "Ionian revolt"? Without question, there was a general uprising in western Anatolia, and, while Herodotus opens this section by describing the events simply as "evils" that came to Ionia (κακά, 5.28), he later refers to it as a revolt either in Ionia (6.1) or of the Ionians that then spread to neighboring regions (5.104.2, 117). Aristagoras' role in the outbreak and the coordination at Panionion ensured that the revolt remained centered on Ionia, but there is ambiguity as to who was involved. In fact, the "Ionian revolt" *was not* a general uprising of a unified Ionia.[61] Consider the case of Ephesus. Some Ephesians helped guide the raid to Sardis in 498 (Hdt. 5.100), but Ephesus itself remained conspicuously detached from the revolt. While the poleis of Lesbos sent seventy ships to fight alongside the Ionians at the battle of Lade in 494 (Hdt. 6.8), the only Ephesian contribution to the battle was to kill some Chian survivors whom they allegedly mistook for raiders (Hdt. 6.16). For later chroniclers, an uprising that met in council at the Panionion could indicate Greek

While the evidence makes it impossible to offer a comparative assessment of Ionian prosperity, Georges, "Persian Ionia," 10, is undoubtedly correct that "the Persian presence . . . redirected, rather than depressed, the Ionian economy." Erik Jensen, *The Greco-Persian Wars* (Indianapolis, IN: Hackett, 2021), 18, offers a modified version of the economic thesis, that Darius' expansionist policies had dramatically increased the demands on Ionia.

58. J. A. S. Evans, "Histiaeus and Aristagoras: Notes on the Ionian Revolt," *AJPh* 84, no. 2 (1963): 113–28, actually declares: "We must realize that the Ionian revolt was a nationalist movement," while other scholars avoid using the n-word, but nevertheless couch their interpretation in terms of "uniquely" Greek notions of "freedom," as A. R. Burn, *Persia and the Greeks: The Defence of the West c.546–478 B.C.* (London: Edward Arnold, 1962), 193; Charles Hignett, *Xerxes' Invasion of Greece* (Oxford: Oxford University Press, 1963), 85; Gaetano de Sanctis, "Aristagora di Mileto," *Rivista di filologia e di istruzione classica* 59 (1931): 48–72. Greaves, Knight, and Rutland, "Milesian élite responses," 70–72, point out that these interpretations rely on a close and uncritical reading of Herodotus.

59. As Balcer, *Sparda*, 232–36.

60. Briant, *From Cyrus to Alexander*, 150–52; Georges, "Persian Ionia," 19–23; cf. P. B. Manville, "Aristagoras and Histiaios: The Leadership Struggle in the Ionian Revolt," *CQ*² 27, no. 1 (1977): 80–91. Recently, Greaves, Knight, and Rutland, "Milesian élite responses," 2018, show how the Milesian elite accommodated Persian rule as a way of turning it to their own ends. Under their interpretation, Aristagoras initiated the revolt to regain the *arētē* he lost in the failure at Naxos.

61. J. Neville, "Was There an Ionian Revolt?," *CQ*² 29, no. 2 (1979): 268–75, takes this argument to the extreme in rejecting altogether that Herodotus saw an "Ionian" revolt, but he goes too far in his zeal to counteract pernicious ideas about Ionian "nationalism."

antipathy toward Persia or a coalescence of regional identity, but the description of the events demonstrates regional fissures.[62]

Despite the stunning raid on Sardis in 498, the inevitability of Persian power quickly set in. Darius's generals regained supremacy on land where they harried the force that captured Sardis (Hdt. 5.116) and hammered a Milesian army in the Maeander plain (Hdt. 5.120). Artaphernes and Otanes soon turned their attentions to Ionia itself, capturing Clazomenae (Hdt. 5.123). For his part, Aristagoras abandoned the revolt and fled to Thrace (Hdt. 5.124–26). The war dragged on for more than four years before the Persian fleet and army finally converged on Miletus. The rebels met the Persians by sea near the island of Lade (Hdt. 5.7–16), but the battle quickly turned sour for the Ionians. All but eleven of the sixty Samian ships deserted, which caused others to follow suit. Moreover, the remaining crews were exhausted from a week of strenuous training, so those who held firm were soon overwhelmed. Persian forces tightened the noose around Miletus after the battle (Hdt. 6.18). Herodotus spares readers the gruesome details of the capture, but it was so traumatic that when Phyrnicus produced a play at Athens called *The Capture of Miletus* not only did the whole theater weep, but the Athenians also fined him a thousand drachmae and banned its performance (Hdt. 6.21.2).[63]

Persian forces stamped out the remaining embers of revolt over the next year, recapturing and executing Histiaeus (Hdt. 6.30), easily (εὐπετέως) subduing Chios (Hdt. 6.31), and exacting revenge by putting temples to flame, castrating boys, and carrying away young women (Hdt. 6.31). Those who could fled (Hdt. 6.22–24), probably to escape retribution more than out of an aversion to living under Persian rule, and the Persians deported people from Miletus to the Red Sea (Hdt. 6.20).

And yet taking Persian actions in their entirety reveals a commitment to mitigating the circumstances that incited the revolt. First, Artaphernes brought the Ionian leaders to Sardis to compel them to stop fighting among themselves and setting a precedent for Persian arbitration between conflicting parties (Hdt. 6.42.1). Then he conducted a survey of Ionia that regularized the tribute payments at a level no higher than it was before (Hdt. 6.42.2).[64] Pericles Georges observed that this tributary burden fell upon fewer citizens than before the revolt, but the fact that Artaphernes based the obligation on the agricultural

62. Cf. Briant, *From Cyrus to Alexander*, 155. On the Panionion, see Appendix 1.

63. Balcer, *Sparda*, 245, suggests that the Persian fury against Miletus was because it had held a privileged position, but it is more likely that this was the center of opposition. It is also likely that reports of the destruction of Miletus were hyperbolic; see Chapter 2.

64. These two measures were linked; changes to the territorial holdings of one polis meant a change in its tributary obligation; see Briant, *From Cyrus to Alexander*, 494–96.

output of each polis meant that it was the contrary of vindictive.[65] Likewise, while Artaphernes initially restored the tyrants to power in the Ionian cities, his successor, Mardonius, reversed that decision and turned local rule over to democracies (Hdt. 6.43).[66] In his account of the end of the Ionian revolt, Diodorus Siculus includes an exchange between Artaphernes and the Milesian historian Hecataeus (10.25.4). Artaphernes muses that he is concerned about the Ionians resenting the Persians for their treatment during the revolt. Hecataeus responds that if suffering evils had engendered mistrust, then good treatment will engender amity (εὐνοούσας). The exchange is likely pure invention, but it is telling, nevertheless. Persian officials gave Ionia considerable latitude for self-governance. When it came time for an invasion of the Balkans just over a decade later, the Ionians numbered among the Persian forces (see Chapter 2).[67]

Archaic Ionia was a dynamic place, but this efflorescence did not take place in isolation. Rather, it developed in tension and cooperation with first Lydia and then Achaemenid Persia. The ruthless suppression of the Ionian revolt must have represented a collective trauma for the people who lived through it, but it is also unfair to describe the last half century of the Archaic period in terms of decline. The imperial regime had changed, but the way that the Ionians interacted with this world had not. In fact, the revolt was largely the result of Ionian elites exploiting an imperial system for their own gain, which we will see again and again throughout the Classical period. Thus, when the Hellenic League "liberated" the region in 479, it was not at all certain that freedom was anything more than a political slogan designed to win support for a new form of hegemony.

---

65. Georges, "Persian Ionia," 34. Diod. 10.25.4 says that Artaphernes assessed tribute to each according to its ability to pay (τακτοὺς φόρους κατὰ δύναμιν ἐπέταξεν). Darius subsequently empowered Mardonius to relieve half of the assessed tribute (Polyaenus 7.11.3; Plut. *Mor.* 172F).

66. Persian support for democracies should not be a surprise. It was, after all, one of the tyrants who had incited the revolt. My interpretation runs contra Georges, "Persian Ionia," 34, who characterizes Artaphernes as "a vindictive incompetent," evidence for which he provides in the restoration of the tyrants.

67. On Persian governance of Ionia, see Briant, *From Cyrus to Alexander*, 493–97; Georges, "Persian Ionia," 34–35.

❦

CHAPTER 2

Orienting toward Athens and the Aegean System

480–454

Ionia was firmly ensconced in the Persian Empire at the start of Xerxes' ill-fated campaign in 480. When Xerxes mustered his forces, therefore, the Ionians came. A contemporary observer would be hard-pressed to imagine that the next two years would see Persian power rolled back or that this development created the playing field that would shape the region for the next two centuries. And yet that is exactly what happened.

Ionia had long been constrained by its relationships with its imperial neighbors, so the development of Athenian hegemony was novel primarily in that the new power in the region was a Greek polis rather than a king. The year 480/79 also marked a subtle change in that Athens held Persian authority at bay without sweeping Persia entirely away, thereby leaving the Ionian poleis to chart a course that accounted for a multipolar imperial arena. Analyzing Ionia within this new environment reveals two recurring themes. First, Ionians were complicit in the practice of empire in the Aegean, both in the Persian system and in the developing Athenian one. This is not a shocking conclusion, but the ebbs and flows of imperial competition offered new avenues to exploit power dynamics, including at the expense of other Greek poleis. Second, imperial competition threatened to exacerbate the long-standing factional conflicts in Ionia, the consequences of which began to appear already in the first half of the fifth century.

Fighting Badly? Ionia and Xerxes' Invasion of Greece

Despite the prominence of the Ionian revolt in Herodotus' history (5.28–55, 97–126, 6.1–42), the Ionians are largely subsumed into the mass of the Persian forces in his account of the campaign in 480. He refers to them as Ionians, as distinct from Greeks, at once highlighting concerns over their loyalty and demonstrating them to be among the most efficient units in the Persian fleet. The result is a tension that closer evaluation reveals to be the result of two competing forces: faction within Ionia at the time of the invasion and a web of pressures around how the Ionian contribution to the Persian invasion ought to be remembered.

According to Herodotus' catalog of the Persian force, the Ionians furnished a hundred ships (7.94; cf. Diod. 11.2.8). The description of this contingent is frustratingly vague and, despite already having described events in Ionia at length, Herodotus hews to the formula in the rest of this section in providing only an ethnographic snapshot about the contingent, saying that they were "equipped like Greeks" (ἐσκευασμένοι ὡς Ἕλληνες, 7.94).[1] Numbers reported by Herodotus are notoriously problematic, but, while the one hundred ships may be inexact, only the Phoenicians supplied more.[2]

In describing the Persian naval forces, Herodotus says Ariabignes, a son of Darius, commanded the Ionian and Carian ships, all of which carried Persian, Median, and Sacae marines (7.96–97).[3] However, it would be a mistake to assume that the Ionians at this moment fought for Persia only under the threat of death and were merely awaiting an opportunity to break free. In fact, Herodotus offers a rare moment of insight into their motivations at the start of the battle of Artemisium, when the Persian fleet had the Hellenic League ships surrounded (8.10.2–3):

> Now, all those among the Ionians sympathetic to the Greeks were sailing involuntarily. They became greatly distressed seeing [the Greeks] surrounded and believed that none would ever return home again, so weak did the Greek position seem to be. But others relished the situation, competing with each other to see who could seize an Attic ship first

---

1. Most of the ships were probably triremes, but this number may have also included biremes and pentekonters. On the composition of Archaic fleets, see Thomas J. Figueira, "Archaic Naval Warfare," *Historika* 5 (2015): 499–515. Herodotus later notes that he omits the names of the leaders of individual contingents on the grounds that they are not soldiers so much as slaves (ὥσπερ οἱ ἄλλοι στρατευόμενοι δοῦλοι, 7.96). Herodotus also describes the Samothracians as Ionians at 8.90, but see below, n. 8.

2. Herodotus' catalog includes no Greeks among the infantry, and O. Kimball Armayor, "Herodotus' Catalogues of the Persian Empire in the Light of the Monuments and the Greek Literary Tradition," *TAPhA* 108 (1978): 7, argues that it has a sense of "predetermination" that reflects the people of the Persian Empire. The presence of Ionian individuals at Plataea, such as the Ephesian Dionysophanes who buried Mardonius after the battle (Hdt. 9.84; Paus. 9.2.2), serves as a reminder that there were people with the campaign other than soldiers.

3. H. T. Wallinga, *Xerxes' Greek Adventure: The Naval Perspective* (Leiden: Brill, 2005), 40–42, suggests thirty Persian marines on each ship.

in order to receive gifts from the king since there was the most talk in camp about the Athenians.

ὅσοι μέν νυν τῶν Ἰώνων ἦσαν εὔνοοι τοῖσι Ἕλλησι, ἀέκοντές τε ἐστρατεύοντο συμφορήν τε ἐποιεῦντο μεγάλην ὁρῶντες περιεχομένους αὐτοὺς καὶ ἐπιστάμενοι ὡς οὐδεὶς αὐτῶν ἀπονοστήσει· οὕτω ἀσθενέα σφι ἐφαίνετο εἶναι τὰ τῶν Ἑλλήνων πρήγματα. ὅσοισι δὲ καὶ ἡδομένοισι ἦν τὸ γινόμενον, ἅμιλλαν ἐποιεῦντο ὅκως αὐτὸς ἕκαστος πρῶτος νέα Ἀττικὴν ἑλὼν παρὰ βασιλέος δῶρα λάμψεται· Ἀθηναίων γὰρ αὐτοῖσι λόγος ἦν πλεῖστος ἀνὰ τὰ στρατόπεδα.

Herodotus only specifies that some of the Ionians felt sympathy the Greeks, thereby leaving open to interpretation the identity of the ship commanders who were eager to attack the Athenians because they saw potential reward, but the parallel construction of his language also suggests that all of the viewpoints described here belonged to Ionians.[4] Indeed, Graham Shipley has argued that the Samians enthusiastically participated in the campaign because they had come to see the Ionian revolt as a mistake, while a strand of historiography suggests that serving in the Persian fleet empowered traditionally disenfranchised classes of people in Ionia in much the same way that ascendancy of the navy in fifth-century Athens endowed the *thētes* with increased political power.[5] Equally important, though, is Herodotus' explanation for the Ionian sympathy: not out of kinship, but at the seemingly hopeless situation of the Greek fleet.

A similar slippage occurs in the description of Themistocles' bid to separate the Ionians from Persia before the battle. Themistocles reportedly believed that the Ionians and Carians were the key to defeating the Persians (Hdt. 8.19.1) and so discretely sailed to locations where the Persian ships would put in for water and there left a message for the Ionians (Hdt. 8.22; Plut. *Them.* 9.1–2). In the Herodotean version, Themistocles wrote:[6]

---

4. Barry S. Strauss, *The Battle of Salamis: The Naval Encounter That Saved Greece—and Western Civilization* (New York: Simon and Schuster Paperbacks, 2005), 21, takes Herodotus as putting the Ionians in one group and the rest of the Persian fleet in the other.

5. Graham Shipley, *A History of Samos, 800–188 BC* (Oxford: Oxford University Press, 1987), 108, following B. M. Mitchell, "Herodotus and Samos," *JHS* 95 (1975): 88–89. Cf. Hdt. 6.14, where most of the Samian fleet refused to fight at the battle of Lade. For the thesis of political opportunity in service to Persia, see H. T. Wallinga, "The Ancient Persian Navy and Its Predecessors," in *Sources, Structures, and Synthesis: Proceedings of the Groningen 1983 Achaemenid History Workshop*, ed. Heleen Sancisi-Weerdenburg (Leiden: Nederlands Instituut voor het Nabije Oosten, 1987), 47–77; Tristan A. Goldman, "Imperializing Hegemony: The Polis and Achaemenid Persia" (PhD diss., University of Washington, 2011), 117–32.

6. Plutarch adds that Themistocles asked the Ionians to foul the Persian forces in battle, but that seems like later embellishment. Polyaenus 1.30.7 contains an abbreviated account of the message

Ionians! You are not acting justly taking up arms against your fatherland and bringing slavery to Hellas. It would be best if joined with us, but if that is not within your power you could still withdraw from this conflict yourselves and beg the Carians to go with you. But if you can do neither of these but are so powerfully compelled such that you cannot resist, then deliberately feign cowardice when battle is joined, remembering that you are our offspring and that these hostilities with the barbarians were your fault from the beginning.

ἄνδρες Ἴωνες, οὐ ποιέετε δίκαια ἐπὶ τοὺς πατέρας στρατευόμενοι καὶ τὴν Ἑλλάδα καταδουλούμενοι. ἀλλὰ μάλιστα μὲν πρὸς ἡμέων γίνεσθε: εἰ δὲ ὑμῖν ἐστι τοῦτο μὴ δυνατὸν ποιῆσαι, ὑμεῖς δὲ ἔτι καὶ νῦν ἐκ τοῦ μέσου ἡμῖν ἕζεσθε καὶ αὐτοὶ καὶ τῶν Καρῶν δέεσθε τὰ αὐτὰ ὑμῖν ποιέειν. εἰ δὲ μηδέτερον τούτων οἷόν τε γίνεσθαι, ἀλλ' ὑπ' ἀναγκαίης μέζονος κατέζευχθε ἢ ὥστε ἀπίστασθαι, ὑμεῖς δὲ ἐν τῷ ἔργῳ, ἐπεὰν συμμίσγωμεν, ἐθελοκακέετε μεμνημένοι ὅτι ἀπ' ἡμέων γεγόνατε καὶ ὅτι ἀρχῆθεν ἡ ἔχθρη πρὸς τὸν βάρβαρον ἀπ' ὑμέων ἡμῖν γέγονε.

Commentators from Herodotus onward have explained this gambit by saying that Themistocles had hoped either to lure the Ionians away from Xerxes' fleet or to sow the seeds of mistrust so that the king would hold them back from battle (Hdt. 8.22; cf. Plut. *Them.* 9.2). Themistocles' actions make for a good story—bravery, risk, and a dramatic flourish appealing to a common heritage— but there is no indication that they made a significant contribution to the Greek cause. Much like Leonidas' "sacrifice" at Thermopylae, Themistocles' attempts to incite a mass defection from Persia held more weight as propaganda and in memory than they did in practice.

After three days of indecisive fighting and a destructive storm (Hdt. 8.9–18; Diod. 11.12–13), the defending ships withdrew south and Xerxes' fleet advanced toward the climactic battle at Salamis.

On the day of battle, the Ionian contingent held the Persian left wing, nearest to Piraeus and facing the Spartan ships, while the Phoenicians faced the Athenians across the strait. Herodotus describes the hours that followed as a tangled and desperate struggle in which the Persian fleet fell to ruin under the eyes of the king himself.[7] However, Herodotus also points out that parts of

---

and simply says that it caused the king to mistrust the Ionians, though see below, "Fighting Badly," on Xerxes' mistrust.

7. For blow-by-blow analyses of the battle, see Jack Martin Balcer, *The Persian Conquest of the Greeks, 545–450 B.C.* (Konstanz: Universitätsverlag Konstanz, 1995), 257–72; John F. Lazenby, *The*

the Persian fleet demonstrated conspicuous bravery amid the carnage. At the height of the battle, the Phoenicians approached Xerxes to accuse the Ionians of treason (προδόντων), only for the king to witness a Samothracian vessel sink an Athenian ship and capture an Aeginetan one in quick succession and therefore dismiss the accusation (8.90).[8] Herodotus also identifies two Samians, Theomestor, the son of Androdamas, and Phylacus, the son of Histiaeus, who received honors from Xerxes on account of their bravery (8.85). Finally, in describing the Ionian conduct, he once again invokes Themistocles' appeal, only to say that most simply ignored it (ἐθελοκάκεον μέντοι αὐτῶν κατὰ τὰς Θεμιστοκλέος ἐντολὰς ὀλίγοι, οἱ δὲ πλεῦνες οὔ, 8.85).

There is reason to be suspicious of Herodotus' account of the Ionian role in the fighting. He singles out Greeks whose conduct in the battle was less than ideal and includes praise for the duplicitous skill of Artemisia of Caria, but the general shape of his narrative extols the naval prowess of the Greeks and the failures of the non-Greek ships. For the Ionians he thus suggests that they exceeded the barbarian contingents and those few who fell short did so only because they heeded Themistocles. While allowing that some of the Ionian ships may well have performed better than the Phoenicians at Salamis, Herodotus' explanation also suits a politically correct memory about the battle from a time when the Ionians were integral members of the Delian League.[9] Herodotus thus redeems those Ionians for the defeat at the battle of Lade even as they fought on the wrong side of the conflict. Diodorus confuses the issue further by preserving the tradition that the east side of the Persian fleet, composed of the Greek contingents, put up the stiffest resistance, but adds that before the battle the Ionians dispatched a Samian man to relate Xerxes' battle plans to the Greek

---

Defense of Greece, 490–479 B.C. (Warminster: Aris & Phillips, 1993), 151–97; Strauss, *The Battle of Salamis*, 157–208; Wallinga, *Xerxes' Greek Adventure*, 114–48.

8. Although Paus. 7.4.3 suggests that Samothrace was a colony of Samos and thus "Ionian," Herodotus more likely picked up the language of his sources for this story since the common Persian word for all Greeks was "Yauna" (Ionian).

9. Contra Wallinga, *Xerxes' Persian Adventure*, 41–42, who argues that the tradition was Athenian slander because Herodotus records only two Samians as *orosangai* (8.85) and the actual fighting would have been done by the Persian marines stationed aboard that prevented sabotage. Herodotus likely published his history in installments throughout the 420s, though the exact chronology is debated; see Justus Cobet, "Wann wurde Herodots Darstellung der Perserkriege publiziert?," *Hermes* 105, no. 1 (1977): 2–27; J. A. S. Evans, "Herodotus' Publication Date," *Athenaeum* 57 (1979): 145–49; J. A. S. Evans, "Herodotus 9.73.3 and the Publication Date of the Histories," *CPh* 82, no. 3 (1987): 226–28; Charles W. Fornara, "Evidence for the Date of Herodotus' Publication," *JHS* 91 (1971): 25–34; Charles W. Fornara, "Herodotus' Knowledge of the Archidamian War," *Hermes* 109, no. 2 (1981): 149–56; David Sansone, "The Date of Herodotus' Publication," *Illinois Classical Studies* 10, no. 1 (1985): 1–9; Rosalind Thomas, "The Intellectual Milieu of Herodotus," in *The Cambridge Companion to Herodotus*, ed. Carolyn Dewald and John Marincola (Cambridge: Cambridge University Press, 2016), 60–75. James Romm, *Herodotus* (New Haven, CT: Yale University Press, 1998), 48–58, lays out the challenges to understanding Herodotus' biography.

commanders, promising to desert during the battle—which they proceeded to not do (11.17.3–4).[10]

In fact, if we trust Herodotus, Xerxes only began to suspect the loyalty of the Ionians *after* suffering defeat at Salamis. Recalling a parallel episode where Ionians were tasked with guarding Darius' bridge over the Danube (Hdt. 4.133–41, 5.23), Herodotus says Xerxes feared that the Ionians would put it into the minds of his enemies to destroy the bridge over the Hellespont and so decided to withdraw his royal person from Europe (8.97).[11] And yet, not only is there no record of Xerxes punishing any Ionian for disloyalty, but he also appointed two Samians *orosangai*. A careful reading of Herodotus' account of Xerxes' campaign thus underscores the continued factionalism in Ionia writ large. The evidence that Ionians fought against people they considered their kin only under compulsion is far slimmer and likely emerged from a need to reha-bilitate them for having been on the wrong side of a war branded as a defense of Greek liberty.

Local and regional conflicts in Ionia meant that the potential for rebellion and revolution bubbled just beneath the surface throughout the Classical period. When the Greek ships mustered at Aegina after Salamis, they were approached by six Chians who had participated in a conspiracy to murder the tyrant Strat-tis, asking that the Greek fleet sail immediately to Ionia (Hdt. 8.132).[12] Nev-ertheless, the region was still firmly Persian in the winter of 480/79. Xerxes dispatched Artemisia to convey his family to Ephesus (Hdt. 8.106) and followed through on his promise to appoint Theomestor tyrant on Samos, where part of the Persian fleet spent the winter (Hdt. 8.130; Diod. 11.27.1). When spring arrived, the Persian fleet, including the Ionian ships, mustered at Samos in order to guard against a potential rebellion, Herodotus says, while adding that "they did not expect the Greeks to come to Ionia" (οὐ μὲν οὐδὲ προσεδέκοντο τοὺς Ἕλληνας ἐλεύσεσθαι ἐς τὴν Ἰωνίην, 8.130.3).[13] They could not have known that 479 would be a year that displayed all of the features that defined Ionia for the subsequent two centuries.

10. This seems to be an inversion of Themistocles' activities as described by Herodotus (8.22). Lazenby, *Defense of Greece*, 185 calls the story "faintly ridiculous." On the contested traditions about the order of battle, see Lazenby, 183–87.

11. In the earlier incident the Ionians remained loyal to Darius, albeit because he ensured their political power; see Chapter 1. In the latter, Herodotus credits Themistocles with the plan to attack the bridge without mentioning the Ionians (8.108.2).

12. Herodotus conspicuously does not use the language of liberty to describe this episode. The Greek commanders were only willing to go as far as Delos.

13. Diodorus also comments on the specter of agitation in Ionia (ὡς ἀλλότρια φρονούντων τῶν Ἰώνων, 11.27.1).

The Year of Liberation? 479 BCE

Buried near the end of Herodotus' history is his account of the battle of Mycale (9.90–107; cf. Diod. 11.34–36), an engagement that ancient tradition implausibly sets on the same day as Plataea (Hdt. 9.90; Diod. 11.24.1).[14] Despite acknowledging the battle's significance in securing the victory over the Persians, Herodotus sets it in the denouement of the war. However, for Ionia, Mycale, not Salamis, led to the "liberation" that framed the rest of the fifth century. Before turning to the battle and its aftermath, it is worth considering what can be gleaned about the regional political currents in Ionia from these passages. Both Herodotus and Diodorus frame Mycale as a moment of liberation for Ionia and put those words in the mouths of the ambassadors from Samos. Persian-appointed officials ruled at least at Samos, Chios, and Miletus, but their positions became increasingly tenuous as the year wore on.[15]

Herodotus records both subversive actions and Persian suspicion. Immediately before the battle, he says that "the Samians" sent Lampon, son of Thrasycles, Athenagoras, son of Archistratides, and Hegesistratus, son of Aristagoras, to make an appeal to the Spartan commander Leutychides on Delos, where Hegisistratus declared (9.90):[16]

> Should the Ionians only see you, they will desert from the Persians and the barbarians will not remain, but if they do, you will never again have such a hunt.

> ὡς ἢν μοῦνον ἴδωνται αὐτοὺς οἱ Ἴωνες ἀποστήσονται ἀπὸ Περσέων, καὶ ὡς οἱ βάρβαροι οὐκ ὑπομενέουσι· ἢν δὲ καὶ ἄρα ὑπομείνωσι, οὐκ ἑτέρην ἄγρην τοιαύτην εὑρεῖν ἄν αὐτούς.

Hegisistratus continued that the Persian ships were unseaworthy and implored the Greeks to liberate them from slavery by defeating the barbarians. Of course,

---

14. Pierre Briant, *From Cyrus to Alexander: A History of the Persian Empire*, trans. Peter T. Daniels (Winona Lake, IN: Eisenbrauns, 2002), 533, offers a more likely chronology whereby the Greek fleet sailed to Delos before Plataea (Hdt. 9.90) and only went on the offensive afterward.

15. Mardonius was supposed to have deposed all Ionian tyrants in 492, replacing them with democracies (Hdt. 6.43). While allowing that Xerxes may have simply made a new decision to appoint Theomestor, it may well be that labeling him and the Chian Strattis (Hdt. 8.132) "tyrants" is slander on account of their collaboration with the Persian authorities.

16. Diodorus 11.34.2 says that the "worthy ambassadors" (πρέσβεις ἀξιοῦντες) came from Samos. Shipley, *History of Samos*, 109, identifies these names as belonging to the other families who had been suppressed and exiled during and after the reign of Polycrates; cf. Sara Forsdyke, *Exile, Ostracism, and Democracy: The Politics of Expulsion in Ancient Greece* (Princeton, NJ: Princeton University Press, 2005), 59–69.

Leutychides rejected both the impassioned plea and all arguments in favor of viewing the name "Hegisistratus" as an auspicious omen, whereupon the two sides bound themselves with an oath of alliance (Hdt. 9.91–92). The Samians had also liberated five hundred Athenian prisoners, whom they supplied with provisions and sent back to Athens, which in turn led to suspicion from the Persians (Hdt. 9.99.2). Herodotus thus establishes Samos as the leading polis in the fight for Greek liberty, a status that is paid off both by having the Samians turn on the Persians at the height of the fighting and with Samos' prominent position within the Delian League. Diodorus' account strengthens this picture not only by saying not only that the Samians dispatched the ambassadors (11.34.2) and had unanimously decided to turn on the Persians, but also that their attack turned the tide of the battle (11.36.2, 4).[17]

Persian suspicions peaked immediately before the battle of Mycale when Leutychides had a ship sail close to shore and repeat Themistocles' ploy from the leadup to Artemisium, with a herald tell the Ionians to turn against the Persians (Hdt. 9.98). The Persian commander Tigranes ordered the Samians stripped of their arms and armor (ὅπλα) and stationed the Milesians on the heights of Mycale away from the battlefield (9.99).[18] Nevertheless, Herodotus says, at the climax of the battle the Ionians effected a second revolt. The Samians led the way by turning on the Persians, causing them to retreat, and then the Milesians, who were ostensibly guarding the passes and guiding the Persians to safety, directed them right back to their enemies (Hdt. 9.103–4).[19] The Ionian role in leading the Greeks of Asia against the Persians and turning the tide of the battle is undoubtedly exaggerated, once again redeeming Greeks who had fought on the "wrong side," but there is no reason to reject more modest contributions.[20]

---

17. Diodorus' use of Ephorus as his source for Mycale and its aftermath likely accounts for the differences from Herodotus.

18. Shipley, *History of Samos*, 109, doubts that the disarmed soldiers were hoplites on account of his contention that Samos had fewer hoplites in proportion to the size of its population than other poleis, but recent scholarship has begun to challenge the primacy of the hoplite at the time of the Persian wars altogether; see, in particular, Roel Konijnendijk, "'Neither the Less Valorous nor the Weaker': Persian Military Might and the Battle of Plataia," *Historia* 61, no. 1 (2012): 1–17.

19. Herodotus' mention of the Milesians here is notable because he had implied that the entire population of Miletus was killed or deported following the Ionian revolt (6.19). As Alan M. Greaves, *Miletos: A History* (New York: Routledge, 2002), 132, suggests, the destruction of Miletus was likely exaggerated, while Vanessa B. Gorman, *Miletos, the Ornament of Ionia* (Ann Arbor: University of Michigan Press, 2001), 146–51, plausibly connects a series of *isopoliteia* treaties between Miletus and its colonies during this period and thus suggests that the new citizens returned from the colonies; see below, "Ionia within the Early Athenian Arche."

20. T. J. Quinn, *Athens and Samos, Lesbos and Chios, 478–404 B.C.* (Manchester: Manchester University Press, 1981), 7. Cf. Mitchell, "Herodotus and Samos," 87–91, who sees a Samian apologia behind Herodotus' account of both the Ionian revolt and the battle of Mycale. Elizabeth

Whether a spontaneous uprising against the Persians as in Herodotus or a premeditated plot as in Diodorus, the Greek sources present the events as the result of a revolutionary sentiment against Persian rule, but there is little evidence from the Ionians specifically that supports this picture. It was this rationale that prompted Jack Balcer to argue that the primary issue was not revolution, but "to find successful means by which to revitalize the particular poleis in order to prevent further disintegration, and to preserve and reorganize the social and political order."[21]

In the immediate aftermath of Mycale, the leaders of the Hellenic League convened a council on Samos to determine what to do with the Ionians since they believed it would only be a matter of time before they faced another threat from the barbarians (9.106.2). The topic at hand was who would give them land. The possibility of relocating the Ionians was not new; Bias of Priene had allegedly made the same proposal in 546, and some of the Phocaeans and Teians had actually followed through (Hdt. 1.164–70). However, the scale of the proposed operation would have dwarfed the earlier proposals and the paucity of the surviving details invites questions about its veracity, in either Herodotus' account or the more exaggerated version in Diodorus, where the Athenians scuttled the plan only after the Ionians and Aeolians had prepared because they would then cease to be the Ionian mother city (11.37).[22] Herodotus does not mention the Aeolians or other Greeks of Asia, for instance, or whether the proposal included islands like Samos and Chios that had been no more successful than their neighbors on the mainland at warding off Persian power. Thus, Herodotus' discussion foreshadows the coming rivalry between Athens and Sparta more than it records a serious proposal. Thucydides blames the violence of Pausanias for the demise of the Hellenic League, but the failure to resolve the underlying tension between its aims of liberating the Greeks and its unwillingness to commit to protecting them spelled its doom.[23]

Irwin, "Herodotus and Samos: Personal or Political," *CW* 102, no. 4 (2009): 395–416, argues, persuasively, that Herodotus' interest in Samos comes from its parallel with fifth-century Athens. She rejects earlier arguments that it was personal, but only brushes on how memory and politics shaped his presentation of Samos (416 n. 65), which necessarily would have included not just Athenian memories, but Samian ones.

21. Jack Martin Balcer, *Sparda by the Bitter Sea: Imperial Interaction in Western Anatolia* (Providence, RI: Brown University Press, 1984), 324. Balcer, in "Fifth Century B.C. Ionia: A Frontier Redefined," *REA* 87, nos. 1–2 (1985): 31–42, and "The Liberation of Ionia: 478 B.C.," *Historia* 46, no. 3 (1997): 374–77, also argues that Persia retained control of the river deltas in Ionia. While he is correct to doubt that liberation of Ionia was clean and complete, I am skeptical of his interpretation that Persian control lay behind local unrest in the region; see Chapter 3, "Domestic Factionalism and the Specter of Persia."

22. Shipley, *History of Samos*, 109. On these myths see Chapter 1.

23. As Donald Kagan, *The Outbreak of the Peloponnesian War* (Ithaca, NY: Cornell University Press, 1969), 34.

Herodotus does not record the fate of Theomestor but concludes by saying that the Greeks enrolled the Samians, Chians, and Lesbians in the Hellenic League before sailing to the Hellespont to dismantle Xerxes' bridge (9.106.4).[24] Through the campaign season of 478, ships from Samos and Chios, at least, sailed with Pausanias first to Cyprus and then to Byzantium, where Spartan leadership collapsed (Thuc. 1.94–95).[25] Persian power remained at Sardis just over the horizon, but, for the moment, Ionia was free.

Founding the Delian League

Sparta might have led the Hellenic League against Persia, but Athens dominated the fifth-century Aegean. From the outset, the Ionians received an outsized amount of blame for undermining the Spartan alliance. Thucydides says that it was the Ionians as a group (οὐχ ἥκιστα οἱ Ἴωνες, 1.95.1) who came to resent the violent (βίαιος) leadership of Pausanias and therefore requested that Athenians lead a new alliance that would better serve their interests, while [Aristotle] says that Aristides stoked the flames of frustration on the part of the Ionians after Pausanias' fall (*Ath. Pol.* 23.4).[26] However, from this early date it is unclear how many of the Ionian poleis had joined the Hellenic League (see above, "The Year of Liberation").[27] Ancient sources present conflicting evidence, oscillating between naming Samos and Chios as specific poleis brought into the league and making general pronouncements about the Ionians being involved in league activities. This contradiction is most pronounced with regard to the Milesians, whose actions at Mycale Herodotus characterized as a second Ionian revolt, but who no ancient source included on the list of poleis enrolled in the Hellenic League.[28]

---

24. Herodotus expands the list of enrollees to "all other islanders who had served with the Greeks," τοὺς ἄλλους νησιώτας, οἳ ἔτυχον συστρατευόμενοι. Distinguishing between the islanders and the mainland poleis is a repeated issue throughout the Classical period.

25. Balcer, *Sparda*, 327–30, frames the campaign to Sparta as a bid to maintain hegemony over the Hellenic League in the face of a challenge from Athens.

26. Plutarch elaborates on Pausanias' violence, describing the punishments he meted out to non-Spartans in contrast to the moderation of the Athenians Cimon and Aristides (*Arist.* 23.2–3).

27. In part this determination is dependent on the strength and longevity of the league. I follow David Yates, "The Tradition of the Hellenic League against Xerxes," *Historia* 64, no. 1 (2015): 1–25, in seeing the Hellenic League as a "tenuous and temporary" association that quickly faded out of existence after 478; cf. Adrian Tronson, "The Hellenic League of 480 B.C.—Fact or Ideological Fiction," *Acta Classica* 34 (1991): 93–110, who regards the Hellenic nature of the league as an "ideological fiction." The interpretation of a strong Hellenic League emerges mostly from the evidence of Diodorus Siculus, following Ephorus, that builds on the model of the fourth-century League of Corinth.

28. This question of original enrollment in the Delian League and, by extension, the Hellenic League, was a debate in the early twentieth century, for discussion see particularly Raphael Sealey,

Presenting Ionian antagonism to Sparta as the driving force behind the creation of the Delian League also leads to the false conclusion that this was an *Ionian* alliance built on kinship.[29] Ancient sources almost universally point to Athenian activities spearheaded by Themistocles and Aristides that caused poleis throughout the Aegean to reject Sparta, leaving Athens as a natural alternative (e.g., Diod. 11.41–46; [Arist.] *Ath. Pol.* 23.4–5).[30] Plutarch identifies commanders from Samos, Chios, and Lesbos generally and Uliades of Samos and Antagoras of Chios specifically as instigating the conspiracy (*Arist.* 23.4–5). He is almost certainly wrong to exonerate his upright subject Aristides on the charge of conspiring against the Spartans, but his suggestion that the non-Athenian actors included only men from the large islands that had joined the Hellenic League after the battle of Mycale is more likely true than is the implication that the Delian League was the result of a general Ionian uprising.

Similarly, no ancient source preserves a list of poleis that inscribed their oath to have the same enemies and friends on lumps of iron before casting them into the sea to render it unbreakable ([Arist.] *Ath. Pol.* 23.5).[31] Subsequently, ancient tradition held, Aristides assessed the allies for tribute, likely preserving the rates that the Persians had set ([Arist.] *Ath. Pol.* 23.5; Plut. *Arist.* 24). Recreating the original roster of the Delian League is complicated further still by the processes of historical memory that surround the purpose of the league and the relationship between the league members and Athens. In Ionia, Chios and Samos were charter members and Miletus likely was as well, but Myus was supposed to have been given to the exiled Themistocles by the Persian king as late as 465 (Plut. *Them.* 29.7).[32] Evidence in either direction for the rest of the

---

"The Origin of the Delian League," in *Ancient Societies and Institutions*, ed. Ernst Badian (New York: Barnes and Noble, 1966), 242–48. However, Gorman, *Miletos*, 215, declares that the Milesian contribution at Mycale must have meant its inclusion.

29. Gorman, *Miletos*, 215, highlights the parallel with 499 in the appeals to Athenian kinship even though Aristagoras had also appealed to Sparta before traveling to Athens. Gordon Shrimpton, "Horton Hears an Ionian," in *Epigraphy and the Greek Historian*, ed. Craig Cooper (Toronto: University of Toronto Press, 2008), 129–49, takes a wider view of Ionian identity suggests that Athens chose Delos as the focal point of its new confederacy because of its religious importance to Ionia, citing it as the birthplace of Artemis and Apollo. However, this is misleading since other traditions located the birth of both deities in the vicinity of the Ionian dodecapolis or Lycia.

30. On the interpretations of the Delian League constitution, see P. J. Rhodes, *Commentary on the Aristotelian Athenaion Politeia*, rev. ed. (Oxford: Oxford University Press, 1993), 294–95.

31. The original roster of the Delian League is a debate begun in the nineteenth century and still unresolved. A. Kirchhoff, "Der Delische Bund im Ersten Decennium Seines Bestehens," *Hermes* 11, no. 1 (1876): 1–48, maintained that the alliance excluded the Ionian and Aeolian poleis other than perhaps those on the islands until after Eurymedon in 465, which Evelyn Abbott, "The Early History of the Delian League," *CR* 3 (1889): 387–90, roundly rejected.

32. Complications with this donation abound. First, the gifts may not be real, given that they fit into a metaphorical schema for a complete diet. Second, by the 460s Myus, located on the Bay of Mycale, may not have been in the power of the king to give except as a symbolic gesture, though see

region is limited. Ephesus remained a crucial transit point for people moving between the Persian Empire and the Aegean world, but it, along with the rest of Ionia, was firmly in the Athenian orbit by 454, and there is no evidence for a military expedition coercing the Ionians to join, as there was elsewhere (Plut. *Cim.* 12.4; see below, "The Tides of War"). Placing the Ionians collectively at the inauguration of the Delian League elides a more complicated reality. In these early years the entire region was likely assessed for contributions even when they were only tenuously within the league's orbit before gradually and spasmodically they joined in earnest.

The process by which Ionia became fully integrated into the Delian League is bound up with its original purpose. Athenian propaganda asserted a league mandate to liberate and protect the Greeks of Asia Minor from Persia (e.g., Thuc. 3.10.1; Diod. 11.41.4), but these were mere words. Closer to the mark is the formulation of Raphael Sealey: "The original purpose of the League was piratical."[33] Indeed, liberation by the Delian League was conquest by another name—its recipients had no choice but to sign on.[34] Athenian willingness to compel obedience tempered any protection it offered and is therefore an inadequate explanation on its own for how Ionia became integrated into this Athenian-Aegean system, regardless of the potential of kinship diplomacy.

In a discussion of Ionian motivations, lodged between the usual explanations I just characterized as inadequate on their own, Jack Balcer offered a third possibility.[35] At least by the reorganization of the Persian Empire under Darius I, and arguably earlier, Ionian commercial prosperity had stemmed from

---

Balcer, "Liberation of Ionia." On the date of Themistocles' arrival in Persia, see Pietro Maria Liuzzo, "L'arrivo di Temistocle in Persia e la successione a Serse: Il breve regno di Artabano," *Rivista storica dell'antichità* 40 (2010): 33–50.

33. Sealey, "Origins of the Delian League," 238, following Thucydides 1.96.1, cf. Noel Robertson, "The True Nature of the 'Delian League,'" *AJAH* 5, no. 1 (1980): 64–96 and Noel Robertson, "The True Nature of the 'Delian League' II," *AJAH* 5, no. 2 (1980): 110–33, who characterizes the league as containing a small group of predatory members. This position is not universally accepted. Some scholars, such as A. H. Jackson, "The Original Purpose of the Delian League," *Historia* 18, no. 1 (1969): 12–16, see the league activity as aiming for strategic advantage rather than conquest. Vincent Azoulay, *Pericles of Athens*, trans. Janet Lloyd (Princeton, NJ: Princeton University Press, 2014), 51–52, notes the new members still had a say in the league *synedrion*, at least at first.

34. As Sealey, "Origins of the Delian League," 241–42, points out. Hunter Rawlings III, "Thucydides on the Purpose of the Delian League," *Phoenix* 31, no. 1 (1977): 1–8, argues that Thucydides meant to imply an ulterior motive behind the Athenian actions in 478/7 and that they only accepted leadership to assert control. While there was more Athenian activity in the coup to topple Pausanias than is sometimes acknowledged, the position that Athens was aiming for an empire from the jump is too aggressive and not supported by Thucydides; see A. French, "Athenian Ambitions and the Delian Alliance," *Phoenix* 33, no. 2 (1979): 134–41. Balcer, *Sparda*, 330–31, holds that the eastern Greeks sought an alliance, which was frequently true but too strong as a blanket statement.

35. Balcer, *Sparda*, 331.

its extensive trading networks throughout Anatolia and the eastern Mediterranean. These markets were closed to Ionian merchants following their "liberation," meaning that this region where the poleis were still recovering from
the revolts of the 490s had to reorient its commerce.[36] The positive incentives
of promised plunder from military campaigns against Persia and economic
opportunity in the Aegean bound the Ionians into this new system more tightly
than did kinship or promises of protection. In fact, Ionian interaction with
the Delian League in these early years appears most clearly in the campaigns
against Persia.

The Tides of War: 478–454

The details of the early history of the Delian League are scarce, which complicates our understanding of how the Ionians interacted with it.[37] Thucydides, for
instance, uses his account to examine the growth of Athenian power to support
his thesis about the origins of the Peloponnesian War.[38] He covers the early
Delian League campaigns to Eion, Scyros, Carystus, and Naxos in a few short
sentences that demonstrate the growth of Athenian power, before recounting
Cimon's campaigns in southern Anatolia and Cyprus that captured Phaselis
and won a victory at the Eurymedon River (Thuc. 1.100; Diod. 11.60–61; Plut.
Cim. 12.4). By the end of this period, Thucydides concludes, the allies were the
cause of their own subjection because they met their obligations with money
and shirked military service. When the time came to fight back, he explains,
they were both "unprepared and inexperienced" (ἀπαράσκευοι καὶ ἄπειροι,
1.98–99). Athens had expanded the league by force, and the subjugation of
Naxos both demonstrated a willingness to compel allies to remain in the league
and temporarily ended any debate about how long it would exist.[39] But Athens

---

36. E.g., Miletus, which Herodotus says was left desolate of Milesians (Μίλητος μέν νυν
Μιλησίων ἠρήμωτο, 6.22.1), though other poleis likely recovered more quickly. The time between
the end of the revolts and 478 is the same as the time between the plague at Athens and the launch
of the Sicilian expedition, when Thucydides suggests that the Athenians had finally recovered from
the first catastrophe.

37. The most thorough account of this period is still Russell Meiggs, The Athenian Empire
(Oxford: Oxford University Press, 1972), 68–91.

38. As A. French, The Athenian Half-Century, 478–431 BC (Sydney: Sydney University Press,
1971), 2, notes, "Outside the strict confines of his subject he leaves the ground virtually untouched."

39. Thucydides' abbreviated chronology is compressed. These campaigns ranged from the 477
into the 460s. Ron K. Unz, "The Chronology of the Pentekontaetia," CQ^2 36, no. 1 (1986): 69–73,
provocatively rejects Thucydides' relative chronology, accepted by most scholars, on the grounds
that it fails to explain why the Naxians would have believed the league no longer necessary and
therefore places the revolt after the battle of Eurymedon. For a traditional order of events, see

did not operate alone, so we need to ask what role the Ionians played in the growth of the league power.

At some time in the first half of the 460s, the Athenians elected Cimon, son of Miltiades, strategos and empowered him to wage war against Persia in order to liberate the Greeks of Asia, as Diodorus characterizes it (11.contents).[40] The highwater mark of Cimon's success and, indeed, of Athenian expansion was a decisive victory over the Persian fleet off Cyprus that he followed up with a second victory over the Persian army at the Eurymedon River (Diod. 11.60–62; cf. Thuc. 1.100.1). Diodorus reports that Cimon captured 340 ships, twenty thousand prisoners, and a sizable amount Persian gold and credits Cimon (11.62.1) and the Athenians (11.60.6) for the victories. Indeed, the two hundred Athenian triremes Cimon had upon leaving the Piraeus formed the core of the fleet, but league forces swelled its size by half again, bringing his total force up to three hundred ships (Diod. 11.60.3; cf. Thuc. 1.100.1). Neither Thucydides nor Diodorus lists the allied contingents individually, but Diodorus specifically says that ships from Ionia joined Cimon's expedition. Determining what he meant by "Ionia" is another matter.

There is always a risk that casual invocations of Ionia in ancient historians merely to refer to the Greeks of Asia Minor (see Chapter 1). Diodorus distinguishes between Ionians and Aeolians elsewhere, but, writing in the first century BCE, he was beholden to sources that, on top of choosing not to elaborate on the non-Athenian contingents, could have applied their own definition of "Ionian." Despite these limitations, there is good reason to believe that a significant portion of the allied ships came from the cities of the Ionian dodecapolis and that most of those came from Chios and Samos, two large island poleis that still maintained substantial fleets at this time. Identifying these poleis as integral to Cimon's expedition is not purely speculative. In his biography of Cimon, Plutarch includes an anecdote about Cimon's ferocity in attacking Phaselis because the city refused Athenian liberation (*Cim.* 12.4). The Chians, he says, were traditionally on good terms with the Phaselites and therefore appealed to Cimon while passing notes to the besieged by shooting arrows over the wall. The details of this episode strain credibility, but an Athenian decree that established a judicial relationship with Phaselis likely uses the relationship between

---

Meiggs, *Athenian Empire*, 68–91, and Brian Rutishauser, *Athens and the Cyclades: Economic Strategies 510–314 BC* (Oxford: Oxford University Press, 2012), 89–90. The lack of evidence has led to numerous proposals; see Rutishauser, 89 n. 52.

40. ὡς Ἀθηναῖοι τὰς κατὰ τὴν Ἀσίαν Ἑλληνίδας πόλεις ἠλευθέρωσαν. Despite a continued tendency in some corners to frame Greek history in terms of freedom from oriental oppression, there is a lack of freedom in these Athenian liberations; see Sealey and Robertson above, n. 33. Azoulay, *Pericles*, 51–60, stresses the violence of the Delian League.

Athens and Chios as a model (*RO* 120 = *IG* I³ 10, ll. 10–11), and the broad out-
lines of an Athenian expedition bolstered by Ionian forces fit neatly within the
consensus picture of the Delian League in this period.

Much the same picture emerges in the Athenian expeditions to Egypt. In
c.464, shortly after the accession of Artaxerxes, the Egyptian Inarus, the son
of Psammetichus, solicited Athens for support for his rebellion against Persia (Thuc. 1.104; Diod. 11.71).[41] The Athenians responded enthusiastically
(Diod: μετὰ πολλῆς προθυμίας) and dispatched hundreds of ships to Egypt.
Thucydides' narrative foreshadows the catastrophe in Sicily a half century later,
right down to the loss of a second fleet sent to relieve the first (Thuc. 1.110.4),
so recent scholarship has cast doubt the enormous size of the expedition.[42]
Thucydides' reliability is beyond the scope of this inquiry, but this expedition
in particular is often seen as a wheel on which he could sharpen his political axe
about the foolishness of democracy.[43] Nevertheless, the Athenian enthusiasm
for the campaign found in all of the available sources is generally explained
by the combination of a fervor to strike a blow against Persia combined with
the economic opportunity that might be found in Egypt and it is worth considering how far beyond Athens these motivations spread.[44] The Ionian poleis
had long had close commercial relationships with Egypt. Chios, Teos, Phocaea,
and Clazomenae were among the nine that contributed to a Hellenion at the
emporium Naucratis, while two others, Samos and Miletus, established their
own precincts for Hera and Apollo, respectively (Hdt. 2.178.2–3).[45] Ionia also

41. These dates are contested. I follow Daniel Kahn, "Inaros' Rebellion against Artaxerxes I
and the Athenian Disaster in Egypt," *CQ*² 58, no. 2 (2008): 424–40, in seeing a short rebellion that
started after the accession of Artaxerxes I in 465 and concluded in 457 following the Persian victory
at Prosopitis, with a second Athenian expedition to Cyprus c.450.

42. Eric W. Robinson, "Thucydidean Sieges, Prosopitis, and the Hellenic Disaster in Egypt,"
CW 18, no. 1 (1999): 132, notes the recent consensus of c.100 ships lost, which, he says, would not
have caused the collapse of Athenian power though he ultimately agrees with Thucydides' emphasis
on the failure of the expedition; cf. A. J. Holladay, "The Hellenic Disaster in Egypt," *JHS* 109 (1989):
178–79. Kahn, "Inaros' Rebellion," 435, points out that Ctesias (F14) and Diodorus (11.77) offer a
different ending to the campaign found in Thucydides 1.110.1, where "most of them were killed"
(οἱ δὲ πλεῖστοι ἀπώλοντο); cf. Eyal Meyer, "The Athenian Expedition to Egypt and the Value of
Ctesias," *Phoenix* 72, nos. 1–2 (2018): 43–61. For many historians, though, Thucydides reigns. E.g.,
Carmela Raccuia, "La tradizione sull'intervento Ateniese in Egitto," *Helikon* 18–19 (1978–79): 210–
27, who dismisses Ctesias and Diodorus as inadequate even while applauding them for fleshing out
Thucydides' brevity. For the parallel with Sicily, see S. Hornblower, *A Commentary on Thucydides*,
vol. 1 (Oxford: Oxford University Press, 1997), 176–77, though this position is not universally
accepted; see Holladay, "Hellenic Disaster," 181–82.

43. H. D. Westlake, "Thucydides and the Athenian Disaster in Egypt," *CPh* 45, no. 4 (1950):
209–16, for instance; cf. Kahn, "Inaros' Rebellion," 436.

44. Meiggs, *Athenian Empire*, 95 and n. 3, points to evidence for a grain shortage in Athens that
made Egypt particularly attractive, though his principal grounds for an early date for the inscription *IG* I² 31.6, the three-barred sigma, is obsolete.

45. The origins of Naucratis are unclear, but Strabo's story about a Milesian foundation

lay on the eastern edge of the confederacy, making ulterior motivations likely. For some, a blow against Persia kept a threat on its heels; for others, a campaign legitimized their regime by unifying the community against a common enemy.

Both ancient and modern authors overwhelmingly focus on the Athenians.[46] Inarus invited their participation, after all, and Athenian ships comprised the largest part of the expedition, but Thucydides makes it clear that the fleet included both the Athenians and their allies (1.104.1). An honorific epigram for Hegesagoras, son of Zoilos, found on a statue base at the Heraion on Samos commemorates the Samian capture of fifteen Phoenician ships on the Nile near Memphis (*IG* XII 6, 279).[47] Despite Westlake's cavalier assertion that this inscription does not substantially revise what we know about the campaign, it is an important reminder that the selective survival of evidence from this period belies the extent to which Athens relied on its allies to fight its wars.[48] The capture of fifteen vessels, a number more reliable than those given for the total size of the Greek fleet, suggests a substantial number of Samians in Egypt!

Unfortunately, this murky picture already strains the limits of our evidence since the sources frequently omit even the mention of Ionian allies. Jack Balcer reasonably "suspected" wider participation in the Athenian campaigns from Chios, which continued to field a fleet until the last decade of the fifth century, and perhaps Erythrae and Miletus, which were among the wealthiest in the region as judged by the assessment on the Athenian tribute lists,[49] but there is little concrete evidence outside of the inscription on Samos and the anecdotal tradition about the capture of Phaselis.

I opened this section with Thucydides' claim that the Athenian allies grew complacent and thereby fell increasingly under the Athenian yoke. Thus, in the terminology of modern scholars, the Delian League metastasized into an Athenian empire. However, we might tentatively challenge Thucydides' authoritative

---

(13.1.18) likely developed from a later tradition that built Miletus up as a colonizing power; see Jan Willem Drijvers, "Strabo 17.1.18 (801C): Inaros, the Milesians and Naucratis," *Mnemosyne*⁴ 52, no. 1 (1999): 16–22. On the organization of Naucratis, see Carl Roebuck, "The Organization of Naukratis," *CPh* 46, no. 4 (1951): 212–20. Locating the Hellenion has been a goal of excavators; see Albert Leonard Jr., "Ancient Naukratis: Excavations at a Greek Emporium in Egypt, Part I: The Excavations at Kom Ge'if," *AASOR* 54 (1997): 1–35.

46. The most common acknowledgment of non-Athenian forces comes in the calculations for how many Athenians might have died in Egypt; see Holladay, "Hellenic Disaster," 179; Robinson, "Thucydidean Sieges," 149–50.

47. This inscription was first published by Werner Peek, "Ein Seegefecht aus den Perserkriegen," *Klio* 32 (1939): 289–306. His reconstruction has largely been accepted, with subsequent scholars debating how much this changes the picture of the campaign found in the textual tradition.

48. Westlake, "Thucydides."

49. Balcer, *Sparda*, 377. For a discussion of these lists, see Chapter 3.

declaration even beyond the usual caveat that Samos, Chios, and Lesbos were exceptions to the rule. Unlike Herodotus' account of the battle of Lade, where he enumerates contingents from the individual poleis, down to the three triremes each outfitted by Phocaea and Myus (6.8), none of the surviving sources for these Athenian operations offers a roll call. Any evidence for their participation emerges instead from ancillary evidence. This alone is hardly proof that Myus, for instance, contributed even a solitary ship, but underscores that, if Myus did, we would likely not know.

Throughout the early years of the Delian League, most of the Ionians were not idle witnesses to the growth of Athenian power, but actively complicit in it. Much as the Chians sought to profit from the Athenian war against Samos in 440/39 (see Chapter 3, "The War Between Samos and Miletus"), both Chios and Samos likely aided in the campaign against Naxos. Similarly, Pausanias records that the inscribed shield the Spartans dedicated at Olympia after the battle of Tanagra in 457 read that it was a "gift from the Argives, Athenians, and Ionians" (δῶρον ἀπ᾽ Ἀργείων καὶ Ἀθαναίων καὶ Ἰώνων, 5.10.4).[50] Once more the question whether "Ionian" was merely a shorthand for the Athenian allies rears its head, but we should not be quick to dismiss the presence of the men of Ionia: they certainly fought in the Peloponnese during the Peloponnesian War (see Chapter 3). The development of the Athenian tribute lists supports Thucydides' argument, but the fixation on naval warfare erases other military contributions, and the earnest declaration about complacency obscures that this was a period during which the Ionians were continually at war.

Ionia within the Early Athenian Arche:
Desolation and Renaissance

In the two decades between the start of the Persian wars and the Athenian expedition to Egypt, Ionia had gone from being embedded in the Persian Empire to being embedded in an Athenian one. The surest sign of this entanglement is the evidence for participation in Athenian expeditions, but there is also copious evidence from this period for the migration of both people and intellectual traditions to Athens. This movement helped construct that city's reputation as a center of learning, even as the influx of immigrants to Athens likely contributed to legislative changes like the Periclean Citizenship Law of 451/0 ([Arist.] *Ath.*

---

50. Fragments survive from an inscription at Olympia that likely was part of the same monument; see P. J. Rhodes and Robin Osborne, *Greek Historical Inscriptions, 478–404 BC* (Oxford: Oxford University Press, 2017), 70–73.

Pol. 26.3).[51] Thus far I have focused on how Ionians navigated the changing currents of imperial competition, but, just as imperial actions responded to and reflected regional and domestic developments, imperial actions had an impact on what happened in the region.

Already in the Archaic period Ionia was filled with traditions about internal conflict, some the residual legacy of interactions with the indigenous Carian and Lydian inhabitants, others stemming from economic inequality. Nowhere are these traditions more evident than at Miletus, where the women allegedly swore an oath to never sit at a table with their husbands or call them by their names because the Milesian men married them after killing their fathers, husbands, and sons (Hdt. 1.146.3; see Appendix 2). However, two other accounts of factional conflict at Miletus describe it along economic lines. In one, [Plutarch] says that Miletus was divided between the *aeinautai* ("forever sailors") and the *cheiromachei* ("manual workers," here perhaps farmers), which might indicate a growing conflict in the sixth century between the burgeoning commercial interests and the traditional landed stratum of society (*Mor.* 298c–d; cf. Hdt. 5.28–30).[52] In the other, Athenaeus preserves a fragment from Heraclides of Pontus about a conflict between the wealthy and the Gergithae, whom he refers to as the δημότης (common people), during which the Gergithae expelled the citizens and had their young children trampled by oxen on the threshing floor (Athen. 12.26 [524a]).[53] When the wealthy regained the upper hand, he says, they smeared the Gergithae with pitch and set them on fire, which caused a

---

51. The so-called Periclean Citizenship Law has open questions both as to its origin and its practical effects. For an overview of the debate, see Josine H. Blok, "Perikles' Citizenship Law: A New Perspective," *Historia* 58, no. 2 (2009): 142–58. On the connection between the law and immigration, see Cynthia B. Patterson, *Pericles' Citizenship Law of 451–50 BC* (New York: Arno Press, 1981), 40–81, and Rebecca Futo Kennedy, *Immigrant Women in Athens: Gender, Ethnicity, and Citizenship in the Classical City* (New York: Routledge, 2014), 14–22. Kennedy, 16, notes that the law did "more to justify social prejudice than to change marriage patterns."

52. On this conflict, see Greaves, *Miletos*, 95; Noel Robertson, "Government and Society at Miletus, 525–442 B.C.," *Phoenix* 41, no. 4 (1987): 381–82. The *aeinautai* might have been a merchant association throughout the Aegean; see Basile Chr. Petrakos, "Dédicae des AEINAYTAI d'Érétrie," *BCH* 87, no. 2 (1963): 545–47, with discussion in Robert K. Sherk, "The Eponymous Officials of Greek Cities: Mainland Greece and the Adjacent Islands," *ZPE* 84 (1990): 238. Carl Roebuck, "Tribal Organization in Ionia," *TAPhA* 92 (1961): 506–7, characterizes *cheiromachei* as "hand-fighters."

53. The story of the Gergithae plausibly suggests that the poorest people in Ionia were the indigenous Carians, since the name resembles Gergithos in the Troad of Herodotus 7.43.2 and Gerga is attested as a town name in Caria; see G. E. Bean, "Gerga in Caria," *Anatolian Studies* 19 (1969): 179–82, though the Roman-era graves and foundation houses at the site could mean that it received its name from these stories rather than vice versa. The Carians around Miletus were more usually called Leleges (Hdt. 1.171; Strabo 14.1). Gorman, *Miletos*, 103–8, rejects the story and evidence for a Carian population altogether, while Greaves, *Miletos*, 25, only mentions it in conjunction with the threshing of grain. Cf. Eckart Schütrumpf, *Heraclides of Pontus: Texts and Translations* (New Brunswick, NJ: Rutgers University Press, 2008), 80–83.

sacred olive tree to burn and thus the oracular powers to be withdrawn from the Milesians.

Noel Robertson juxtaposes the evidence of Heraclides with a reference in the Suda that "Gergethes" was a derogatory term the wealthy used to refer to manual laborers (Γέργηθες gamma, 189; cf. tau, 1192). "It is clear that the Gergithes are country-folk," he declares, noting the particularly agrarian methods used in the reprisals and comparing them to another group of village-dwelling noncitizens in Ionia, the *Pedieis* at Priene.[54] His proposal, therefore, is that the Gergithae "occupied some of the best land near Miletus," which prompted violent conflict between them and Milesian landowners.[55] Robertson's evidence for the connection between the Gergithes and the countryside is the Suda definition of καὶ οἱ χειρώνακτες οὕτως καλοῦνται παρὰ τοῖς Μιλησίοις τοῖς ἐν περιβολῇ ("the handworkers, as they are called among the Milesians"), where he interprets τοῖς ἐν περιβολῇ as "used by the Milesians living 'in the periphery.'" However, taking τοῖς ἐν περιβολῇ literally mistakes the meaning of the passage, in that it may better refer to refer to those in rarefied circles, as the entry continues τουτέστι τοῖς πλουσίοις ("that is to say, the rich") who dismissively call the craftsmen Gergithae. In other words, the *Suda* does not invalidate an economic interpretation of this conflict.[56]

These traditions reflect generations of conflict rather than individual moments. Herodotus explains that arbiters from Paros surveyed Miletus after two generations of strife and ushered in a period of prosperity by giving rule to those citizens with the best-managed farms (5.28–30.1). This arbitration is often tentatively dated to 525 because that year inaugurates the list of names on an early Hellenistic inscription that purports to record the polis' eponymous officials (*aesymnetes*; *Milet* I.3, no. 122).[57] However, as with almost all evidence for this period in the history of Miletus, the dates are a problem. For the purposes of this discussion, the list includes no hint of a period between 494 and 479, when some scholars have suggested that Miletus was left desolate

---

54. Robertson, "Government and Society at Miletus," 374. On the *Pedieis*, see Appendix 2.

55. Robertson, "Government and Society at Miletus," 375.

56. This is not meant to deny that the Milesians clashed with their neighbors over farmland since, as Robertson, "Government and Society at Miletus," 376, rightly points out, there is evidence for a conflict with Lydia that resulted in the desecration of sacred property and subsequent withdrawal of oracular privileges in the first half of the sixth century (Hdt. 1.19.1), an episode that appears to remember the mirror image of the one preserved by Heraclitus.

57. E.g., Robertson, "Government and Society at Miletus," 376, though Greaves, *Miletos*, 113–15, who decouples the arbitration from the list, challenges the assumption that its start can be calculated by counting entries back from when it was inscribed. Cf. A. J. Graham, "Teos and Abdera," *JHS* 112 (1992): 71–72. Robert K. Sherk, "The Eponymous Officials of Greek Cities IV: The Register: Part III: Thrace, Black Sea Area, Asia Minor (Continued)," *ZPE* 93 (1992): 230, notes that the eponymous official was also sometimes called a *stephanephoros*.

after the Persians ended the Ionian revolt with fire and blood.[58] This inscription instead offers an unbroken list of names that represents an artificial memory about Milesian history more than its historical reality.[59] Inasmuch as the ruined Didyma came to represent Ionian opposition to Persia, the desolation of Miletus bloomed in Greek propaganda. In fact, Milesians likely began to rebuild Miletus probably as early as 492, establishing what Alexander Herda terms a "copy" on the same footprint of the late-Archaic city.[60]

These stasis narratives are filtered through the lens of the Classical period, as Dina Guth has recently demonstrated, but I believe that is even more reason to take seriously their importance to Classical Miletus.[61] The public ritual calendar at Miletus may also reflect statutes designed to preserve the unity of the community, with the Molpoi Decree establishing protocols for the procession from the intramural Delphinion to the sanctuary of Didyma that began the year.[62] Although it resided in the Milesia, Didyma had only come under control of Miletus in the late seventh or early sixth century, and the sanctuary maintained its autonomy under the control of the Branchidae, a non-Greek priestly family (Hdt. 1.157.3; Paus. 7.2.6).[63] According to tradition, the Branchidae betrayed the city to Persia at the conclusion of the Ionian revolt, leading to the sack of the temple and their own deportation (Hdt. 6.19).[64] And yet, even in ruin, the nominal inde-

---

58. E.g., Graham, "Abdera and Teos," 71; Gorman, *Miletos*, 145–51, but see Alexander Herda, "Copy and Paste? Miletos before and after the Persian Wars," in *Reconstruire les villes: Modes, motifs et récits*, ed. Emmanuelle Capet, C. Dogniez, M. Gorea, R. Koch Piettre, F. Mass, and H. Rouillard-Bonraisin (Turnhout: Brepols, 2019), 93–96. This interpretation is built both on Herodotus and limited archaeological evidence for occupation in these years.

59. There are multiple difficulties. The list masks known periods of conflict and equally may skip years or include multiple names for a single year. Likewise, the annual reckoning is based on a count back from Alexander that could belong in either 334 or 332. Cf. Chapter 7.

60. Herda, "Copy and Paste." In a recent chapter, Hans Lohmann, "Miletus after the Disaster of 494 B.C.," in *The Destruction of Cities in the Ancient Greek World*, ed. Sylvian Fachard and Edward M. Harris (Cambridge: Cambridge University Press, 2021), 50–69, argues that Miletus shrank as a result of the sack and that the diminished urban center took on characteristics like the orthogonal grid only after 479, but also that the continuity of cult institutions argues against an actual "refoundation."

61. Dina Guth, "The 'Rise and Fall' of Archaic Miletus," *Historia* 66, no. 1 (2017): 2–20.

62. As with many pieces of evidence for early Ionia, the date of the Molpoi decree is unknown. The extant inscription is a Hellenistic copy of a decree dated to 450/49 based on juxtaposing the named *aesymnetes* with the evidence from the *aesymnetes* list (*Milet* I.3 no. 122), but the core text of the decree likely belongs to an earlier period, perhaps even before the inauguration of the list; see Alexander Herda, *Der Apollon-Delphinios-Kult in Milet und die Neujahrsprozession nach Didyma* (Darmstadt: Verlag Philipp von Zabern, 2006), 15–20, with bibliography.

63. See Chapter 9.

64. N. G. L. Hammond, "The Branchidae at Didyma and in Sogdiana," *CQ²* 48, no. 2 (1998): 339–44, argues that the betrayal belonged in 479, when the retreating Persians destroyed the temple, largely because some early Hellenistic sources name Xerxes as the king responsible. However, this date is unlikely for several reasons. Retributive destruction of sacred precincts was part of the motivation for the Persian campaigns, and Herodotus mentions the oracle at the close of the Ionian revolt, but not again after Mycale, making it more likely that any betrayal and subsequent destruction took place during the reign of Darius.

pendence of the sanctuary and its ambivalently Greek identity turned it into an important site of reconciliation for a fragmented community.

These provisions did not ensure internal stability. A fragmentary decree from the middle of the fifth century records a partial list of individuals banished in perpetuity, along with declarations that they had forfeited their property and establishing provisions to reward any citizen who would kill them should they ever return (*RO* 123 = *Milet* VI.1, no. 187).[65] The context of this inscription defies capture. Scholars traditionally interpreted it as evidence for an oligarchic challenge to the nascent Milesian democracy in the 450s led by the powerful Neleid clan that traced its lineage back to the mythical founder of the city. Indeed, among the exiles were the sons of Nympharetus, a Milesian whose name appeared on the *aesymnetes* list, possibly for the year 503/2 (*Milet* I.3 no. 122, l. 24), which creates a tidy picture of the domestic instability in the 450s that would have explained this date for the Athenian regulatory decrees at Miletus that most likely date to several decades later (see Chapter 3).[66] The circumstantial evidence for dating this inscription has led Noel Robertson to push its date to just after 479 and plausibly identify the Nympharetus of this inscription with man named on the *aesymnetes* list.[67] Although most of the critical information about this decree, including the authorities who passed it, the identities of the perpetrators, and the nature of their threat to Miletus, remain unknown, it is a powerful reminder that the deep domestic divisions that existed in Miletus throughout the Archaic period remained unresolved into the Classical.

We should be cautious about regarding the domestic turmoil at Miletus as typical given the relative surfeit of evidence elsewhere in Ionia, but neither should we dismiss it as entirely unusual. An imprecation inscribed at Teos offers a counterpoint the Milesian example. According to both Strabo and Herodotus, the Teians opted to leave Ionia rather than submit to Persian rule in 545, and instead sailed to Abdera where they founded a new city, only to return to their original settlement sometime later (Hdt. 1.168.1; Strabo 14.1.30).[68] Much like the dating of the Milesian stasis, the return date relies on inference and suppo-

---

65. On the οἱ ἐπιμήνιοι, the board of officials tasked with carrying out the punishments, see Robertson, "Government and Society at Miletus," 378–84.

66. See, e.g., John P. Barron, "Milesian Politics and Athenian Propaganda, c.460–440 B.C.," *JHS* 82 (1962): 3–6.

67. Robertson, "Government and Society at Miletus," 378–84.

68. Herodotus uses the verb κτίζω, Strabo ἀποικέω, but both convey the same action. Herodotus records an earlier phase of colonization by Clazomenae but says that that settlement was driven out by the Thracians. Based on the Phoenician character of the name, Abdera may have originally been a Phoenician emporium, as argued by Benjamin H. Isaac, *The Greek Settlements in Thrace until the Macedonian Conquest* (Leiden: Brill, 1986), 76–77, but there is no archaeological evidence to support this connection; see Katerina Chryssanthaki, "Les trois fondations d'Abdère," *REG* 114 (2001): 386; Graham, "Abdera and Teos."

sition. The Teians equipped seventeen ships at Lade in 494 (Hdt. 6.8), leading to the suggestion that refoundation took place shortly after Darius conquered Thrace between 512 and 510 on the grounds that, if they had no choice but to accept Persian rule, they preferred their home to constant struggle against Thracian and Paeonian tribes attested by Pindar's Second Paean.[69] This set of motivations and chronology is improbable, though, given that Teos began minting coins at least by 520–515—that is, before Darius' invasion of Thrace.[70]

The Teians likely suffered at the end of the Ionian revolt. Herodotus says that the Persians deported young men and women and set fire to the Ionian poleis along with their holy places (τὰς πόλιας ἐνεπίμπρασαν αὐτοῖσι τοῖσι ἱροῖσι, 6.32). But there is nothing like Herodotus' description of Miletus (6.25.1) to suggest that Teos was left depopulated in 494. Nevertheless, the close relationship between Teos and Abdera likely resulted in a reciprocal relationship by which some Abderans returned.[71] Any Persian-imposed tyranny in this period was likely short-lived since Mardonius installed democracies in 492 (Hdt. 6.43.3). This official decision to support democracies may strain belief until one recalls that it was in fact Ionian tyrants who had stirred up the Ionian revolt. However, we might question how *democratic* these democracies were given that the overhaul seems designed to offer the appearance of local control while undermining the position of potential troublemakers. Most likely these constitutions included limited suffrage, and the prominent leaders could count on the backing of Persia. In Teos, the eponymous official in this period was probably the *aesymnetes*, paralleling the office at Miletus. Association with factions that rose to prominence because of Persian power set the stage for the charge that they abused their position, and, in the wake of the battle of Mycale in 479, the Teians established a set of imprecations against those who would abuse the position of *aesymnetes* to set themselves up as tyrants (*RO* 102 = *SIG*³ 37, 38).[72]

---

69. Graham, "Abdera and Teos," 49–51; Jonathan R. Strang, "The City of Dionysos: A Social and Historical Study of the Ionian City of Teos" (PhD diss., SUNY Buffalo, 2007), 60.

70. Chryssanthaki, "Les trois fondations d'Abdère," 394–97.

71. Pindar's Second Paean alludes to the refoundation of Teos following a fire, but A. J. Graham, "'Adopted Teians': A Passage in the New Inscription of Public Imprecations from Teos," *JHS* 111 (1991): 177, notes that it is impossible to know whether the fire describes the destruction in 545 or 494. Strang, "City of Dionysos," 59–60, not altogether convincingly, makes a positive identification of the fire with the end of the Ionian revolt, while offering a synthesis position that there were two waves of Abderan resettlement; cf. Giovan Battista D'Alessio, "Immigrati a Teo e ad Abdera (SEG XXXI 985; Pind. Fr. 52b Sn.–M.)," *ZPE* 92 (1992): 77–78, who finds Pindar's tone and terminology for Teians and Abderans incompatible with a refoundation early in the history of Abdera. Pindar celebrates Abdera as both the mother and daughter of Teos, as Carol Dougherty, "Pindar's Second Paean: Civic Identity on Parade," *CPh* 89, no. 3 (1994): 212, points out, and the two cities had a close relationship, but the loose allusion to a fire that preceded the refoundation of Teos is too little evidence to indicate a large-scale refoundation after 494.

72. Paul J. Kosmin, "A Phenomenology of Democracy: Ostracism as Political Ritual," *CA* 34, no. 1 (2015): 133, compares this inscription to the imprecations read out at every assembly meet-

It is thus tempting to interpret domestic conflicts in Ionia as responses to the changes in the imperial landscape. Jack Balcer, for instance, regarded Ionian history as the result of its location at the intersection of competing imperial systems such that whenever one imperial power became too onerous there was another power waiting in the wings to offer an attractive combination of protection and autonomy.[73] This might have been true on a larger scale, but it does not adequately explain either the complicity of the Ionians in the development of the Athenian empire or the domestic turmoil of the sort on display at Miletus and Teos. Rather, the imprecation at Teos speaks more to the general instability in the form of piracy and threats to the grain supply than to imperial competition, while the domestic conflicts at Miletus ran deep and predated the appearance of these imperial systems. To be clear: imperial competition did not improve local stability in Ionia and often constrained local decision-making, but neither should every local action be interpreted in light of imperial competition. Just as Persian imperial policy required working with local notables, so too did Athenian hegemony respond to the preexisting conditions on the ground in Ionia. This period saw Ionia excised from Persian hegemony only to become entangled in an Athenian one and, as Athenian control tightened, the consequences of the local conditions, rivalries, and demands only became more apparent.

---

ing in Athens condemning medism, tyranny, and subversion of laws, making them a protective function that looks forward rather than backward. *Aesymnete* and tyrant were firmly connected at least by the time of Aristotle, who described the position as an "elected tyranny" (αἱρετὴ τυραννίς, *Politics* 3.1285a 30). On this inscription, cf. Henri van Effenterre and Françoise Ruzé, *Nomima: Recueil d'inscriptions politiques et juridiques de l'archaisme grec*, vol. 1 (Paris: De Boccard, 1994), 366–70, no. 104, whose text diverges from Rhodes and Osborne at several points, albeit in ways that do not change my argument.

73. Balcer, *Sparda*, 19–25. Balcer's model is flawed when it comes to Ionia, and overly reliant on a clash of civilizations given that his stage 1 "defensive" phase was allegedly driven by "a fear of foreign military intervention and fear of foreign domination of the institutions of art" (19–20). More recently, scholars such as Kostas Vlassopoulos, *Greeks and Barbarians* (Cambridge: Cambridge University Press, 2013), have challenged some of the assumptions about these interactions.

CHAPTER 3

❦

Under the Athenian Empire

454–412

The Delian League drew the Ionian poleis into an Aegean system in the aftermath of the Persian wars, but Athens exerted progressively more control over league institutions and members as open conflict with Persia ground to a halt (Plut. *Cim.* 19.1–2).[1] What had begun ostensibly as a defensive alliance guided by Athenian hegemony became frozen under Athenian imperial control (Thuc. 1.96). The relationship between Ionia and Athens changed in the 450s, in step with the evolution of the Delian League.[2] Any history of Ionia in the second half of the fifth century must therefore begin with development of an Athenian empire. The metastasis took place over the course of the years 454–449, which inaugurated a period of conspicuous building projects and the apogee of Athenian power.[3] Nevertheless, it was not primarily the renaissance in Athens, but

---

1. The change is often attributed to the Peace of Callias, which has inspired an extensive bibliography debating its existence and its date, with Klaus Meister, *Die Ungeschichtlichkeit des Kalliasfriedens und deren historische Folgen* (Stuttgart: Franz Steiner, 1982), 124–30, tallying a since-superseded list of 162 contributions. The general, albeit not unanimous, consensus is that some sort of treaty did take place. Ernst Badian, "The Peace of Callias," *JHS* 107 (1987): 38, declared, "It is time scholars stopped disputing the authenticity of the peace at excessive length and started discussing its cardinal importance both in the history of relations between the King and the Greeks and in the history of Athens." John Hyland, *Persian Interventions: The Achaemenid Empire, Athens, and Sparta, 450–386 BCE* (Baltimore, MD: Johns Hopkins University Press, 2018), 15–35, has recently argued the cessation of hostilities only makes sense from the Persian point of view if the king presented it as his delegating authority over the Aegean to a client state, which would have required a formal treaty. I am sympathetic to Hyland's argument and accept a possible diplomatic resolution even though the positive evidence for the treaty stems from fourth-century anachronisms. On the Peace of Callias in the fourth century, see C. L. Murison, "The Peace of Callias: Its Historical Context," *Phoenix* 25, no. 1 (1971): 12–31, and Wesley E. Thompson, "The Peace of Callias in the Fourth Century," *Historia* 30, no. 2 (1981): 164–77.

2. Noel Robertson, "The True Nature of the 'Delian League' II," *AJAH* 5, no. 2 (1980): 110–33, argues convincingly that the key changes happened quickly and in the 460s. I follow a conventional chronology here because it is after 454 that evidence of the evolution appears in Ionia.

3. There is a voluminous bibliography on the development of the Athenian empire; for recent discussion see Vincent Azoulay, *Pericles of Athens*, trans. Janet Lloyd (Princeton, NJ: Princeton University Press, 2014), 51–66; Lisa Kallet, "Democracy, Empire and Epigraphy in the Twenti-

the intersection of imperial systems with local and regional tensions that predated the Delian League, that shaped the direction of Ionia in the fifth century.

The Development of the Athenian Empire

One of the first outward signs of a change in the Delian League's operating
procedure was the transfer of the league treasury. The coffers had been in the
sanctuary of Apollo on Delos from the league's inception, but in 454 they were
moved to Athens (Diod. 12.38.2; Plut. *Arist.* 25.2). Apologists and defenders
of the decision pointed to the strategic vulnerability of Delos after the naval
disaster in Egypt (Thuc. 1.104, 109–10; Ctesias 32–37), and there were plausible rumors that Artaxerxes ordered a raid on the Aegean in retaliation for
Athenian attacks.[4] Others, including the Athenian Aristides, cautioned that
while the move would be expedient, it was unjust (ὡς οὐ δίκαιον μέν, συμφέρον
δὲ τοῦτ᾽ ἐστί, Plut. *Arist.* 25.2).[5] Moreover, the Periclean building program
began in earnest after the transfer of the treasury, and Plutarch records twin
complaints, from the allies that Athens was misappropriating the funds and
from political enemies that Pericles was ornamenting Athens "like a shameless
woman" (ὥσπερ ἀλαζόνα γυναῖκα, Plut. *Per.* 12.1–2).[6] It is important to note,
however, that Plutarch also describes these claims as slander (διαβάλλειν),
which suggests that the accusations were politically motivated hyperbole.[7]

---

eth Century," John Ma, "Empires, Statuses and Realities," and John Ma, "Afterword: Whither the
Athenian Empire?," all in *Interpreting the Athenian Empire*, ed. John Ma, Nikolaos Papazarkadas,
and Robert Parker (London: Duckworth, 2009), 43–66, 125–48, and 223–30, respectively. Notable
among the older bibliography are Harold B. Mattingly, "The Growth of Athenian Imperialism," in
The Athenian Empire Restored (Ann Arbor: University of Michigan Press, 1996), 87–106 (= *Historia*
12, no. 3 [1963]: 257–73); Malcolm F. McGregor, *The Athenians and Their Empire* (Vancouver: UBC
Press, 1987), 75–83; and Russell Meiggs, *The Athenian Empire* (Oxford: Oxford University Press,
1973), 205–72.

4. H. D. Westlake, "Thucydides and the Athenian Disaster in Egypt," *CPh* 45, no. 4 (1950): 209–
16; W. Kendrick Pritchett, "The Transfer of the Delian Treasury," *Historia* 18, no. 1 (1969): 17–21.
John P. Barron, "Milesian Politics and Athenian Propaganda, c.460–440 B.C.," *JHS* 82 (1962): 5,
implausibly argues that revolts in Ionia forced Athens to transfer the treasury.

5. Aristides had died in 467, but the statement could have been delivered in the original deliberations about where to establish the treasury, since he is said to have made the first assessment
([Arist.] *Ath. Pol.* 23.3–5; Plut. *Arist.* 24).

6. The popularity of the Athenian hegemony is disputed. Arguing for unpopularity: T. J. Quinn,
"Thucydides and the Unpopularity of the Athenian Empire," *Historia* 13, no. 3 (1964): 257–66;
Donald W. Bradeen, "The Popularity of the Athenian Empire," *Historia* 9, no. 3 (1960): 257–69; for
popularity: G. E. M. de Ste. Croix, "The Character of the Athenian Empire," *Historia* 3, no. 1 (1954):
1–41; H. K. Pleket, "Thasos and the Popularity of the Athenian Empire," *Historia* 12, no. 1 (1963):
70–77. Charles W. Fornara, "*IG* I², 39.52–57 and the 'Popularity' of the Athenian Empire," *CSCA*
10 (1977): 39–55, argues that, before 431, when the alternative to Athens was autonomy, Athenian
hegemony was unpopular, but that changed once it was a choice between masters. For most Ionian
poleis, complete autonomy was never an alternative.

7. Modern opinions on whether the Athenians used league funds to pay for the domestic

The symbolism of moving the league treasury to Athens could not have been lost on the allies, but neither was it necessarily a unilateral decision. Ancient tradition, in fact, has the proposal coming from the Samian delegates (Plut. *Arist.* 25.2). Samos did not pay the *phoros*, and it is certainly possible that the Athenians used the delegates as a proxy to soften opposition to the move, but the surrounding circumstances provided sufficient cause that one need not posit ulterior motives or cloak-and-dagger political maneuvering. Nor is there anything in the contemporary record to suggest a particular significance to the transfer of the treasury even though it represents a clear, identifiable change to the league structure. The pattern connecting the transfer with other signs of imperial control emerges only in hindsight.

Athens installed a variety of regulations on the league and on individual members in the two subsequent decades, but none of these immediately followed the transfer of the treasury. The only contemporary development that warrants mention was the creation of the so-called Athenian Tribute Lists, marble stelae on the Acropolis that record *aparchai* (first-fruit offerings) from the annual *phoros* (tribute) payments made by league members.[8] The dedication of *aparchai* was probably regular part of league ceremony, with the offerings originally dedicated to Apollo. While there is no evidence for comparable inscriptions on Delos, the Delian lists might have been inscribed on wood that has since decayed. On the Athenian Acropolis, the marble tribute lists stood as a monument to Athenian hegemony and undoubtedly could have provided fuel

---

building program vary widely. Lisa Kallet, "Did Tribute Fund the Parthenon?," *CA* 8, no. 2 (1989): 252–66, argues that the passage should not be dismissed, as do A. Andrewes, "The Opposition to Perikles," *JHS* 98 (1978): 1–8, and Walter Ameling, "Plutarch, *Perikles* 12–14," *Historia* 34, no. 1 (1985): 47–63, but also that the tribute did not fund the Parthenon, while Loren J. Samons II, "Athenian Finance and the Treasury of Athena," *Historia* 42, no. 2 (1993): 129–38, argues that the treasury of Athena became the war chest of the league. Adalberto Giovannini, "Le Parthenon, le tresor d'Athena et le tribut des allies," *Historia* 39, no. 2 (1990): 129–48, emphasizes the Parthenon as a Hellenic monument to victory over the barbarians, and, as Azoulay, *Pericles*, 65–66, points out, the building was a treasury and monument rather than a temple. Jeffrey M. Hurwit, *The Acropolis in the Age of Pericles* (Cambridge: Cambridge University Press, 2004) 94–102, identifies at least one public work, a well-house in Athens, built solely from tribute. Recently, T. Leslie Shear, *Trophies of Victory: Public Building in Periklean Athens* (Princeton, NJ: Princeton University Press, 2016), 21–26, connected the transfer of the treasury with the building program, but he also suggests that Plutarch did not understand the economics of Greek temple building. See Kallet, "Did Tribute Fund the Parthenon?," n. 1 for a list of works that accept as fact that the Parthenon was funded with allied tribute payments.

8. The Athenian Tribute Lists (*IG* I³ 259–91) were compiled from fragments found on the Athenian Acropolis and Agora and first published in three volumes edited by Benjamin D. Meritt, H. T. Wade-Gery, and Malcolm F. McGregor. On the offerings, see Catherine M. Keesling, *The Votive Statues on the Athenian Acropolis* (Cambridge: Cambridge University Press, 2003), 7; Bjørn Paarmann, "Aparchai and Phoroi: A New Commented Edition of the Athenian Tribute Lists and Assessment Decrees" (PhD diss., University of Fribourg, 2009), 40–52; Theodora Suk Fong Jim, *Sharing with the Gods: Aparchai and Dekatai in Ancient Greece* (Oxford: Oxford University Press, 2014), 36. The inscriptions for the assessment decrees only began to stand alongside the dedications in 425.

for outrage throughout the Delian League, but this does not explain the conditions in Ionia, where the thesis of local anti-Athenianism is poorly supported in isolation.[9]

Accustomed to a prominent role in the league, the Ionians are generally thought to have chaffed at the new regulations, with the discontent resulting in a series of revolts between 454 and 449.[10] This interpretation, however, rests on shaky foundations. The regulatory decrees that were long seen as a metastasizing of Athenian hegemony have been down-dated away from this period,[11] and the remaining evidence for local resistance to Athens emerges from a simple reading of the tribute stelae, which are lacunate and inconsistent. Only Colophon and Clazomenae appear on each of the first three lists, but every Ionian community is recorded making *phoros* payments on at least one. Scholars nevertheless often isolate Miletus and Erythrae for special scrutiny.[12]

9. On opposition to Athenian hegemony beyond Athens and Athenian responses, see Jack Martin Balcer, "Separatism and Anti-separatism in the Athenian Empire (478–433 B.C.)," *Historia* 23, no. 1 (1974): 21–39; Martin Ostwald, "Athens and Chalkis: A Study in Imperial Control," *JHS* 122 (2002): 134–43; Cristophe Pébarthe, "Thasos, l'empire d'Athènes et les emporia de Thrace," *ZPE* 126 (1999): 131–54; Pleket, "Thasos," 70–77; Brian Rutishauser, *Athens and the Cyclades: Economic Strategies, 510–314 BC* (Oxford: Oxford University Press, 2012), 85–91; R. Zelnick-Abramovitz, "Settlers and Dispossessed in the Athenian Empire," *Mnemosyne*⁴ 57, no. 3 (2004): 325–45.

10. On this connection, see, for instance, Jack Martin Balcer, *Sparda by the Bitter Sea: Imperial Interaction in Western Anatolia* (Providence, RI: Brown University Press, 1984), 380–81; Barron, "Milesian Politics and Athenian Propaganda," 5; Vanessa B. Gorman, *Miletos, the Ornament of Ionia* (Ann Arbor: University of Michigan Press, 2001), 235–36; David M. Lewis, "The Athenian Tribute-Quota Lists, 453–450," *ABSA* 89 (1994): 294; Meiggs, *Athenian Empire*, 152–64; James Henry Oliver, "The Athenian Decree concerning Miletus in 450/49 B.C.," *TAPhA* 66 (1935): 177–98; Noel Robertson, "Government and Society at Miletus, 525–442 B.C.," *Phoenix* 41, no. 4 (1987): 384–90. Charles W. Fornara, "The Date of the 'Regulations for Miletus,'" *AJPh* 92, no. 3 (1971): 473–75, argues for a date of 442.

11. Down-dating the regulations for Miletus was first proposed by Harold B. Mattingly in three articles, "The Athenian Coinage Decree" (= *Historia* 10, no. 2 [1961]: 148–88), "'Epigraphically the Twenties Are Too Late . . .'" (= *ABSA* 65 [1970]: 129–49], and "The Athenian Decree for Miletos (*IG* I², 22+ = *ATL* II, D 11): A Postscript" (= *Historia* 30, no. 1 [1981]: 113–17], all in *The Athenian Empire Restored* (Ann Arbor: University of Michigan Press, 1996), 35–44, 308–11, and 453–60 and is followed by Paarman, "Aparchai and Phoroi," 121–40; Nikolaos Papazarkadas, "Epigraphy and the Athenian Empire: Reshuffling the Chronological Cards," in *Interpreting the Athenian Empire*, ed. John Ma, Nikolaos Papazarkadas, and Rorbert Parker (London: Duckworth, 2009), 67–77; P. J. Rhodes, "After the Three-Bar 'Sigma' Controversy: The History of Athenian Imperialism Reassessed," *CQ*² 58, no. 2 (2008): 503–4; and P. J. Rhodes, "Milesian 'Stephanephoroi': Applying Cavaignac Correctly," *ZPE* 157 (2006): 116. The provenance of the decree at Erythrae is more problematic. It was found on the Athenian Acropolis by Fauvel in the early nineteenth century, but both the stone and the original transcription are lost. See Russell Meiggs and David M. Lewis, *A Selection of Greek Historical Inscriptions* (Oxford: Oxford University Press, 1969), 91, with bibliography; cf. Georgia E. Malachou, "A Second Facsimile of the Erythrai Decree (*IG* I³ 14)," and Akiko Moroo, "The Erythrai Decrees Reconsidered: *IG* I³ 14, 15 & 16," both in ΑΘΗΝΑΙΩΝ ΕΠΙΣΚΟΠΟΣ: *Studies in Honour of Harold B. Mattingly*, ed. Angelos P. Matthaiou and Robert K. Pitt (Athens: Greek Epigraphical Society, 2014), 73–96 and 97–120, respectively.

12. Colophon is a third polis subject to Athenian regulations, which probably date to a later period; see below "Chaffing at the Athenian Bit."

Milesians from Leros and Teichoussa both appear apart from Miletus proper in 454/3, inscribed among the very last entries on the inaugural list. Similarly, Boutheia on the Mimas peninsula made a payment independent of Erythrae in 453/2 but was grouped with the rest of the Erythraean syntely in the 440s.[13] What should be made of these contradictions?

Miletus and Erythrae were both subject to Athenian regulatory decrees, so the orthodox interpretation links these inconsistencies in the 450s to the Athenian impositions. I follow a later chronology for these regulatory decrees, but it is nevertheless appropriate to review them here in brief. Although the two decrees conform to the unique contexts of the poleis in which they appear, they share a common structure. Both were meant to resolve social conflict in the respective citizen bodies, with one group having appealed to Athens for support and the other to Persia. From the Athenian perspective, much as John Hyland has recently argued for Persian policy,[14] local stability was a means to an end because it ensured a steady flow of tribute. Losers in Ionian political conflicts appealed to Persia, and the resolving of these conflicts not only protected Athenian interests, but also supported the Athenian claim to leadership because the very existence of the Delian League in this early period was predicated on resisting Persia. Persian satraps regularly offered refuge to political exiles, but only in rare instances did they extend substantial military or financial support.

The problems regarding these decrees stem from the twin pillars that support the traditional chronology for Athenian intervention in Ionia. The first pillar is composed of letterforms. Both inscriptions contain the so-called three-barred sigma that was thought to have fallen out of use in Athenian inscriptions by c.450. The second is formed of lacunae and inconsistencies on the early tribute lists. Both arguments are porous. Scholarly opinion about letterforms has begun to shift, confirming Harold Mattingly's old thesis that the three-barred sigma remained in use while, simultaneously, the lacunae in the early tribute lists have begun to be filled in.[15] Thus, at the same time that the possibility of a

---

13. Meiggs and Lewis, *Selection of Greek Historical Inscriptions*, 93; Meiggs, *Athenian Empire*, 112; P. J. Rhodes, "The Delian League to 449 B.C.," in *Cambridge Ancient History²*, vol. 5, ed. David M. Lewis, John Boardman, J. K. Davies, and Martin Ostwald (Cambridge: Cambridge University Press, 1992), 54–59. In an examination of local settlements on the Mimas Peninsula, Ismail Gezgin, "The Localization Problems of Erythrae's Hinterland," trans. A. Aykurt, *Arkeoloji Dergisi* 14, no. 2 (2009): 95–108, argues that there is no archaeological evidence for a settlement named Boutheia. On the cycles of formation of dissolution (*apotaxis*) of the Erythraean syntely, which he attributes to local elites negotiating the Delian League system to minimize their obligations, see Sean R. Jensen, "Tribute and *Syntely* at Erythrai," *CW* 105, no. 4 (2012): 479–96.

14. Hyland, *Persian Interventions*, 28–33.

15. On the three-barred sigma debate see Rhodes, "Three-Bar Sigma Controversy," 503–

later context for both decrees became fashionable, the validity of dating regulations based on the lacunae on the tribute lists was called into question. Most
likely, decrees of this sort only became common after the Samian crisis of 440.[16]

If the regulations were not put in place in the 450s and the resistance to the
phoros is not necessarily supported by the tribute lists, then it is necessary to
reconsider the Ionian responses to the development of the Athenian empire. As
discussed in the previous chapter, the Ionian poleis were unstable even without
the Athenian decrees. Earlier inscriptions from the region record imprecations
against individuals and families that threatened domestic harmony (e.g., *RO*
123 = *Milet* 1.6, no. 187),[17] but these were local inscriptions addressing local
problems. Further, the records of Athenian *phoros* collection in Ionia changed
shape, and while Erythrae and Miletus are unique in that the lists continue link
the satellites in connection to the polis, they are not the only instances where
communities that had previously paid along with a larger neighbor began to
do so on their own.[18] By 443/2, for instance, the Ephesian *aparche* fell from 750
drachmae to 600, while Pygela and Isinda, both former dependents of Ephesus,
appear on the Athenian Tribute Lists for the first time, with a combined *phoros*
slightly less than the difference in the Ephesian levels.[19] This change inaugurated
a period of nearly two centuries during which Ephesus tried to regain control
over Pygela and the Pygelans appealed to Miletus and local dynasts in order to
remain independent. There were undoubtedly Ionians who approached Persia
for support, but probably because they were on the losing side of local power
struggles rather than out of anti-Athenianism.

The consequences of the development of the Athenian empire were not
immediately evident in Ionia and probably remained hidden though much of

---

4; Mattingly, "Epigraphically," 284–85; Papazarkadas, "Epigraphy and the Athenian Empire," 77.
Reevaluating the dates does not require inscriptions with the three-barred sigma to be down-dated
but opens a wider range of possible contexts. For the lacunae, see, e.g., Paarman, "Aparchai and
Phoroi," 125–37.

16. There are still strong grounds to date two comparable inscriptions relating to Euboea (*IG* I³
39 and *SIG³* 64) to the mid-440s; see Ostwald, "Athens and Chalkis," 134–43.

17. As described above, Chapter 2, Miletus had a long history of domestic conflict. Cf. [Plut.]
Mor. 298c–d; Hdt. 5.28–30. On the imprecations in this inscription, see Gorman, *Miletos*, 229–34;
Robertson, "Government and Society at Miletus," 358–59; Barron, "Milesian Politics and Athenian
Propaganda," 1–2.

18. Sean R. Jensen, "Rethinking Athenian Imperialism" (PhD diss., Rutgers University, 2010),
along with "Tribute and *Syntely* at Erythrai," and "*Synteleia* and *Apotaxis* on the Athenian Tribute
Lists," in *Hegemonic Finances: Funding Athenian Domination in the 5th and 4th Centuries BC*, ed.
Thomas J. Figueira and Sean R. Jensen (London: Bloomsbury 2019), 55–77, has made a compelling
case that "sub-hegemonies" persisted under the Athenian empire.

19. Pygela's *aparche* was one hundred drachmae and Isinda fourteen and four obols. Creating a larger number of payers in time resulted in higher tribute levels, but, since it did not make a
significant financial impact in the short term, this was more likely an administrative response to
local discontent.

the 440s even as resistance to Athenian hegemony cropped up in places like Euboea (Thuc. 1.114). In short, an Athenian alliance still served the purposes the ruling classes in Ionia. This situation would not last. A storm loomed on the horizon: the resumption of a regional conflict between Samos and Miletus that threatened to shatter the precarious balance in Ionia.

Domestic Factionalism and the Specter of Persia

Persian power continued to cast a long shadow over the eastern marches of the developing Athenian empire, and so it is necessary to examine the relationship between Ionia and the neighbors to the east before turning to the domestic conflicts. Despite the tradition that Athenian arms and diplomacy made it impossible for Persian forces to approach the Aegean littoral, satraps remained firmly installed at Sardis and Dascylium and in a position to meddle in Greek affairs. Xerxes never relinquished his claim to Ionia, leading Pierre Briant to argue that Artaxerxes I encouraged the satraps of western Asia Minor to test Athenian weakness and, if possible, to recover these revenues. Thus, scholars frequently interpret domestic friction in Ionia as the result of a pro-Persian fifth column.[20] Anecdotal evidence such as Pissouthnes' intervention on Samos supports this argument, but it is usually based on a structuralist interpretation of Ionian politics most fully articulated by Jack Balcer whereby each community consisted of two groups: the demos, or citizen body that both gravitated toward and was supported by Athens, and a landed aristocracy with an affinity for Persia.

These categories rely on intellectual pirouettes. First, there is an assumption that these categories were unified and determined geographically or ideologically, rather than both riven by their own rivalries and feuds and capable of finding common ground with their "natural" opponents. Here there is a tendency to interpret domestic politics primarily in terms of factionalism exploited by imperial politics. Regional competition over land and in matters of prestige plays a subordinate role in these interpretations even though it continued to play a critical role in the history of Ionia. Second, this paradigm implies that

---

20. Balcer, "Separatism and Anti-separatism," 27; Pierre Briant, *From Cyrus to Alexander: A History of the Persian Empire*, trans. Peter T. Daniels (Winona Lake, IN: Eisenbrauns, 2002), 580–81; Matt Waters, "Applied Royal Directive: Pissouthnes and Samos," in *The Achaemenid Court*, ed. Bruno Jacobs and Robert Rollinger (Wiesbaden: Harrassowitz, 2010), 817–28, but cf. Hyland, *Persian Interventions*, 15–36, who argues that Athens was a de facto Persian client. Recently Eyal Meyer, "The Satrap of Western Anatolia and the Greeks" (PhD diss., University of Pennsylvania, 2017) has shown that the Persian system gave satraps in western Anatolia broad latitude to act so long as it did not directly contravene the king's interests.

Athens supported democratic governments, while Persia sought to install oligarchies.[21] Like the model of American foreign policy during the Cold War that inspired this interpretation, Athenian actions were more complex in practice. Despite the ancient testimony of Diodorus Siculus (12.27), there is no contemporary evidence for a formal Athenian policy of promoting democracy within its fifth-century empire.[22] In Ionia, for instance, Chios in the fifth century never had a democratic constitution, and the anonymous "Old Oligarch" explicitly says that Athens threw its lot in with oligarchs at Miletus ([Xen.] *Ath. Pol.* 3.11). The primary case where a formal conflict between democrats and oligarchs is attested in the ancient evidence is on Samos in 411, when the demos enacted a bloody coup primarily because the leadership proposed to break with Athens (Thuc. 8.14), but years of increased inequality lay behind this democratic revolution (see Chapter 4, "Contempt for Athenian Hegemony").

While the structuralist paradigm of Ionian politics needs to be abandoned, the specter of Persia remains central to understanding the political situation in Ionia. In every instance for which evidence exists, the intervening Persian satrap did so at the behest of a group in, or recently exiled from, an Ionian polis. The significance of Persia therefore lay in its potential to widen preexisting regional and domestic conflicts rather than in creating factions by suborning otherwise loyal citizens. Put another way, if regional conflict and the growth of Athenian power provided the kindling and fuel for a fire in Ionia, Persia could provide a spark.

The War between Samos and Miletus

One of the most brutal episodes in fifth-century Ionia began one night in the spring of 440. Under the cover of darkness, Thucydides says, exiles from Samos crossed back to the island with seven hundred mercenaries and staged an uprising with some popular support. With the backing of the Samian demos and aid from the Persian satrap Pissouthnes, the erstwhile exiles rescued their hostages then held on Lemnos (Thuc. 1.115.4–5; Diod. 12.27.3; Plut. 25.3). Both moves flouted Athenian hegemony; in short order, Athens and Samos were embroiled in a war that lasted for more than nine months.

21. Matthew Simonton, *Classical Greek Oligarchy: A Political History* (Princeton, NJ: Princeton University Press, 2017) articulates the significance of "oligarchs" as a political category in classical Greece, but the idea that Persia universally supported them in Ionia is based on a flawed hypothesis of oligarchy's "natural" opposition to Athens.

22. Sarah Bolmarcich, "The Athenian Regulations for Samos (IG I³ 48) Again," *Chiron* 39 (2009): 59–62, offers a compelling rebuttal to the scholarly orthodoxy about Athenian support for democracies.

The seeds of this war were planted more than a year earlier. In 441, war broke out between Samos and Miletus, probably the resumption of a long-standing conflict over farmland near Priene on the Mycale peninsula.[23] No details about this conflict survive, but it went poorly for the Milesians, who appealed to Athens for arbitration as hegemon of the Delian League. According to Thucydides, they were joined by private Samian citizens who wanted regime change (1.115.2). There was nothing untoward about the Milesian appeal or the Athenian decision to intervene according to Greek interstate norms, but there was, no doubt, gossip.

Pericles, the first man at Athens, had a notorious relationship with a Milesian woman, Aspasia. Poets referred to the relationship as developing out of love or lust such that Pericles was supposed to have kissed her affectionately when both leaving and arriving home (Plut. *Per.* 24.5–6), and Aspasia is adorned with slanders frequently given to women in the ancient world, including that she perverted men she was involved with, supplied Pericles with free women as prostitutes, and, eventually, became a new Helen.[24] There was a practical explanation for the relationship, though. Aspasia's sister was married to Alcibiades (the grandfather of the Peloponnesian War's scandalous general and turncoat of the same name), so becoming involved with Aspasia was a way for Pericles to shore up political alliances.[25] In 451/0, Pericles had enacted a citizenship law that granted full rights only to children with two citizen parents, meaning that although he could marry Aspasia, his own actions limited the options of their children.[26] The Samians were probably not interested in the nuances of Athe-

---

23. The traditional reading of this conflict is that Samos and Miletus fought over control of Priene, but see Joshua P. Nudell, "The War between Miletus and Samos περὶ Πριήνης (Thuc. 1.115.2; Diod. 12.27.2; and Plut. 'Per.' 25.1)," *CQ*² 66, no. 2 (2016): 772–74.

24. Cratinus *Dionysalexandros* 115K–A; Aristoph. *Ach.* 516–39; Duris of Samos, *BNJ* 76 F 65; Walter Ameling, "Komoedie und Politik zwischen Kratinos und Aristophanes: Das Beispiel Perikles," *QC* 3, no. 6 (1981): 411. These slanders are baseless.

25. The relationship to the family of Alcibiades is nowhere attested by the written sources but is reconstructed through an onomastic analysis. Plutarch names Aspasia's father Axiochos (*Per.* 24.2), which begins to appear in Athens in the second half of the fifth century with Axiochos Alkibiadou (Axiochus, son of Alcibiades), who was either a cousin or uncle of the scandalous politician; see Phillip V. Stanley, "The Family Connection of Alcibiades and Axiochus," *GRBS* 27, no. 2 (1986): 173–81. The simplest explanation is that the elder Alcibiades married Aspasia's sister after his ostracism in c.460; see Peter J. Bicknell, "Axiochos Alkibiadou, Aspasia and Aspasios," *L'antiquité classique* 51 (1982): 240–47. Cf. Madeleine M. Henry, *Prisoner of History: Aspasia of Miletus and Her Biographical Tradition* (Oxford: Oxford University Press, 1995), 9–10; Rebecca Futo Kennedy, *Immigrant Women in Athens: Gender, Ethnicity, and Citizenship in the Classical City* (New York: Routledge, 2014), 21; A. J. Podlecki, *Perikles and His Circle* (New York: Routledge, 1998), 109–10; Kathleen Wider, "Women Philosophers in the Ancient Greek World: Donning the Mantle," *Hypatia* 1, no. 1 (1986): 40–42. Alcibiades' ostracism is attested by a scholion on Aristophanes' *Knights* (855), and the name appears on *ostraka* found in the Athenian agora; see Eugene Vanderpool, "The Ostracism of the Elder Alkibiades," *Hesperia* 21, no. 1 (1952): 1–8. A political relationship does not necessarily invalidate the evidence that Pericles genuinely cared for Aspasia.

26. Diodorus the Periegete, *BNJ* 372 F 40, refers to her Pericles' γυνὴ (wife). On Aspasia's posi-

nian citizenship laws, but, if Pericles were smitten with this Milesian woman, as people were no doubt saying (e.g., the jokes in Aristoph. *Acharn.* 525–34), then, surely, the arbitration would be biased against them (Diod. 12.27.1; Plut. *Per.* 25.1).

Blaming Aspasia is malicious libel. Not only was Plutarch's source, the early third-century historian Duris of Samos, hardly a neutral commentator, but apparent partiality was just one of the underlying causes of the conflict. There had been a gradual change within the hierarchy of the Delian League that gave Athens ever more power. This evolution had not yet resulted in revolts in Ionia, but tensions were growing. Samos still had a fleet of at least fifty warships in 440 (Plut. *Per.* 25.3), which gave it both an advantage during its conflict with Miletus and a privileged place within the league. The Samians therefore rejected the Athenian offer to arbitrate the conflict; in so doing, they asserted their independence and challenged Athenian hegemony. There was just one problem: under Greek interstate norms, arbitration did not require the consent of the disputants.[27] When the Samians spurned Athens, the conflict ceased to be between Samos and Miletus and became one that would shape the future direction of the Delian League.

In June or July 441, an Athenian fleet sailed to Samos and toppled the government that had rejected the arbitration, installing in its place a faction that had been looking for an opening to take power (Thuc. 1.115.2).[28] The leading Samians surrendered hostages, whom the Athenians deposited on Lemnos. Lastly, among the measures to smother the inchoate resistance, the Athenians installed a garrison on the island (Thuc. 1.115.3–4; Diod. 12.27.1–3). As was common for political exiles in ancient Ionia, the deposed Samians fled to Persian territory, where they appealed to the satrap Pissouthnes for aid. There they plotted their return, which they accomplished about eight months later with the seven hundred mercenaries paid for by the satrap.

The Athenian policies designed to pacify Samos, including meddling in local politics and installing a garrison, probably did not have their intended effect. Thucydides notes that the exiles schemed with the most powerful people remaining in the polis and undermined any potential popular opposition

---

tion in Athens, see Henry, *Aspasia*, 14; Kennedy, *Immigrant Women*, 76–78; Cynthia B. Patterson, "Those Athenian Bastards," *CA* 9, no. 1 (1990): 41–42; Podlecki, *Perikles*, 109–10; Raphael Sealey, "On Lawful Concubinage in Athens," *CA* 3, no. 1 (1984): 111–33.

27. Sheila L. Ager, "Interstate Governance: Arbitration and Peacekeeping," in *A Companion to Ancient Greek Government*, ed. Hans Beck (Malden, MA: Wiley-Blackwell, 2013), 499.

28. Marathesium appears on the ATL for the first time in 442/1 (List 13, col. 1 l. 6), when the brewing conflict might have offered an opportunity for the Marathesioi to break away from Samos; see Jensen, "Rethinking Athenian Imperialism," 205–7; Meiggs, *Athenian Empire*, 428.

to their plans. His terminology is vague, using a markedly oppositional word meaning "to raise an insurrection against" (ἐπανίστημι) for how they behaved toward the demos. It is clear from this word choice that Thucydides regarded the conspirators' return as a revolution, but there is no evidence for the mechanism they used to enact the coup. The revolutionaries had some popular support and quickly overcame the Athenian garrison, turning them over to the care of Pissouthnes (Thuc. 1.115.5). Moreover, the rebels must have been confident in their position because they immediately prepared an expedition against Miletus, thus resuming the original conflict.

When news of the coup reached Athens, the Athenians immediately dispatched a fleet of sixty ships and the entire board of strategoi to the eastern Aegean.[29] Most of the ships in the first wave sailed directly to Samos, but some carried orders to other league states to muster for war, and others sailed south as a precaution against the possible arrival of a fleet from Phoenicia (Thuc. 1.116.1).[30] After defeating the Samians returning from Miletus off the island of Tragia, the Athenians disembarked on Samos and lay siege to the city. However, before reinforcements arrived, Pericles took most of the fleet south toward Caria, supposedly because of a rumor that the Phoenician fleet was approaching (Thuc. 1.116.3), but also to make a show of force that offered reassurances to the Milesians and other league members. With the bulk of the Athenian fleet gone, the Samian commander Melissus attacked the Athenian camp, destroying the guard ships and seizing control of the sea around the island for the two weeks until Pericles returned to close the siege and reinforcements from Athens, Chios, and Mytilene swelled the besieging fleet to as many as 239 ships (Diod. 12.28).[31]

The siege of Samos lasted for more than eight months and, despite a notable silence in Thucydides' narrative, was bitterly fought. Both sides allegedly branded captured enemy soldiers, the Samians marking Athenians with an owl, and the Athenians using the *Samaena*, which perhaps caused Aristophanes to joke in *Babylonians* of 426 that they were a "lettered" people (Plut. *Per.* 26.3–4). However, as Vincent Azoulay has recently pointed out, the real significance lay

---

29. There were probably sixteen Athenian strategoi who operated around Samos during the war; see Bolmarcich, "Athenian Regulations for Samos," 52; Robert Develin, *Athenian Officials, 684–321 B.C.* (Cambridge: Cambridge University Press, 1989), 89–90; Charles W. Fornara and David M. Lewis, "On the Chronology of the Samian War," *JHS* 99 (1979): 7–19; Charles W. Fornara, *The Athenian Board of Generals from 501 to 404* (Stuttgart: Franz Steiner, 1971), 48–50; Androtion, *BNJ* 324 F 38; Strabo 14.1.14; Plut. *Per.* 24.1; Diod. 12.27.4–5.

30. Hyland, *Persian Interventions*, 23, questions the tradition that this fleet was meant to confront a Persian fleet, calling it a "token" force. The show of force was certainly directed at Athenian tributaries in southwest Anatolia.

31. For this calculation, see Bolmarcich, "Athenian Regulations for Samos," 52.

in transforming captives into monetary symbols.[32] Pericles is also reputed to have brought more siege engines to bear against Samos than had ever been used in Greek warfare (Diod. 12.28.3; Plut. *Per.* 27.3), and the Athenian supremacy on both land and sea made the surrender of Samos inevitable.

According to Duris of Samos, Pericles ordered the Samian trierarchs and *epibatoi* (marines) chained to planks in the Milesian agora after they surrendered. There, he says, they were exposed to the elements for ten days before Pericles ordered their heads destroyed with clubs and their bodies disposed of without burial rites (*BNJ* 76 F 67).[33] Plutarch, whose biography of Pericles preserves the story, accuses Duris of embellishing the horrors suffered by the Samians and therefore dismisses its veracity (Plut. *Per.* 28.1–2), but he is being overly exculpatory to Pericles. Modern scholars tend to attribute this episode to an extension of the siege's brutality,[34] but the Milesian agora was an odd choice of venue if the display was meant as a warning for the Samians or as punishment for the atrocities during the war (Duris calls it a warning to the rest of the allies). More likely, this punishment was the conclusion of the regional conflict between Samos and Miletus. Almost nothing is known about the raid on Miletus, but the trierarchs were likely among its leaders and the *epibatoi* some of the mercenaries employed in the coup. It is therefore reasonable to assume that Pericles ordered the crucifixion, execution, and disposal of the bodies of these individuals for crimes committed in Miletus.

Samos retained its independence in the aftermath of the war, free of both *phoros* and garrison, but its challenge to Athenian hegemony was not without consequences. First, the Samian ringleaders were once more forced into exile and hostages were surrendered. The Samians were also forced to tear down their walls and give up their fleet (Thuc. 1.117.3; Diod. 12.28.3; Plut. *Per.* 28), as well as repay the Athenian war expenses, which totaled more than fourteen hundred talents, in annual installments of fifty talents (*ML* 55 = *IG* I³ 363).[35]

---

32. Azoulay, *Pericles*, 58.

33. Armand D'Angour, *Socrates in Love: The Making of a Philosopher* (London: Bloomsbury, 2019), 127, speculates that Melissus would have been among the executed Samians, but there is no evidence either way.

34. Graham Shipley, *A History of Samos, 800–188 BC* (Oxford: Oxford University Press, 1987), 117; cf. Philip S. Stadter, *A Commentary on Plutarch's Pericles* (Chapel Hill: University of North Carolina Press, 1989), 258–59; Meiggs, *Athenian Empire*, 192; Frances Pownall, "Duris of Samos (76)," *BNJ* F 67 commentary. Peter Karavites, "Enduring Problems of the Samian Revolt," *RhM* 128, no. 1 (1985): 47–51, argues that the punishment ought to be associated with a second revolt in 412, but see Azoulay, *Pericles*, 57–61, for Pericles' violence.

35. There are three sums recording cost of the war, which Fornara in Fornara and Lewis, "Chronology of the Samian War," 12–14, argues corresponds to the three consecutive boards of treasurers responsible for the expedition, while Benjamin D. Meritt, "The Samian Revolt from Athens in 440–439 B.C.," *PAPhS* 128, no. 2 (1984): 128–29, holds that the largest refers to the war

Finally, the Samian boule swore a loyalty oath to defend both its own demos and Athens (*ML* 56 = *IG* I³ 48, l. 22), which set the precedent for the resolution of future conflicts in the Delian League.[36]

Samos had been one of the staunchest supporters of the league before 454, and it had held pride of place as one of three members outside Athens to retain its fleet when the rest of the league transitioned to providing *phoros* payments. In the absence of evidence for increasing discontent with Athenian hegemony, it is necessary to ask what changed. Samos had traditionally been one of the dominant poleis in the Aegean, and the tipping point was simply that the Samians called the Athenian bluff concerning its willingness to intervene in disputes between Delian League members. Thucydides' brief narrative elides that Samos' challenge posed a real threat that nearly broke Athenian hegemony. The war was not only a demonstration of Athenian will, but also of its ability to exert power over the league members.[37] After 439, Samos fell into an anomalous position, no longer a naval power, but also explicitly paying reparations to Athens rather than a *phoros* to the Delian League. Despite the lingering resentment toward Athens that some Samians must have harbored on account of the financial demands, time heals most wounds, and Samos would become Athens' staunchest ally again before the end of the Peloponnesian War. Those Samians who refused to surrender took refuge at Anaia in the Samian *peraea*.

A Horse Not in Need of a Whip: Chios and Athens

Chios had also held a special position within the Delian League after 454. Like Samos, it was wealthy because of its strategic position astride maritime trade routes and was therefore able to maintain a fleet of warships. Once Samos sur-

---

with Samos, while the other two were for related expeditions. Cf. Alec Blamire, "Athenian Finance, 454–404 B.C.," *Hesperia* 70, no. 1 (2001): 101–3; G. Marginesu and A. A. Themos, "Ἀνέλοσαν ἐς τὸν πρὸς Σαμίος πόλεμον: A New Fragment of the Samian War Expenses (*IG* I³ 363 + 454)," in ΑΘΗΝΑΙΩΝ ΕΠΙΣΚΟΠΟΣ: *Studies in Honour of Harold B. Mattingly*, ed. Angelos P. Matthaiou and Robert K. Pitt (Athens: Greek Epigraphical Society, 2014), 171–84; Shipley, *Samos*, 117–18, with n. 32. Ancient authors give various sums for the cost: Diodorus Siculus 12.28.3 (200 talents), Isocrates 15.111 (1000 talents), and Cornelius Nepos *Timotheus* (1,200 talents).

36. Meiggs and Lewis, *Greek Historical Inscriptions*, 153, saw this line as a reciprocity clause sworn by the Athenian representatives, but see Fornara and Lewis, "Chronology of the Samian War," 17–18. For the most recent reconstruction, see Angelos P. Matthaiou, "The Treaty of Athens with Samos (*IG* I³ 48)," in ΑΘΗΝΑΙΩΝ ΕΠΙΣΚΟΠΟΣ: *Studies in Honour of Harold B. Mattingly*, ed. Angelos P. Matthaiou and Robert K. Pitt (Athens: Greek Epigraphical Society, 2014), 141–70.

37. This is one of the strongest points of evidence in favor of Hyland's revisionist argument that Persian satraps were under orders not to interfere in the Aegean. Pissouthnes supported the Samian exiles in their domestic conflict but stopped short of giving them aid against Athens.

rendered in 439, Chios alone among the Ionian poleis continued to provide ships to the Delian League. But did the Chians watch the resolution of the war around Samos with trepidation? Looking back from the twenty-first century, it is hard to imagine that they did not recognize the metastasis of Athenian imperialism as it was happening, but money is a powerful drug. Pottery shards from amphorae demonstrate the extent of the Chian commercial reach, including in the Athenian Agora and the Black Sea, and Chian merchants were deeply involved in the slave trade, particularly from the Caucasus.[38] Chios profited from Athenian campaigns, not only through its share of the booty, but also by victualing the forces on league expeditions.

Chian ships joined the Athenian blockade, and its merchants likely provided supplies to the besiegers (Diod. 12.27.4). Anecdotes from the siege, such as the Athenian *proxenos* at Chios, Hermisilaus, hosting a dinner party attended by Sophocles and Ion of Chios (Ion, *BNJ* 392 T 5b, F 6), suggest that personal, as well as economic, relationships caused the Chians to turn a blind eye to Athens crushing resistance to its hegemony. Certainly, the power of personal relationships should not be dismissed, but Thucydides suggests an alternate explanation. In an encomium of Chios in 411, he says that it was the only community other than Sparta that grew more stable as it grew larger and attributes this situation to its reluctance to act rashly (8.24.4). This combination of internal stability and caution was probably equally important in the lack of resistance to the expansion of Athenian hegemony since Athens never had cause to intervene in its domestic affairs the way that it did on Samos.

It is possible that the progression of Athenian imperialism was evident to people on Chios after the war on Samos made clear the limits of allied autonomy, but this does not necessarily mean that they would have launched their

---

38. Theopompus claims that the Chians were the first Greek people to have purchased enslaved people (*BNJ* 115 F 122a). On slaves being imported from the Black Sea region, see D. C. Braund and G. R. Tsetzkhladze, "The Export of Slaves from Colchis," *CQ*² 39, no. 1 (1989): 114–25, though David M. Lewis, *Greek Slave Systems in Their Eastern Mediterranean Context, c. 800–146 BC* (Oxford: Oxford University Press, 2018) and "Near Eastern Slaves in Classical Attica and the Slave Trade with Persian Territories," *CQ*² 61, no. 1 (2011): 91–113, has recently explored the problems with identifying the Black Sea as the primary vector of this trade. For the spread of Chian pottery finds, see R. M. Cook, "The Distribution of Chiot Pottery," *ABSA* 44 (1949): 154–61; Michail J. Treister and Yuri G. Vinogradov, "Archaeology on the Northern Coast of the Black Sea," *AJA* 97, no. 3 (1993): 532; Miron I. Zolotarev, "A Hellenistic Ceramic Deposit from the North-eastern Sector of the Chersonesos," in *Chronologies of the Black Sea Area, C. 400–100 BC*, ed. Lise Hannestad and Vladimir F. Stolba (Aarhus: Aarhus University Press, 2006), 194–95; Valeria P. Bylkova, "The Chronology of Settlements in the Lower Dnieper Region (400–100 BC)," in *Chronologies of the Black Sea Area, c. 400–100 BC*, ed. Lise Hannestad and Vladimir F. Stolba (Aarhus: Aarhus University Press, 2006), 218–20; T. C. Sarikakis, "Commercial Relations between Chios and Other Greek Cities in Antiquity," in *Chios: A Conference at the Homereion in Chios*, ed. John Boardman and C. E. Vaphopoulou-Richardson (Oxford: Oxford University Press, 1986), 121–32.

own challenge. In fact, there is no evidence of growing concern on Chios. Commerce continued between the two poleis and intellectuals such as the playwright Ion and the mathematician Hippocrates frequented Athens, attending and giving lectures and, in the case of Ion, winning dramatic competitions (Ion, *BNJ* 392 T 1, 2).[39] Chian forces also continued to accompany Athenian military expeditions (e.g., Thuc. 2.56.2, 4.129.2, 5.85, 7.57.3). From an Athenian perspective Chios was the perfect subject, such that in 422 the Athenian comic poet Eupolis quipped that Chios was like a horse that did not require a whip because it obediently provided ships and men whenever needed (*Poleis*, F. 232).[40]

Chaffing at the Athenian Bit

Signs of stasis began to appear with increasing regularity throughout Ionia starting in the 430s. The first incident was at Erythrae. An Athenian regulatory decree c.434 installed an Athenian-style democracy with a council approved by the Athenian *phrourarchos* (garrison commander, *RO* 121 = *IG* I³ 14, l.13–14).[41] Another decree addressed the issue of exiles, specifying a group that had taken refuge with Persia and requiring Erythrae to seek Athenian approval before any new expulsions or restorations (*RO* 122 = *I.Ery.* 2, l. 27). These decrees conjure the specter of Persia along with the mention of exiles, so the conflict that Athens intervened in is often interpreted as being between Athenian loyalists and a faction that intended to turn Erythrae over to the Persians. Thus, the standard line goes, the Athenian garrison was intended to "protect Erythrai from mediz-

---

39. Ion allegedly procured a jar of wine for every Athenian citizen after his victory (*BNJ* 392 T 1, 2). On his participation in the tragedy category, see Kenneth J. Dover, "Ion of Chios: His Place in the History of Greek Literature," in *Chios: A Conference at the Homereion in Chios*, ed. John Boardman and C. E. Vaphopoulou-Richardson (Oxford: Oxford University Press 1986), 27–37, and T. B. L. Webster, "Sophocles and Ion of Chios," *Hermes* 71, no. 3 (1936): 263–74. Ion also warranted mention in Aristophanes' *Peace* (832–37). Hippocrates was a Pythagorean mathematician who allegedly came to Athens to lodge a court case after being swindled out of his cargo; Arist. *Eudemian Ethics*, 8.2.5.

40. αὕτη Χίος, καλὸν καλῶν πόλις<μα>|πέμπει γὰρ ὑμῖν ναῦς μακρὰς ἄνδρας θ᾽ ὅταν δεήσμη | καὶ τ᾽ ἄλλα πειθαρχεῖ καλῶς, ἄπληκτος ὥσπερ ἵππος. Text after John M. Edmonds, *Fragments of Attic Comedy*, vol. 1 (Leiden: Brill, 1957).

41. The dating of this decree is complicated by the absence of a named archon. On a late date, see Moroo, "The Erythrai Decrees Reconsidered," 97–120; Papazarkadas, "Epigraphy and the Athenian Empire," 78. For an earlier date c.450, see Meiggs and Lewis, *Greek Historical Inscriptions*, 453/2; Jensen, *Rethinking Athenian Imperialism*, 52–54; P. J. Rhodes and Robin Osborne, *Greek Historical Inscriptions, 478–404 BC* (Oxford: Oxford University Press, 2017), 119–23; Matthew Simonton, "The Local History of Hippias of Erythrai: Politics, Place, Memory, and Monumentality," *Hesperia* 87, no. 3 (2018): 497–543. Harold B. Mattingly, "What Are the Right Dating Criteria for Fifth-Century Attic Texts?," *ZPE* 126 (1999): 117–22, renounced his late dating.

ers," even while acknowledging that it was part of a broader policy of protecting Athenian imperial interests.[42]

Before examining the local conditions at Erythrae in more detail, it is necessary to question the usual characterization of conflicts of this type as a direct outgrowth of a cold war between Athens and Persia.[43] The inscription erected at Erythrae invites a reading of a conflict stirred up by meddlesome Persians and a handful of malcontents, but there is reason to be skeptical. It was in the Athenian interest to exonerate most of the population, blaming the people who had already gone into exile, and implying that the current impositions were protection against barbarians and tyrants. The display was itself a piece of rhetoric. The exiles had taken refuge with Persia, and it is an easy leap to paint them as patsies working to undermine Greek freedom by inviting in the Persians, which thereby justified the Athenian intervention. And yet, Persia was a common destination for Greek (including Athenian!) political refugees banned from the Delian League, and Persian territory was just a few kilometers from Erythrae. It is therefore natural to have expected the Erythraean exiles to decamp for Persia in 434 without their actions necessarily having been motivated by either gold or Persian sympathies.

What, then, do these decrees indicate about the local political situation in Erythrae? First, the provisions concerning government were designed to circumvent several local problems at once. The Athenian-style democracy would in theory make it more difficult for a few individuals to seize power, while the *phrourarchos'* power to vet the incoming council provided Athens a measure of control over prospective legislation. This new arrangement, combined with the provision concerning exiles, also gave the *phrourarchos* authority to mediate local disputes. Despite the benevolent veneer of the decree, the combination of restrictions and garrison indicates that the crisis at Erythrae went beyond just a group of malignant medizers and extended into the population at large.

Panning back from Erythrae reveals a similar pattern throughout Ionia. In 430, a faction in Colophon called for and received aid from Persia, forcing their rivals to flee to the port of Notium (Thuc. 3.34.1). There, the refugees again split into factions, with the Persian satrap Pissouthnes sending merce-

---

42. Meiggs and Lewis, *Greek Historical Inscriptions*, 92; cf. Briant, *From Cyrus to Alexander*, 579, 581; Rhodes, "Delian League," 56–57. Curiously, the medizing faction is typically described as "small."

43. Samuel K. Eddy, "The Cold War between Athens and Persia, ca. 448–412 B.C.," *CPh* 68, no. 4 (1973): 241–58, draws the parallel between his modern setting and the ancient world, but the basic relationship is implicitly accepted elsewhere. Hyland, *Persian Interventions*, 24, rightly critiques Eddy as mistaking "sporadic episodes for an overarching strategy." I agree with Hyland that the decree does not record active Persian involvement.

he revolt.

naries to support one side. Once the conflict broke out in Colophon, Pissouthnes took advantage of the schism, but Thucydides gives no indication that he had actively been working to cause the conflict. With their backs to the wall, the other faction appealed to the Athenian admiral Paches, who detained the mercenary commander during a parley and immediately attacked and defeated the Persian force (Thuc. 3.34.2-3). Paches restored the exiled Colophonians and established them in a new settlement at Notium with other refugees from around the Aegean (*ML* 47 = *IG* I³ 37; Thuc. 3.34.4).[44] In 427, there were thus two Colophons, one in Notium and one in the original *astu*, because this was the most expedient solution for Athens to resolve a deep rift in the Colophonian citizen body.

Another regulatory decree appears on an inscription from Miletus, probably from 426/5 (*IG* I³ 22).[45] As at Erythrae, the Athenians installed a garrison and restrictions on the Milesian political and legal systems (ll. 28-51), as well as installing five archons (officers), one for each of the five natural divisions of the Milesian territory.[46] Other than the number of archons, which was probably no more significant than a practical consideration in terms of the Milesian civic structure, the most notable difference was that the Milesian officials swore to uphold the decree, rather than swearing an oath of loyalty to Athens. This is a significant change, but one that even more strongly reflects the need to resolve a bitter internal conflict, rather than to quell a nascent revolt.

Domestic conflicts in Ionia did not exist in isolation, and imperial competition over Ionia exacerbated the conflicts because factions could exploit the imperial actors for local ends. These conflicts became deep-seated in time, but they should not be taken to reflect a political preference on the part of the community. Looking at the Athenian regulations in Ionia as an outgrowth of local conflict moreover avoids the trap where every local development is a reaction to specific imperial actions in Athens. The signs of unrest extended even to Chios, but before turning to these, it is necessary examine the only incident where fighting from the Archidamian War spilled across the Aegean into Ionia.

In 427, a Peloponnesian fleet under the command of the Spartan Alcidas crossed the Aegean to support Mytilene, which had revolted from Athenian leadership. According to Thucydides, the Peloponnesians did not sail with

44. As with the other regulatory decrees for Ionia, the date of this inscription is debated. It is frequently dated as part of a series in the 440s, but see Papazarkadas, "Epigraphy and the Athenian Empire," for the connection to Thucydides.

45. On this inscription, see Mattingly, "Athenian Decree for Miletos," 453-60; Paarman, "Aparchai and Phoroi," 121-40; Robertson, "Government and Society at Miletus," 356-98.

46. For the importance of these Milesian districts, see Robertson, "Government and Society at Miletus," 356-98.

enough urgency and arrived in Asia Minor unaware that Mytilene had fallen about a week earlier. The fleet thus put in at Embata in Erythrae to debate a course of action. An Elean named Teutiaplus proposed an attack, anyway, claiming the Athenians could be taken unawares (Thuc. 3.30). Alcidas was unimpressed, and Ionian exiles and Lesbians who had joined the expedition urged him instead to capture a city in Ionia or Cyme just into Aeolis to use as a base to incite revolution throughout the region. The exiles reassured Alcidas that the Ionians would welcome Spartan intervention and that their plan was prudent because they could induce Pissouthnes to support them and it would deprive Athens of a significant part of its revenue (πρόσοδον ταύτην μεγίστην, Thuc. 3.31.1).[47]

Alcidas was ultimately not persuaded, but the proposal is revealing about the circumstances in Ionia in 427. First, this war council took place at a town in Ionian territory, which is clear indication that the capture of outlying settlements was well within the capacity of the fleet. Second, the proposal was made by unnamed and unprovenanced Ionian exiles. Thucydides does not indicate when they joined Alcidas, but the fact that among them were Lesbians and the ostensible aim of the expedition was to relieve the siege of Mytilene, it is reasonable to assume that they had accompanied it from the Peloponnesus and thus had a voice in the deliberations. Third, the basic structure of the plan, from using an Ionian polis as a Spartan base to appealing to the Persian satrap to envisioning widespread popular support for revolution is identical to the outcome fifteen years later during the Ionian War (see Chapter 4). While it cannot be ruled out that Thucydides meant this debate to foreshadow the later revolt, it still invites the question whether it is an accurate assessment of Ionian popular opinion.

The exiles were overly optimistic in more than one respect. There is no indication that, when news spread that a Peloponnesian fleet was in the Erythraeid, any other Ionians approached Alcidas. On the contrary, Thucydides says that the Ionians reacted with fear and immediately sent messengers to Paches and the Athenian fleet (3.33.2). It was ultimately continuous intervention on the parts of Tissaphernes and Cyrus the Younger during the Ionian War that pried Ionia away from Athens. The exiles also misjudged Pissouthnes, who received support from Athenian mercenaries when he went into revolt soon after Artaxerxes' death in 424 (Ctesias, F 52).[48]

---

47. Examination of the Athenian Tribute Lists does not support their boast. The Ionian-Carian district was one of the poorest.
48. On Pissouthnes' revolt, see Briant, *From Cyrus to Alexander*, 591; D. M. Lewis, *Sparta and Persia* (Leiden: Brill, 1977), 80–81; Meiggs, *Athenian Empire*, 349; Lloyd Llewellyn-Jones and James Robson, *Ctesias' History of Persia: Tales of the Orient* (Routledge: New York, 2009), 194–95.

But if Pissouthnes was no Cyrus, neither was Alcidas Lysander. With Mytilene fallen, Alcidas decided to return to the Peloponnese. Thucydides preserves a compressed sketch of Alcidas' voyage, but it began with a tour of Ionia. Setting out from Embata, the Spartan fleet sailed south along the shore to the Teian town of Myonnesus. During the expedition, Alcidas' fleet had been conducting piratical raids on Chios and other Ionian communities. Mistaking the Peloponnesian vessels for Athenians, the Ionians had come up to the ships and been captured (Thuc. 3.32.3). At Myonnesus, Alcidas ordered most of these prisoners executed. Continuing southward, Alcidas put in at Ephesus, where he received envoys from the Samian exiles at Anaea who rebuked him for executing the prisoners, saying that they were Athenian allies under coercion and that his current actions were turning potential friends into enemies (Thuc. 3.32.2).[49] After releasing the remaining prisoners, probably in return for ransoms, Alcidas' fleet beat a hasty retreat from Ephesus.

So ended the only Spartan expedition to Ionia during the Archidamian War, but local conflict continued. According to Thucydides, one of the factors working in Alcidas' favor in 427 was that Ionia was unfortified (3.33.2). The lack of defensive walls is clearly explained in some instances, such as on Samos, where they were destroyed as part of the resolution to the war in 440/39. In others, the information is sketchier. It is possible that the Ionian communities were without walls because of because of imperial mandate, either by Persia or Athens.[50] Indeed, a fragment from the lost comic poet Telecleides chides the Athenians for giving Pericles power over the walls of their subjects (Plut. *Per.* 16.2), and other evidence indicates that Athens intervened when local conditions threatened its interests, including at Chios in 427 (Thuc. 4.51). Little is known about this local conflict, but a fragmentary inscription from Athens dated to 425/4 honors Philippos and Ach[illes], two Chians plausibly from the poet Ion's family who preserved the *pisteis* between Chios and Athens.[51] However, other

---

49. There is a lack of evidence for Ephesus in the second half of the fifth century even though it remained an important waypoint for people making their way to Persia (Thuc. 1.137; 4.50). Simon Hornblower, *A Commentary on Thucydides*, 3 vols. (Oxford: Oxford University Press, 1991–2008), 2.414–15, attributes its apparent willingness to treat with Alcidas to its being unwalled (Thuc. 3.33.2). A. W. Gomme, *A Historical Commentary on Thucydides*, 2 vols. (Oxford: Oxford University Press, 1956), 2.294–95, believes that Alcidas only stayed long enough to take on water.

50. It is a commonly held position that the destruction of walls was a stipulation of the Peace of Callias that both Athens and Persia desired; see Badian, "Peace of Callias," 35; George L. Cawkwell, *The Greek Wars: The Failure of Persia* (Oxford: Oxford University Press, 2005), 141; Hornblower, *A Commentary on Thucydides*, vol. 1, 415; cf. Lewis, *Sparta and Persia*, 153 and n. 118; H. T. Wade-Gery, *Essays in Greek History* (Oxford: Oxford University Press, 1958), 219; Meiggs, *Athenian Empire*, 149–50; Gomme, *Historical Commentary on Thucydides*, vol. 1, 295; J. M. Cook, "The Problem of Classical Ionia," *PCPhS* 187, no. 7 (1961): 9–11. Gorman, *Miletos*, 237, rejects this explanation for Miletus.

51. See Benjamin D. Meritt, "Attic Inscriptions of the Fifth Century," *Hesperia* 14, no. 2 (1945): 115–17; John P. Barron, "Chios in the Athenian Empire," in *Chios: A Conference at the Homereion in*

Ionian poleis may have been unfortified because they were decentralized and walls were expensive to build, rather than by imperial fiat.

Alcidas' meeting with Ionian emissaries at Ephesus in 427 also poses a riddle. There is no direct evidence for the political leanings of fifth-century Ephesus before 411, but indirect evidence leads to several divergent interpretations. On the one hand, the tribute lists indicate a stable record of *phoros* payments, and no evidence suggests that Ephesus was subject to special regulations or a garrison. On the other hand, Ephesus stood apart from the Ionian revolt, even slaughtering Chian survivors after the battle of Lade (Hdt. 6.16; see Chapter 1). There was no such thing as a "purely" Greek culture anywhere in the eastern Aegean, least of all in Ionia, but acculturation was particularly pronounced at Ephesus. These processes are epitomized by the Persianization of the cult of Artemis, where the priest took on the title "Megabyxos" (Xen. *Anab.* 5.3.6), Persian items appeared among the dedicatory offerings, and friezes show figures in Persian garb participating in the rituals.[52] What should be made of this disparate evidence? Was Ephesus a quiescent subject or a hotbed of anti-Athenian medism?

The answer is, of course, both—and neither. Ephesus was a natural port for Sardis and therefore had deep, long-standing ties the Lydian capital.[53] Moreover, after Cyrus II annexed Lydia in the mid-sixth century, Ephesus became integrated into the Persian royal road system (Hdt. 5.54; Strabo 1.6).[54] The fame of the

---

Chios, ed. John Boardman and C. E. Vaphopoulou-Richardson (Oxford: Oxford University Press: 1986), 101–2.

52. Margaret C. Miller, "Clothes and Identity: The Case of Greeks in Ionia c.400 BC," in *Culture, Identity and Politics in the Ancient Mediterranean World*, ed. Paul J. Burton (Canberra: Australasian Society for Classical Studies, 2013), 25–33. On the cultural identity of Ephesus, see also Appendix 2.

53. Other ports in the region, including Cyme and Smyrna, also had close ties to Sardis, but Ephesus may have served as the harbor for Croesus' fleet (Hdt. 1.27; Diod. 9.25.1–2; Friederike Stock et al., "The Palaeogeographies of Ephesos [Turkey], Its Harbours, and the Artemision: A Geoarchaeological Reconstruction for the Timespan 1500–300 BC," *Zeitschrift für Geomorphologie* 98, no. 2 [2014]: 33–66). Croesus lavished dedications on the Artemisium (see Chapter 9), and the sanctuary shows numerous votives of Lydian make; see Michael Kerschner, "Die Lyder und das Artemision von Ephesos," in *Die Archäologie der ephischen Artemis: Gestalt und Ritual eines Heiligtums*, ed. Ulrike Muss (Vienna: Phoibos, 2008), 223–33; Sabine Ladstätter, "Ephesus," in *Spear Won Land: Sardis from the King's Peace to the Peace of Apamea*, ed. Andrea M. Berlin and Paul J. Kosmin (Madison: University of Wisconsin Press, 2019), 191–92. For the identification of the Ephesian harbors and the evolution of the coastline, see Stock et al., "Palaeogeographies of Ephesos."

54. David French, "Pre- and Early-Roman Roads of Asia Minor: The Persian Royal Road," *Iran* 36 (1998): 20–21; Alan M. Greaves, *The Land of Ionia: Society and Economy in the Archaic Period* (Malden, MA: Wiley-Blackwell, 2010), 101. On the Persian road system, see Briant, *From Cyrus to Alexander*, 357–87, and Pierre Briant, "From the Indus to the Mediterranean: The Administrative Organization and Logistics of the Great Roads of the Achaemenid Empire," in *Highways, Byways, and Road Systems in the Pre-modern World*, ed. Susan E. Alcock, John Bodel, and Richard J. A. Talbert (Malden, MA: Wiley-Blackwell, 2012), 185–201. When the Athenians returned Artaphernes to Persia in 425/4, they made first for Ephesus (4.50), and Alexander's route in 334 took him from Sardis to Ephesus; see Chapter 7.

sanctuary of Artemis, which had prominent Anatolian features despite its Greek name, made it a natural magnet for dedications from prominent Persians. Processes of acculturation and religious propaganda, however visible at Ephesus, are not synonymous with political sympathies. Where local conflicts drove factions in most other Ionian poleis to appeal to Persia for support, there is no indication that the same happened at Ephesus. The significance given to the acculturation of the Ionian poleis emerged from the later historiographical record that created an east-west cultural binary that defined Greeks in opposition to the barbarian Persians.[55] Only after years of war and increasing financial demands when all of Ionia was ripe for revolt did Ephesus reject Athenian hegemony.

Ionians and the Peloponnesian War

Excepting only Alcidas' expedition in 427, Ionia was spared the direct effects of the Archidamian War. Nevertheless, the years of conflict between Athens and Sparta affected the region in two ways.

The first was economic. War likely led to an uptick in piracy in the Aegean, at least with expeditions like that of Alcidas, which, in turn, had an immeasurable, but certainly deleterious effect on Ionian commerce.[56] The same can be said about the relationship between Ionian trade and the Greek states in European Greece. The war would have restricted commercial opportunities with, for instance, Corinth, but there is no balance sheet recording the actual change. Further, the effects of the war on Ionian commerce were not constant. Not only did Ionian merchants continue to ply the sea-lanes, fulfilling both military and civilian demands for goods irrespective of the war, but also the Peloponnesian War was in fact a series of interconnected conflicts punctuated by truces, so the interruption of trade was neither constant nor complete.

Somewhat more detail is known about the evolution of the Athenian impe-

---

55. Lynette G. Mitchell, *Panhellenism and the Barbarian in Archaic and Classical Greece* (Swansea: Classical Press of Wales, 2007), 10–19; Kostas Vlassopoulos, *Unthinking the Greek Polis: Ancient Greek History beyond Eurocentrism* (Cambridge: Cambridge University Press, 2007) 46–53; cf. Appendix 2.

56. On speculation about the expansion of trade during peacetime, see Hyland, *Persian Interventions*, 28–30. Tracking the level of piracy in the fifth century is a challenge because of the nature of our sources. Thucydides implies that Athens suppressed piracy, but recently Philip de Souza, *Piracy in the Greco-Roman World* (Cambridge: Cambridge University Press, 1999), 15–30, and Rutishauser, *Athens and the Cyclades*, 17, have suggested it continued unabated, contra Hornblower, *A Commentary on Thucydides*, vol. 1, 150. I believe there was a decline in piracy in the middle two quarters of the fifth century, but because the maritime courts had offered redress within the Athenian *arche* rather than because of Athenian policy. The Athenian activities that Thucydides describes as antipiratical, like the expedition to Scyros (1.98.2), look suspiciously like imperialism.

rial structures. Every four years since 454 Athenian officials had conducted a new assessment that revised the levels of *phoros* due for the next period. During the Archidamian War, however, the new assessments came more frequently and at irregular intervals. The most infamous of these assessments was the ninth (A9), conducted in 425/4. The changes in the ninth assessment have traditionally been attributed to the malice of Cleon, who used it as an opportunity to double or even treble the imperial revenue because the war fund had been depleted (*ML* 69 = *IG* I^3 71).[57]

Benjamin Meritt and Allen West, two of the original editors of the Athenian Tribute Lists, believed that the sum of tribute payments on A9 could be reconstructed as either 960[---] or 1460[---] talents based on a lost first digit, which is either five hundred or one thousand.[58] (The reconstructed inscription is also missing the final three digits of the total.) The inscription recording this assessment is lacunate, and many of the figures, including all of those from Ionia, are lost, but the surviving amounts regularly reveal a substantial uptick in *phoros* obligations. The *ATL* editors took the increased obligations in places such as Thrace as confirmation of the larger sum and inferred exorbitant increases in the assessed *phoros* in Ionia, some as high as fifty talents.[59] They nevertheless conceded that the Athenian income from tribute payments never exceeded about one thousand talents, so either the system was wildly inefficient or, more likely, support for the larger figure is misplaced. The ninth assessment did constitute a substantial overhaul of tribute levels, but, as Lisa Kallet has recently demonstrated,[60] this did not mean an across-the-board increase. Moreover, there is no evidence, either in surviving *phoros* payments in the years after 425 or in the form of new unrest, for particularly onerous obligations in Ionia. This is not to say that this assessment did not increase the Ionian *phoros* obligations. Most likely, the overall assessment was close to 960 talents, and Ionian obligations remained at or near their historical maximum levels.[61]

It is tempting to see the assessment of 425 as the cause of the Milesian revolt against Athens described above. The problem with this interpretation is the chronology. The regulatory decree is dated 426/5 based on the archon in whose

---

57. See, for instance, Blamire, "Athenian Finance," 111; Donald Kagan, *The Archidamian War* (Ithaca, NY: Cornell University Press, 1990), 250–51.

58. Benjamin D. Merritt and Allen B. West, *The Athenian Assessment of 425 B.C.* (Ann Arbor: University of Michigan Press, 1934), 88–89.

59. Meritt and West, *Athenian Assessment*, 89.

60. Lisa Kallet, "Epigraphic Geography: The Tribute Quota Fragments Assigned to 421/0–415/4 B.C.," *Hesperia* 73, no. 4 (2004): 492–95.

61. The exception to this general trend did not appear until 415/4 when Clazomenae's payment was a staggering fifteen talents (EM 6653), before dropping to a more typical five and a third talents the next year.

term it was enacted, while the assessment was in 425/4. The two periods overlap, but face in different directions. Where the assessment took place *in* 425/4, the regulatory decree in 426/5 records the resolution of a conflict that had been going on *before* that year. The two decrees therefore took place consecutively and were not connected. With this explanation eliminated, it opens the door again for the regulatory decree to be considered in light of chronic factional conflict that plagued fifth-century Miletus. The Ionians almost certainly availed themselves of the special appeals court created in the decree since, as still holds true when it comes to taxes, there were great financial rewards to crying poverty in the fifth century BCE, but there is no reason to interpret local stasis as anti-Athenianism in the wake of a cruel assessment.

Although the assessment of 425 did not lead to substantial changes in Ionia, two other wartime measures did. The first, the so-called Standards Decree (*ML* 45 = *IG* I³ 1453), is traditionally dated to the mid-440s as part of the tightening imperial regulations, but recent scholarship has revised this date to either the mid-420s or, more likely, c.415/4.[62] While the revisionist argument began on the basis of the character of Athenian leaders, namely to exonerate Pericles and pin the blame on the "bloody-minded" Cleon,[63] there is nevertheless good reason to read the decree as wartime financial expediency. The Standards Decree itself is a misnomer in that it was a body of regulatory decrees concerning economic activity and erected on stelae in markets throughout the Delian League.[64] These

---

62. For the 440s date, see Azoulay, *Pericles*, 54; Balcer, *Sparda*, 396–405; Samuel K. Eddy, "Some Irregular Amounts of Athenian Tribute," *AJPh* 94, no. 1 (1973): 47–70; Meiggs and Lewis, *Greek Historical Inscriptions*, 111–16; E. S. G. Robinson, "The Athenian Coinage Decree and the Coinages of the Allies," *Hesperia* suppl. 8 (1949): 328–40; Mario Segre, "La Legge Ateniese sull' unificazione della moneta," *Clara Rhodos* 9, no. 4 (1938): 151–78; for the 420s, see Loren J. Samons II, *Empire of the Owl: Athenian Imperial Finance* (Stuttgart: Franz Steiner, 2000), 330–31; C. Howgego, *Ancient History from Coins* (New York: Routledge, 1995), 44; Harold B. Mattingly, "New Light on the Athenian Standards Decree," in *From Coins to History: Selected Numismatic Studies* (Ann Arbor: University of Michigan Press, 2003), 24–29 (= *Klio* 75 [1993]: 99–102); Michael Vickers, "Fifth Century Chronology and the Coinage Decree," *JHS* 116 (1996): 171–74. Lisa Kallet, *Money and Corrosion of Power in Thucydides: The Sicilian Expedition and Its Aftermath* (Berkeley: University of California Press, 2001), 205–26, and Athena Hadji and Zoe Kontes, "The Athenian Coinage Decree: Inscriptions, Coins and Athenian Politics," in *Proceedings of the XIII Congress of International Numismatics*, ed. Carmen Alfaro Asins, Carmen Marcos Alonso, and Paloma Otero Morán (Madrid: Ministerio de Cultura, Secretería General Técnica, 2005), 263–68, favor a date around 415 at the transition from *phoros* to *eikoste*.

63. Loren J. Samons II, "Periklean Imperialism and Imperial Finance in Context," in *Hegemonic Finances: Funding Athenian Domination in the 5th and 4th Centuries BC*, ed. Thomas J. Figueira and Sean R. Jensen (London: Bloomsbury 2019), 14, has recently pointed out the weakness of this premise, declaring that "the imperialists were the Athenians themselves." He argues that Pericles was only moderate in contrast to the normal extremes.

64. There are no extant copies of the inscription from Ionia, but the district is mentioned specifically (ll. 25–26), so the decree took effect there. For epigraphical reconstructions of the decree, see Thomas J. Figueira, *The Power of Money: Coinage and Politics in the Athenian Empire* (Philadelphia: University of Pennsylvania Press, 1998), 319–423; for a synopsis of debates, see David M.

decrees had two primary effects. First, they mandated that all economic activity in Delian League markets had to use Attic weights and measures and, second, they required that allied coins used in tribute payments be reminted into Athenian Owls, the famous silver tetradrachmae. The decrees likewise installed procedures for carrying out the new regulations and penalties for infractions.

The fundamental question is how much of an imposition these policies were on the Athenian allies. The Ionian poleis had produced some of the earliest Greek coinage, but they had an inconsistent record of minting coins in silver, electrum, and perhaps smaller denominations in the fifth century. The comparatively rich evidence from Chios reveals an unexpected pattern.[65] Starting in the mid-fifth century, Chian mints abandoned the production of staters in favor of tetradrachmae marked with a Chian amphora, but on their own standard. Then there was a transition in the 430s in the amphorae type produced on Chios that brought the amphora into closer alignment with Attic measures, and the iconographic representation on coins follows suit.[66] The pattern, then, is that Chios made a spasmodic and irregular transition toward Attic measures and denominations over the course of the second half of the fifth century, but never completed the process.

Lewis, "The Athenian Coinage Decree," in *Coinage and Administration in the Athenian and Persian Empires*, ed. Ian Carradice (Oxford: Oxford University Press, 1987), 53–63, and, more recently, Hadji and Kontes, "Athenian Coinage Decree," 263–68, with bibliography.

65. Ironically, while Athenian Owls are found only rarely in Aegean hoards from this period, Chian coin finds are plentiful; see Peter G. van Alfen, "The Coinage of Athens, Sixth to First Centuries B.C.," in *The Oxford Handbook of Greek and Roman Coinage*, ed. William E. Metcalf (Oxford: Oxford University Press, 2012), 94, and N. M. M. Hardwick, "The Coinage of Chios, 6th–4th century BC," in *Proceedings of the XI International Numismatic Congress*, ed. Catherine Courtois, Harry Dewit, and Véronique Van Driessche (Louvain: Séminaire de Numismatique Marcel Hoc, 1993), 213–16, 221. Recently, seven thousand to ten thousand Athenian coins (between four and six talents) turned up in southeastern Turkey; see Richard Buxton, "The Northern Syria 2007 Hoard of Athenian Owls: Behavioral Aspects," *AJN*[2] 21 (2009): 1–27. John H. Kroll and Alan S. Walker, *The Athenian Agora: Results of Excavations Conducted by the American School of Classical Studies in Athens, vol. 26: The Greek Coins* (Princeton: The American School of Classical Studies at Athens, 1993), 4, note that Athenian tetradrachmae make up only a small percentage of the coins found at the Agora in Athens.

66. On this process, see Harold B. Mattingly, "Coins and Amphoras: Chios, Samos and Thasos in the Fifth Century B.C.," in *The Athenian Empire Restored* (Ann Arbor: University of Michigan Press, 1996), 435–52 (= *JHS* 101 [1981], 78–86); Harold B. Mattingly, "Chios and the Athenian Standards Decree," in *The Athenian Empire Restored* (Ann Arbor: University of Michigan Press, 1996), 521; Figueira, *Power of Money*, 154–55; Barron, "Chios in the Athenian Empire," 97; Andrew R. Meadows, "A Chian Revolution," in *Nomisma: La circulation monetaire dans le monde grec antique*, ed. Thomas Faucher, Marie-Christine Marcellesi, and Olivier Picard (Athens: Ecole française d'Athènes, 2011), 275. An inscription from the Treasurers of the Other Gods at Athens from 429/8 (*IG* I^3 383) indicates an offering of 485 Chian drachmae and four obols, which may have included both old and new coin issues. See N. M. M. Hardwick, "The Coinage of Chios from the Sixth to the Fourth Century B.C." (PhD diss., Oxford University, 1991), 209, for the possible combinations.

The Athenian regulations therefore likely formalized the de facto situation in Ionia where the weights and measures had come into alignment with the Attic standard over the course of the fifth century and Athenian Owls had largely supplanted local issues. Coins of many denominations continued to circulate in the Aegean, and the economic standards had changed already before the enactment of these decrees, but the regulations were nonetheless regarded as ham-handed imperialism. It was in this context that Aristophanes in *Birds* of 414 lampoons the Standards Decree by having a decree-peddler demand that the citizens of Cloudcuckooland use the same measures, weights, and decrees as the Olophyxians (1040–41). The economic effect of the Standards Decree on Ionia is difficult to measure, particularly if, as I have suggested, it was not as onerous as is frequently assumed, but it nevertheless needs to be interpreted as a factor contributing to Ionian frustration with Athenian hegemony by the time of the Sicilian Expedition in 415.

The second wartime change was the replacement of the *phoros* with a 5 percent harbor tax in 413 (Thuc. 7.28.4). The change replaced an indirect levy on the communities with direct taxation on merchants, but, more importantly, was designed to raise revenue for the war. In short, the symbolic capital in which the allies acknowledged Athenian hegemony through tribute became less important than the money direct taxation could bring in.[67] Arable land and natural resources had probably constituted the largest part of the previous assessment, so the transition to taxation based on commercial activity that affected all harbors in the league, including Chios and Samos, significantly increased the imperial burden on Ionia and was likely a contributing factor in the outbreak of the Ionian War in 411.

The Peloponnesian War also affected Ionia more directly: while Thucydides focuses on the triumphs and tragedies of Athens, Ionians fought. Milesians went on the Athenian expeditions to Corinth and Cythera in 425 (Thuc. 4.42, 4.54); Chians accompanied the invasion of the Argolid in 429 (Thuc. 2.56.2), helped Nicias subdue Mende and Scione in 423 (Thuc. 4.129.2), and aided in the capture of Melos in 416 (Thuc. 5.84.1); and Chians, Samians, and Milesians contributed to the invasion of Sicily in 415 (Thuc. 6.31.2; 7.20.2; 7.57.3).[68] Athe-

---

67. Kallet, *Money and Power*, 195–226. Hyland, *Persian Interventions*, 45–46 describes the change in Athenian economic policy as symbolically giving up the *phoros* collection that had been granted by the Persian king. This may have been true from the Persian perspective, but there is nothing to indicate that the Athenians took this symbolism into consideration. Gorman, *Miletos*, 236–37, argues that the tax was in addition to the *phoros*; cf. Hornblower, *A Commentary on Thucydides*, vol. 3, 594–95.

68. Hornblower, *A Commentary on Thucydides*, vol. 3, 226–28, argues that the Ionians happily participated in expeditions like the one to Melos to coerce Dorians, but there is little evidence for ethnolinguistic tribalism during the Peloponnesian War outside of the written histories.

nian soldiers and sailors made up the bulk of the fighting forces, and Athenian commanders may not have trusted Ionian soldiers since, at least in the battle at Cythera, they played no role in the fighting,[69] but their repeated appearance as well as the size of the contingents (two thousand Milesian hoplites at Cythera) indicates a substantial contribution to the Athenian war effort. Moreover, the Ionian casualties, particularly in the expedition to Sicily, likely contributed to growing anti-Athenian sentiment. Too, Athenian honorific decrees testify to the presence of Ionians who collaborated with the Athenian imperial state, such as Apollonophanes of Colophon, who was rewarded for his aid of Athenian troops in 427 (*IG* I³ 65), and Heracleides of Clazomenae, who received honors for his cooperation with an embassy to the king of Persia in perhaps 423 (*RO* 157 = *IG* I³ 227).[70] However, even before the disaster in Sicily, Pisthetairus in Aristophanes' *Birds* (414) quips that he likes the custom of always adding Chios to things (Χίοισιν ἥσθην πανταχοῦ προσκειμένοις, 879–80). It is possible that these lines were a polite echo of Eupolis' commentary about the nature of the alliance, but that is not the way of Attic comedy. More likely, they were a dark joke referring to the scarcity of Athenian allies and therefore to actions that marked Chios as unique.[71] Aristophanes was not celebrating Chios' special relationship but poking at a grim situation. The Athenians in 414 were concerned that the Chians, and by extension the other Ionians, were not so well trained.

The relationship between the Ionian poleis and the Athenian empire in the second half of the fifth century swung between extremes. It was here that the greatest threats to Athenian hegemony emerged, but also where Athens often found collaborators for its imperial project who saw opportunities for profit and power. The Sicilian Expedition marked the end of Athenian hegemony over Ionia, but these were also the last years of the fifth century when Ionia itself was largely untouched by war. What is more, the long-simmering stasis in Ionia only grew more pronounced as the Athenian grip weakened.

---

69. Hornblower, *A Commentary on Thucydides*, vol. 3, 217.

70. These honors, which included making Heracleides *proxenos*, likely made it a target of the Thirty. It survives in a copy made after the restoration of the democracy.

71. Barron, "Chios in the Athenian Empire," 102; followed by Alastair Blanshard, "Trapped between Athens and Chios: A Relationship in Fragments," in *The World of Ion of Chios*, ed. Victoria Jennings and Andrea Katsaros (Leiden: Brill, 2007), 155.

CHAPTER 4

❦

Contempt for Athenian Hegemony

413/412–401

Athenian control over Ionia crumbled close on the heels of the disaster in Sicily. Diodorus Siculus connects the two developments, saying that the failure created contempt for Athenian hegemony (τὴν ἡγεμονίαν αὐτῶν καταφρονηθῆναι, 13.34.1). However, the unraveling of Athenian power had multiple causes. While Diodorus intimates that the Chians, Samians, Byzantines and others had a nearly primal sense of Athenian weakness, the defeat in Sicily had also sacrificed their men and ships for what is presented in our sources as Athenian ambition. At the same time, Athens increased the financial burden on the league through the imposition of the harbor tax, which, John Hyland has recently argued, led to a change in Persian imperial policy to reclaim the tribute from Ionia that had, at least tacitly, been granted to Athens.[1]

These conditions seem to support Thucydides' framing, that the Ionians were primed (ἑτοῖμοι) to reject Athenian hegemony when presented with the opportunity (8.2.2). Scholars have traditionally followed this interpretation, based both on the earlier challenges to Athenian rule and because we know the outcome: the Ionians *did* break away from Athens.[2] The question is, what happened?

This chapter examines how Ionia became disentangled from Athenian

---

1. John Hyland, *Persian Interventions: The Achaemenid Empire, Athens, and Sparta, 450–386 BCE* (Baltimore, MD: Johns Hopkins University Press, 2018), 38–46; cf. Pierre Debord, *L'Asie Mineure au IVᵉ siècle (412–323 a.C.)* (Pessac: Ausonius Éditions, 1999), 214.

2. E.g., Donald. Kagan, *The Fall of the Athenian Empire* (Ithaca, NY: Cornell University Press, 1987), 10–11; David M. Lewis, *Sparta and Persia* (Leiden: Brill, 1977), 114–16; Jacqueline de Romilly, "Thucydides and the Cities of the Athenian Empire," *BICS* 13 (1966): 1–12. Some scholars have modified Thucydides' declaration. Simon Hornblower, *A Commentary on Thucydides*, vol. 3 (Oxford: Oxford University Press, 2008), 754, refers to the opposition to Athens in Ionia as an "ephemeral mood," while H. D. Westlake, "Ionians in the Ionian War," *CQ²* 29, no. 1 (1979): 9–10, maintains that the Ionians were eager to recover their liberty, notes variations in regional attitudes; see below, "Contempt for Athenian Hegemony."

hegemony only to be caught up in a convoluted snarl of rapidly changing power relationships in the eastern Aegean that continued until the King's Peace brought them to a sudden halt in 386. The Ionian War also marked a change in how Ionia interacted with imperial powers.[3] For the next quarter century the Ionian poleis oscillated between allegiances as the strength and interest of the competing powers waxed and waned, usually for reasons entirely separate from the machinations over Ionia. In this period, Ionia was a setting for military campaigns designed to reclaim the Ionians as subjects or that used the region as a beachhead to reach another enemy, and ambitious men set their sights on the Ionian cities, once again making the region a cornerstone of the Aegean system.

Contempt for Athenian Hegemony

In 412, an embassy arrived in Sparta (Thuc. 8.5.4). The ambassadors included representatives of the Persian satrap Tissaphernes and conspirators from Chios and Erythrae.[4] In a reprise of the start of the Ionian revolt of 499 (Hdt. 5.39–41, 49–51), these Ionians intended to draw the Spartans into a war in Asia Minor, but, bypassing the king Agis at Decelea, they went directly to Sparta. Once there, though, they discovered that the real challenge was not inciting the Spartans to action but persuading them to sail to Ionia. At about the same time, Calligeitus of Megara and Timagoras of Cyzicus had come to Sparta on behalf of Pharnabazus, another Persian satrap (Thuc. 8.6.1).[5]

The two embassies made the same argument: support the liberation of the eastern Aegean and join with Persia because it will cripple Athens. The criti-

---

3. Debord, L'Asie Mineure, 203, regards the period 413–404 as a hinge that allows for the understanding of the fourth century. There is slippage in the naming conventions for the individual conflicts that made up the Peloponnesian War. The conventional term for the final years had become the Decelean War already in antiquity, probably reflecting the attitudes of Athenian writers, as Westlake, "Ionians in the Ionian War," n. 1, suggests, but Thucydides refers to the war in Ionia as τοῦ Ἰωνικοῦ πολέμου (8.11.3). Since my focus is on the Ionian theater, I will use "Ionian War" to refer broadly to the final decade of the Peloponnesian War even though conventionally it only lasted from c.411 to 407/6.

4. As Hornblower, A Commentary on Thucydides, 763–64, notes, Thucydides leaves out the article when identifying the ambassadors, indicating that they did not represent a unified group. Hyland, Persian Interventions, 50, suggests "careful prearrangement" to place the ambassadors there simultaneously, seeing these embassies as the culmination of Tissaphernes' attempts to court Ionian elites. Cf. Marcel Piérart, "Chios entre Athènes et Sparte: La contribution des exiles de Chios à l'effort de guerre lacédémonien pendant la guerre du Péloponèse IG V 1, 1+SEG 39, 370," BCH 119, no. 1 (1995): 253–82; T. J. Quinn, "Political Groups at Chios: 412 B.C.," Historia 18, no. 1 (1969): 26–30.

5. The simultaneous arrival of the two embassies was not a coincidence but reflects the changed stance of Persian central authority; see Hyland, Persian Interventions, 50–53.

cal difference was the destination of the campaign, the Hellespont or Ionia. Choosing Pharnabazus and the Hellespontine Greeks would have severed the Athenian lifeline, the trade route that brought grain from the Black Sea, and Pharnabazus' emissaries brought with them a sweetener of twenty-five talents (Thuc. 8.8.1). A campaign in Ionia did not offer such immediate rewards. The Chians, however, talked up the strength of their fleet in order to demonstrate their importance to the Athenian war effort. The Spartans were still skeptical, according to Thucydides, but the Ionians had the support of Alcibiades and, through him, the ephor Endius (8.6.3; 8.12).[6] Rather than rushing into action, the Spartans discretely dispatched Phrynis, a *perioikos*, to reconnoiter and discover whether the Chians were exaggerating their strength (Thuc. 8.6.4). Satisfied with the report in the summer of 412, the Spartans agreed to send Chalcideus in command of a fleet and with Alcibiades in tow.

Haste was of the utmost importance, despite the delay. The Chians had traveled in secret, and every additional day increased the risk of discovery. The expedition, however, required conveying ships across the isthmus of Corinth, which would have required the Corinthians to violate the Isthmian truce, and they simply refused. It was during this final delay, when their representatives to the Isthmian games saw preparations for an expedition (Thuc. 8.10.1), that the Athenians became suspicious (Thuc. 8.9.2). They sent the general Aristagoras to Chios with accusations of treachery. Most of the Chians had no knowledge of the plot, and the conspirators, whom Thucydides describes as the few in the know (οἱ δὲ ὀλίγοι καὶ ξυνειδότες), were unwilling to act without Spartan support, so they roundly denied the accusations and agreed to send seven ships to join the Athenian fleet as a demonstration of good faith (8.9.2–3).

Their initial efforts were thwarted by Athenian blockades, but the Spartans persisted, and the fleet eventually arrived in Ionia. At the behest of the Chian conspirators, they sailed directly into the town of Chios, where the council was in session. Chalcideus and Alcibiades, Thucydides says, gave speeches to the assembled Chians and, with the promise of more Peloponnesian ships on the way, persuaded them to revolt from Athens before doing the same in Erythrae and Clazomenae (Thuc. 8.14.2–4). The revolutions in Ionia unfolded quickly, but this is not necessarily a sign of popularity. The Spartans remained suspicious of the Chian resolve, and probably for good reason since the rebellion had been carried out through a conspiracy that circumvented any popular opposition.[7] Since the Chians were also more experienced sailors than his Pelopon-

---

6. On the debate at Sparta, see Hornblower, *A Commentary on Thucydides*, 774–76.

7. See Matthew Simonton, *Classical Greek Oligarchy: A Political History* (Princeton, NJ: Princeton University Press, 2017), 193–94. On the divisions in the Chian polity in 412, cf. Jack Martin

nesians, Chalcideus elected to kill two birds with one stone by forcing the Chians to man his ships while arming his Peloponnesians and leaving them behind on the island as a garrison (8.17.2).

The Athenians responded swiftly by recalling the seven Chian ships, arresting the free crews on the charge of being involved in the conspiracy, and emancipating the enslaved rowers (Thuc. 8.15.2). The Athenians then authorized up to forty-nine warships to be sent to Ionia in the hopes of turning public opinion again before the dominoes all fell.

What followed was a period of moves and countermoves during which Ionia was up for grabs. The first Athenian squadron, eight ships under the command of Strombichides, arrived at Samos and tried to interrupt the cascade by sailing on to Teos (8.16.1). Their arrival, Thucydides says, at first had the intended effect on the Teians, who closed their gates against the Erythraean and Clazomenaean infantry who had arrived by land (8.16.1). When Chalcideus arrived from Chios with his twenty-three ships, Strombichides put to sea and was chased back toward Samos. Deprived of Athenian support, Teos capitulated and the Erythraeans, Clazomenaeans, and mercenaries in Tissaphernes' pay began to dismantle the walls (Thuc. 8.16.3). Chalcideus and Alcibiades sailed next from Chios to Miletus, their fleet reinforced with twenty ships from Chios, arriving just ahead of two Athenian squadrons under Strombichides and Thrasycles (Thuc. 8.17.2–3). Alcibiades had a family connection to influential Milesians and therefore believed that he would be able to induce a revolt and thereby claim credit for winning the war (Thuc. 8.17.1).[8] Failing to intercept the Peloponnesians, the Athenians established a blockade of Miletus from the island of Lade until reinforced by thirty-five hundred additional troops under the command of three generals, Phrynicus, Onomacles, and Scironides (Thuc. 8.17.3, 24.1).[9] The subsequent battle between this Athenian force and combined forces of Miletus, Tissaphernes, and a handful of Peloponnesians ended in a draw, with Thucydides noting that each sides' ethnic Ionians triumphed over the ethnic Dorians (8.25.5). Despite being prepared to besiege Miletus, the Athenian forces withdrew when a larger Peloponnesian fleet threatened to cut them off from their allies (8.27).[10] Other Chian ships fomenting rebellion in

Balcer, *Sparda by the Bitter Sea: Imperial Interaction in Western Anatolia* (Providence, RI: Brown University Press, 1984), 525; Quinn, "Political Groups at Chios," 22–30.

8. For the use of informal networks for political ends, see Lynette G. Mitchell, *Greeks Bearing Gifts: The Public Use of Private Relationships in the Greek World, 435–323 BCE* (Cambridge: Cambridge University Press, 1998), 47–48. On Alcibiades' family, see Chapter 3 n. 25.

9. On Phrynicus, who subsequently became a supporter of the oligarchy of 411, see Nikos Karkavelias, "Phrynichus Stratonidou Deiradiotes and the Ionia Campaign in 412 BC: Thuc. 8.25–27," *AHB* 27 (2013): 149–61.

10. Curiously, Thucydides says that the setbacks at Miletus so enraged the Argives who made

Ionia were less fortunate and took refuge in Ephesus and Teos when they ran into Athenian reinforcements.

But what did the Ionians think of this turn of events? It is a common position of modern historiography that the Ionians invariably turned away from Athens out of a desire to restore their liberty lost in the development of the Athenian empire.[11] This position, however, fails to appreciate the complexities of the Ionian polities and the role of regional interactions. Thucydides' narrative for the outbreak of the Ionian War makes it clear that the Ionians were anything but of one mind. At Chios, the people conspiring to use Sparta and Persia as counterweights to Athens were not doing so from exile, but as prominent members of the community who arranged for the boule to meet just when Endius and Alcibiades arrived (Thuc. 8.14.1–2). In Thucydides' telling, moreover, the general population was hesitant to make a rash move, but also was not set against the idea. Most other Ionian poleis did not play as active a role, but between dissatisfaction with Athens and the threat of force from Sparta, Persia, and their fellow Ionians, the choice was easy. And yet the situation was not irreversible. At Erythrae, a particularly decentralized polis, Athenian vessels continued to use Sidoussa and Pteleum as bases from which to harass Chios (Thuc. 8.24.2). When the Athenian commander Diomedon arrived at Teos sometime after its walls were demolished, the citizens received him and offered to rejoin Athens (Thuc. 8.20.2). Similarly, when Athenian forces captured a fort at Polichna and forced the men who caused the revolt at Clazomenae to flee (τῶν αἰτίων τῆς ἀποστάσεως), the city reverted to Athens (Thuc. 8.23.6). In the end, almost every polis in Ionia left the Athenian orbit, but this brief survey reveals considerable reticence already in 411/0. Far from a popular uprising against tyrannical Athenian overreach, this was a rebellion that broke out in fits and starts, complicated by long-standing internal tensions and the threat of force.

The lone Ionian polis never to abandon Athens was Samos, which served as the primary Athenian outpost in the eastern Aegean for the remainder of the war. But neither was Samos exempted from the schisms erupting throughout the region. Diodorus includes Samos in the list of poleis that felt contempt at Athenian hegemony (13.34.1), and its leadership in 411 was suspected of plot-

---

up about a quarter of the Athenian force that they picked up and went home (καὶ οἱ Ἀργεῖοι κατὰ τάχος καὶ πρὸς ὀργὴν τῆς ξυμφορᾶς ἀπέπλευσαν ἐκ τῆς Σάμου ἐπ᾽ οἴκου, 8.27.6).

11. Westlake, "Ionians in the Ionian War," 9–44; Lewis, *Sparta and Persia*, 114–16. Debord, *L'Asie Mineure*, 232 cautions that whatever Ionian enthusiasm existed in the early years rapidly waned. Balcer, *Sparda*, 425, limits enthusiasm to small factions in Ionia, while Akiko Nakamura-Moroo, "The Attitude of Greeks in Asia Minor to Athens and Persia: The Deceleian War," in *Forms of Control and Subordination in Antiquity*, ed. Tōru Yuge and Masaoki Doi (Leiden: Brill, 1988), 568, rightly, I believe, rejects the premise of a Greek-Persian antithesis in Ionian thinking.

ting with Sparta, as had happened in Chios. The result was a brutal coup. The demos took it upon itself to overthrow the men in power, summarily executing two hundred and sending another four hundred into exile after confiscating their property (Thuc. 8.21; cf. Xen. *Hell.* 2.2.6). Later in 411, the Samian demos with Athenian military aid defeated an attempted countercoup carried out by three hundred oligarchic conspirators, executing thirty more and banishing three ringleaders. When he heard about the factionalism on Samos, the Spartan navarch sensed an opportunity to appease discontents within his own ranks by making an assault on the island. He launched his entire fleet and instructed the Milesians to meet them on the Mycale promontory across from Samos, but a brief show of force from the Athenian fleet and reinforcements from the Hellespont prompted him to withdraw without offering battle (Thuc. 8.78–79).

Some modern scholars look at these events on Samos as a constitutional crisis between oligarchs and democrats, but it is reductive to treat it exclusively in these terms.[12] The conflict as described by Thucydides was along class lines, with the poor strata of society overthrowing the ruling landowners and instituting new laws to deprive them of their position, which, in turn created new schisms within the Samian state (Thuc. 8.73).[13] But equally important was the orientation of Samos toward Athens and Sparta.[14] Since 439 and as late as 412, the authorities in Samos had been in step with Athens to maintain leverage against the exiles at Anaea. This situation had preserved a status quo for more than a quarter century, but as Athenian power in Ionia waned, the ruling class on Samos considered seeking Spartan support toward the same end. Unlike on Chios, where the presence of Spartan ships and the honeyed tongue of Alcibiades persuaded the citizen body to abandon Athens, popular sentiment on Samos, supported by three Athenian ships, ran the other way. The result was a

12. Ronald P. Legon, "Samos in the Delian League," *Historia* 21, no. 2 (1972): 156; Martin Ostwald, "*Stasis* and *Autonomia* in Samos: A Comment on an Ideological Fallacy," *SCI* 12 (1993): 51–66; Graham Shipley, *A History of Samos, 800–188 BC* (Oxford: Oxford University Press, 1987), 124–28. T. J. Quinn, *Athens and Samos, Lesbos and Chios, 478–404 B.C.* (Manchester: Manchester University Press, 1981), 21, argues that the coup was contained to the ruling oligarchy. Cf. Hornblower, *A Commentary on Thucydides*, 808–9.

13. Ionia had a long history of endemic political conflict between those with land and those without it; see Alan M. Greaves, *The Land of Ionia: Society and Economy in the Archaic Period* (Malden, MA: Wiley-Blackwell, 2010), 91–94; and Chapter 2 in this volume. Thucydides labels the targets of this purge as οἱ γεόμοροι and τῶν δυνατωτάτων. The γεόμοροι are often identified as the landed aristocracy on the suspect evidence of Plutarch's *Graec. Quest.* 57; see Marcello Lupi, "Il duplice massacro dei 'geomoroi,'" in *Da Elea a Samo: Filosofi e politici di fronte all'impero ateniese*, ed. Luisa Breglia and Marcello Lupi (Naples: Arte Tipografica Editrice, 2005), 259–86. Cf. the discussion in A. Andrewes, *A Historical Commentary on Thucydides*, vol. 5 (Oxford: Oxford University Press, 1981), 79, and Hornblower, *A Commentary on Thucydides*, 809. On regime breakdown and the development of this oligarchic faction, see Simonton, *Oligarchy*, 239–41.

14. Andrewes, *Historical Commentary on Thucydides*, 44–49.

bloody purge that Thucydides says the Athenians took as a sign of loyalty. They legitimized the new leadership and sent the fleet to the island to ensure that it remained in the Athenian orbit.

The Spartan decision to precipitate a general uprising in Ionia paid off. The Chians, in particular, threw themselves into the Spartan venture, even sending an expedition of their own ships to Lesbos to incite a revolution there (Thuc. 8.22.1). The response was more muted, even tepid, elsewhere in Ionia, but neither was resistance stiff except on Samos, which remained an Athenian ally to the bitter end.

Battlefield Ionia

After the initial wave of revolutions in 411 and 410 Ionia became a battlefield. The conflict between Athens and Sparta took center stage in this development, but the situation was rarely that simple. Already in 412/1, Tissaphernes began to recover Persian suzerainty over Ionia by building and garrisoning a fort in Milesian territory, which may have been interpreted as a precursor to a regime change (Thuc. 8.84.4).[15] Outraged, the Milesians drove the Persian forces out, to the acclaim of their Greek allies—except Sparta.[16] The Spartan commander in Miletus, Lichas, chastised them, saying that because they lived in Persian territory, they ought to obey the satrap (τε χρῆναι Τισσαφέρνει καὶ δουλεύειν Μιλησίους καὶ τοὺς ἄλλους τοὺς ἐν τῇ βασιλέως τὰ μέτρια καὶ ἐπιθεραπεύειν, Thuc. 8.84.5).[17]

Lichas' admonition followed official Spartan policy based on the treaty established in 411. Although never ratified, the first iteration of the treaty negotiated between Chalcideus and Tissaphernes framed terms of debate. According to Thucydides, this agreement read (8.18):

---

15. Hyland, *Persian Interventions*, 83, is skeptical that "reintegration" of Miletus to Persia alone would have been enough to create this violent reaction, while the possibility of regime change might have. On Tissaphernes' defensive strategy, see John W. I. Lee, "Tissaphernes and the Achaemenid Defense of Western Anatolia, 412–395 BC," in *Circum Mare: Themes in Ancient Warfare*, ed. Jeremy Armstrong (Leiden: Brill, 2016), 264–69.

16. Cnidus also expelled a Persian garrison (Thuc. 8.109), while the Greek sailors were angry with Tissaphernes over money; see Lee, "Tissaphernes," 268; Hyland, *Persian Interventions*, 80–83.

17. Lichas had connections throughout the Aegean (Plut. *Cim.* 10.5–6). On the proliferation of the name, see Simon Hornblower, "Λίχας καλος Σαμιος," *Chiron* 32 (2002): 237–46. R. W. V. Catling, "Sparta's Friends at Ephesos: The Onomastic Evidence," in *Onomatologos: Studies in Greek Personal Names Presented to Elaine Matthews*, ed. R. W. V. Catling and Fabienne Marchand (Oxford: Oxford University Press, 2010), 195–237, evaluates Laconian names in Ionia more broadly and notes that the name Lichas appears at Miletus.

Whatever land and cities the king has and that the ancestors of the king had are the king's. And whatever money or other profit came to the Athenians from these cities, the king and the Lacedaemonians and their allies together shall intercept, such that the Athenians receive neither money nor anything else. The king, the Lacedaemonians, and their allies shall wage war in tandem against the Athenians. . . . Should any [poleis] revolt from the king, then they are enemies of the Lacedaemonians and their allies; and if any revolt from the Spartans and their allies, they are enemies to the king.

ὁπόσην χώραν καὶ πόλεις βασιλεὺς ἔχει καὶ οἱ πατέρες οἱ βασιλέως εἶχον, βασιλέως ἔστω· καὶ ἐκ τούτων τῶν πόλεων ὁπόσα Ἀθηναίοις ἐφοίτα χρήματα ἢ ἄλλο τι, κωλυόντων κοινῇ βασιλεὺς καὶ Λακεδαιμόνιοι καὶ οἱ ξύμμαχοι ὅπως μήτε χρήματα λαμβάνωσιν Ἀθηναῖοι μήτε ἄλλο μηδέν. καὶ τὸν πόλεμον τὸν πρὸς Ἀθηναίους κοινῇ πολεμούντων βασιλεὺς καὶ Λακεδαιμόνιοι καὶ οἱ ξύμμαχοι . . . ἢν δέ τινες ἀφιστῶνται ἀπὸ βασιλέως, πολέμιοι ὄντων καὶ Λακεδαιμονίοις καὶ τοῖς ξυμμάχοις· καὶ ἤν τινες ἀφιστῶνται ἀπὸ Λακεδαιμονίων καὶ τῶν ξυμμάχων, πολέμιοι ὄντων βασιλεῖ κατὰ ταὐτά.

Delegates revised this agreement the following year, adding provisions that forbade the Spartans from collecting tribute from the territory belonging to the king, thereby making them more reliant on Persian patronage. The new language that explicitly prevented the Spartans and their allied forces from attacking Persian domains testifies as much to the strained relationships between the Peloponnesian forces and the Persians as it does to their acquiescence that Ionia now belonged to Persia.[18] Following a topos in fourth-century Athenian rhetoric, modern treatments of these treaties often focus on whether Sparta sold out the Ionians in its haste to defeat Athens.[19] Compounding this interpretation

---

18. Hyland, *Persian Interventions*, 63. On the awkward phrasing of this treaty at Thuc. 8.37.5, see Hyland, *Persian Interventions*, n. 76. He is certainly correct that the τις τῶν πόλεων ὁπόσαι ξυνέθεντο βασιλεῖ is limited to poleis beyond Persian territory, meaning that most Ionians, once more claimed as Persian subjects, were not considered to have signed on to this treaty. Chios was in a different category.

19. On this topos, see Joshua P. Nudell, "'Who Cares about the Greeks Living in Asia?': Ionia and Attic Orators in the Fourth Century," *CJ* 114, no. 1 (2018): 163–90. On the treaties, see Hornblower, *A Commentary on Thucydides*, 800–802; Edmond Lévy, "Les trois traités entre Sparte et le Roi," *BCH* 107, no. 1 (1983): 221–41; Lewis, *Sparta and Persia*, 91; Pavel Nyvlt, "Sparta and Persia between the Second and the Third Treaty in 412/411 BCE: A Chronology," *Eirene* 50, nos. 1–2 (2014): 39–60; Noel Robertson, "The Sequence of Events in the Aegean in 408 and 407 B.C.," *Historia* 29, no. 3 (1980): 282–301; Christopher Tuplin, "The Treaty of Boiotios," in *Achaemenid History*, vol. 2, ed. Heleen Sancisi-Weerdenburg and Amelie Kuhrt (Leiden: Brill, 1984), 138–42.

is the implication found in Thucydides that, for as much as the Spartans conceded, Tissaphernes was unprepared to hold up the Persian side of the bargain (Thuc. 8.59; 87). John Hyland has recently reexamined these treaties, showing that they reflect the standard expression of a benevolent, just, and exacting king now reclaiming territory that was rightfully his.[20] There are ultimately no grounds to vilify the Spartans for betraying the Ionians to Persia with this treaty because their motivation for inciting revolts in 411 was to cripple Athens, not to liberate Ionia. As was often the case, declarations of freedom were little more than hollow-point rounds in a weapon aimed at another target. However, as the example from Miletus demonstrates, this does not mean that the Ionian poleis were without a role to play.

As Sparta and Persia negotiated these treaties, Athenian squadrons sent to Lesbos under the command of Diomedon attacked a fort at Clazomenae (8.23.6) and proceeded to raid Chios (8.24.2–3). They defeated the Chians in three battles on the island, and the Chians afterward refused to give battle. This occasion prompted Thucydides to provide a eulogy for the prudent decision-making that had made Chios wealthy (8.24.4–5).[21] His praise falls immediately after a description of the spoliation of the countryside, implying that the economic complications stemmed from agricultural devastation. However, although repeated attacks shattered any sense of inviolability, the more severe consequences came from the disruption of trade routes and the loss of their enslaved people after the Athenians fortified Delphinium on the north side of the island (Thuc. 8.40).[22] These reverses strained the relationship with Sparta, and some in Chios entertained second opinions about the wisdom of their choice. When the men who had led Chios into revolt caught wind of a conspiracy against Sparta and, by extension, against them, they summoned aid from the Spartan navarch Astyochus. According to Thucydides, Astyochus tried to resolve the conflict with minimal bloodshed by taking hostages (8.24–25), but the situation continued to deteriorate.[23] Their plight was also complicated by

---

20. Hyland, *Persian Interventions*, 71–74. He is also likely correct to largely redeem Tissaphernes of his alleged duplicity.

21. On this eulogy, see Hornblower, *A Commentary on Thucydides*, 819–20.

22. Mark Lawall, "Ceramics and Positivism Revisited: Greek Transport Amphoras and History," in *Trade, Traders and the Ancient City*, ed. Helen Parkins and Christopher Smith (New York: Routledge, 1998), 86–89, 95, notes a decline in datable Chian finds at both Athens and Gordion in this period. The Athenians also liberated the rowers on Chian ships (Thuc. 8.15), and Thucydides notes that there was a larger number of enslaved people in Chios than in any polis other than Sparta (8.40.2).

23. Astyochus is often blamed for early Spartan setbacks, but Caroline Faulkner, "Astyochus, Sparta's Incompetent Navarch?," *Phoenix* 53, nos. 3–4 (1999): 206–21, explains his actions and points out both the possible sources of Thucydides' biases and the extreme difficulties facing any Spartan commander.

the relationship between Astyochus and the harmost Pedaritus, who kept Chios in line with a reign of terror. Pedaritus executed one Tydeus, a leading citizen and possibly the son of the poet Ion, allegedly for conspiring to restore the Athenian alliance (Thuc. 8.38).[24] When Astyochus ordered the Chians to send ships to Lesbos to encourage rebellions on that island, Pedaritus informed him that none would go (Thuc. 8.32.3). Despite Pedaritus' intervention, Astyochus nevertheless blamed the Chians, repeatedly threatening them that he would not come to their aid should they ever require it (8.33.1). When some Chians expressed a lack of confidence in their forces and Pedaritus' mercenaries to protect the polis after Athenian reinforcements landed on the island, Astyochus was good to his word (Thuc. 8.38).

Regional tensions also continued to influence Ionian behavior. When Athenian forces under the command of Thrasyllus besieged Pygela, a small community that had once been dominated by Ephesus, it was Milesian hoplites who came to their relief. The two hundred Milesian hoplites chased the scattered Athenian light troops upon arriving at the scene but were almost entirely wiped out when confronted by a contingent of Athenian peltasts and hoplites (Xen. Hell. 1.2.2–3; Diod. 13.64). Despite some attempts to use this episode to deride the military capacities of the Milesians,[25] disciplined peltasts posed a particular threat to hoplites, and it is probable that the Milesians were both outnumbered and disorganized, having pursued the first Athenians they came upon.[26] From a military perspective the more important question is why relief came from so far away.[27] The answer lies in the regional politics of Ionia. The Milesian hoplites were two or three days' march from home when they clashed with Thrasyllus' forces, but requesting help from Ephesus would have given it an opening to recapture its erstwhile dependent, something it would repeatedly aspire to in the fourth century, leading the Pygelans to use Miletus and Mausolus of

24. Pedaritus is never referred to as ἁρμοστήν, which is a rare word that appears just once in Thucydides' text (8.5.1, in reference to Euboea). Xenophon uses it once in the Anabasis (5.5.19) and eleven times in the Hellenica, including in reference to Lysander's appointment to put down the revolt against the Thirty (2.4.28) and in reference to Thibron's appointment in Ionia (3.1.4). Xenophon makes it clear that this was the standard term for Spartan governors, so we can reasonably assume that this was in fact Pedaritus' position. On harmosts and decarchies, see below, "Enter Lysander."

25. E.g., Westlake, "Ionians in the Ionian War," 26, 34.

26. Xen. Hell. 4.5.13; Arist. Pol. 1321a14–21; Paul Cartledge, Agesilaos and the Crisis of Sparta (London: Duckworth, 2000), 45–46; Louis Rawlings, The Ancient Greeks at War (Manchester: Manchester University Press, 2007), 85–86; H. van Wees, ed., War and Violence in Ancient Greece (Swansea: Classical Press of Wales, 2000), 62–65.

27. A question asked, but not answered, by John F. Lazenby, The Peloponnesian War: A Military Study (New York: Routledge, 2004), 208–9.

Caria as a counterweight to Ephesian ambitions.[28] As John Lee characterizes it: "Thrasyllus had hit a weak spot in Tissaphernes' defenses, where local politics trumped military practicalities."[29] Almost all of the Ionians might have sided with Sparta, but this did not mean that they were on each other's side.

The anti-Athenian forces ultimately defeated Thrasyllus at the foot of Mount Coressus, just outside of Ephesus. However, while the Ephesians contributed to their own defense and subsequently awarded honors to the Syracusans and Selinuntines whose ships were stationed at Ephesus at the time (Xen. *Hell.* 1.2.10), the bulk of the credit for the victory belonged to Tissaphernes. When the satrap heard that Thrasyllus was planning a return to Ephesus, Xenophon says, Tissaphernes mustered his forces with the rallying cry to defend the sanctuary of Artemis (Xen. *Hell.* 1.2.6–10). The sanctuary was a natural focal point for this effort given its regional prominence, and Tissaphernes capitalized on the victory with a series of bronze coins that included an image of Artemis.[30] Unlike at Miletus, Tissaphernes did not attempt to install a garrison at Ephesus. Lee reasonably explains his decision as a calculation that protecting a local religious institution would be more effective at securing loyalty than would a garrison, but this also allowed him to maintain maximum flexibility to respond to Athenian hit-and-run raids in a theater characterized by multiple river valleys.[31] Although Lee is correct that Tissaphernes' deft touch at Ephesus ruffled fewer feathers than at Miletus, Xenophon offers no indication that his defense of Artemis and Ephesus won him any affection from the citizens.

The situation in Ionia began to change in 408 when Sparta ratified a new treaty that set the terms for cooperation in the war against Athens (Xen. *Hell.* 1.4.2–3). In the wake of the treaty, Darius II appointed his son Cyrus as *karanos* over western Anatolia, a position akin the Greek strategos. This office gave the prince broad powers to oversee the war effort that to this point had been limited by competition between Tissaphernes and Pharnabazus (Xen. *Hell.* 1.4.3, 5.3; cf. *Anab.* 1.9.7).[32] According to Xenophon, Cyrus arrived in Asia Minor

---

28. See Lene Rubinstein, "Ionia," in *An Inventory of Archaic and Classical Poleis*, ed. Mogens Herman Hansen and Thomas Heine Nielsen (Oxford: Oxford University Press, 2004), 1094, and Chapter 6 in this volume.

29. Lee, "Tissaphernes," 270.

30. The coins may be reflected by a series from Astyra in Aeolis, which also had a shrine for Artemis. Hyland, *Persian Interventions*, 102, shows that the series was designed to associate this small shrine with the famous sanctuary at Ephesus. This coin series was traditionally dated to Tissaphernes' second stint in Ionia, 400–395; see Herbert Cahn, "Tissaphernes in Astyra," *AA* 4 (1985): 592–93, but has been redated by Jarosław Bodzek, "On the Dating of the Bronze Issues of Tissaphernes," *Studies in Ancient Art and Civilization* 16 (2012): 110–15.

31. Lee, "Tissaphernes," 273.

32. On competition between satraps and the limited resources available to Pharnabazus and Tissaphernes compared with Cyrus' wide remit, see Pierre Briant, *From Cyrus to Alexander: A His-*

bearing the king's seal stamped on a letter addressed to all "those who dwell by the sea" (πάντων τῶν ἐπὶ θαλάττῃ, Xen. *Hell.* 1.4.3), which certainly included the Ionians. It is unknown whether the letter addressed specific actions or the renewed status of Ionia as subjects of Persia because Xenophon only preserves part of the text. Tissaphernes had, to the Greeks at least, coordinated the war against Athens piecemeal, on his own terms, and always with a sense that he anticipated that if Athens and Sparta exhausted each other, it would further his position. Certainly, these were the charges the Spartans leveled against Tissaphernes when Cyrus arrived (e.g., Plut. *Lys.* 4.1). However, it was the resources available to Cyrus, not the attitude toward the Ionian poleis or relationship between the poleis and the Persian satrap, that changed. Greek authors ascribe a cunning malice to Tissaphernes, but with respect to Ionia he was following orders.[33] His methods aroused more enmity than did Cyrus' flattery, but the expectation of the Great King throughout the fifth century had been that he was sovereign over Ionia. Accommodations about revenue could be made to support the Spartan war effort, and the treaty negotiated in 408 was aimed at this end, not toward securing new freedoms for the Ionians. But the war over Ionia was entering a new phase in 408, one powered by the personality of the new Spartan navarch, Lysander.

Enter Lysander

Lysander took command of the Spartan war effort in Ionia in autumn 408, initiating wide-ranging changes in the region that would shape its history for a decade. One of his first actions was to move the Spartan base of operations from Miletus to Ephesus (Plut. *Lys.* 3.2). Plutarch makes a big deal about the move because he claims that Lysander rescued Ephesus from barbarity, but this is exaggerated.[34] The absence of a Persian garrison might have contributed to

tory of the Persian Empire, trans. Peter T. Daniels (Winona Lake, IN: Eisenbrauns, 2002), 593–96. Cyrus probably replaced Tissaphernes in this capacity; see Hyland, *Persian Interventions*, 107–8, who also notes the etymological link between *karanos* and *strategos*. Stephen Ruzicka, "Cyrus and Tissaphernes, 407–401 B.C.," *CJ* 80, no. 3 (1985): 205–8, argues that Tissaphernes incorporated into Cyrus' entourage to advise the inexperienced prince but received an appointment again in 404 as a reward for betraying him.

    33. Hyland, *Persian Interventions*, 149; John Hyland, "Thucydides' Portrait of Tissaphernes Re-examined," in *Persian Responses*, ed. Christopher Tuplin (Swansea: Classical Press of Wales, 2007), 1–25; Ruzicka, "Cyrus and Tissaphernes," 204–11; H. D. Westlake, "Tissaphernes in Thucydides," *CQ*² 35, no. 1 (1985): 43–54.

    34. Lewis, *Sparta and Persia*, 115, and Westlake, "Ionians in the Ionian War," 40–41, deny any Persian presence, while Jack Martin Balcer, "The Greeks and the Persians: Processes of Accultura-tion," *Historia* 32, no. 3 (1983): 257–67, follows Plutarch in seeing acculturation as a recent devel-

Lysander's decision, but other considerations were likely more important. Miletus was the southernmost Ionian city and was separated from the other centers of Spartan activity by the Athenian fleet on Samos. Ephesus neatly sidestepped a repeat of 411, when Lichas ordered the Milesians to accommodate Tissaphernes, but it also put the Spartan fleet in a better position to counter Athenian activities. More important, though, and critical for the history of Ionia, was the close connection between Ephesus and Sardis, where the Persian prince Cyrus had recently taken up residence. With these regional and strategic considerations in mind, Lysander assembled the Spartan fleet at Ephesus.

Lysander's primary concern when he assumed command was to secure a steady supply of money to pay for the naval war. John Hyland has recently estimated the Persian subsidy, including direct payments and the Ionian tribute remitted in 405/4, at between 3,272 and 3,672 talents over the course of roughly seven years.[35] These resources, in turn, allowed Lysander to inaugurate a massive stimulus project at Ephesus that brought merchant vessels to convey supplies to the city and dispensed contracts for trireme construction (Plut. Lys. 3.3). Even absent the remission of tribute, these contracts brought an infusion of wealth to Ephesus that likely lay behind an honorific statue erected at the Artemisium (Paus. 6.3.15).[36]

However, Persian money proved unreliable, which led to Spartan demands that the Ionians themselves underwrite the costs of the fleet. In turn, these demands reignited preexisting tensions.[37] Already in 411, for instance, the Spartan navarch Mindaros demanded that the Chians pay each of his sailors three "fortieths" (Thuc. 8.101.1), an amount that totaled about 4.5 talents,[38]

---

opment in Ionia. Margaret C. Miller, "Clothes and Identity: The Case of Greeks in Ionia c.400 BC," in *Culture, Identity and Politics in the Ancient Mediterranean World*, ed. Paul J. Burton (Canberra: Australasian Society for Classical Studies, 2013), 18–38, however, demonstrates that Persian and Anatolian features had become inextricable from local identity, where the Priest of Artemis held the Persian title Megabyxos (Xen. *Anab.* 5.3.4; Pliny *N.H.* 35.36, 40), cf. Chapter 9 and Appendix 2.

35. Hyland, *Persian Interventions*, 118–21. His calculation excludes ancillary costs like mercenary salaries and pay for loggers and shipbuilders.

36. On this honor, which is usually tied to Ephesus' oligarchic regime, see Westlake, "Ionians in the Ionian War," 41; Nakamura-Moroo, "Attitude of Greeks in Asia Minor," 570; Kagan, *Fall of the Athenian Empire*, 302–3.

37. Most of the Ionian contributions to the so-called Spartan War Fund (*RO* 151 = *IG* V 1, 1) likely belong in this context, as suggested by Piérart, "Chios entre Athènes et Sparte," 253–82, but Rhodes and Osborne observe that there is no one date that works for all entries. They follow Angelos P. Matthaiou and G. A. Pikoulas, "Ἔδον Λακεδαιμονίοις ποττὸν πόλεμον," *Horos* 7 (1988): 77–124, in suggesting that it was inscribed in phases starting in c.427 and concluding in the c.409. Cartledge, *Agesilaos*, 72–73, maintains a later date c.403, but the relatively small amount in the inscription (maybe just over thirteen talents total), as William T. Loomis, *The Spartan War Fund: IG V 1, 1 and a New Fragment* (Stuttgart: Franz Steiner, 1992), notes, suggests that it belongs in an early phase of Spartan fiscal management.

38. What, exactly, Thucydides meant by "fortieth" (τεσσαρακοστός) is a matter of heated

and the demands for cash steadily grew as the war dragged on. In 408/7, Diodorus reports, the Spartan navarch Cratesippidas took a bribe to restore Chian exiles to their home, where they exiled six hundred of their political opponents in turn (Diod. 13.65.3–4). The new exiles seized Atarneus, from whence they continued to harass Chios. But these strains also extended beyond the endemic factional conflict and further drained Ionian resources. Lysander's immediate successor after his first term as navarch, Callicratidas, convinced the people of both Miletus and Chios in 406/5 to give him additional money when he thought that Cyrus was balking at providing what he promised (Xen. Hell. 1.6).[39] Xenophon says that he demanded from Chios a pentedrachmia (πεντεδραχμία) for each of his sailors, probably about 23.1 talents of silver in sum, that would pay the wages for just ten days (Xen. Hell. 1.6.12).[40] The soldiers serving under the Spartan Eteonicus had been forced to work for hire in the winter of 406, but they subsequently planned a coup against their supposed ally when the seasonal employment dried up (Xen. Hell. 2.1.1–5).[41] Eteonicus thwarted their plan and restored discipline, but also demanded that the Chians give him up to some fifty talents of silver to appease the soldiers.[42] The Chians paid up, but they also joined the other Ionian allies to formally petition Sparta for Lysander's return (Xen. Hell. 2.1.6–7).

The Spartans had entered the war against Athens woefully ignorant about how much money was required to operate a fleet and about the mechanisms of finance. Recent research has demonstrated how their approach to financ-

debate because this term does not correspond to any denomination of coin used in the Greek world. N. M. M. Hardwick, "The Coinage of Chios, 6th–4th century BC," in *Proceedings of the XI International Numismatic Congress*, ed. Catherine Courtois, Harry Dewit, and Véronique Van Driessche (Louvain: Séminaire de Numismatique Marcel Hoc, 1993), 211–22, proposes that "fortieth" was in effect an exchange rate where forty of a given Chian coin was equivalent to a single coin, in the case probably a Persian daric. Aneurin Ellis-Evans, "Mytilene, Lampsakos, Chios and the Financing of the Spartan Fleet (406–404)," *NC* 176 (2016): 11–12, identifies this Chian coin as likely being a third-stater coin.

39. According to Plutarch, Lysander had returned to Cyrus the money he had not yet spent and told Callicratidas to ask for it himself (Plut. *Lys.* 6.1). Diodorus paints a portrait of Callicratidas as an upright young Spartan, saying that he punished anyone who tried to bribe him (13.76.2), and both Diodorus and Xenophon describe him as an energetic commander whose fleet aggressively pursued the war in Ionia.

40. Like the "fortieth" (see n. 38), "pentedrachmia" is a term without correspondence to a denomination of Greek coin. Ellis-Evans, "Mytilene, Lampsakos, Chios," 12–14, reasonably suggests the term indicates the amount paid rather than the denominations distributed.

41. The lack of money to pay the soldiers is often attributed to a personal conflict between Lysander's replacement Callicratidas and Cyrus (Xen. *Hell.* 1.6.6–7; Plut. *Lys.* 6.5–6), but Hyland, *Persian Interventions*, 112, argues that the tension arose because Cyrus' readily available money was depleted.

42. On the estimate of fifty talents, see Ellis-Evans, "Mytilene, Lampsakos, Chios," 14, who astutely notes that Eteonicus' forces had already been depleted by losses at Arginousae earlier in the year.

ing the war both slowly evolved over the course of the conflict and ultimately allowed them to eventually emerge triumphant.[43] By the time that Lysander returned in 405/4, the Spartan fiscal system had reached maturity, funneling Persian subsidies, ad hoc requisitions from allied poleis, and the tributes from Persian subjects in Asia Minor (Xen. *Hell.* 2.1.14) into pay for the maintenance, upkeep, and operation of fleets throughout the Aegean. The enforcement of this system resulted in the widespread adoption of the Chian weight standard to facilitate conversion between the coinages of different poleis and the so-called ΣΥΝ coinage minted at Rhodes, Iasus, Cnidus, Ephesus, Samos, Byzantium, and Cyzicus.[44]

But where did these changes leave the Ionians? The second century CE travel writer Pausanias records an Ionian proverb about their political loyalties saying that they preferred to "paint both sides of the walls" because "the Ionians, just like all men, do service to strength" (τοὺς τοίχους τοὺς δύο ἐπαλείφοντες . . . καὶ Ἴωσιν ὡσαύτως οἱ πάντες ἄνθρωποι θεραπεύουσι τὰ ὑπερέχοντα τῇ ἰσχύι, 6.3.15–16). They paid court to Alcibiades, he says, with the Samians erecting a statue of him in the Heraion, as easily as they did to the Spartans, since the Ephesians erected statues not only of Lysander, Eteonicus, and Pharax, but also of Spartans of no particular repute! Indeed, there is little unambiguous evidence that the Ionians as a whole favored one side over the other, which fits in a world where nobody was altogether on the side of the Ionians. These statues therefore need to be interpreted as early examples of honorific statues that became a prominent feature of diplomacy in the Hellenistic period, while paying court was the surest way to minimize property damage. Spontaneous displays of support for the war against Athens disappeared after the first years, and poleis without strategic importance had been allowed to slip from Spartan control. Teos, for instance, which had lost its walls in 411, had subsequently readmitted Athenian forces, ostensibly in return for protection (Thuc. 8.20), only to see Callicratidas sneak his forces inside the restored fortifications and plunder the city in 406/5 (Diod. 13.76.4). Being forced to turn over increasingly large sums of money for the Spartan war efforts could not have been popular,

---

43. Particularly Ellis-Evans, "Mytilene, Lampsakos, Chios," 14–16.

44. Earlier scholarship dated this coinage alliance to after the battle of Cnidus in 394, as John Buckler, *Aegean Greece in the Fourth Century BC* (Leiden: Brill, 2003), 133; George L. Cawkwell, "A Note on the Heracles Coinage Alliance of 394 B.C.," *NC* 16 (1956): 69–75; George L. Cawkwell, "The ΣΥΝ Coins Again," *JHS* 83 (1963): 152–54; Charles D. Hamilton, *Sparta's Bitter Victories: Politics and Diplomacy in the Corinthian War* (Ithaca, NY: Cornell University Press, 1979), 230. More recent studies have convincingly redated the coins to Lysander's second term in 405/4 following Stefan Karwiese, "Lysander as Herakliskos Krakonopnigon: ('Heracles the Snake-Strangler')," *NC* 140 (1980): 1–27; cf. Ellis-Evans, "Mytilene, Lampsakos, Chios," 14–16. The Samian examples must date to the period shortly after his capture of the island.

but neither those demands nor the fact that the Spartans symbolically curtailed Ionian liberty by betraying them to Persia resulted in widespread uprisings and Ionian ships and sailors remained essential to the Spartan fleets throughout the war (e.g., Xen. *Hell.* 1.6.3; Diod. 13.70.2).[45] When Lysander erected an ostentatious monument at Delphi to commemorate his victory at Aegospotamoi, he paid tribute to these contributions with statues of not only three Chians, but also men from Ephesus, Miletus, a Samian from Anaea, and likely an Erythraean (Paus. 10.9.9)— nearly a quarter of the twenty-nine naval commanders honored in the monument, in all.[46]

By the last years of the Ionian War only Samos and pockets of Athenian-held territory resisted the overwhelming tide of Spartan successes. It is easy see an element of coercion in this continued resistance since Samos continued to be the principal Athenian naval base in the eastern Aegean, but this was not the only reason that Samos continued to fight alongside Athens. Xenophon associates the Samian loyalty to Athens with fact that they had enacted a slaughter of the wealthy on the island (σφαγὰς τῶν γνωρίμων ποιήσαντες) when those men had conspired to revolt (*Hell.* 2.2.6). The Samian *demos* had clearly wanted to keep its relationship with Athens and in 405/4 were rewarded en masse for their dedication with a decree of Athenian citizenship (*RO* 2 = *IG* I³ 127, ll. 12–13), as well as receiving other honors and gifts, including the Athenian triremes on Samos (ll. 25–26).[47] There was, however, another reason that the Samians looked to Athens. The Samian exiles living in Asia Minor make frequent appearance throughout the fifth century, including sending ten ships to fight with the Spartans at Arginousae (Xen. *Hell.* 1.6.29). Thucydides and Xenophon present the bloodshed on Samos as a class conflict caused by the question of

---

45. Lazenby, *Peloponnesian War*, 254–55; Hyland, *Persian Interventions*, 115.

46. Erythrae is a restoration of a lacuna preferred by Hyland, *Persian Interventions*, 115 n. 107, following Lewis, *Sparta and Persia*, 115 n. 50 and contra Westlake, "Ionians in the Ionian War," 27 n. 3, whose objection is that there would be no cause to refer to Erythrae in relation to Mount Mimas. Hyland aptly notes that the reference to Mimas is more likely specifying a place within the Erythraeid, perhaps indicating an otherwise unattested local conflict, than indicating contributions to some anonymous community. Cf. John Hyland, "The Aftermath of Aegospotamoi and the Decline of Spartan Naval Power," *AHB* 33 (2019): 21–22, who notes that the allied contributions diminished after 404 in part because Lysander kept the captured Athenian fleet under Spartan control.

47. The unusual features of this inscription, including its pictural relief and its destruction during the period of the Thirty Tyrants and subsequent reinscription by the restored democracy, have received a great deal of recent scholarly attention. Jas Elsner, "Visual Culture and Ancient History: Issues of Empiricism and Ideology in the Samos Stele at Athens," *CA* 34, no. 1 (2015): 33–73, and Alastair Blanshard, "The Problem with Honouring Samos: An Athenian Documentary Relief and Its Interpretation," in *Art and Inscriptions in the Ancient World*, ed. Zahra Newby and Ruth Leader-Newby (Cambridge: Cambridge University Press, 2007), 19–37, are the two more complete treatments of the stele, incorporating both the inscription and the images. For a summary of approaches, see Elsner, 46–48.

loyalty to Athens, but this was only the proximate cause. These exiles were the root of the conflict.

Samos continued to hold out against Sparta after the battle of Aegospotamoi in 405 (Xen. *Hell.* 2.2.6, 3.6) and the fall of Athens in 404, surrendering only in 403 after a long siege (Xen. *Hell.* 2.3.6–7). The long resistance may have worsened Lysander's punishment of the Samians, but his actions nonetheless capture the new status of Ionia. Lysander returned the exiles to power, as well as installing a Spartan named Thorax as harmost, stationing a garrison on the island, and appointing a narrow oligarchy (Xen. *Hell.* 2.3.6–7).[48] These arrangements also created a new wave of exiles, many of whom probably went to Athens, while others sought refuge nearby in poleis such as Ephesus and Notium (*RO* 2 = *IG* I³ 127, ll. 49–50). On top of paying the Spartan war tax, the restored Samians offered ostentatious honors for Lysander, including a statue of him at Olympia erected at public expense (Paus. 6.3.14–15), couplets from poet Ion of Samos decorating his victory monument at Delphi (*ML* 95 = *SEG* 23.324b) and renaming the festival for Hera the "Lysandreia" (Duris, *BNJ* 76 F 26).[49] The festival occurred under this name at least four times, probably only being abolished in 394 after the battle of Cnidus. While Lysander was unsuccessful in persuading the poet Choerilus of Samos to compose an epic poem about his triumphs (Plut. *Lys.* 18.4), multiple winners of the poetic competitions at the Lysandreia took up the theme of his greatness.[50] It was in this context that Duris of Samos says that the Samians dedicated altars and a cult to Lysander as though he were a god (*BNJ* 76 F 71).[51] While honorific statues became a normal diplomatic practice, the creation of the Lysandreia was likely indicative of more sinister processes at work.

---

48. Shipley, *Samos*, 131, highlights that Xenophon calls the new regime "its one-time citizens," probably indicating the exiles at Anaia.

49. Shipley, *Samos*, 133–34, suggests that the epigram may have been added later.

50. Lysander likely intended Choerilus to compose a contemporary epic along the lines of his *Persica* that debuted in Athens to such acclaim that the Assembly allegedly awarded him a gold stater per line and decreed that it should be recited alongside the works of Homer (*Suda* s.v. Χοιρίλος). George Huxley, "Choirilos of Samos," *GRBS* 10, no. 1 (1969): 13, correctly notes that there is no evidence that Choerilus ever began this poem. On Choerilus' treatment of the contemporary in the form of epic, see Kelly A. MacFarlane, "Choerilus of Samos' Lament (SH 317) and the Revitalization of Epic," *AJPh* 130, no. 2 (2009): 219–34. The Lysandreia became one of the preeminent literary festivals in Ionia during this period and is attested by inscriptions recording victories such as *IG* XII 6.1 334. The Lysandreia attracted poets such as Antimachus of Colophon, who wrote an acclaimed *Thebaid*, about the Seven Against Thebes, and whose poetry was equated with Homer and Hesiod and sought after by Plato because it was unavailable in Athens. He evidently lost in his appearance at the Lysandreia, though perhaps not strictly because Lysander approved more of Niceratus of Heracleia's poem, as Plutarch suggests (*Lys* 18.4).

51. Michael A. Flower, "Agesilaus of Sparta and the Origins of the Ruler Cult," *CQ²* 38, no. 1 (1988): 132–33; Frances Pownall, "Duris of Samos (76)," *BNJ* F 71 commentary. Simonton, *Oligarchy*, 208–10, incisively demonstrates how these rituals served to reinforce the new regime.

The Spartan victory in 404 made Lysander arguably the most powerful man in the Aegean world, and our surviving sources suggest that he had been preparing for this moment since 407. According to one of these sources, Lysander summoned oligarchic-minded men to Ephesus, instructing them to form *hetaireia* in their communities and to integrate themselves into public affairs with the promise that he would appoint them to what Plutarch calls "revolutionary decarchies" (γενομένων δεκαδαρχιῶν, *Lys.* 5.3–4; cf. Diod. 13.70.4). Thus, it is thought, Lysander cultivated supporters who would be loyal to him and used them as a seed to create a system of decarchies throughout the Aegean in 404/3.[52] However, this tradition is riddled with source problems. The only polis in Ionia where we know that Lysander established a decarchy was Samos, which had remained allied with Athens throughout the war and thus was likely regarded as particularly suspect, though Chios, which lay outside of Persian territory, likely had one as well. Moreover, *hetaireia* were a normal part of elite Greek life even in the most radical of democratic poleis, so it is implausible that Lysander himself introduced a substantial, widespread change in Ionia. This is not to say either that Lysander did not build close relationships with Ionian aristocrats or that he did not support these allies in overthrowing what remained of the popular governments in Ionia (Plut. *Lys.* 7.2). Rather, this was a negotiated and reciprocal relationship that he never formalized on a wide scale.[53] Lysander's generosity won him allies who chaffed at Callicratidas' frugality and therefore requested his reappointment.

Exemplary of these political currents was a particularly brutal coup at Miletus in c.405. According to Diodorus, events transpired as follows (13.104.5–6):

> At the same time in Miletus certain men with oligarchic proclivities dissolved the demos with Spartan aid. First, during the Dionysia, they

---

52. E.g., E. Cavaignac, "Les dékarchies de Lysandre," *REH* 90 (1924): 292–93; C. D. Hamilton, "Spartan Politics and Policy, 405–401 B.C.," *AJPh* 91, no. 3 (1970): 297–98; Kagan, *Fall of the Athenian Empire*, 397; H. W. Parke, "The Development of the Second Spartan Empire (405–371 B.C.)," *JHS* 50, no. 1 (1930): 51–53, though Parke acknowledges, "A precise answer to the question, where . . . Lysander left harmosts and decarchies, and where harmosts without decarchies, or merely ungarrisoned oligarchies, is precluded by our lack of evidence." The source problems surrounding the decarchies has led to a notably slim modern bibliography. The two clearest discussions are Hamilton, *Sparta's Bitter Victories*, 37; David M. Lewis, "Sparta as Victor," in *Cambridge Ancient History*[2], vol. 6, ed. David M. Lewis, John Boardman, Simon Hornblower, and Martin Ostwald (Cambridge: Cambridge University Press, 1994), 29–30.

53. Xenophon says that Lysander went to Ionia in the 390s so that he could "restore with the help of Agesilaus the decarchies he had established in the cities and dissolved by the ephors" (ὅπως τὰς δεκαρχίας τὰς κατασταθείσας ὑπ᾽ἐκείνου ἐν ταῖς πόλεσιν ἐκπεπτωκυίας δὲ διὰ τοὺς ἐφόρους . . . πάλιν καταστήσειε μετ᾽Ἀγησιλάου, 3.4.2), but makes no mention of which cities had had decarchies. In reporting Lysander's motivations for the campaign, Xenophon likely makes general a practice that had been more limited.

abducted their principal opponents from their homes and slit the throat
of some forty men; then, after that, when the agora was full, they killed
three hundred chosen for their wealth. The most accomplished of those
who favored the demos, who numbered not fewer than a thousand,
fled to the satrap [Tissaphernes][54] because they feared their situation.
He received them generously, giving each a stater and settling them in
Blaudos,[55] a citadel in Lydia.

καθ᾽ ὃν δὴ χρόνον ἐν τῇ Μιλήτῳ τινὲς ὀλιγαρχίας ὀρεγόμενοι
κατέλυσαν τὸν δῆμον, συμπραξάντων αὐτοῖς Λακεδαιμονίων. καὶ τὸ μὲν
πρῶτον Διονυσίων ὄντων ἐν ταῖς οἰκίαις τοὺς μάλιστα ἀντιπράττοντας
συνήρπασαν καὶ περὶ τεσσαράκοντα ὄντας ἀπέσφαξαν, μετὰ δέ, τῆς
ἀγορᾶς πληθούσης, τριακοσίους ἐπιλέξαντες τοὺς εὐπορωτάτους
ἀνεῖλον. οἱ δὲ χαριέστατοι τῶν τὰ τοῦ δήμου φρονούντων, ὄντες οὐκ
ἐλάττους χιλίων, φοβηθέντες τὴν περίστασιν ἔφυγον πρὸς Φαρνάβαζον
τὸν σατράπην. οὗτος δὲ φιλοφρόνως αὐτοὺς δεξάμενος, καὶ στατῆρα
χρυσοῦν ἑκάστῳ δωρησάμενος, κατῴκισεν εἰς Βλαῦδα, φρούριόν τι τῆς
Λυδίας.

Diodorus notes that the conspirators had Spartan backing for their coup, but
later traditions tie the entire episode to Lysander specifically, whether through
his willingness to lull the people into a false sense of security (Polyaenus 1.45.1)
or by saying that he provoked them to action when they seemed prepared to
settle with their domestic opponents (Plut. *Lys.* 8). However, as Vanessa Gorman notes, contemporary sources for this coup, including Xenophon's account
of the period and the Milesian epigraphical record, make no mention of the
atrocities—let alone attest to Lysander's involvement.[56] This incongruity creates a problem for understanding Miletus in this period. Oligarchic regimes as
a rule did not produce inscriptions for public consumption, and the specificity
of detail in Diodorus' account generally follows the violence of contemporary

54. Diodorus' text says that the Milesian exiles took refuge with Pharnabazus, but A. Andrewes, "Two Notes on Lysander," *Phoenix* 25, no. 3 (1971): n. 15 notes confusion and conflation of the Persian satraps, whom Diodorus at times calls "Pharnabazos" interchangeably, and thus reasonably amends the satrap in this passage to Tissaphernes. Lydia is also significantly closer to Miletus than Hellespontine Phrygia, and we hear of Milesian "friends" of Tissaphernes who formed part of his retinue until his death in 395 (Polyaenus 8.16).
55. The toponym "Blauda" is unknown, but Strabo locates a "Blaudos" in Lydia (12.5.2), making an identification likely; see Andrewes, "Two Notes on Lysander," n. 15.
56. Vanessa B. Gorman, *Miletos, the Ornament of Ionia* (Ann Arbor: University of Michigan Press, 2001), 240–41. Diodorus mentions Lysander in the aftermath of the coup (13.104.7), but not in connection to it.

oligarchic regimes, both of which suggest that the massacre could have taken place. Further, it was followed by another round of exiles just a few years later (see below, "Persian Dynastic Politics"), and there was no democratic reconciliation that would necessitate public acknowledgment of events. At the same time, this is the last that we hear of the exiles at Blaudos specifically—in marked contrast to the exiles from Chios and Samos—and there is no indication of a regime change on the *aesymnetes* list (*Milet* I.3, no. 122).[57] The coup at Miletus fits the wider context of political restructuring that took place throughout the Aegean, where local oligarchs took advantage of Spartan hegemony to seize power against their populist rivals.[58] However, where both Samos and likely Chios were saddled with Spartan harmosts upon the conclusion of the war (Diod. 14.10), there is no evidence for a comparable arrangement on the mainland. Those poleis belonged to Persia.[59]

Domestic backlash against Lysander's power ultimately caused the Spartans to withdraw support from his imperial arrangements in 403/2.[60] The ephors declared their support for ancestral constitutions in Ionia (Xen. *Hell.* 3.4.2) and recalled Lysander's appointed harmosts, ultimately executing Thorax, who held that position at Samos (Plut. *Lys.* 19.4). Both actions were strikes against the navarch, but we ought to be careful not to overstate how big a change this was in Ionia. The constitutions in question were unlikely to have been democratic, even in poleis with strong democratic traditions, and, regardless of how repugnant these oligarchic regimes were thought to be, there is no evidence that they entirely crumbled in the absence of Spartan support. The Samians for instance, held the Lysandreia for at least two more cycles after Lysander's recall, while the only documented instance of imminent regime change was not a popular uprising, but an outgrowth of Persian dynastic politics. The change in attitude

57. As a source of evidence for specific trends in Milesian political history this inscription should be taken with extreme skepticism, but the second column (II. l.2) *may* begin with the repudiation of Athens, and the names could be read as a particular faction becoming ascendent since entries for Hegemon, son of Eodemos (II. 1.4, in perhaps 410/9), and Eodemos, son of Hegemon (II. l.12, 402/1), two names that together appear only once elsewhere on the list (Eodemos, I. l. 90), may indicate a father-son pair. Recently, however, Eric W. Driscoll, "The Milesian Eponym List and the Revolt of 412 B.C.," *The Journal of Epigraphic Studies* 2 (2019): 11–32, has argued that a new fragment of the list ought to be interpreted as indicating that the stele first went up in 412 as a way of galvanizing the divided community." There is also a double entry, likely in 403/2 at II. l. 11, but should that quirk hold any significance it would be to the conflict between Tissaphernes and Cyrus. On the inscription, see Chapter 2 and Chapter 7.
58. Hamilton, "Spartan Politics and Policy," 294–314. Flower, "Agesilaus of Sparta," 123–34, suggests that the development of the ruler cults lay behind the falling out between Agesilaus and Lysander, while Graham Wylie, "Lysander and the Devil," *AC* 66 (1997): 75–88, implies that Lysander was corrupt and rotted to the core. On the end of the decarchies, see Andrewes, "Two Notes on Lysander," 206–14.
59. Contra Andrewes, "Two Notes on Lysander," 216, who argues that Cyrus allowed Lysander an entirely free hand throughout Ionia until it was no longer politically expedient.
60. Andrewes, "Two Notes on Lysander," 216.

in Sparta might have prompted a withdrawal from the eastern Aegean following the Peloponnesian War, but it neither caused widespread political upheaval
in Ionia nor dissolved the relationships that had been formed.

Persian Dynastic Politics, 404–401

At the conclusion of the Peloponnesian War in 404, Cyrus and Tissaphernes
reasserted Persian control over Ionia.[61] Treaties between Sparta and Persia in
the preceding years had recognized the legitimacy of Persian authority in return
for military and financial support for the war, and the Spartan commander
Lichas had chastised the Milesians for asserting their autonomy against Tissaphernes (Thuc. 8.84.5). Cyrus' arrival in western Anatolia changed the Persian hierarchy by giving him control over multiple existing satrapies (Xen. *Hell.*
1.4.3; *Anab.* 1.9.7) but did not fundamentally change the relationship between
Ionia and Persia.[62] For the Ionians, though, this situation was one of limbo.
Spartan commanders were generally unwilling to support Ionians against Persia, but Lysander also enrolled the Ionians into the Spartan alliance system.
When Spartan enthusiasm for projecting power into Asia Minor waned after
404, the Ionian poleis became embroiled in the Persian conflict between Cyrus,
Tissaphernes, and, ultimately, Artaxerxes II.

Darius II died in 405/4, elevating Cyrus' older brother Artaxerxes to the
throne. The royal intrigues of Parsyatis, Cyrus, Artaxerxes II, and Tissaphernes
and the campaign that culminated in the battle of Cunaxa in 401 are largely
beyond the scope of this study, but they need to be addressed in brief since the
campaign began in Ionia. Cyrus left Anatolia for a time in 405 before his father
died, likely to answer charges that he had overstepped his mandate by executing a member of the Persian nobility (Xen. *Hell.* 2.1.8). Cyrus was exonerated
and, at the behest of their mother, Parsyatis, Artaxerxes II initially reconfirmed
his brother's position. When Tissaphernes accused Cyrus of plotting a coup,
Artaxerxes reversed course and had him arrested (Xen. *Anab.* 1.1.3; Ctesias F
19.59; Plut. *Artax.* 3.4).[63] Parsyatis again intervened to prevent her son's execu-

---

61. Hamilton, "Two Notes on Lysander," 294–314; Lewis, "Sparta as Victor," 40–41; Lewis,
Sparta and Persia, 137. For a revised interpretation of the power dynamics, see Hyland, *Persian
Interventions*, 99–12. Jeffrey Rop, *Greek Military Service in the Ancient Near East, 401–330 BCE*
(Cambridge: Cambridge University Press, 2019), argues that the subsequent service of Greeks in
Persian forces indicates the influence of Persian political patronage in the Aegean during the fourth
century.

62. See Debord, *L'Asie Mineure*, 120–24, 166, 224; Jack Martin Balcer, "The Ancient Persian
Satrapies and Satraps in Western Anatolia," *AMI* 26 (1993): 81–90; Ruzicka, "Cyrus and Tissaphernes," 204; Lewis, *Sparta and Persia*, 129–32.

63. Ruzicka, "Cyrus and Tissaphernes," 207–8; Lloyd Llewellyn-Jones and James Robson, *Cte-*

tion, and Cyrus returned to Sardis, where he began in earnest to plot against his brother. Artaxerxes acknowledged Cyrus' position in Sardis, but also created a new satrapy for Tissaphernes in Caria, to which he appended the Ionian poleis (Xen. *Anab.* 1.1.6).[64] This situation in western Anatolia was an uneasy post hoc arrangement. The revenues from Ionia belonged to Tissaphernes on paper, but therein lay the rub.

Most Ionian poleis simply ignored Artaxerxes' order to pay their tribute to Tissaphernes and instead submitted to Cyrus. Their choice was easy. The Ionians undoubtedly mistrusted Tissaphernes based on earlier interactions, while Cyrus entertained them lavishly, promising to remit their tribute should they support his cause. As Hyland notes, Xenophon also glosses over Cyrus' coercive activities to present the prince in the most positive light (Xen. *Anab.* 1.1.8).[65] Only Miletus resisted Cyrus' charms, and not for want of enticement. When Tissaphernes learned that some Milesians were considering Cyrus' offer, he seized the city, exiled Cyrus' supporters, and installed men who would be loyal to him, perhaps by restoring those who had been exiled to Blauda in c.405 (Xen. *Anab.* 1.1.6–7). Once again, the stark divisions within a citizen body of an Ionian polis entered the realm of imperial politics. The opening move of Cyrus' anabasis therefore did not entail a march upland at all, but a brief siege of Miletus with the stated aim of restoring the exiles. This campaign, however, was a feint, and Cyrus soon abandoned Miletus to embark on his campaign against Artaxerxes (Xen. *Anab.* 1.2.2).[66]

Liberation from Athens never actually aimed at an independent Ionia. Rather the intersection of local agendas with Spartan and Persian interests had brought about change. In this same vein, the Ionian ambivalence toward the project that appeared almost as soon as the fighting started can be better explained by the presence of war that most Ionians had no interest in than by dissolution at betrayed promises. The only respite came when events elsewhere meant that the imperial collaborators were too occupied to intervene in Ionia. Cyrus' quixotic bid for the Persian throne drew both him and Tissaphernes toward the Persian heartland and left Ionia free from Persian intervention for a time. Following Cyrus' death at Cunaxa in 401, Artaxerxes once more gave

sias' *History of Persia: Tales of the Orient* (New York: Routledge, 2009), 197; Briant, *From Cyrus to Alexander*, 615–16.

64. Ruzicka, "Cyrus and Tissaphernes," 208–9. Cf. Briant, *From Cyrus to Alexander*, 616–17; Debord, *L'Asie Mineure*, 124–26.

65. Hyland, *Persian Interventions*, 125–26.

66. Briant, *From Cyrus to Alexander*, 616–20; Hamilton, *Sparta's Bitter Victories*, 103–4; Ruzicka, "Cyrus and Tissaphernes," 210–11; M. Waters, *Ancient Persia: A Concise History* (Cambridge: Cambridge University Press, 2013), 177–81.

Tissaphernes control over Ionia. Xenophon says, unsurprisingly, that the Ionians feared retribution for having sided with Cyrus (Xen. *Hell.* 3.1.3). When Tissaphernes demanded their surrender, they responded with another appeal to Sparta. There had not been a clean break between the two, and the ties cultivated during the Ionian War prompted a series of expeditions to Asia Minor in the 390s that only ended when the Corinthian War demanded Spartan attention closer to home.[67]

---

67. Contra Hamilton, *Sparta's Bitter Victories*, 107–8, who argues that the ascendancy of a conservative faction in Sparta at the end of the Peloponnesian War meant a complete withdrawal of ties.

❦

CHAPTER 5

Centered on the Periphery

401/400–387

Tissaphernes returned to Ionia in triumph after Cyrus' defeat at Cunaxa in 401 and demanded the immediate surrender of all Ionian poleis (*Hell.* 3.1.3). Despite the ultimatum, Tissaphernes refrained from attacking the Ionians. John Hyland explains his apparent hesitation by noting that most of western Anatolia *did* submit and express regret for supporting insurrection (e.g., Diod. 14.35.3).[1] Thus, Tissaphernes waited.

According to Xenophon, the Ionians responded with alarm because they preferred freedom, and they were fearful about reprisals for having been loyal to a prince-turned-traitor (*Hell.* 3.1.3). However, Xenophon's account of these events includes a severe rhetorical gloss between Tissaphernes' imperial language that asserted control over both the Ionians loyal to Cyrus and those loyal to himself, and the "they" who desired freedom and feared retribution. The latter category *does not* include the entirety of the former, but conflating the two lent urgency to their plight.[2] In fact, local political calculations likely played a bigger role than the ambassadors let on. Tissaphernes had already toppled the regime at Miletus at the outset of the conflict with Cyrus and installed men who would be loyal to him (see Chapter 4), while the revolutions of the Ionian War had created new groups of exiles. For the regimes at Ephesus and nearby poleis that had come to power with the support of Cyrus and the Spartans, therefore, Tissaphernes' arrival posed dire risk. Thus, in 401/0, Ionian ambas-

---

1. John Hyland, *Persian Interventions: The Achaemenid Empire, Athens, and Sparta, 450–386 BCE* (Baltimore, MD: Johns Hopkins University Press, 2018), 128–29.

2. Cf. Hyland, *Persian Interventions*, 128–29, who rightly challenges the assertion of David M. Lewis, *Sparta and Persia* (Leiden: Brill, 1977), 121–22, 138–39, that the Ionian response was universal and based on the grounds that Tissaphernes overstepped his remit and trampled the Greek principle of autonomy. Hyland points out that out that paying tribute was not incompatible with political autonomy.

sadors traveled to Sparta asking that they protect the Greeks of Asia (τῇ Ἀσίᾳ Ἑλλήνων, Xen. *Hell.* 3.1.3; Cf. Diod. 14.35.6).[3] Although Xenophon's narrative likely elides internal debate at Sparta, he says that the Spartans agreed to help and mustered one thousand *neodamodeis*, four thousand Peloponnesian allies, and three hundred Athenian cavalry under the command of the general Thibron (Xen. *Hell.* 3.1.4).[4]

"Liberation" discourse was nothing new in Ionia, but it could be a powerful tool. Although a conservative faction had gained prominence in Sparta after the fall of Athens, fighting for the defense of the Greeks of Asia—a claim that sounded grander even than protecting Spartan allies—allowed the proponents of Spartan imperialism such as Thibron and Lysander to once more rise in prominence.[5] Thus, these Ionians who had worked with the Spartans during the previous decade once more pulled their allies into a conflict centered squarely on Ionia, with not inconsequential results. The new conflict further constrained Ionian actions until the outbreak of the Corinthian War in 395 drew Sparta's attention back to across the Aegean and left Persia with a nearly free hand in Ionia.

---

3. By the Hellenistic period it was common to refer to the Greeks of Asia as a corporate body that had one set of interests, but this is the earliest appearance of the slogan in a political sense; see Robin Seager and Christopher Tuplin, "The Freedom of the Greeks of Asia: On the Origins of a Concept and the Creation of a Slogan," *JHS* 100 (1980): 144, with n. 37. This naturally introduces the question to whom it refers. Seager and Tuplin reasonably argue that it only encapsulated those Greeks in Asia who were making the appeal, though the contention of H. D. Westlake, "Spartan Intervention in Asia, 400–397 B.C.," *Historia* 35, no. 4 (1986): 406 n. 6, that the appellants were the Greeks of Asia broadly seems misguided. Xenophon says that the request came from the threatened Ionians, who appealed to Sparta ostensibly on behalf of the rest of the Greeks of Asia.

4. Thibron also hired the mercenaries who had accompanied Cyrus (Diod. 14.37.4). On the makeup of the Spartan force, see John Buckler, *Aegean Greece in the Fourth Century BC* (Leiden: Brill, 2003), 44–45; Peter Krentz, *Xenophon: Hellenika II.3.11–IV.2.8* (Warminster: Aris & Phillips, 1995), 159. Xenophon says that the newly restored Athenian democracy dispatched cavalrymen who had served the Thirty. The *neodamodeis* are often characterized as emancipated helots based on Thucydides 4.80, but that is an oversimplification. R. F. Willetts, "The Neodamodeis," *CPh* 49, no. 1 (1954): 28, characterizes them as one of several "underprivileged sections of the Spartan community," which together made up the great majority of the population."

5. On the Spartan factions in this period, see Charles D. Hamilton, "Spartan Politics and Policy, 405–401 B.C.," *AJPh* 91, no. 3 (1970): 294–314, though he likely overstates the influence of the conservative faction. Daniel Tober, "'Politeiai' and Spartan Local History," *Historia* 59, no. 4 (2010): 414–20, follows Jacoby *FGrHist* 581 in identifying Thibron as the author of a Spartan *politeia* that claimed imperialism was the ultimate end of the Lycurgan constitution (Arist. *Pol.* 7.1333b12)—in marked contrast to Xenophon's conclusions. The date of Thibron's *politeia* is unknown. Jacoby suggested the text either advertised Sparta to the Ionian poleis or was a project of his exile. I follow Kenneth Nigel and Anton Powell "Thibron (581)," *BNJ*, who prefer the latter context. For other chronological possibilities, see Tober, 415 n. 18 and n.19.

Sparta in Anatolia: Crusades for Greek Liberty? 399–394

When Thibron arrived in Ionia, he instructed the poleis to raise soldiers, with some two thousand Ionians joining his expedition (Diod. 14.36.2; Xen. *Hell.* 3.1.5). The historian H. D. Westlake declares that the "significantly small number" of Ionians was "evidence of their inability to defend themselves," but this is a hasty assessment.[6] The ancient sources are vague about the origin of these troops, with Xenophon flippantly declaring that "at that time all poleis obeyed any order that a Lacedaemonian man might give them."[7] But it is nonetheless possible to provide the boundary for Spartan influence. Xenophon says that the Ionians came from the mainland (ἐκ τῶν ἐν τῇ ἠπείρῳ Ἑλληνίδων πόλεων), while Diodorus adds that Thibron enlisted them from his own (Ephesus) and other poleis (ἐκεῖ δὲ ἔκ τε τῶν ἰδίων πόλεων καὶ τῶν ἄλλων). In the south of Ionia, Miletus and Magnesia near the mouth of the Maeander both remained loyal to Tissaphernes, so it is reasonable to assume that Myus stayed out of the conflict. In the north, Tissaphernes had recently raided the territory of Cyme in Aeolis and took prisoners (Diod. 14.35.7), which probably resulted in pushing Clazomenae and Erythrae toward Sparta. Thus, most of Thibron's Asian Greeks likely came from Ephesus and the Ionian communities in the Cayster River valley and to the north. The only city in the Maeander River valley that certainly contributed soldiers was Priene, on the north side of the bay (Xen. *Hell.* 3.2.17). With these bounds established, some observations about the Ionians who joined the Spartan expedition are in order. First, there is no information about how many troops Thibron demanded from the Ionians or how many mouths he was prepared to feed. Similarly, these two thousand troops represented a muster from part of Ionia that *excluded* three of the four largest poleis in the region.[8] Neither was this a mass conscription, which would have left the communities defenseless and fields uncultivated and caused more problems for Thibron than it solved. Finally, two thousand soldiers, more than a quarter of the entire expedition, was not an insignificant number. Westlake may be correct that the Ionians were unable to defend themselves against Tissaphernes, but their contributions to the campaign should not be dismissed.

Based at Ephesus, Thibron led his army north along the Aegean coast, capturing multiple settlements, including Pergamum, but when the campaign bogged down in an expensive siege of Larisa, the ephors ordered him to invade

---

6. Westlake, "Spartan Intervention in Asia," 410.

7. πᾶσαι γὰρ τότε αἱ πόλεις ἐπείθοντο ὅ τι Λακεδαιμόνιος ἀνὴρ ἐπιτάττοι.

8. Chios and possibly Samos were still within the sphere of Spartan influence and may have been garrisoned, but while they both supplied ships for Sparta at times in the 390s there is no evidence that either contributed to Thibron's expedition.

Caria, which would threaten Tissaphernes' estates and Miletus (Xen. *Hell.* 3.1.6–7).[9] Before Thibron could comply he was recalled on the accusation that he had allowed his army to raid the territory of Spartan allies and was replaced by Dercylidas (Xen. *Hell.* 3.1.8). We are told that the new commander nursed a grudge against Pharnabazus that stemmed back to the Peloponnesian War and so led his soldiers from Ionia to campaign in the north Aegean, albeit while preventing them from pillaging friendly territory (Xen. *Hell.* 3.1.9–10).[10]

It was not until the middle of the next campaign season, in 398, that Dercylidas led his soldiers back south toward Ionia. According to Xenophon, that spring began with Dercylidas meeting with inspectors from Sparta at Abydus on the Hellespont. He dismissed them to continue their journey to Ephesus content in the knowledge that they would see the Greek cities they passed through in a state of "well-governed peace" (ἐν εἰρήνῃ εὐδαιμονικῶς, *Hell.* 3.2.9). Nevertheless, Xenophon's subsequent narrative puts a lie to that rosy characterization and hints at the lingering scars from the Peloponnesian War. After a brief foray into the Chersonese, Dercylidas returned south in the summer of 398, where he "discovered" that exiles from Chios held a well-defended fortress of Atarneus in Aeolis from which they had been raiding the rest of Ionia (Xen. *Hell.* 3.2.11). Xenophon twice says that Decylidas believed the Ionian poleis to be at peace (*Hell.* 3.2.9, 11), downplaying the disruption caused by these exiles, but it is hard to believe that he did not know about them during his initial campaign through Aeolis. These exiles had resided at Atarneus since 408/7, when their political opponents bribed the Spartan navarch Cratesippidas to restore them to Chios. Diodorus says that they had continually been at war with Chios, at least implying that they disrupted Dercylidas' imagined peace (13.65.3–5). This time, Dercylidas surrounded Atarneus and besieged it for seven months before the defenders surrendered (Xen. *Hell.* 3.2.11). Xenophon ends his discussion of Atarneus by noting that Dercylidas appointed Dracon of Pellene to command the post and supplied it with equipment for his own use. What happened to the Chian exiles is unknown.[11]

---

9. Paul Cartledge, *Agesilaos and the Crisis of Sparta* (London: Duckworth, 2000), 210–11; Charles D. Hamilton, *Sparta's Bitter Victories: Politics and Diplomacy in the Corinthian War* (Ithaca, NY: Cornell University Press, 1979), 113–19; Westlake, "Spartan Intervention in Asia," 413–26.

10. Dercylidas' campaigns in Aeolis, Bithynia, and Thrace are largely beyond the scope of this inquiry, but Xenophon indicates their success. Dercylidas allegedly captured Larisa, Hamaxitus, and Colonae in a single day and incited other settlements to revolt against Pharnabazus, mostly through diplomacy (*Hell.* 3.1.16). All three of Larisa, Hamaxitus, and Colonae had recently been captured by Mania, whom Pharnabazus had appointed to rule Aeolis (Xen. *Hell.* 3.1.11–13). Xenophon also explains Dercylidas' decision to campaign in the north as a means of not burdening his allies with feeding his soldiers (*Hell.* 3.2.1).

11. Alexander's so-called letters to Chios between 334 and 332 attest to the continuing problem of exiles in the region (see Chapter 7), but there is little explicit evidence for its redress in the new Chian constitution established after the battle of Cnidus in 394.

According to Xenophon, the Ionians sent emissaries to Sparta in 398/7 saying that it was within Tissaphernes' power to leave Ionia autonomous and urging a campaign against Caria to gain favorable terms (*Hell.* 3.2.12). This claim, however, introduces more questions than it answers. On the one hand, it is easy to label the Ionians here as being credulous regarding promises made by Tissaphernes. Further, Xenophon goes on to say that the king had to ratify the treaty that would guarantee Ionian autonomy (*Hell.* 3.2.20), which indicates a limit to the satrap's power and suggests that the Ionians misrepresented the situation to their own advantage.[12] Tissaphernes might have been able to follow Cyrus' example by remitting tribute from the Ionian poleis and making up the deficit in his obligation to the king elsewhere, but this guarantee would have come as a privilege of acknowledging his suzerainty, not one of autonomy. On the other hand, Xenophon does not specify who these ambassadors were, saying only that they were from the poleis of Ionia (πρέσβεις εἰς Λακεδαίμονα ἀπὸ τῶν Ἰωνίδων πόλεων). While it is possible that these ambassadors were exiles or dissidents from poleis like Miletus that were under Tissaphernes' control, the most likely scenario is that they came from the communities that had sent soldiers to join Thibron and Dercylidas and who were concerned because the Spartans had not yet attacked the man who threatened them.

Dercylidas led his army south into the Maeander plain only after learning that the Persians were on the offensive.[13] Nevertheless, the army marched unprepared to fight, believing that the Persian force was advancing toward Ephesus (Xen. *Hell.* 3.2.14).[14] It was therefore a shock when they blundered into the combined Persian army of Tissaphernes and Pharnabazus arrayed for battle across the road. Dercylidas ordered his soldiers into a battle formation, and while the Peloponnesians prepared in disciplined silence, Xenophon says, the Ionian hoplites dropped their weapons in the grain fields and fled, while those who remained looked as though they would soon run away (*Hell.* 3.2.17).[15]

---

12. As noted by Christopher Tuplin, "The Treaty of Boiotios," in *Achaemenid History*, vol. 2, ed. Heleen Sancisi-Weerdenburg and Amelie Kuhrt (Leiden: Brill, 1984), 149–51, and Matt Waters, "Applied Royal Directive: Pissouthnes and Samos," in *The Achaemenid Court*, ed. Bruno Jacobs and Robert Rollinger (Wiesbaden: Harrassowitz, 2010), 817–28.

13. Dercylidas' target was one of Tissaphernes' residences. For an evaluation of the Persian and Spartan moves in this campaign, see Hyland, *Persian Interventions*, 131–32, with John Hyland, "The Aftermath of Aegospotamoi and the Decline of Spartan Naval Power," *AHB* 33 (2019): 25, for the small-scale naval operation that operated concurrently. There is no evidence for naval contributions from the Ionian allies before Agesilaus ordered them to construct 120 new vessels in 395 (Xen. *Hell.* 3.4.28).

14. The ancient sources that describe this showdown are contradictory. Xenophon provides the most detail, but Diodorus 14.39.4–6 places it in the vicinity of Ephesus and claims that the Persian satraps outnumbered Dercylidas' army by nearly 3:1.

15. ὅσοι δὲ ἦσαν ἀπὸ Πριήνης τε καὶ Ἀχιλλείου καὶ ἀπὸ νήσων καὶ τῶν Ἰωνικῶν πόλεων, οἱ μέν τινες καταλιπόντες ἐν τῷ σίτῳ τὰ ὅπλα ἀπεδίδρασκον· καὶ γὰρ ἦν βαθὺς ὁ σῖτος ἐν τῷ Μαιάνδρου πεδίῳ· ὅσοι δὲ καὶ ἔμενον, δῆλοι ἦσαν οὐ μενοῦντες. Krentz *Xenophon*, 170, suggests that Xeno-

Fleeing before the start of battle in their territory was not a good look for the Ionians, particularly because Tissaphernes and Dercylidas proceeded to negotiate a truce. This episode is potent evidence to support the long-held view that the Ionians were weak, yet, curiously, Xenophon offers neither explanation nor condemnation for their cowardice. Instead, he focuses on the leaders, Dercylidas and Tissaphernes. Despite having commanded this army for the better part of a year, there is no evidence that Dercylidas took the time to train his comparatively inexperienced troops. His successes in Aeolis had demonstrated his diplomatic cunning and ability to organize the logistics to carry on a lengthy siege but had not tested his soldiers on the battlefield. When he took these raw soldiers into battle, he proceeded to put them at a disadvantage, which led to their flight. At the same time, Xenophon exaggerates the episode to deride Tissaphernes' decision to negotiate despite having the upper hand.[16]

The truce struck between Dercylidas and Tissaphernes required the Spartans to withdraw their forces and harmosts from Ionia in return for a promise from both sides guaranteeing Ionian autonomy (Xen. *Hell.* 3.2.18–20).[17] This proposal was a nonstarter. Reports immediately circulated that the Persians were assembling a new fleet in Phoenicia for war in the Aegean (Xen. *Hell.* 3.4.1; Diod. 14.39.2–4), and Lysander asked his friends in Ionia to appeal for a new expedition (Plut. *Lys.* 23.1; cf. Plut. *Ages.* 6.1).[18] Thus, in 396, King Agesilaus left Sparta at the head of a force of thirty full Spartans, two thousand *neodamodeis*, and six thousand allies. Xenophon indicates that Lysander's true objective was to restore his decarchies (Xen. *Hell.* 3.4.2), while about the rest of the Spartans he says, "What was esteemed the most was not fighting for Greece but conquering Asia" (κάλλιστον δὲ πάντων ἐκρίνετο τὸ μὴ περὶ τῆς Ἑλλάδος ἀλλὰ περὶ τῆς Ἀσίας τὸν ἀγῶνα καθιστάναι, *Ages.* 1.8).[19]

Upon arriving at Ephesus, Agesilaus embarked on a propaganda campaign to win support for his expedition, declaring to Tissaphernes his intention that

phon specifically mentions Prienians because, as inhabitants of the Maeander Valley, they might be expected to fight most fiercely. Cf. Buckler, *Aegean Greece*, 58–59; Westlake, "Spartan Intervention in Asia," 414. Diodorus says nothing about the alleged flight of the Ionians.

16. See Hyland, *Persian Interventions*, 132, on Xenophon's scorn for Tissaphernes.

17. Pierre Briant, *From Cyrus to Alexander: A History of the Persian Empire*, trans. Peter T. Daniels (Winona Lake, IN: Eisenbrauns, 2002), 365; Hamilton, *Sparta's Bitter Victories*, 118–19. Hyland, *Persian Interventions*, 132, explains Tissaphernes' willingness to entertain the autonomy of Ionia within the longer continuum of Persian policy, noting again that autonomy did not preclude the collection of tribute.

18. Briant, *From Cyrus to Alexander*, 635–37; Buckler, *Aegean Greece*, 59–60; Westlake, "Spartan Intervention in Asia," 422–23.

19. Where Lysander wanted to restore the decarchies is left unstated, suggesting that they existed throughout Ionia, but see Chapter 4, "Enter Lysander." A campaign might present opportunities to expand his system beyond its original bounds, but Lysander returned to Sparta after a falling out with Agesilaus. Xenophon describes the campaign as revenge for the Persian Wars; see John Dillery, *Xenophon and the History of His Times* (New York: Routledge 1995), 116.

the poleis in Asia would be autonomous, like those across the Aegean (Xen. *Hell.* 3.4.5). The surviving accounts of Agesilaus' expedition depict him as an energetic commander determined to offer the Ionians more than just words. Like Thibron and Dercylidas, he instructed them, as well as the communities of Aeolis and the Hellespont, to send soldiers to Ephesus when he arrived in Asia in 396 (Xen. *Hell.* 3.4.11–12; Xen. *Ages.* 1.14).[20] Xenophon goes on to explain how the Spartan king transformed the city until it appeared as though it was a workshop of war (πολέμου ἐργαστήριον) and put his army through a rigorous training regimen before the start of his second campaigning season (*Hell.* 3.4.16–19; cf. Nepos *Ages.* 3).[21] Xenophon marvels: "What a sight it would have been to see: Agesilaus first, and then the other soldiers processing, garlanded, from the gymnasium, dedicating the garlands to Artemis" (Xen. *Ages.* 1.27; cf. *Hell.* 3.4.18).[22] While it is tempting to dismiss Xenophon's description as hyperbolic, almost like a cinematic training montage, it is also representative of the extent of Sparta's investment in Ephesus in particular, which complicated Ionian decision-making after his departure. Agesilaus also went further to cultivate a relationship with the sanctuary of Artemis, and an inscription bearing his name likely indicates an otherwise unattested building phase at the temple during and after the campaign.[23]

His army newly energized, Agesilaus won a victory over the Persians outside Sardis in early 395.[24] The conduct of the Ionian levies is unrecorded, but Agesilaus intended to bring them to Europe when he was recalled later that year (Xen. *Hell.* 4.2.4–5). According to Xenophon, Agesilaus realized that many of the Asian Greeks did not want to fight against Greeks, but a more likely explanation is that most did not want to cross to Europe because it meant leaving their homes. Moreover, in his speech to these soldiers, Xenophon has the king address them as his allies (ὦ ἄνδρες σύμμαχοι, *Hell.* 4.2.3). Yet, in the same scene in his biography of Agesilaus, Xenophon says that the Ionians mourned the king's departure not just as they would their ruler, but their father or close

---

20. Cartledge, *Agesilaos*, 212–13.

21. Cartledge, *Agesilaos*, 214.

22. ἐπερρώσθη δ' ἄν τις κἀκεῖνο ἰδών, Ἀγησίλαον μὲν πρῶτον, ἔπειτα δὲ καὶ τοὺς ἄλλους στρατιώτας ἐστεφανωμένους τε ὅπου ἀπὸ τῶν γυμνασίων ἴοιεν, καὶ ἀνατιθέντας τοὺς στεφάνους τῇ Ἀρτέμιδι.

23. Christoph Börker, "König Agesilaos von Sparta und der Artemis-Tempel in Ephesus," *ZPE* 37 (1980): 69–70; Burkhardt Wesenberg, "Agesilaos im Artemision," *ZPE* 41 (1981): 175–80; cf. Chapter 9.

24. J. K. Anderson, "The Battle of Sardis in 395 B.C.," *California Studies in Classical Antiquity* 7 (1974): 27–53; Cartledge, *Agesilaos*, 214–17; Vivienne J. Gray, "Two Different Approaches to the Battle of Sardis in 395 B.C.," *California Studies in Classical Antiquity* 12 (1979): 183–200; Charles D. Hamilton, *Agesilaus and the Failure of the Spartan Hegemony* (Ithaca, NY: Cornell University Press, 1991), 98–100.

friend (οὐχ ὡς ἄρχοντος μόνον ἀλλὰ καὶ ὡς πατρὸς καὶ ἑταίρου, *Ages.* 1.38).[25]
Allied forces were supposed to follow Spartan leadership, but Agesilaus gave
the soldiers the option, thus tacitly admitting an end to ambitions in Asia.
Some Ionians continued to serve with Agesilaus after he returned to Europe
and even fought at the battle of Coronea in 394, where they routed their opponents (Xen. *Hell.* 4.3.15–17).[26]

For all of Agesilaus' successes on land, failures at sea dictated the Spartan
withdrawal from Ionia. The expedition had corresponded with a surge in the
size of the Spartan fleet, including 120 new triremes that Agesilaus commissioned his allies to construct (Xen. *Hell.* 3.4.28). As Hyland has recently noted,
the cost of this new Spartan fleet would have been staggering.[27] According to
Xenophon, the poleis, including those of Ionia, and some private individuals
paid for the initial construction out of a desire to please Agesilaus, but the construction costs were only a fraction of the bill. The largest expense came in the
form of operational costs for veteran crews, and not only did Agesilaus not ben-
efit from Persian subsidies, but also there is little evidence that he was able to
tap into the same fiscal systems that a series of Spartan commanders had established in the last phase of the Peloponnesian War (see Chapter 4). It defies belief
that Ionians would not have had any financial obligations during this period
given the expectations both before and afterward, but the Spartans' sphere of
influence did not include all of Ionia, and their ability to coerce resources out
of their allies was decidedly more limited than when the pressure came from
both Sparta and Persia.

These fiscal and military limitations brought an end to Spartan intervention
in Anatolia. The Spartans recalled Agesilaus and his forces from Ionia in 395/4
because of the outbreak of the Corinthian War (Diod. 14.83.1), but the Spartan presence continued into 394 when the fleet, still beset by financial problems that reduced the crew sizes, campaigned south of Ionia.[28] This campaign
ended with the battle of Cnidus, where a Persian fleet under the command of
the satrap Pharnabazus and the Athenian exile Conon defeated the Spartans.[29]

25. Dillery, *Xenophon*, 117.
26. Cartledge, *Agesilaos*, 219–22; Hamilton, *Agesilaus*, 106–11. Ancient authors laud Agesilaus
for his generalship at Coronea (Xen. *Ages.* 6.2; Frontinus, *Strat.* 2.6.6; Nepos *Ages.* 4; Polyaenus,
2.1.19), but Cartledge is skeptical.
27. Hyland, "Aftermath of Aegospotamoi," 35–36.
28. On the issue of crew sizes, see Hyland, "Aftermath of Aegospotamoi," 33.
29. The Greek sources give overwhelming credit to Conon for the campaign, but Hyland, *Persian Interventions*, 145, rightly notes that Pharnabazus was Conon's superior. Evidence from both
Ctesias (F 63) and Diodorus (14.39.1) indicates that he was responsible for the king's selection
of Conon, but Duane A. March, "Konon and the Great King's Fleet, 396–394," *Historia* 46, no. 3
(1997): 257–59, implausibly concludes that Conon came to hold supreme command, and Briant,
From Cyrus to Alexander, 646, likewise gives Conon credit for the victory. On the battle of Cni-

In the aftermath of Cnidus, Conon and Pharnabazus swept away the Spartan arrangements in Anatolia, accepting the surrender of Teos, Erythrae, Ephesus, and Chios, and dissolving the pro-Spartan governments (Xen. *Hell.* 4.8.1–3; Diod. 14.84.4; see below, "Athens Resurgent?").[30] These changes marked a watershed moment in Ionia and the end of the Spartan relationships that had governed its history for nearly two decades, offering an opportunity to evaluate this Spartan period. From the start, the purported principle behind Spartan actions was the cause of Greek liberty, but, for exactly as long, Ionia had been at the center of a political arena where principles were a tool rather than an objective. The result was that Persian and Spartan financial mechanisms replaced the Athenian *phoros* that was supposed to have been so reviled. Moreover, while the Spartan garrisons in Ionia during the Ionian War might have been explained as a temporary measure, intermittent evidence indicates a Spartan presence in the 390s. At Chios, the arrival of Pharnabazus and Conon in 394 resulted in the expulsion of the garrison that may have been in place continuously for more than a decade. And yet, I argued above, the oligarchic regimes that came to power after 411 did not collapse with Lysander's recall in 403. Their continued existence explains not only the new wave of expeditions in the 390s, but also how a grievance against Thibron prompted a change in Spartan leadership. Likewise, the fact that Ionian soldiers during this period repeatedly campaigned with or at the behest of Spartan commanders is indicative of the reciprocal relationship that developed between factions in the Ionian poleis and Spartans with imperial aspirations. The Spartans bound the Ionians to them and expected contributions in return, the same as any other ally.[31]

Although Xenophon provides evidence for concern about certain friends of the Spartans in Ionia (*Hell.* 4.8.23), the circumstances and course of the final,

dus itself, see Xen. *Hell.* 4.3.11–12; Diod. 14.83.5–7; Polyaenus 1.48.5; Nepos *Conon* 4; Ctesias 63; Cartledge, *Agesilaos*, 218, 363; Hamilton, *Sparta's Bitter Victories*, 228–29; Buckler, *Aegean Greece*, 128–41; Robin Seager, "Thrasybulus, Conon and Athenian Imperialism, 396–386 B.C.," *JHS* 87 (1967): 101; Robin Seager, "The Corinthian War," in *Cambridge Ancient History*², vol. 6, ed. David M. Lewis, John Boardman, Simon Hornblower, and Martin Ostwald (Cambridge: Cambridge University Press, 1994), 103–4; S. Perlman, "Athenian Democracy and the Revival of Imperialistic Expansion at the Beginning of the Fourth Century B.C.," *CPh* 63, no. 4 (1968): 261–62. Hyland, "Aftermath of Aegospotamoi," 36, points out that Conon also had issues paying his crews and had to put down a mutiny while at Rhodes before receiving a new influx of money; cf. Hyland, *Persian Interventions*, 143–47.

30. Briant, *From Cyrus to Alexander*, 645; Seager, "Thrasybulus, Conon and Athenian Imperialism," 101.

31. The soldiers who remained with Agesilaus in 394 were likely employed as mercenaries since even Sparta employed them in increasing numbers during this period; see Louis Rawlings, *The Ancient Greeks at War* (Manchester: Manchester University Press, 2007), 169–73; Harvey F. Miller, "The Practical and Economic Background to the Greek Mercenary Explosion," *G&R* 31, no. 2 (1984): 153–60.

abortive Spartan expedition to Ionia in 392/1 under the command of Thibron indicates how that relationship had been waning. Ephesus and Priene still aided the Spartan forces (Xen. *Hell.* 4.8.17–19),[32] but only a passing reference in Diodorus Siculus suggests that he employed soldiers from Asia (14.99.2).[33] There is also reason to doubt Xenophon's claim that Thibron used Ephesus as a base, as he instead settled for seizing a fortified settlement, perhaps near Mount Solmissus, from which to raid Persian territory.[34] Local factors shaped this reception. On the one hand, men who had profited from the deep Spartan investment in Ephesus were likely willing to help him, and he might have garnered support by promising to help the Ephesians recover dependencies lost in the fifth century, while others at Ephesus intended to stand apart in the face of renewed Persian power.[35] One day, Xenophon says, Persian horsemen launched an attack on Thibron while he was exercising with a discus after breakfast (Xen. *Hell.* 4.8.19).[36] Thibron lost his life in the attack, and his routed soldiers took temporary refuge in unnamed friendly cities, perhaps including Ephesus. So ended the Spartan presence in Ionia.

Athens Resurgent? 394–387

If the battle of Cnidus marked a watershed moment in Ionia, one might ask what came next for the region. John Hyland has thoroughly refuted the traditional interpretation that the Persian king's primary objective in supporting either Athens or Sparta was a "defensive balancing strategy" designed to

---

32. ὁ δὲ διαβάς τε καὶ ὁρμώμενος ἐξ Ἐφέσου τε καὶ τῶν ἐν Μαιάνδρου πεδίῳ πόλεων Πριήνης τε καὶ Λευκόφρους καὶ Ἀχιλλείου, ἔφερε καὶ ἦγε τὴν βασιλέως.

33. Hyland, *Persian Interventions*, 161, suggests that Thibron's forces consisted of mercenaries but offers no provenance for their origin.

34. Hyland, *Persian Interventions*, 161, with n. 94, makes this proposal based on the Ephesian participation in an arbitration called by Struthas at about the same time. Diodorus calls the fort "Ionda" and the mountain Cornissus, which might be corruptions of the erstwhile Ephesian dependency Isinda and Mount Solmissus, though both identifications are highly speculative and run contrary to the idea that he operated primarily in the Maeander River valley.

35. On the relationship between Ephesus and Isinda, see Chapter 3; for Ephesian imperial ambitions, see Chapter 6. It is tempting to ascribe Thibron's cool reception in Ionia as the result of the Spartan betrayal of Ionians' autonomy in peace negotiations the previous year, as Noboru Sato, "Athens, Persia, Clazomenae, Erythrae: An Analysis of International Relationships in Asia Minor at the Beginning of the Fourth Century BCE," *BICS* 49 (2006): 26, but this fails to account for the continuing existence of Ionian "friends" of Sparta, for the waxing and waning of enthusiasm for Spartan intervention over the preceding two decades, and for the fact that the Persian authorities were taking actions meant to demonstrate that Persian rule would be *less* intrusive than the Spartan equivalent.

36. Diodorus 14.99 records a different, more heroic, account of Thibron's demise, saying that Struthas caught up to him while he returned from a successful raid.

exhaust two warring states that might otherwise meddle with his subjects. Instead, Hyland and others have demonstrated that the king's primary objective in the Aegean was to reassert imperial control over western Anatolia such that he put resources behind whichever contender was willing to recognize that authority.[37] And yet Persian officials in the region, including Pharnabazus and Struthas, initially applied a light touch to the reins of imperial control in ways that allowed local and regional wounds to fester.[38]

The minimal Persian presence and Conon's campaign set the stage for Athens to play a leading role in Ionia during the last years of the 390s. Conon himself had a complex relationship with Athens. He had been one of the generals responsible for the catastrophic defeat at Aegospotamoi in 405 that broke Athenian power and had subsequently fled to Cyprus before entering Persian service (Xen. *Hell.* 2.1.29). Pharnabazus nevertheless dispatched him to Athens in 393, where he was greeted as a liberator and granted a statue (Dem. 20.69; Diod. 14.39).[39] Conon's return was not without issue, as it reignited an old political rivalry with Thrasybulus. Despite their hostility, both men shared the ambition of restoring Athens while conspicuously avoiding its being seen as a threat to Persian dominance.[40] In 393 or early 392, these activities began with Conon reestablishing Athenian diplomatic relationships in Ionia in ways that neither precluded nor superseded the Ionian obligations to Persia, particularly on the mainland.[41]

The clearest signs of the Athenian presence in Ionia at this time were the honors Conon received throughout the region. Ephesus and Samos erected

---

37. Hyland, *Persian Interventions*, 148–49; cf. José Pascual, "Conon, the Persian Fleet and a Second Naval Campaign in 393 BC," *Historia* 65, no. 1 (2016): 16–17.

38. I follow Hyland's interpretation of Persian policy, which sees the apparent inactivity as a deliberate choice, rather than Briant, *From Cyrus to Alexander*, 646, who characterizes the Persian triumph as "fragile and uncertain" and suggests that "the Persians, willy-nilly, were once against squeezed between Sparta's desire to maintain its dominion and Athens's wish to reestablish its own."

39. The Athenians principally honored Conon for liberating the allies (ἠλευθέρωσε τοὺς Ἀθηναίων συμμάχους, Dem. 20.69); see Seager, "Thrasybulus, Conon and Athenian Imperialism," 99–100.

40. Barry S. Strauss, "Thrasybulus and Conon: A Rivalry in Athens in the 390s B.C.," *AJPh* 105, no. 1 (1984): 37–48, suggests personal enmity rather than antipathy over Conon's service with Persia, contra particularly George L. Cawkwell, "The Imperialism of Thrasybulus," *CQ²* 26, no. 2 (1976): 270–77, but also Perlman, "Athenian Democracy," 257–67; Seager, "Thrasybulus, Conon and Athenian Imperialism," 95–115. I diverge from Strauss in his belief that "had [Conon and Thrasybulus] cooperated in the 390s, Athens could only have benefited" (38), in that this line seems derived from an outdated interpretation of Athenian and Persian power as roughly equal. The Persian satrap Tiribazus had Conon arrested when he arrived to negotiate a treaty on behalf of Athens in 392 (Xen. *Hell.* 4.8.16; Diod. 14.85.4; Nepos *Conon* 5). Sometime thereafter he made his way back to Cyprus, where he died (Lysias 19.39).

41. On Conon's activities, see Dem. 20.69; Diod. 14.39.3; Nepos *Conon* 5; Justin 6.3.4; Buckler, *Aegean Greece*, 137. George L. Cawkwell, *The Greek Wars: The Failure of Persia* (Oxford: Oxford University Press, 2005), 168, suggests that the Athenians rejected Conon's prudent advice and set about entirely restoring its empire.

statues of Conon (Paus. 6.3.16), and an inscription from Erythrae praises him for his benefaction (*RO* 8 = *I.Ery.* 6, l. 3) and gave him a series of standard honors, including making him *proxenos* (l. 4) and giving him front seats at the theater at Erythrae (ll. 4–6), immunity to import dues (ll. 6–9), and, if he desired it, citizenship (ll. 10–11).[42] The Erythraeans also granted Conon the unusual honor of choosing where to erect the statue, which was a practice that only became common in the Hellenistic period (Dem. 20.68–71; cf. Paus. 1.3.2).[43] Erythrae probably gave these honors to Conon for his liberation of the polis after Cnidus, but the decree cannot be securely dated to 394, when Conon was still in Persian service. There is no mention of Pharnabazus on the stele, which underscored that these were Greek honors, but also likely indicates that they were offered after Conon returned to Athens as part of strengthening economic relationships between the two poleis.[44] Thus, rather than merely indicating the change in imperial power, this decree was a sign of restored diplomatic activity between Erythrae and Athens.

Nowhere was Conon's presence felt more deeply than on Chios, where he sent the rhetorician Isocrates to rewrite its constitution ([Plut.] *Mor.* 837b).[45] Isocrates had no known connection to Ionia before this assignment, but he had close ties to Conon, whose son Timotheus was his most notorious pupil. While on Chios, he took students such as the local politician Metrodorus, who later trained the orator Theocritus (*Suda* theta 166).[46] The details of the constitution Isocrates designed are unknown, but internal conflict and exiles contin-

---

42. On the institution of *proxenia*, see William Mack, *Proxeny and Polis: Institutional Networks in the Ancient Greek World* (Oxford: Oxford University Press, 2015).

43. Andrew Stewart, *Attika: Studies in Athenian Sculpture of the Hellenistic Age* (London: Society for the Promotion of Hellenic Studies, 1979), 115–32; M. K. Welsh, "Honorary Statues in Ancient Greece," *ABSA* 11 (1904–5): 40; Ian Worthington, *A Historical Commentary on Dinarchus: Rhetoric and Conspiracy in Later Fourth-Century Athens* (Ann Arbor: University of Michigan Press, 1992), 153–54. On the location of the statue, see John Ma, "A Gilt Statue for Konon at Erythrae?," *ZPE* 157 (2006): 124–26; cf. John Ma, *Statues and Cities: Honorific Portraits and Civic Identity in the Hellenistic World* (Oxford: Oxford University Press, 2013), 103–7, for negotiations in where to place honorific statues.

44. On honors being a regular commodity in Greek economic practice, see Darel Tai Engen, *Honor and Profit: Athenian Trade Policy and the Economy and Society of Greece, 415–307 BCE* (Ann Arbor: University of Michigan Press, 2010), particularly 8–12.

45. Joseph Roisman and Ian Worthington, *Lives of the Attic Orators: Texts from Pseudo-Plutarch, Photius and the Suda* (Oxford: Oxford University Press, 2015), 150; Slobodan Dušanić, "Isocrates, the Chian Intellectuals, and the Political Context of the Euthydemus," *JHS* 119 (1999): 2.

46. Isocrates supposedly opened a school on Chios that did not outlive his stay on the island, but he likely had other Chian students both there and when he opened his Athenian school. Ancient tradition suggested that the historian Theopompus was his pupil, but Michael A. Flower, *Theopompus of Chios: History and Rhetoric in the Fourth Century BC* (Oxford: Oxford University Press, 1994), 62, argues that "the pupil-teacher relationship . . . was an invention of Hellenistic biography and literary criticism," based on Theopompos, *BNJ* 115 F 25, where he claimed to be Isocrates' contemporary. Contra Gordon S. Shrimpton, *Theopompus the Historian* (Montreal: McGill University Press, 1991), 9–10.

ued to be a problem. Perhaps in 394/3, Demasistratus, the father of the histo-rian Theopompus, was forced to go into exile on the charge of *laconism* (ἐπὶ λακωνισμῶι, *BNJ* 115 T 2), and the son was able to return to Chios only after Alexander conquered the island in 334/3 and decreed the return of exiles.[47] Equally important, though, Isocrates' constitution empowered a new faction in Chios. A Chian embassy came to forge a new alliance with Athens roughly a decade later in 384, and Slobodan Dušanić posits that it consisted of "relatives, intellectuals and party friends who had entertained close relations and collabo-rated politically along pro-Athenian lines, with Isocrates after c.393."[48]

Developments like these on Chios fueled Spartan concerns that poleis like Ephesus and Priene might suffer repercussions for having welcomed Thibron (see above, "Sparta in Anatolia").[49] The official Persian policy might have been to proceed a light touch, but this did not preclude local actors from using the realignment to purge their opponents as had happened to them during the Ionian War (Chapter 4). The Spartans therefore dispatched a fleet to the eastern Aegean in late 391 or early 390 that they reinforced with additional ships when they determined that the initial effort was too small to help their friends (αὐτὸν ἐλάττω ἔχοντα δύναμιν ἢ ὥστε τοὺς φίλους ὠφελεῖν, Xen. *Hell.* 4.8.22–23).[50] The Spartan ships sailed first to Samos, flipping its allegiance once more and conscripting additional ships to reinforce the flotilla, before doing the same at Cnidus and Rhodes (Xen. *Hell.* 4.8.23; Diod. 14.97.3–5). This Spartan fleet con-tinued to operate in the eastern Aegean into the summer of 390, but primarily in the southern theater near Rhodes, while the Persian authorities confronted Evagoras' rebellion on Cyprus.

While Hyland suggests that Struthas remanded Ionian ships to the control of the Carian dynast Hecatomnus for operations on Cyprus (Diod. 14.98.3–4; Theopompos, *BNJ* 115 F 103.4), the limited Persian oversight and Spartan

---

47. The date that Demasistratus went into exile is unknown. Flower, *Theopompus*, 13–17, posits an earlier date in 394 after the battle of Cnidus, while Shrimpton, *Theopompos*, 4, puts it on the opposite end of the spectrum c.340. See additional discussions in W. Robert Connor, *Theopompus and Fifth-Century Athens* (Washington, DC: Center for Hellenic Studies, 1968), 2; Simon Horn-blower, *Mausolus* (Oxford: Oxford University Press, 1982), 131; William S. Morison, "Theopompus of Chios (115)," *BNJ* biographical commentary. I believe a date c.394/3 is most likely, but the same domestic competition that led to exile in the 390s could also have led to exile in the 380s when Agesilaus again advocated for Spartan intervention in Ionia (Diod. 15.5.2). For the relationship between Theopompus, Theocritus, and Alexander, see Chapter 7.

48. Dušanić, "Isocrates," 7.

49. Xenophon uses the verb ὑποδέχομαι, which was frequently used for the act of admitting, receiving, or welcoming into one's home, as well as for harboring fugitives.

50. Diod. 14.97.3 records just one fleet with three commanders, whom he calls Diphilas (Diph-ridas), Eudocimus (probably Ecdicus of Xen. *Hell.* 4.8.20), and Philodocus.

activities opened the door to renewed diplomatic relationships with Athens.[51] The next phase of Athenian involvement in Ionia came in 390, when Thrasybulus began again to extend Athenian imperial and economic power.[52] The primary focus of Thrasybulus' expedition, and the aim of Athenian imperialism, was securing the grain route from the Black Sea, but Diodorus explicitly says that his expedition sailed first to Ionia, where he collected tribute from the allies.[53] Thrasybulus' collections may well have been extortionate, and he died in an attack on Aspendus in 389 (Xen. *Hell.* 14.99.4), but evidence from soon thereafter indicates the partial restoration of financial systems from two decades before. An Athenian decree for Clazomenae from 387/6, for instance, praises the Clazomenaeans for both their past and their present devotion (πρόθυμός) to Athens and lays down the terms of the relationship between the two communities (*RO* 18 = *IG* II² 28).[54] According to the decree, Thrasybulus had established a new 5 percent harbor tax on Clazomenae (ll. 7–8), but also suggests that once he was no longer around to demand payment, they had stopped remitting it regularly (ll. 5–6). Now, though, representatives from Clazomenae wanted Athenian help. The decree goes on to discuss a renegade faction at Chyton from whom they had collected hostages (ll. 9–10),[55] issues of who had the authority to create and readmit exiles (ll. 12–13), the imposition of garrisons and governors (ll. 13–17), and the importation of grain (17–20).[56] The inscription included additional provisions that are too fragmentary

51. Hyland, *Persian Interventions*, 163. Evagoras was in revolt against Persia for much of the 380s; see Briant, *From Cyrus to Alexander*, 646–49, for a summary of Persian operations. In a survey of the diplomatic relationships between Cyprus and Persia in this period, Eugene A. Costa Jr., "Evagoras I and the Persians, ca. 411 to 391 B.C.," *Historia* 23, no. 1 (1974): 40–56, characterizes the rebellion as a war of Persian aggression.

52. Xenophon *Hell.* 4.8.25 and Diodorus 14.94.4 both record Thrasybulus' expedition. Seager, "Thrasybulus, Conon and Athenian Imperialism," 109; Perlman, "Athenian Democracy," 265–66. Strauss, "Thrasybulus and Conon," 39–40, notes that the Ionians swapped the statues of Lysander for ones of Conon.

53. Cawkwell, "Imperialism of Thrasybulus," 271; P. J. Stylianou, *Historical Commentary on Diodorus Siculus Book 15* (Oxford: Oxford University Press, 1999), 466–67. On the Black Sea grain trade, see Alfonso Moreno, *Feeding the Democracy: The Athenian Grain Supply in the Fifth and Fourth Centuries BC* (Oxford: Oxford University Press, 2007), 145–208.

54. I follow the Greek text of *AIO* 800, which includes fragment d published in Angelos P. Matthaiou, "Νέες Ἀττικές ἐπιγραφές," *Horos* 17–21 (2004–9): 14–15 no. 6 (l. 8–18 = fr. d) that confirms an earlier reading that the inscription refers to Athenian generals operating in the vicinity of Clazomenae. *IG* II² 28 includes στρατηγοὺς at l. 20, but not στρατηγ[ῶν at l. 11. The surviving relief includes depiction of two sheep, perhaps to visually represent the treaty partner Clazomenae that frequently depicted rams on its coins.

55. Stephen Ruzicka, "Clazomenae and Persian Foreign Policy, 387/6 B.C.," *Phoenix* 37, no. 2 (1983): 107. Chyton is probably the same as the Chryton mentioned by Aristotle (*Pol.* 5.1303b9); see Lene Rubinstein, "Ionia," in *An Inventory of Archaic and Classical Poleis*, ed. Mogens Herman Hansen and Thomas Heine Nielsen (Oxford: Oxford University Press, 2004), 1069–71; Victor Parker, "Ephoros (70)," *BNJ* F 78, commentary. Cf. Ephoros, *BNJ* 70 F 78; Strabo 14.1.36.

56. Stylianou, *Historical Commentary*, 467, argues that this clause means that the inscription

to make much of, but the surviving sections reveal a slate of local concerns that must have been common in Ionia after the events of the previous several decades. Certainly, an inscription found at Erythrae at roughly the same period addresses similar provisions that both reveal the continuing presence of local stasis and an assertion that the local community had the final authority to resolve their affairs (*RO* 17 = *SEG* xxvi 1282).[57] In return for Athenian support, the Ionian poleis had to submit to Athenian hegemony in the form of the harbor tax. Critically, both inscriptions make provisions *against* the assertion of Athenian power even as they reveal the presence of Athenian generals. Thus, they reveal the extent to which this new Athenian imperialism was contingent upon responding to local concerns.

It has been suggested that there was a great deal of goodwill in Athens toward Clazomenae at the time of the decree, particularly since it offered surety of autonomy in contrast to the treaty with Erythrae.[58] Noboru Sato, however, shows that the Athenian decision stemmed from two distinct factors. First, in Clazomenae itself the faction looking to side with Athens was firmly entrenched, having received hostages from the dissidents in Chyton, meaning that the Athenians did not fear that reconciliation would undermine the polis' alignment the way that the same policy in Erythrae might have.[59] Second, Athenian propaganda could play up the magnanimous support of Clazomenaean freedom, particularly to Athenians who wanted to continue an aggressive anti-Persian policy, while also allowing them to avoid getting entangled in an unwinnable war.[60] From the Ionian perspective, groups within both Erythrae and Clazomenae believed that they could use Athenian support to consolidate control of the poleis against factions supported by Persia and were willing to offer concessions to Athens in exchange. Certainly not everyone in Erythrae and Clazomenae favored an alliance with Athens, and it may be that the opposition parties in both poleis believed that Persia would support them, conjecture that leads to the suggestion that such an appeal to the Persian king caused him to include Clazomenae within his domain in the King's Peace (see below, "The Road to Peace").[61]

---

dates to before Antalcidas blockaded the Hellespont in late summer 487, while P. J. Rhodes and Robin Osborne, *Greek Historical Inscriptions, 404–323* (Oxford: Oxford University Press, 2007), 79, highlight that the Clazomenaeans purchased grain from local sources, though the listed cities may represent waypoints rather than origins, as Errietta M. A. Bissa, *Governmental Intervention in Foreign Trade in Archaic and Classical Greece* (Leiden: Brill, 2009), 203.

57. The inscription at Erythrae also includes provisions against handing the city over to the barbarian.

58. Kunihiro Aikyo, "Clazomene, Eritre ed Atene prima della Pace di Antalcida (385 A.C.)," *ACME* 41 (1988): 17–33.

59. Sato, "Athens, Persia, Clazomenae, Erythrae," 27–28.

60. Sato, "Athens, Persia, Clazomenae, Erythrae," 30–33.

61. Ferdinand Nolte, *Die historisch-politischen Voraussetzungen des Königsfriedens von 386 v. Chr.* (Bamberg: Universität Frankfurt am Main, 1923), 7–8. However, there is no evidence for

The Road to Peace

The honors visited upon Conon and the apparent restoration of Athenian power mask the larger consequence of the Cnidus campaign: that is, the restoration of Persian hegemony in Ionia. Sometime between 391 and 388 Miletus and Myus submitted a dispute over land in the Maeander valley to the satrap Struthas (*RO* 16 = *I.Priene* 458). The outcome of the arbitration was inscribed on a stele in Miletus.

Two fragments from the inscription survive. The upper fragment contains substantial lacunae along the left side, but the surviving text indicates the location of the disputed territory (l. 5) and the involvement of the Persian king and Struthas (ll. 9–10),[62] and that a certain group of people assembled (l. 11). Rhodes and Osborne accept the reconstruction of line 11, where about twenty letters are missing as ὅπ[ως οἱ τῶν Ἰώνων δικασταὶ συ]νελθό[ν]-[τες], translating it "so that the Ionians' jurors may assemble."[63] Their reading is strengthened by the lower fragment, which includes a list of jurors from Erythrae, Chios, Clazomenae, Lebedus, and Ephesus. Rhodes and Osborne plausibly speculate that the names of the jurors from Phocaea, Teos, Colophon, Samos, and Priene fall into a lacuna between the two fragments. Their list includes the entirety of the dodecapolis listed by Herodotus, excepting only the disputants (1.142), but it is equally plausible that the list also included Smyrna, or, conversely, that one or more of the poleis did not send jurors, and thus "Ionian" is used as a general description rather than a specific group.[64] In principle, though, I agree that Struthas used the member poleis of the Panionion as arbitrators, thus following the Persian precedent set by Artaphernes (Hdt. 6.42).[65] Before the jurors heard the case, the Myesians dropped the suit, a fact the Milesians submitted as evidence (ll. 37–40).

---

regime change after the treaty and there was a difference between a small polis like Clazomenae and the larger Chios and Samos.

62. The reconstructed name Στ]ρούσης, is identified with Στρούθας at Xen. *Hell.* 4.8.17–19 and Diod. 14.99.1–3.

63. *Greek Historical Inscriptions*, 70–71.

64. Diodorus 15.49, lists nine poleis as members of the Ionian League; see Stylianou, *Historical Commentary*, 49. Thomas Lenschau, "Alexander der Grosse und Chios," *Klio* 33 (1940): 220–21, suggests that Diodorus excluded the island poleis Samos and Chios (one of whom sent jurors) and that he records the Panionia taking place at Ephesus because Priene did not properly exist this point. Priene was refounded in the fourth century; see Hornblower, *Mausolus*, 323–26; cf. Nancy Demand, "The Relocation of Priene Reconsidered," *Phoenix* 40, no. 1 (1986): 35–44, but since Xenophon (*Hell.* 3.2.17) mentions Priene by name during the Spartan campaigns there is no reason to assume that it had ceased to exist.

65. Briant, *From Cyrus to Alexander*, 495, says that Struthas' use of the other Ionian poleis confirms the quality of evidence in Herodotus. Cf. 646. For the interpretation that Struthas gave the arbitration to the Ionian League, see Frank Adcock and D. J. Mosley, *Diplomacy in Ancient Greece* (London: Thames and Hudson, 1975), 213; Luigi Piccirilli, *Gli arbitrati interstatali Greci: Dalle origini al 338 A.C.* (Pisa: Marlin, 1973), 158.

Despite its limitations, this inscription is a remarkable document. It is the only positive evidence for the Ionian poleis resolving a secular dispute as a collective group, albeit at the direction of the Persian satrap. It is for this reason that it is suggested that the Ionian League, supposedly defunct since the Persian Wars, had been revived at least by the 390s, perhaps as part of the Spartan intervention in the region (see Appendix 1). Yet there is no indication that the league took on a new political substance at this time. It is more likely that Struthas did not delegate the arbitration *to* the Ionian League but used membership in the *koinon* to choose which communities would send arbitrators. His actions also shared the responsibility for the decision among the other communities, thereby giving a veneer of regional agency while maintaining imperial control in Ionia—even before the creation of the King's Peace in 387.

A group of Spartans led by Antalcidas had been trying to bargain with Persia for an end of the hostilities in the Aegean since 392, and they had been willing to give up claim to the freedom of the Ionians to achieve that end (Xen. *Hell.* 4.8.12–15, Andoc. 3; Plut. *Ages.* 23.1–2).[66] At the same time, Athens continued its imperial pretensions in the region, which the Ionian poleis were willing to indulge so long as it meant that they kept their autonomy.[67] In 387/6 the warring parties agreed to the King's Peace, which formally recognized a distinction between the Ionian islands, which were to be autonomous, and the Anatolian littoral, which belonged to the Persian king (Xen. *Hell.* 5.1.25–31; Diod. 14.110.3).[68]

According to Xenophon, the King's Peace read (*Hell.* 5.1.31):[69]

> King Artaxerxes thinks it just that the poleis in Asia should belong to him, as well as Clazomenae and Cyprus among the islands, and that the other Greek poleis, both small and great, should be left independent, except Lemnos, Imbros, and Scyros; and these should belong, as of old, to

---

66. Hamilton, *Sparta's Bitter Victories*, 236–37; Lewis, *Sparta and Persia*, 144–45; Cartledge, *Agesilaos*, 194–95, 365–65; Jack Cargill, *The Second Athenian League: Empire or Free Alliance* (Berkeley: University of California Press, 1981), 7–8; James G. Devoto, "Agesilaus, Antalcidas, and the Failed Peace of 392/91 B.C.," *CPh* 81, no. 3 (1986): 191–202; Antony G. Keen, "A 'Confused' Passage of Philochoros (F 149a) and the Peace of 392/1 B.C.," *Historia* 44, no. 1 (1995): 1–10; Simon Hornblower, "Persia," in *Cambridge Ancient History²*, vol. 6, ed. David M. Lewis, John Boardman, Simon Hornblower, and Martin Ostwald (Cambridge: Cambridge University Press, 1994), 74–75; Seager, "Corinthian War," 106–9.

67. Seager, "Thrasybulus, Conon and Athenian Imperialism," 105–6, 115.

68. Buckler, *Aegean Greece*, 169. This formulation emphasizes the difference between the two groups in terms of autonomy but had greater significance for the two "autonomous" poleis than those on the mainland.

69. Diod. 14.110.2–4 preserves a truncated account of the treaty that does not contradict Xenophon's version; see Dillery, *Xenophon*, 201. Xenophon translation adapted from C. L. Brownson in the Loeb edition.

the Athenians. I will make war upon whoever does not accept this peace in company with those who desire this arrangement, both by land and by sea, with ships and with money.

Ἀρταξέρξης βασιλεὺς νομίζει δίκαιον τὰς μὲν ἐν τῇ Ἀσίᾳ πόλεις ἑαυτοῦ εἶναι καὶ τῶν νήσων Κλαζομενὰς καὶ Κύπρον, τὰς δὲ ἄλλας Ἑλληνίδας πόλεις καὶ μικρὰς καὶ μεγάλας αὐτονόμους ἀφεῖναι πλὴν Λήμνου καὶ Ἴμρου καὶ Σκύρου: ταύτας δὲ ὥσπερ τὸ ἀρχαῖον εἶναι Ἀθηναίων. ὁπότεροι δὲ ταύτην τὴν εἰρήνην μὴ δέχονται, τούτοις ἐγὼ πολεμήσω μετὰ τῶν ταῦτα βουλομένων καὶ πεζῇ καὶ κατὰ θάλατταν καὶ ναυσὶ καὶ χρήμασιν.

Using the traditional language of benevolent imperialism, Artaxerxes declared his authority over the Aegean. As Hyland has recently argued, the King's Peace was not a bilateral treaty between equals, but one in which the king delegated authority over the Aegean to Sparta and made few concessions to Athens.[70] The inclusion of Clazomenae among the king's possessions stands out in the extant text of the treaty because this small Ionian polis situated on an island close by the coast is paired with the large island of Cyprus as exceptions to the rule that the islands would remain autonomous. Stephen Ruzicka offers the most thorough assessment, arguing that "Clazomenae naturally and necessarily accompanied the claim to Cyprus" because the Gulf of Smyrna was an essential staging ground for operations against the larger island.[71] Athenian support for Evagoras on Cyprus in the early 380s that coincided with imperialism in the Gulf of Smyrna revealed the potential for meddling in Persian affairs, even as they acknowledged the king's rights on the mainland (e.g., *RO* 18 = *IG* II^2 28, l. 25).[72] Ruzicka overstates the Athenian threat to Persian suzerainty in Ionia, but he makes an important point, that the inclusion of both islands stood as a clear warning to the Athenians about how far the king's power extended.

The King's Peace formally divided Ionia, drawing a line between Clazomenae and the mainland cities on one side and Chios and Samos on the other. Poleis on the mainland, including Ephesus and Miletus, formally became Persian subjects; Chios and Samos, in contrast, received autonomy, extracted from their preexisting relationships with Athens and Sparta and protected by the general peace (*koine eirene*).[73] This arrangement was one that Sparta, Athens,

---

70. Hyland, *Persian Interventions*, 165–66.

71. Ruzicka, "Clazomenae and Persian Foreign Policy," 108.

72. Rhodes and Osborne, *Greek Historical Inscriptions*, 79–80; T. T. B. Ryder, *Koine Eirene: General Peace and Local Independence in Ancient Greece* (Oxford: Oxford University Press, 1965), 34.

73. The description of autonomy as a privilege granted by the king rather than a simple right was not itself an innovation, but a development from the later part of the Peloponnesian War. On

and Thebes wielded like a bludgeon against each other, by the grace of the Persian king, but these wrangles had limited impact on the eastern Aegean. Artaxerxes had a strategic motivation to break the Athenian sway over Clazomenae, but Chios and Samos stood as testaments to the Persian resolve to uphold Greek autonomy, even though they too had been conquered by Persia in the Archaic period. The statuses of Chian and Samian territories on the continent is unknown, but they were likely held in arrangements that acknowledged Persian suzerainty through taxes even as the owners had citizenship within an autonomous polis.[74]

Thus, the stage was set for the next half century in Ionia. The Spartans, erstwhile allies of the Ionians, could be accused of abandoning the Greeks of Asia, even if this allegation was a rhetorical trope more than a political reality. With the King's Peace still in effect three decades later in 354/3, an inscription testifies to an Erythraean dedication of a gold crown on the Athenian Acropolis (*IG* II² 1437, l. 12). Even more tellingly, there continued a lively trans-Aegean intellectual community that freely crossed the imaginary line drawn by the King's Peace. Kings and dynasts around the Aegean, including the Hecatomnids of Caria and the Argeads in Macedonia, patronized Greek intellectuals, and Ionian elites continued to frequent Athens for education. On one occasion, Heraclides of Pontus made the trip from Athens to Colophon to acquire works by the poet Antimachus unavailable in Athens.[75] The complete picture is in this way disjointed. Athenian authors, and particularly Isocrates and Demosthenes, place great rhetorical stock on the political landscape of the Aegean, but the King's Peace did not radically alter the situation in Ionia.[76]

---

the *koine eirene* see Martin Jehne, *Koine Eirene: Untersuchungen zu den Befriedungs- und Stabilisierungsbemühungen in der griechischen Poliswelt des 4. Jahrhunderts v. Chrs.* (Stuttgart: Franz Steiner Verlag, 1994), 31, 53, 99–100; K. Moritani, "*Koine Eirene*: Control, Peace, and *Autonomia* in Fourth-Century Greece," in *Forms of Control and Subordination in Antiquity*, ed. T. Yuge and M. Doi (Leiden: Brill, 1988), 574; Julia Wilker, "War and Peace at the Beginning of the Fourth Century: The Emergence of the *Koine Eirene*," in *Maintaining Peace and Interstate Stability in Archaic and Classical Greece*, ed. Julia Wilker (Mainz: Verlag Antike, 2012), 93, 106. Cf. Polly Low, "Peace, Common Peace, and War in Mid-Fourth-Century Greece," in *Maintaining Peace and Interstate Stability in Archaic and Classical Greece*, ed. Julia Wilker (Mainz: Verlag Antike, 2012), 118–34.

74. It is also likely, albeit impossible to prove, that the treaty had additional clauses that addressed such unresolved issues; see George L. Cawkwell, "The Foundation of the Second Athenian Confederacy," *CQ²* 23, no. 1 (1973): 52; Pierre Debord, *L'Asie Mineure au IVᵉ siècle (412–323 a.C.)* (Pessac: Ausonius Éditions, 1999), 278–79; Dillery, *Xenophon*, 201; Hornblower, "Persia," 80; Seager, "Corinthian War," 117–19; Ryder, *Koine Eirene*, 27–36.

75. Victor J. Matthews, *Antimachus of Colophon: Text and Commentary* (Leiden: Brill, 1996), T 4; Eckart Schütrumpf, ed., *Heraclides of Pontus: Texts and Translations* (New Brunswick, NJ: Rutgers University Press, 2008), F 8.

76. On these Athenian discourses about Ionia, see Joshua P. Nudell, "'Who Cares about the Greeks Living in Asia?': Ionia and Attic Orators in the Fourth Century," *CJ* 114, no. 1 (2018): 163–90.

CHAPTER 6

❦

A Region Divided

386–336

The wars of the 390s ended with a whimper in Ionia. After Spartan hegemony ebbed back toward the Peloponnese, Ionian political establishments looked once more to Athens for support. The result was a piecemeal restoration of Athenian economic hegemony over Clazomenae, Erythrae, and other poleis in northern Ionia in the early 380s. Even so, Persia maintained political control, as demonstrated by the appeal to Struthas to mediate between Miletus and Myus (see Chapter 5). The King's Peace of 386, generally heralded as a triumph for the king, established new ground rules for political activity. The treaty stipulated that the mainland, including those mainland territories of Chios and Samos, belonged to Persia, but mandated the end to all other political arrangements in the Aegean under the banner of protecting autonomy. The half century that followed is commonly regarded as the darkness before the dawn in the eastern Aegean. With the Persian Empire decaying and the Greek poleis exhausted from decades of war, the fourth century was seen as a nadir in Ionia that would only pick up again with the conquests of Alexander the Great.

This characterization is misleading. The King's Peace did constrain Ionian activity, but it did not mark as substantial a sea-change as is sometimes thought. Persian satraps continued to respond to local pressures in Ionia, and the Ionian poleis like Chios continued to find ways to work around the new restrictions. The years that followed the King's Peace were turbulent, with the Athenian conquest of Samos and Ionia becoming engulfed by the Satrap's Revolt, but it also saw the first phases of revitalization. Regional competition continued with hardly an interruption, but, unlike in European Greece, where new forms of regional cooperation also emerged, nothing of the sort took place in Ionia.

109

Chios and the Second Naval Confederacy

Chios had a long history of alliance with Athens, punctuated by a period of extreme hostility. It had been one of the few Delian League states to continue providing ships until the outbreak of the Ionian War in 412 and had been an Athenian ally again in the Corinthian War after 394. The King's Peace formally ended the second period of alliance in 386, but the separation lasted just two years. In 384 Chios and Athens ratified a defensive alliance that reaffirmed Chian autonomy (*RO* 20 = *IG* II² 34, ll. 19–20) and created a mutual defense pact (ll. 25–29) to last in perpetuity (l. 35).[1] This treaty between Chios and Athens was constructed to exist in the new world of the King's Peace, but it owed its creation to the earlier relationships between the two communities. The inscription concludes with a list of four members from the Chian delegation, Bryon, Apelles, Theocritus, and Archelaus (ll. 42–43).[2] Bryon and Theocritus belonged to a cadre of influential Chians who had collaborated and studied with Isocrates when he established his school on the island in 393 ([Plut.] *Mor.* 837C), which indicates a continuity of the political regime supported by Athens from the 390s.[3] Yet the fact that a treaty of this sort might have been construed as contravening the new peace—hence the careful language explaining that it *did not* do so (ll. 21–23)—makes it is necessary to ask whether something happened in 385/4 to prompt an embassy to Athens.

Diodorus Siculus claims that the Athenians sent embassies to Chios and other cities subject to Sparta, encouraging them to join a cause of liberty (15.28.1–3), but his account is confused. The inclusion of Byzantium and other Greek poleis clearly indicates that Diodorus describes the foundation of the Second Naval Confederacy in 379, but those poleis, including Chios, were not Spartan subjects.[4] There is no reason to doubt that there was Athenian initiative behind the foundation of the Second Naval Confederacy, but Diodorus' source skews heavily toward an anti-Spartan agenda and thus should be accepted

---

1. A similar alliance appears in the fragmentary *IG* II² 35 without the Athenian partner, which, if it refers to the same treaty, may be a copy or a reaffirmation several years later.

2. There is a lacuna in the inscription, meaning that the names Apelles and Theocritus are restored.

3. Slobodan Dušanić, "Isocrates, the Chian Intellectuals, and the Political Context of the *Euthydemus*," *JHS* 119 (1999): 7; Egidia Occhipinti, "Political Conflicts in Chios between the End of the 5th and the First Half of the 4th Century B.C.," *AHB* 24 (2010): 33–35. On this school, see Joseph Roisman and Ian Worthington, *Lives of the Attic Orators: Texts from Pseudo-Plutarch, Photius and the Suda* (Oxford: Oxford University Press, 2015), 150–51.

4. P. J. Stylianou, *Historical Commentary on Diodorus Siculus Book 15* (Oxford: Oxford University Press, 1999), 252. Cf. George L. Cawkwell, "The Foundation of the Second Athenian Confederacy," *CQ*² 23, no. 1 (1973): 60.

warily when considering the motivations of the new members, let alone Chios in 384.[5]

Another possible explanation is the threat of war in the eastern Aegean. In his *Panegyricus* of 380, Isocrates warned of the Persian threat to Chios along with Samos and Rhodes should they strengthen the garrisons in the coastal poleis (4.163).[6] Slobodan Dušanić, however, has highlighted the inconsistencies behind this declaration. While Isocrates warns about the Persian threat, he also obscures a more complicated reality. The most pressing threat to Chios came in the person of Glos, a rebel Persian admiral with Spartan support who may have been called "Persian" (Diod. 15.9.5).[7] Moreover, if Isocrates is correct that there was a Persian military buildup in mainland Ionia in the second half of the 380s, it was part of the campaign against Glos and his successor Tachus, rather than one designed to threaten Chios.[8] Dušanić's interpretation is attractive because he supplies a clear and present danger that the Chians reacted to and explains the lengthy duration of the Persian military presence in Ionia. Further, he reconciles the statement from Isocrates that Chios would join Persia with Diodorus' claim that the Chians wished to rebel from Sparta and clears the Persians of any violation of the peace. There is just one difficulty: the dates.

Dušanić argues that the fighting in Cyprus, which began in 386/5, lasted no more than two years, and that it was during that time that Tiribazus was arrested and Glos led his rebellion. This argument generally accepts the Diodoran chronology and places Glos' revolt early in 384,[9] but it runs counter to the consensus of modern scholarship, which pushes the end of the Cyprian War and Glos' revolt into the last years of the 380s, sometimes as late as 380/79 and

5. Cinzia Bearzot, "L'Impero del Mare come Egemonia subaltern nel IV secolo (Diodoro, Libri XIV–XV)," *Aevum* 89 (2015): 83–91, argues that the historiographical tradition Diodorus uses in this section leans Boeotian, based on its characterization of maritime and terrestrial hegemony.

6. I. A. F. Bruce, "The Alliance between Athens and Chios in 384 B.C.," *Phoenix* 19, no. 4 (1965): 284.

7. Slobodan Dušanić, "The Attic-Chian Alliance ('IG' II² 34) and the 'Troubles in Greece' of the Late 380's BC," *ZPE* 133 (2000): 22–28. Glos was probably an Egyptian who had inherited from his father estates in Ionia and married the daughter of the Persian satrap Tiribazus, whose patronage had helped secure his position in the campaign against Evagoras. After Tiribazus was arrested, Glos took the soldiers under his command and tried to set himself up as an independent dynast in western Anatolia. Cf. Simon Hornblower, "Persia," in *Cambridge Ancient History²*, vol. 6, ed. David M. Lewis, John Boardman, Simon Hornblower, and Martin Ostwald (Cambridge: Cambridge University Press, 1994), 81–82; Stephen Ruzicka, "Glos, Son of Tamos, and the End of the Cypriot War," *Historia* 48, no. 1 (1999): 23–43. Stylianou, *Historical Commentary*, 161, suggests that he was Carian. Dušanić argues that that sudden reversal of Spartan policy was the result of internal divisions and a party in Sparta led by Agesilaus that had not been in favor of the peace to begin with, which also corresponds with Diod. 15.5.2, who says that the Spartans began encouraging stasis in poleis throughout Greece in the latter half of the 380s; see Stylianou, 168–74.

8. Dušanić, "The Attic-Chian Alliance," 27.

9. Dušanić, "The Attic-Chian Alliance," 28–29.

thus after the treaty between Athens and Chios.[10] Diodorus places two years of fighting in Cyprus in between the battle of Citium, in which Glos played a critical role, and when Evagoras was bottled up in Salamis, with other events that took place between 386 and 384. But Evagoras had begun his revolt in c.390 and did not finally surrender until 380, so some scholars have moved the date of Citium to 383 to align the two years of fighting attested by Ephorus (by way of Diodorus) with the two years immediately preceding Evagoras' surrender.[11] Gordon Shrimpton, like Dušanić, supports the Diodoran chronology and argues that the war in Cyprus had effectively ended in 384. However, he maintains that Evagoras negotiated a conditional surrender with Orontes and the two men conspired to have Glos' father-in-law Tiribazus arrested that year, which both prompted Glos' rebellion and bought Evagoras several years of a cold war in which to negotiate for a lenient surrender with Artaxerxes.[12] Thus Shrimpton dates Glos' rebellion late in 384 or 383, still postdating the new Chian-Attic alliance.

Glos did threaten Chios in the late 380s before he was assassinated in 383/2 (Diod. 15.18.1),[13] but, even if his revolt was underway in 384, the Chian-Attic alliance was not a response to that specific threat. The eastern Aegean in the 380s was particularly volatile. There had been a Persian civil war within recent memory, there were multiple ambitious satraps with various levels of independence from Persia conniving against one another, and Evagoras schemed against Persia on Cyprus. In other words, as soon as the peace was established the threat of war emerged. Likewise, the Spartan imperialist party centered on Agesilaus probably began to fan the flames of existing domestic tensions as early as 386/5 (Diod. 15.5.2), before Glos' revolt, and could equally have caused the Chians to seek an alliance with Athens. Once Glos went into revolt, the

---

10. See, for instance, Pierre Briant, *From Cyrus to Alexander: A History of the Persian Empire*, trans. Peter T. Daniels (Winona Lake, IN: Eisenbrauns, 2002), 652–53; Ruzicka, "Glos," 40. T. T. B. Ryder, "Spartan Relations with Persia after the King's Peace: A Strange Story in Diodorus 15.9," *CQ*[2] 13, no. 1 (1963): 105–9, argues that a volte-face in the Spartan relationship with Persia so soon after 386 is unlikely, while the evidence is stronger for that change by 380. Michael J. Osborne, "Orontes," *Historia* 22, no. 4 (1973): 522–23, argues that Diodorus collapses events that took place over the course of ten years into his narrative for two of those years.

11. Briant, *From Cyrus to Alexander*, 653; Ruzicka, "Glos," 23–43.

12. Gordon S. Shrimpton, "Persian Strategy against Egypt and the Date for the Battle of Citium," *Phoenix* 45, no. 1 (1991): 1–20. His suggestion also reconciles one of the contradictions in the sources highlighted by Osborne, "Orontes," 522–37, in that Theopompus says that Evagoras implicated Tiribazus, while Diodorus, probably following Ephorus, says it was Orobantes acting alone. Stylianou, *Historical Commentary*, 185, likewise dates Glos' rebellion to 383/2.

13. Diodorus' account of the end of Glos' rebellion ends abruptly with an aside about the dispute between Clazomenae and Cyme, probably because his source for this section, Ephorus, related the story about his native community losing to the tricky Ionians; see Stylianou, *Historical Commentary*, 208–9.

Chians would not have sought an alliance because they saw a war brewing, but because a war was upon them. The circumstances were therefore ripe for Chios to look for an alliance in 384, without needing to tie the cause to the appearance of Glos.

The wording of the Attic-Chian alliance of 384 makes it clear that its composers intended to abide by the terms of the King's Peace (*RO* 20 = *IG* II² 34, ll. 7–22).[14] There are parallels between this treaty and the alliance between Athens and Corcyra in 433 (Thuc. 1.44) that incited conflict even though it did not violate the letter of the Thirty Years Peace, and it is tempting to see an instance of Athenian imperial policy repeating itself. However, the Chians declare in the treaty that "they have come offering good things to the people of Athens and to all of Greece and to the king; be it decreed by the people" (καὶ ἥκοσιν ἀγαθὰ [ἐπαγγελλόμενοι τῶ]|ι δήμωι τῶι Ἀθηνα[ίων καὶ ἁπάσηι τῆι Ἑ]|λλάδι καὶ βασιλεῖ, [ἐψηφίσθαι τῶι δ]ήμ|ωι, *RO* 20 = *IG* II² 34, ll. 13–16).[15] They, at least, had a particular interest in making sure that the treaty did not antagonize Persia. Further, both parties treated 386 as a watershed, so while the preexisting relationship between Chios and Athens helped lead to the treaty in 384, they meticulously avoided that justification for the alliance in the treaty's language.[16] Reverting to an earlier alliance would have violated the peace by retying the knot of animosities that had drawn Greece into the Corinthian War and risked Persian retaliation. Isocrates may have claimed, in an Orwellian moment, that Chios and Athens had never not been allies (14.27–28), but the sentiment was, predictably, mere rhetoric.

The Attic-Chian alliance of 384 established the diplomatic framework for the Second Athenian League. In 378, Chios and Byzantium, along with Rhodes and the Lesbian poleis Methymna and Mytilene, renewed their treaties with Athens under the framework of the new confederacy (Diod. 15.30.2).[17] A stele

---

14. P. J. Rhodes and Robin Osborne, *Greek Historical Inscriptions, 404–323* (Oxford: Oxford University Press, 2007), 86; cf. Bruce, "Alliance between Athens and Chios," 283; Dušanić, "The Attic-Chian Alliance," 22; Ryder, "Spartan Relations with Persia," 49, for how the treaty was designed specifically to abide by the terms of the peace.

15. Trans. *RO* 20.

16. Dušanić, "The Attic-Chian Alliance," 25–26, argues that the Athenian leaders were under immense pressure from "hoi polloi" to help Chios, in part stemming from "the tradition about the Chian-Attic kinship," such as appears in Plato's *Euthydemus* (302 B–D), but this is speculative. On the manipulation of kinship myths for political ends, see Naoíse Mac Sweeney, *Foundation Myths and Politics in Ancient Ionia* (Cambridge: Cambridge University Press, 2013), 161; Lee Patterson, *Kinship Myth in Ancient Greece* (Austin: University of Texas Press: 2010), 5–6; S. Perlman, "The Historical Example, Its Use and Importance as Political Propaganda in the Attic Orators," *SH* 7 (1961): 162.

17. Cawkwell, "Foundation," 50–51; Stylianou, *Historical Commentary*, 272–78; Jack Cargill, *The Second Athenian League: Empire or Free Alliance* (Berkeley: University of California Press, 1981), 51–52.

from the Athenian agora (*RO* 22 = *IG* I² 43) establishing the prospectus for the new league states that the terms would be the same for new allies as they were for Chios, in a callback to the treaty in 384 (μήτε φρορὰν εἰσδεχομένωι μήτε ἄρχοντα ὑποδεχομένωι μήτε φόρον φέροντι, ἐπὶ δὲ τοῖς αὐτοῖς ἐφ᾽ οἷσπερ Χῖοι, ll. 21–24).[18] Appropriately, Chios appears at the head of the list of member states (l. 79; cf. Diod. 15.28.3). Moreover, in the same way that the Attic-Chian alliance had explicitly described how it did not violate the King's Peace, the new confederacy professed to be defensive in nature and in accordance with the peace (ll. 9–15):[19]

> So that the Spartans shall allow the Greeks to be free and autonomous, and to live in their own territory in security, [[and so that the peace and friendship sworn by the Greeks and the king in accordance with the agreements may be in force and endure,]] be it decreed by the people.

> ὅπως ἂν Λακεδ[αιμό]νιοι ἐῶσι τὸς Ἕλλη-
> νας ἐλευθέ[ρ]ος [καὶ] αὐτονόμος ἡσυχίαν
> ἄγειν, τὴ[ν χώραν] ἔχοντας ἐμ βεβαίωι τὴ-
> [ν ἑαυτῶν πᾶσαν, [[κα]ὶ [ὅπ]ω[ς κ]υ[ρ]ία ἦι κ[α]ὶ δι-
> [αμένηι ἥ τε εἰρήνη καὶ ἡ φιλία ἣν ὤμοσ]α-
> [ν οἱ Ἕλληνες] καὶ [βα]σιλεὺς κατὰ τὰ[ς σ]υν-
> [θήκας]], ἐψηφί]σθαι τῶι δήμωι

The decree is especially lacunose, but there is general agreement about the thrust of the text. In the early years of its existence, the confederacy was guided by the

---

18. The fragmentary Aristoteles Decree (*IG* II² 43) is not without controversy, because the inscription shows evidence that the membership roll evolved over time; see, e.g., Christopher A. Baron, "The Aristoteles Decree and the Expansion of the Second Athenian League," *Hesperia* 75, no. 3 (2006): 379–95. Cf. Sviatoslav Dmitriev, *The Greek Slogan of Freedom and Early Roman Politics in Greece* (Oxford: Oxford University Press, 2011), 381–90; Martin Dreher, *Hegemon und Symmachoi: Untersuchen zum Zweiten Athenischen Seebund* (Berlin: de Gruyter, 1995), 110–41; C. M. Fauber, "Was Kerkyra a Member of the Second Athenian League?," *CQ²* 48, no. 1 (1998), 110–16; Brian Rutishauser, *Athens and the Cyclades: Economic Strategies, 510–314 BC* (Oxford: Oxford University Press, 2012), 158–70; A. G. Woodhead, "IG II² 43 and Jason of Pherae," *AJA* 61, no. 4 (1957): 367–73; A. G. Woodhead, "Chabrias, Timotheus, and the Aegean Allies, 375–373 B.C.," *Phoenix* 16, no. 4 (1962): 258–66.

19. Trans. *RO* 22. There is a controversy over the second declaration of purpose in the Aristoteles Decree, which may have been later erased. In the sense that it followed the precedent of the Attic-Chian alliance, I accept this reconstruction. On the difficulties of this decree, see Jack Cargill, "Hegemony Not Empire: The Second Athenian League," *AncW* 5, nos. 3–4 (1982): 91–102; Jack Cargill, "The Decree of Aristoteles: Some Epigraphical Details," *AncW* 27, no. 1 (1996): 39–51; Rhodes and Osborne, *Greek Historical Inscriptions*, 100–101; cf. Sheila L. Ager, "4th Century Thera and the Second Athenian Sea League," *AncW* 32, no. 1 (2001): 99–119. Hornblower, "Persia," 83, notes the decree threatens anyone who attacked a league member, implying that the Persian king could indeed violate the treaty.

synedrion chaired by one of the delegates.[20] The *synedrion* met in Athens, but the Athenians stood apart from it, holding no vote. In principle, the confederacy was a voluntary association to protest high-handed Spartan actions such as garrisons in Boeotia (e.g., Xen. *Hell.* 5.4.10) and Sphodrias' raid on the Pireaeus in 378 (Xen. *Hell.* 5.4.20; Diod. 15.29.5–6).[21] The council had legal protections, and the Athenians likely swore to abide by the decisions of the *koinon*,[22] but a long Athenian shadow lay over the league. Not only did the *synedrion* meet in Athens, but it was also created by a decree of the Athenian Assembly.[23] The league also established a *syntaxis* (contribution) required of the allies, changing the term from *phoros* to avoid associations with the fifth-century empire.[24] The league also afforded certain protections, particularly against piracy. Everyone outside this racket was still covered by the King's Peace in theory, but their security depended on the willingness and ability of the Persian king and his proxies in the Aegean to enforce the agreement. In practice, this was a paper shield, as the Samians would discover in 366.

The Destruction of Samos?

Samos never joined the new Athenian alliance. As early as Isocrates' *Panegyricus* in 380, there was a possible estrangement between the two, since Isocrates groups Samos with Chios and Rhodes as communities with the potential for

---

20. Silvio Accame, *La lega Ateniese del secolo IV a.C.* (Rome: Angelo Signorelli, 1941), 111–14; George L. Cawkwell, "Notes on the Failure of the Second Athenian Confederacy," *JHS* 101 (1981): 46–47; Cargill, *Second Athenian League*, 115–28.

21. On the Spartan garrisons in Boeotia, see John M. Wickersham, "Spartan Garrisons in Boeotia 382–379/8 B.C.," *Historia* 56, no. 2 (2007): 243–46, with bibliography. There is a debate whether the foundation of the confederacy belongs before the raid, as recorded by Diodorus and argued by Cawkwell, "Foundation," 56–60 and Stylianou, *Historical Commentary*, 261–65, or after the raid, as argued by Robert Morstein Kallet-Marx, "Athens, Thebes, and the Foundation of the Second Athenian League," *CA* 4, no. 2 (1985): 127–51, and D. G. Rice, "Xenophon, Diodorus and the Year 379/8 B.C.," *YCS* 24 (1975): 112. I prefer to follow Victor Parker, "Sphodrias' Raid and the Liberation of Thebes: A Study of Ephorus and Xenophon," *Hermes* 135, no. 1 (2007): 13 n. 1 in seeing the foundation of the league as a process rather than a response to an event, though I believe the main framework of the confederacy predates the raid, whereas he argues it follows.

22. Stylianou, *Historical Commentary*, 254. Accame, *La lega Ateniese*, 34–35, believes that *IG* II² 35, possibly a copy of *IG* II² 34, should be read as an updated treaty to accommodate the new confederacy. Cf. Cargill, *Second Athenian League*, 52.

23. Stylianou, *Historical Commentary*, 256–57.

24. Rutishauser, *Athens and the Cyclades*, 168–69, notes the issues in interpreting the *syntaxis*, including that there is contradictory evidence for who set the rates, the *synedrion* or the Athenian *ecclesia*, and that its existence is not securely dated before 371, though Dreher, *Hegemon und Symmachoi*, 41–89, concludes that it was in place from the inception. On the *syntaxis*, see Patrice Brun, *Eisphora-Syntaxis-Stratiotika: Recherches sur les finances militaires d'Athènes au IVe siècle av. J.-C.* (Paris: Les Belles Lettres, 1983), 74–142, with 100–105 on how the allies received the shift. Most of the evidence for the *syntaxis* postdates Chios' departure from the league, so I will not explore the issue in depth here.

Persian sympathies (4.163). Isocrates' inclusion of Chios, an ally for multiple years at the time of publication, underscores the potential threat to Athenian interests in the eastern Aegean and might imply otherwise unattested domestic tensions on the island. Rhodes, moreover, was a founding member of the new Athenian confederacy. It might be expected that Samos, an Athenian ally to the bitter end of the Peloponnesian War, might follow suit, but nothing of the sort happened.

Sometime in the early 360s, Tigranes, a Persian *hyparch*, fulfilled Isocrates' prophecy by establishing a garrison on Samos. The circumstances of this garrison, which Athenian sources present as a violation of the King's Peace (e.g., Dem. 15.9), are unknown. The most probable suggestion is that Tigranes was a deputy of Mausolus, the satrap of Caria, and that the garrison was an early instance of his imperial ambition.[25] It is also possible that Tigranes worked for another satrap who installed the garrison in response to either Mausolus' aggression or the overtures of Ariobarzanes, a satrap then in revolt. The picture changes somewhat when considering the Samians. The competing satrapal agendas combined with the lack of evidence for a regime change in support of exiles makes it likely that this garrison was invited rather than imposed. Nevertheless, in 366, Timotheus led an Athenian fleet to the eastern Aegean. Nominally he was there to support Ariobarzanes, the satrap of Hellespontine Phyrgia, but in fact he landed on Samos and captured it after a ten-month siege (Isoc. 14.111; [Arist.] *Oec.* 2.1350b; cf. Polyaenus 3.10.9–10).[26]

Timotheus' capture of Samos in 366/5 had long-lasting effects on Ionia. Within a year, the Athenians dissolved the Samian demos and established the first-wave cleruchies, placing an estimated six thousand to twelve thousand new residents on the island over the next decade (Philochorus, *BNJ* 328 F 154; Strabo 14.1.18).[27] Because of a comment by the contemporary philosopher

25. Graham Shipley, *A History of Samos, 800–188 BC* (Oxford: Oxford University Press, 1987), 137; Simon Hornblower, *Mausolus* (Oxford: Oxford University Press, 1982), 198–99, who offers as evidence Mausolan coins on Samos. John Buckler, *Aegean Greece in the Fourth Century BC* (Leiden: Brill, 2003), 353, suggests that Tigranes acted on orders from Autophradates, whom Diodorus names as satrap of Lydia (15.90).

26. Lisa Kallet, "Iphikrates, Timotheos, and Athens, 371–360 B.C.," *GRBS* 24, no. 3 (1983): 246. There is also evidence of a skirmish near Chios during the siege (Isaeus 6.27), which came about after Timotheus dispatched ships to Erythrae. On the date of the skirmish, see Eugene Schweigert, "The Athenian Cleruchy on Samos," *AJPh* 61, no. 2 (1940): 198. On Timotheus' ambitions, see Stephen Ruzicka, *Politics of a Persian Dynasty: The Hecatomnids in the Fourth Century* (Norman: University of Oklahoma Press, 1992), 73–74.

27. Jack Cargill, "*IG* II² 1 and the Athenian Kleruchy on Samos," *GRBS* 23, no. 4 (1983): particularly 326–29. Cargill advances a more sophisticated position from G. T. Griffith, "Athens in the Fourth Century," in *Imperialism in the Ancient World*, ed. P. D. A. Garnsey and C. R. Whittaker (Cambridge: Cambridge University Press, 1978), 139–40, who imagines a bifurcated state on Samos with the Samian demos initially enjoying a symbiotic relationship with Athens, only to end

Heraclides Ponticus that Aristotle quoted in the *Samian Politeia* (οἱ δὲ ἐλθόντες πάντας ἐξέβαλον, Arist. F. 611.35 Rose), a common assumption is that these cleruchs displaced the entire population of Samos.[28] In time, this action came to be regarded as a grave injustice committed by Athens, and inscriptions testify to individuals and poleis that gave aid to the exiles during this period, while the Athenians maintained that they liberated the island.[29] Before turning to the consequences, it is worth examining in more detail the circumstances of how this conquest came about. In capturing Samos, Timotheus violated the King's Peace but not the charter of the Second Naval Confederacy (Dem. 15.9).[30] Where the King's Peace had guaranteed protection for every polis, the Athenian treaty offered protection only to members of the confederacy (*RO* 22 = *IG* I² 43; Xen. *Hell.* 6.5.2).[31] The lack of sources for the event complicates any attempt at reconstruction in that it requires parsing convoluted historical memory that offers little plausible causality. Most scholars interpret the expedition as naked imperialism against a polis outside of the league, rightfully mistrusting Athenian protestations of Panhellenic altruism.[32] Nevertheless, there is another interpretation that considers the local conditions on Samos.

---

up oppressed or in exile after 352. There is no evidence of a Samian polis after 365 until Alexander's decision in 324/3. Shipley, *Samos*, 141–42, suggests many now-disenfranchised citizens retreated to the mountains and lived on the fringes of society. All scholars accept that *some* of the cleruchs were ancestral Samians and that the exiled population centered on those who had resisted Athens. Thus Shipley, *Samos*, 140: "Only the ruling oligarchs had anything to fear." The differences of opinion come from where one sits on the sliding scale of the two extremes. The larger the ancestral Samian component, the smaller the number of exiles, and vice versa. Cf. Hornblower, *Mausolus*, 198–200; Shipley, *Samos*, 141–43; Raphael Sealey, "*IG* II² 1609 and the Transformation of the Athenian Sea-League," *Phoenix* 11, no. 3 (1957): 95–97, 108; Raphael Sealey, *Demosthenes and His Time* (Oxford: Oxford University Press, 1993), 106. The cleruchy is also attested by a partial list of settlers, *IG* II² 1952. Cf. *IG* II² 108; Isoc. 15.111–12; Dem 15.9; Nepos *Timotheus* 1.2.

28. Hornblower, *Mausolus*, 199, with n. 132; Shipley, *Samos*, 132–33, 141; and R. Zelnick-Abramovitz, "Settlers and Dispossessed in the Athenian Empire," *Mnemosyne*[4] 57, no. 3 (2004): 330, are rightly skeptical of the "total expulsion" from an island with the population of Samos. The quotation is exceedingly terse, and Rosalind Thomas, *Polis Histories, Collective Memories and the Greek World* (Cambridge: Cambridge University Press, 2019), 313, takes it to refer to a cleruchy in the fifth century. Cf. Diod. 18.8.7.

29. There were two competing cultural memories about Timotheus' conquest at work, with the anti-Athenian one winning out in part because it was a tool to reunify the polis after the return of the exiles in 323/2; see Joshua P. Nudell, "Remembering Injustice as the Perpetrator? Athenian Orators, Cultural Memory, and the Athenian Conquest of Samos," in *The Orators and Their Treatment of the Recent Past*, ed. Aggelos Kapellos (Berlin: de Gruyter, 2022), 447–63.

30. Pierre Debord, *L'Asie Mineure au IVᵉ siècle (412–323 a.C.)* (Pessac: Ausonius Éditions, 1999), 293; Hornblower, "Persia," 89.

31. Cargill, *Second Athenian League*, 12. It has been posited that the Athenian takeover of Samos was a response to the Theban naval construction at about the same time; see J. M. Cook, "Cnidian Peraea and Spartan Coins," *JHS* 81 (1961): 70 n. 81, and Hornblower, *Mausolus*, 198, but such an explanation reverses the causation.

32. This would have been in keeping with fifth-century practice except that the Athenians enrolled "liberated" poleis into the Delian League instead of dissolving the polis.

An Athenian Decree at the end of the Peloponnesian War granted Samians Athenian citizenship, which they reinscribed after the original stele was destroyed by the Thirty (RO 2 = IG I³ 127, ll.12–13; see Chapter 4). Further, Timotheus' family had long had close ties to Ionia. After a triumphant campaign in 394 his father, Conon, had received honorary statues at Erythrae (RO 8 = SIG³ 134), Ephesus, and Samos (Paus. 6.3.16) and had commissioned Isocrates to establish a new constitution on Chios ([Plut.] Mor. 837b), but a subsequent Spartan campaign had overturned the regime on Samos again (Xen. Hell. 4.8.23; Diod. 14.97.3–5; see Chapter 5). There is no further information on the Samian constitution, and Shipley believes that the expulsion of the Spartan decarchy might have still not put to rights the preceding decades of social upheaval. By 366/5, therefore, it is entirely plausible that Timotheus responded to a direct appeal from a group of Samians who benefited from the close ties to Athens and felt threatened by the presence of Tigranes. Instead of restoring Samos, though, subsequent Athenian actions created a hybrid community where ancestral Samians, some with Athenian citizenship, mingled with Athenians in the subordinate polis on Samos.³³ The transition created Samian exiles, and their numbers likely grew in step with the arrival of additional cleruchs, but an arrangement of the sort I just described helps explain why there is no evidence for the widespread consequences one might expect from the complete expulsion of a polis with the population of Samos.

Where does that leave the exiles, whom Hornblower describes as "Samians who had been put on the streets of Greece by Athens, [who] were walking mementoes to the power of Fortune, τύχη, no less than of the πλεονεξία, the Greed, of the Athenians"?³⁴ Shipley notes that the Samians did not form a community in exile in their mainland peraea, perhaps because most of the land no longer belonged to them.³⁵ Instead, the exiles dispersed, possibly settling as far away as Sicily.³⁶ Most probably took refuge in nearby cities, including Ery-

---

33. The new community on Samos appears in inscriptions as the "demos on Samos" (IG II² 1437, l. 20) or "the Athenian demos on Samos" (Syll.³ 276A–C). Strikingly, the weight of the crown dedicated at Delphi in Syll.³. 276A and C is given not in drachmae but in a combination of obols and darics (ll. 12–15)! On the naming conventions for the status of the community see Jack Cargill, Athenian Settlements of the Fourth Century B.C. (Leiden: Brill, 1995), 62, with n. 24. Some residents also maintained Athenian citizenship (e.g., Epicurus: Strabo 14.1.18; Diog. Laert. 10.1), but this need not have been universal.

34. Hornblower, Mausolus, 199.

35. Shipley, Samos, 155–56.

36. Robert B. Kebric, In the Shadow of Macedon, Duris of Samos (Wiesbaden: Franz Steiner, 1977), 4–5; Robert B. Kebric, "Duris of Samos: Early Ties with Sicily," AJA 79, no. 1 (1975): 89; Shipley, Samos, 163–64. According to Christian Habicht, "Samische Volksbeschlüsse der hellenistischen Zeit," MDAI(A) 72 (1957): 152–274, no. 23 is a decree from Heraclea for Duris' brother. There are multiple communities named "Heracleia," though. The one in Sicily is its usual identifica-

thrae and Miletus, which received decrees of thanks after the Samians recovered their island after 322 (see Chapter 8). The Samians might have received an outpouring of pan-Ionian generosity, but there is only evidence for aid from cities within Mausolus' sphere of influence, suggesting that they did so out at his behest. Timotheus had supported his rival Ariobarzanes, and the gesture cost Mausolus nothing. Exile and oppression by Athens were powerful stories to help forge a viable polis in the early Hellenistic period, but they give a misleading impression of what happened on Samos in 366/5.

The Satrap's Revolt

The Persian Empire was facing imminent doom in the late 360s and early 350s, at least according to Diodorus (15.90.3).[37] He claims that the entire Mediterranean coast from Anatolia to Egypt went into revolt, cutting off a full half of the annual tribute, and that the problems caused by the death of Artaxerxes II and the accession of Artaxerxes III in 358 compounded these crises (15.90.3–4, 93.1).[38] Diodorus' pronouncements of Persian weakness are greatly exaggerated. The empire remained structurally sound, though that fact was probably difficult to tell from Ionia on its fringes. There *was* a fracturing of royal control in Anatolia, troubles that Pierre Briant declares "had always been there in latent form."[39]

The so-called Great Satrap's Revolt erupted into open warfare in the early 360s. Far from an organized coalition of rebel satraps led by Orontes, Artaxerxes II confronted a series of local uprisings. Ariobarzanes, the satrap of Hellespontine Phrygia, may have quietly renounced his loyalty to Persia as early as the 370s, but he openly declared his revolt sometime before 366, and Datames, the satrap of Cappadocia, joined him.[40] Artaxerxes ordered the satrap of Lydia, Autophradates, and the Hecatomnid dynast Mausolus to defeat the rebels and, at this juncture, Orontes, a Persian possibly in disgrace for slandering Tiribazus in Cyprus in the 380s (assuming it is the same man), expanded his position in Mysia.[41] Diodorus implies that this was a spontaneous rebellion, but "revolt"

---

tion, but the Hellespont may be more probable.

37. On the contradictions in this passage, see Stylianou, *Historical Commentary*, 527–36.

38. Briant, *From Cyrus to Alexander*, 680–81; Matt Waters, *Ancient Persia: A Concise History* (Cambridge: Cambridge University Press, 2013), 192–93.

39. Briant, *From Cyrus to Alexander*, 656–75, 680–81; Debord, *L'Asie Mineure*, 302–66; Michael Weiskopf, *The So-Called "Great Satraps' Revolt," 366–360 BC: Concerning Local Instability in the Achaemenid Far West* (Wiesbaden: Franz Steiner, 1989), 94–99. Cf. Waters, *Ancient Persia*, 192–93.

40. Briant, *From Cyrus to Alexander*, 661–62.

41. Briant, *From Cyrus to Alexander*, 662; Simon Hornblower, "Asia Minor," in *Cambridge*

was endemic in Anatolia, where semiautonomous satraps and dynasts con-
tended with Greek poleis.[42] Indeed, Maria Brosius describes Persian diplomacy
within and beyond Persian territory as guided by "pragmatism and political
expediency."[43] Among the exaggerated number of regions in revolt listed by
Diodorus is Ionia (15.90.3–4), but this is a feature of the relevant satraps going
into revolt rather than any action taken by the Ionian poleis. When the Ionians
were ordered to pay tribute to a loyal satrap, they readily did so, and, since the
satrap was the representative of the king, the communities were not subject to
punishment.[44]

The Rising Power in the South: Caria and Ionia

Mainland Ionia was unambiguously part of the Achaemenid empire in the
360s, but administration of the region was split between the Autophradates,
the satrap at Sardis, and Mausolus of Caria. The two rivals undoubtedly both
recruited mercenaries from Ionia (Diod. 15.91.2–4). However, while rivalry
between satraps was nothing new, the fact that Mausolus was also the hereditary dynast over Caria, which had increasing exchange with Ionia in this
period, put him in a unique position to exert influence in ways not often seen
before. In this way, the Satrap's Revolt manifested as another competition over
Ionia. Mausolus played an ambiguous role in these events, first helping the loyal
Persian forces, and later withdrawing from the campaign, and then supporting
the Spartans, and Diodorus lists him among the enemies of Artaxerxes (Diod.
15.90.3). Similarly, it is possible that Mausolus withdrew from the campaign
because he needed to safeguard his own territory from Athenian attacks while
Timotheus besieged Samos.[45] The most probable explanation is that the Carian dynast hedged his bets by supporting both sides of the conflict, joining the

---

Ancient History[2], vol. 6, ed. David M. Lewis, John Boardman, Simon Hornblower, and Martin
Ostwald (Cambridge: Cambridge University Press, 1994), 220. Orontes first appears in historical
sources as the satrap of Armenia in 401. He participated in the campaign in 384 against Evagoras in
Cyprus, but then disappears from the sources until the late 360s. A career that spanned more than
forty years is certainly possible but is far from certain. Diodorus includes Autophradates in his list
of rebels, but Xen. *Ages.* 2.26 indicates otherwise.

42. Briant, *From Cyrus to Alexander*, 663.

43. Maria Brosius, "Persian Diplomacy between 'Pax Persica,' and 'Zero Tolerance,'" in *Maintaining Peace and Interstate Stability in Archaic and Classical Greece*, ed. Julia Wilker (Mainz: Verlag
Antike, 2012), 153–54.

44. Brosius, "Persian Diplomacy," 163, notes that the only revolts punished by Persia were those
that threatened the Persian peace.

45. Ruzicka, *Politics of a Persian Dynasty*, 69.

revolt but not so deeply that he could not return to being loyal, while also trying to enhance his local position.[46] Between the conclusion of the Satraps' Revolt in the late 360s and the start of the Social War in 357 there is no clear evidence for Mausolus' activity in Ionia, but he likely used the pretext of the revolt to plant his seeds, the fruits of which he reaped in the 350s. There is a frustrating lack of chronological detail for Ionia during these years, but they were dominated by interaction with Caria.

One example of this interaction comes from Erythrae. Sometime in the mid-fourth century, the Erythraeans abandoned the first site of their polis and moved some nineteen kilometers around the bay.[47] Simon Hornblower suggests that the relocation was prompted, or at least had been enabled, by Mausolus, whose relationship with the polis blossomed shortly thereafter.[48] In either c.365 or c.357, Erythrae granted honors to Mausolus and his sister-wife Artemisia because he was an *aner agathos* (*RO* 56 = *SIG*^{3} 168, l. 3).[49] The decree declared that Mausolus was an *euergetes* to the polis, and awarded notable honors in making him *proxenos* and citizen and giving the right to sail into and out of the harbor without needing permission through a treaty (ll. 5–8).[50] The Erythraeans also erected a bronze statue of Mausolus in the agora and a stone one of Artemisia beside the temple of Athena, both with crowns, albeit hers at a lesser expense (ll. 10–13). Whether the decree ought to date to Mausolus' first spate of activity in the gulf of Smyrna in the 360s or the second in 357, which I prefer, it points to his direct involvement in local Ionian politics. The rhetor Naucrates

46. Briant, *From Cyrus to Alexander*, 668–70; Hornblower, *Mausolus*, 172–82.

47. J. M. Cook, "Old Smyrna," *ABSA* 53–54 (1958–59): 21–22; Hornblower, "Asia Minor," 224–25. Philip Kinns, "Ionia: The Pattern of Coinage during the Last Century of the Persian Empire," *REA* 91, nos. 1–2 (1989): 186, identifies series of coins minted in c.350–340 that may be associated with the need for a new public works program, noting that Erythrae did not have widespread coinage before this series. However, this series could have been used to pay for ongoing construction.

48. Hornblower, *Mausolus*, 100, 108. Mausolus is, notably, granted the honors by the Erythraean boule, not the demos, indicating that a narrow faction in Erythrae dominated the political decision-making.

49. Rhodes and Osborne, *Greek Historical Inscriptions*, 267, and Debord, *L'Asie Mineure*, 392, date the inscription vaguely to the mid-350s at the same time that Mausolus sent aid to Chios, though Hornblower, *Mausolus*, 110, and Ruzicka, *Politics of a Persian Dynasty*, 73, plausibly suggest that it may date to the mid-360s after the Athenian conquest of Samos, when the Erythraeans offered aid to refugees. The terminus ante quem for the honors must be 353, when Mausolus died. I generally follow Ernst Badian, "A document of Artaxerxes IV?," in *Greece and the Eastern Mediterranean in ancient history and prehistory*, ed. Konrad H. Kinzel (Berlin: De Gruyter, 1977), 44 n. 6 in believing that there is not enough evidence to positively date the decree.

50. Mack, *Proxeny and Polis*, 230, observes that premier Hellenistic kings did *not* receive *proxenia*, which makes this honor for Mausolus particularly of note, and citizenship was even more substantial than *proxeny*. I believe it speaks to various avenues through which Mausolus approached the poleis of Ionia. His willingness to project conspicuously Greek symbolic language set him apart from other Persian administrators.

from Erythrae was one of the Greek intellectuals who gave an encomium at Mausolus' funeral, which was also attended by the exiled Chian Theopompus (Theopompus, *BNJ* 115 T 6a and b).[51]

Despite the close relationship between Erythrae and Mausolus, as early as the mid-360s Timotheus probably sent ships to the city. The result was a naval battle against Carian ships off Chios (Isaeus 6.27; cf. Dem. 8.24).[52] The mission of this flotilla is unknown, but it could have been for the purposes of extorting funds for his campaign war chest, to enact regime change, or, most likely, both. Timotheus had a family connection with Erythrae where the citizens had honored his father Conon after the battle of Cnidus in 394 by making him proxenos (*RO* 8 = *SIG*³ 134), a position Timotheus would have inherited.[53] It is likely that Timotheus' contacts in Erythrae were marginalized by Mausolus' activities and that he promised Timotheus resources in return for his support, which also explains why Mausolus was willing to commit to the defense of Erythrae. This did not, however, mean that Erythrae ceased to be in contact with Athens, where its citizens dedicated a crown on the Athenian Acropolis in c.350 (*IG* II² 1437, l. 12).

Though less well documented, Mausolus' relationship with other Ionian poleis parallels the one with Erythrae. Miletus, the Ionian city closest to Caria, must have been within the Hecatomnid sphere of influence from an early date, albeit with its government propped up by the Hecatomnid dynast rather than direct rule.[54] Polyaenus records that Mausolus sent one Aegyptus to Miletus, but his scheme to capture the polis failed (6.8). Hornblower surmises that Mausolus wanted to annex the Milesian hinterland,[55] but that he acted through a subordinate so that he was not directly implicated. It is impossible to know when, if at all, the plot took place, but the story fits plausibly before 365, when Mausolus first asserted his influence in Ionia. Another strategem records how Mausolus captured Latmus.[56] Polyaenus says that Mausolus first returned Latmian hostages and appointed others to his bodyguard and indulged the community in all ways (7.23.2).[57] He then pretended to lead his forces to Pygela,

---

51. Hornblower, *Mausolus*, 109–10, 334, with n. 9.

52. Ruzicka, *Politics of a Persian Dynasty*, 73; Schweigert, "Athenian Cleruchy on Samos," 197–98; George L. Cawkwell, "Notes on the Social War," *C&M* 23 (1962): 34–49.

53. Ruzicka, *Politics of a Persian Dynasty*, 73; Brosius, "Persian Diplomacy," 160.

54. Hornblower, *Mausolus*, 111; Ruzicka, *Politics of a Persian Dynasty*, 72–73.

55. Hornblower, *Mausolus*, 111.

56. Lene Rubinstein, "Ionia," in *An Inventory of Archaic and Classical Poleis*, ed. Mogens Herman Hansen and Thomas Heine Nielsen (Oxford: Oxford University Press, 2004), 1082.

57. Cf. Polyaenus 8.53.4, who attributes the same trick to Artemisia. The ploy more plausibly belongs to Mausolus; confusion stems from the name of his sister-wife, another Artemisia. There

which took him past Latmus. When the citizens came out to greet him, his forces captured the community. Many details about this episode are vague, but it demonstrates not only that Mausolus was already active in the region, but also that he sought to strengthen his position through flattery and force.

And yet Miletus must have been on friendly terms with Caria by Mausolus' death since, shortly thereafter, the citizens honored his successors Idreius and Ada with statues at Delphi (Tod 2 161B = SIG^3 225).[58] Moreover, silver coins of a Milesian type that date to the fourth century and bear the letters EKA and MA, probably abbreviations of MA[αύσσολλος] and EKA[τόμνος], have been discovered between Halicarnassus and Miletus.[59] Simon Hornblower believes that these coins, rather than mimicking the Milesian type, are the Milesian type, indicating that Miletus minted Hecatomnid coinage.[60] Miletus, like Erythrae, aided Samian refugees, perhaps at the behest of Mausolus, and Hornblower posits that Miletus may have introduced the worship of the Carian deity Zeus Labraundeus during this same period.[61] Much as was the case in Ephesus, however, seeking a purely Greek culture in Miletus is a fallacy. Miletus contained a large Carian population (Hdt. 1.146) so the appearance of a Carian deity need not have been introduced by Mausolus.

Hecatomnid influence also manifested in Priene, but the nature of this interaction is subject to debate. Excavations at Priene in the early twentieth century did not discover evidence of a settlement on the site before the Hellenistic period. They concluded that the polis was refounded in the middle of the fourth century, perhaps moving from the port city of Naulochon, which produced coins in its own name around this period.[62] Supporting their hypothesis was that the early fourth-century Oxyrhynchus Historian said that Priene was situated near the mouth of the Maeander River (12.3), while Strabo said that the city in his day (and still today) lay more than forty stadia from the sea

---

are several places in the region that carry the topnym "Latmus." While one of those belonged to Miletus, this episode more likely refers to a separate polis of the same name that was later absorbed into Heracleia; see Pernille Flensted-Jensen, "Caria," in An Inventory of Archaic and Classical Poleis, ed. Mogens Herman Hansen and Thomas Heine Nielsen (Oxford: Oxford University Press, 2004), 1126–27.

58. Cf. Waldemar Heckel, Who's Who in the Age of Alexander the Great (New York: Routledge, 2005), 3. Ada and Idreius were Mausolus' younger siblings and inherited his position. Ruzicka, Politics of a Persian Dynasty, 112, suggests that erecting at Delphi signaled to Athens that their loyalty belonged to Caria. Cf. Hornblower, "Asia Minor," 229–30.

59. Philip Kinns, "The Coinage of Miletus," NC 146 (1986): 237, 249–50; Kinns, "Ionia," 191.

60. Hornblower, Mausolus, 111.

61. Hornblower, Mausolus, 111–12.

62. Kinns, "Ionia," 191.

(12.18.17).[63] Although not every scholar accepts the relocation hypothesis,[64] the predominant issue was whether the excavator's thesis that Alexander refounded the city in the 330s should be accepted or whether the facts that Priene contributed delegates to the Amphyctyonic Council in 343 (Aesch. 2.116) and that the temple of Athena was nearing completion when Alexander passed through the region indicate Hecatomnid influence.[65] As Nancy Demand aptly notes in her rejection of the refoundation hypothesis, much of the scholarship on fourth-century Priene is based on the absence of evidence.

The most recent analysis of the monuments suggest that the Hellenistic foundation level was established c.370.[66] This chronology rules out both Mausolus and Alexander as the driving force behind the rebirth of Priene, but it nevertheless fell within the Carian sphere of influence. There is no direct evidence connecting Mausolus and his successors to the new building projects, but Priene was a beneficiary of the Ionian renaissance that saw widespread cultural exchange between Ionia and Caria.[67] It was during this period that work began on a new temple of Athena Polias, and Vitruvius identifies its architect as Pytheus, who also worked on the Mausoleum in Halicarnassus.[68] Yet it is precisely the establishment of this cult that leads Simon Hornblower to deny Mausolus a role in patronizing the city on the grounds that it, and others with Attic implications such as Demeter and Kore, would have run counter to the

---

63. See also Pseudo-Skylax 98.

64. See particularly Nancy Demand, "The Relocation of Priene Reconsidered," *Phoenix* 40, no. 1 (1986): 35–44, who raises pertinent objections, particularly about how the silting of the Maeander would have changed the distance between the city and the sea.

65. For arguments in favor of Alexander, see Theodor Weigand and Hans Schrader, *Priene: Ergebnisse der Ausgrabungen und Untersuchungen von den Jahren 1895–1898* (Berlin: Reimer, 1904), 35; Getzel Cohen, *The Hellenistic Settlements in Europe, the Islands, and Asia Minor* (Berkeley: University of California Press, 1996), 187; Hornblower, *Mausolus*, 323–30; for the Hecatomnids, see G. E. Bean and J. M. Cook, "The Carian Coast III," *ABSA* 52 (1957): 138–42; Alexander Herda, "Greek (and Our) Views on the Karians," in *Luwian Identities: Culture, Language and Religion between Anatolia and the Aegean*, ed. Alice Mouton, Ian Rutherford, and Ilya Yakubovich (Leiden: Brill, 2013), 421–505; Eloisa Paganoni, "Priene, il *Panionion* e gli Ecatomnidi," *Aevum* 88 (2014): 37–58; Sotiris G. Patronos, "Public Architecture and Civic Identity in Classical and Hellenistic Ionia" (PhD diss., Oxford University, 2002), 115–21, 124–27. Mikhail Rostovtzeff, *Social and Economic History of the Hellenistic World*, vol. 1 (Oxford: Oxford University Press, 1941), 178, proposed Athens as a sponsor for the relocation.

66. Wolfram Hoepfner, "Old and New Priene—Pythius and Aristotle," in *Priene²*, ed. Kleopatra Ferla (Cambridge, MA: Harvard University Press, 2005), 29–31.

67. Poul Pedersen, "The 4th Century BC 'Ionian Renaissance' and Karian Identity," in *4th Century Karia: Defining a Karian Identity under the Hekatomnids*, ed. Olivier Henry (Paris: De Boccard, 2013), 33–46.

68. Vitruv. 1.1.12 and 7.pref.12; see Helga Botermann, "Wer Baute das Neue Priene? Zur Interpretation der Inschriften von Priene Nr. 1 und 156," *Hermes* 122, no. 2 (1994): 178–81. On the interrelationship of construction in fourth-century Asia Minor, see also Walter Voigtlander, *Der jüngste Apollotempel von Didyma: Geschichte seine Baudekors* (Tübingen: Wasmuth, 1975), 14–28.

Carian interests.[69] Nor is the name Pytheus appearing in both contexts concrete evidence that Mausolus or Ada financed both projects. But these projects nevertheless fit within a larger context of civic projects undertaken in Caria around this same time.[70] Eloisa Paganoni has recently proposed a new explanation for Hecatomnid influence, connecting it with a concerted effort on the part of Mausolus to gain influence at the Panionion sanctuary on Mount Mycale, of which Priene was a traditional supervisor.[71] This thesis accounts for neither Ionian competition over the sanctuary nor the absence of evidence for direct patronage, but offers an attractive explanation for why the Hecatomnids might have taken an interest in the city. Moreover, Hecatomnid patronage of Priene did not mean that the citizen body was completely beholden to the Carians.

However, not every Ionian polis fell under the sway of Mausolus. Ephesus had become a regional power in its own right. Under the leadership of one Heropythos in the 350s, the Ephesians began to reassert their claim over neighbors such as Pygela, which, in turn, appealed to Mausolus for political support (Polyaenus 7.23.3).[72] For his efforts in restoring the prominence of Ephesus, Heropythos received the unusual honor of a tomb in the agora, which was desecrated during the unrest in 335/4 (Arr. 1.17.11).[73] Probably with the support of the satrap in Sardis, Ephesus remained the largest producer of silver coinage in the eastern Aegean.[74] Indeed, the economic strength of Ephesus in the fourth century was on display after the temple of Artemis burned in 356, when the Ephesians were in a position to carry out the restoration without needing extravagant dedications from wealthy patrons like Mausolus or Alexander the Great.[75]

---

69. Hornblower, *Mausolus*, 323–30. On the Sanctuary of Demeter and Kore, see Kleopatra Ferla, ed., *Priene*² (Cambridge, MA: Harvard University Press, 2005), 126–30. Prienian coins from the mid-fourth century include seemingly Attic iconography; see Kinns, "Ionia," 191–92.

70. On these reorganizations, see Bean and Cook, "Carian Coast," 141; Hornblower, *Mausolus*, 78–105.

71. Paganoni, "Priene," 37–58. Cf. Appendix 1.

72. On the date, see Hornblower, *Mausolus*, 112. These events may have been the context for Theopompus' digression on Ionian history in his *Philippic History*; see William S. Morison, "Theopompus of Chios (115)," *BNJ* F 59, 305, commentary.

73. Polyaenus records the name as "Herophytus," but this is probably mistaken; see T. Corsten, *Lexicon of Greek Personal Names*, vol. 5A (Oxford: Oxford University Press, 2010), 206.

74. Kinns, "Ionia," 188–89. On the limited production of Persian sigloi, which may have led to an increased production in Ephesian coins, see Ian Carradice, "The Regal Coinage of the Persian Empire," in *Coinage and Administration in the Athenian and Persian Empires*, ed. Ian Carradice (Oxford: Oxford University Press, 1987), 73–95. Cf. Chapter 1 on the relationship between Ephesus and Sardis.

75. In fact, Dieter Knibbe, *Ephesos-Ephesus: Geschichte einer bedeutenden antiken Stadt und Portrait einer modern Großgrabung* (Bern: Peter Lang, 1998), 88–89, suggests that the temple administration sabotaged the temple as an excuse to move its location because the sanctuary had been struggling against the rising floodwaters of the Cayster River. On the restoration of the temple of Artemis, see Chapter 9.

The Social War

War in the eastern Aegean resumed in 357 when Chios, Byzantium, and Rhodes formed an alliance against their erstwhile ally Athens. The origins of this conflict are not well understood, and Diodorus Siculus introduces it with a perfunctory announcement that the war had begun (16.7.3). But spontaneous revolts tend to have underlying causes, and the pressures that led to the Social War had been gestating for about a decade. The battle of Leuctra in 371 had broken the Spartan hegemony over Greece, and the Athenians had perhaps begun to incrementally strengthen their grip over the league with increases in the *syntaxis*. At the same time, it was during this period that Athens conquered poleis like Samos that remained outside its protection racket, thereby raising the specter of Athenian imperialism once more. There is no evidence for a wave of revolts from the Second Naval Confederacy the way there was from the fifth-century Delian League, so Jack Cargill is probably right that the organization remained generally fair to the weaker members of the league.[76] The same cannot be said for the larger members like Chios that had entered this arrangement first through bilateral treaties with Athens and became targets for those who wanted to render the league toothless.

The Theban leader Epaminondas himself sailed to Ionia in 364/3. He chased away the Athenian general Laches and persuaded the Chians to flip their loyalties (Diod. 15.79.1), but his death at the battle of Mantineia in 362 ended Theban efforts to wrest control of the sea from Athens. Stephen Ruzicka also suggests that, despite the testimony of Diodorus, Chios and Rhodes formed an alliance with the Thebans in hope of avoiding war with Persia. They probably had not actually yet withdrawn from the Athenian confederacy, but the arrival of Laches's squadron must have given another indication that Athens was willing to compel compliance.[77] At the same time, the incident at Samos likely prompted Mausolus to put garrisons on the mainland opposite the island.[78]

Throughout the 360s the Athenians took an increasingly presumptive attitude toward the allies in the new confederacy;[79] Isocrates even records that some Athenians advocated denying allies that had fallen behind on payments

---

76. Cargill, *Second Athenian League*, 128–60.

77. Stephen Ruzicka, "The Eastern Greek World," in *The Greek World in the Fourth Century*, ed. Lawrence A. Tritle (New York: Routledge, 1997), 121. Hornblower, *Mausolus*, 131; Sealey, *Demosthenes*, 103; and Stylianou, *Historical Commentary*, 494–97, argue that Byzantium withdrew from the confederacy in 364, while Chios and Rhodes remained until 357. But, as Cargill, *Second Athenian League*, 169, argues, neither is there evidence that Theban efforts incited revolts. The connection between Mausolus and the rejection of Athens is clearer.

78. Ruzicka, "Eastern Greek World," 120.

79. Cawkwell, "Notes on the Failure," 51–52.

access to the sea (8.36). There is also other evidence that, unsurprisingly, the other poleis believed the Athenians to be plotting against them in the early 350s, which, in turn, became the pretext for the Social War (Dem. 15.3).[80] Chios and Rhodes broke with the confederacy in 357, having concluded an alliance with Byzantium, Cos, and the Hecatomnid dynast Mausolus the year before. While it is possible that the root cause of the Social War lies in the alliance between the eastern Greek poleis and Thebes under Epaminondas, as is implied by Diodorus, Ruzicka persuasively argues that they would have yielded to Athenian pressure to return to the league in 357 had it not been for new alliances with Mausolus.[81] Mausolus manipulated the concerns over Athenian actions in the Aegean islands in order to start the war and shatter Athenian influence in the region,[82] while the cities that left the confederacy were merely waiting for Athens to be occupied somewhere besides Samos.[83]

Athens attacked Chios twice in 356. Each time Mausolus came its defense, and in the lull between attacks he raided Samos and other Athenian territories (Diod. 16.7.2–4) and won a battle over the Athenian fleet at Embata near Erythrae (Diod.16.21).[84] By 354, Athens was forced to again recognize the autonomy of Chios and Rhodes, but those poleis maintained their defensive alliances with each other and, more importantly, found themselves within the Carian sphere of influence until the entrée of Macedonia into the eastern Aegean.[85] Carian garrisons, while not common, did exist, but, perhaps more telling of the new status quo is that hoards of Carian coins depicting Mausolus and Pixodarus have been discovered on Chios.[86] Among these is a Mausolan drachm minted on the Chian standard, which Simon Hornblower posits as a sign of

---

80. Ernst Badian, "The Ghost of Empire: Reflections on Athenian Foreign Policy in the Fourth Century," in *Die athenische Demokratie im 4. Jahrhundert v. Chr.*, ed. Walter Eder and Christoph Auffarth (Stuttgart: Franz Steiner Verlag, 1995), 94–95; Cawkwell, "Notes on the Failure," 51–63; Ian Worthington, *Demosthenes of Athens and the Fall of Classical Greece* (Oxford: Oxford University Press, 2013), 65.

81. Stephen Ruzicka, "Epaminondas and the Genesis of the Social War," *CPh* 93, no. 1 (1998): 68.

82. Hornblower, *Mausolus*, 183, 208–9, and Ruzicka, *Politics of a Persian Dynasty*, 93–94, follow Demosthenes' claim (15.3) that Mausolus started the conflict. Buckler, *Aegean Greece*, 379, suggests that though Mausolus benefited from the war, he was not the instigator.

83. Cawkwell, "Notes on the Failure," 55. The two explanations are not mutually exclusive; see Sealey, *Demosthenes*, 106–7.

84. Hornblower, *Mausolus*, 212; Ruzicka, "Eastern Greek World," 121; Sealey, *Demosthenes*, 104–5; Worthington, *Demosthenes*, 65–67. The raids on Athenian territory were probably not possible without the aid of Chian ships since the Athenians returned in force later that year. On the fallout from the battle of Embata at Athens, see Raphael Sealey, "Athens after the Social War," *JHS* 75 (1955): 74–81.

85. Ruzicka, "Eastern Greek World," 122–23.

86. Hornblower, *Mausolus*, 132.

political interference, declaring that "the coin is not likely to be a mere stray."[87] Hornblower's suggestion is certainly possible, but too little is known about the series or context to infer direct interference even though it offers clear indication of a general orientation toward Caria.

A Calm before the Storm

Mausolus died in 353 and was succeeded in turn by his sister-wife Artemisia until 351, Idrieus (351/0–344/3) and his sister-wife Ada (until 341/0), and finally another brother, Pixodarus (340–336).[88] Carian power did not disappear in this period, but the arrival of new figures such as Hermias of Atarneus and the satrap Rhosaces led to renewed imperial competition for influence in Ionia that gradually eroded the Hecatomnid position.[89] Idrieus, like Mausolus before him, patronized building projects in Ionian poleis and the Milesians dedicated statues of him and his sister-wife Ada at Delphi in the 340s, which indicates that plans to rebuild the sanctuary at Didyma were not yet formed (Tod 2 161 B = SIG^3 225).[90] At Erythrae, an inscription records grants of honors to Idrieus, perhaps displayed next to the inscription for Mausolus. Like Mausolus, Idreius became *euergetes*, proxenos, and citizen, and received freedom from commercial taxation and rights in the courts.[91] Shortly after 351, however, Artemisia had installed a garrison on Chios (Dem. 5.25), indicating that the Carian ability to coerce Ionians by means other than force was on the wane.[92] Chios was exceptional, however, and the garrison also reflects that it was the Ionian polis best positioned to assert its independence.

The weakening of Hecatomnid power was also on display beyond Ionia. In c.351, Rhodian ships sailed to and attacked Halicarnassus and were paid back

87. Hornblower, *Mausolus*, 109, with n. 19; cf. Robin Lane Fox, "Theopompus of Chios and the Greek World," in *Chios: A Conference at the Homerion in Chios*, ed. John Boardman and C. E. Vaphopoulou-Richardson (Oxford: Oxford University Press, 1986), 109.

88. The Athenians may have used his passing as an opportunity to reinforce their position on Samos and thus sent new cleruchs in 352/1. See Ruzicka, *Politics of a Persian Dynasty*, 106.

89. Hornblower, "Asia Minor," 216; Hornblower, "Persia," 94. Rhosaces probably governed the territory formerly known as Sparda from the regional capital, Sardis, since he is described as the satrap of both Ionia and Lydia (Diod. 16.47) and receives mention in a Lydian inscription from 343/2; see Christopher H. Roosevelt, *The Archaeology of Lydia, from Gyges to Alexander* (Cambridge: Cambridge University Press, 2009), 30. His son Spithridates inherited the post.

90. Ruzicka, *Politics of a Persian Dynasty*, 104, 112.

91. Ender Varınlıoğlu, "Inscriptions from Erythrae," *ZPE* 44 (1981): 45–47, no. 1; cf. Ruzicka, *Politics of a Persian Dynasty*, 111–12.

92. Hornblower, *Mausolus*, 39–40.

in kind by Artemisia (Vitruv. 2.8.14–15).[93] This demonstration of force may have also prompted the outpouring of honors and dedications for the dynasts, lest other poleis suffer a similar fate.[94] Carian coercion, along with continued patronage, worked in the short term, but resentment at the treatment and fear of heavy-handed Carian policies encouraged the Ionian poleis to look for new friends. At this juncture, the one most forthcoming was Hermias of Atarneus.

At around the same time that they honored Idrieus, the Erythraeans concluded a treaty with Hermias (*RO* 68 = *I.Ery.* 9), who was in the process of extending his diplomatic influence.[95] The treaty assured both parties of economic rights and protections in the case of war. It has also been suggested that Chios negotiated a treaty with Hermias to recover its lost *peraea*, largely based on a fragment from Theopompus (*BNJ* 115 F 291).[96] This passage is opaque and thus obscures the relationship between Chios, Mytilene, and Hermias, but it preserves Theopompus' scorn for how the dynast treated the Ionians (κ(αὶ) προεπηλάκισε πλείστους Ἰώνων). A close relationship between Chios and Hermias is, however, unlikely, since Atarneus had been part of the Chian *peraea* until 387.

In 342, Artaxerxes III assigned Mentor to Anatolia with the instructions to defeat Hermias. After luring the tyrant out under false pretenses and arresting him, Mentor reestablished royal control over the entirety of western Anatolia (Diod. 16.52.2–7). According to Diodorus, Mentor managed this peacefully, writing to cities using Hermias' seal, professing that he and the king were reconciled. Convinced that the hostilities had ended such that yesterday's protector was about to become today's enemy, they surrendered.[97]

The account of these events preserved by Diodorus is compressed, but it does show that the Persian territorial boundaries in Anatolia were the same in 336 as they were at the conclusion of the King's Peace in 386. Yet it also indicates that Carian hegemony over Ionia weakened in the 340s to the point

---

93. Ruzicka, *Politics of a Persian Dynasty*, 110–12. Richard M. Berthold, *Rhodes in the Hellenistic Age* (Ithaca, NY: Cornell University Press, 1984), 32 n. 44, and Richard M. Berthold, "A Historical Fiction in Vitruvius," *CPh* 73, no. 2 (1978): 129–34, believe the episode to be fictional.

94. Ruzicka, *Politics of a Persian Dynasty*, 113–14.

95. Hermias had formed an alliance with Philip as early as 348 (Dem. 10.32; Diod. 16.52.5–8). Buckler, *Aegean Greece*, 473, argues that Hermias did not possess sufficient resources to provide a bridgehead to Asia, as Philip's opponents claimed was the motivation behind the alliance. Cf. Ruzicka, *Politics of a Persian Dynasty*, 122–23; Ian Worthington, *Philip II of Macedonia* (New Haven, CT: Yale University Press, 2008), 127; Worthington, *Demosthenes*, 224–26; Briant, *From Cyrus to Alexander*, 688–89; Peter Green, "Politics, Philosophy, and Propaganda: Hermias of Atarneus and His Friendship with Aristotle," in *Crossroads of History: The Age of Alexander the Great*, ed. Waldemar Heckel and Lawrence A. Tritle (Claremont, CA: Regina Books, 2003), 29–46.

96. Hornblower, "Persia," 81.

97. Briant, *From Cyrus to Alexander*, 688.

where it was virtually nonexistent outside Miletus. The decline made it possible for factions within an increasing number of Ionian polities to break free and consider themselves independent. Hermias was a useful ally to help them resist Caria, but this was a practical, rather than ideological, decision. This process probably included expelling the faction that had benefited from Persian or Carian rule in some instances, but it seems it was frequently just a shift in policy. Chios, for instance, sent ships to aid its old ally Byzantium in 340 after the Athenian ambassador Hyperides persuaded Chios to join a coalition against Philip of Macedon.[98] The expedition was a fiasco and resulted in the Chian ships, including a grain fleet, being captured. When Philip released their ships, the Chians withdrew from the conflict.[99]

The period from 386 to 336 in Ionia began with the cities off the coast technically autonomous and those on Anatolia both de jure and de facto part of the Persian Empire. The intervening years were tumultuous, with periods when powerful dynasts, not all of whom were Persian vassals, were able to exert a great deal of control over both the mainland and the islands. In addition, there were periods when anti-Persian factions in the mainland poleis were able to draw on their contacts from the wider Greek world to exert their own independence. Multiple competing imperial powers vied for control of Ionia during this period, which led in turn to extended periods of stasis, but in 336 Macedonia was poised to radically change the balance of power.

---

98. Hyperides delivered a speech about Chios in the Assembly of which only the title survives. Hyperides advocated for an aggressive policy against Macedonian power; see Craig Cooper, *Dinarchus, Hyperides, and Lycurgus* (Austin: University of Texas Press 2001), 63; Chris Carey et al., "Fragments of Hyperides' 'Against Diondas' from the Archimedes Palimpsest," *ZPE* 165 (2008): 1–19; Worthington, *Demosthenes*, 129–30.

99. A. B. Bosworth, *Conquest and Empire: The Reign of Alexander the Great* (Cambridge: Cambridge University Press 1993), 192; Buckler, *Aegean Greece*, 485; Rubenstein, "Ionia," 1064–65; Worthington, *Philip II*, 134–35. By contrast, Philip simply sold the cargo in the Athenian ships (Dem. 18.139; Justin 9.1.5).

CHAPTER 7

☙

Free at Last?

336–323

Ionia had been subject to the King's Peace for more than fifty years by the spring of 336. This half century had seen the waxing and waning of the Hecatomnids' hegemony in Ionia. Their last foothold in the region was in Miletus, which may have helped pique Philip's interested in an alliance with Pixodarus in 337/6.[1] Hecatomnid power was diminished further that year when the new Persian king, Darius III, replaced Pixodarus with the Persian Orontobates (Strabo 14.2.17; Arr. 1.23.8).[2] The same spring, Philip II launched his invasion of Persia by sending a vanguard to Anatolia (Diod. 16.81; Justin 9.5.8).[3] The introduction of new forces to both the north and the south exposed old fissures within Ionia that threatened domestic stability.

Philip's and Alexander's campaigns to Asia Minor were presented under the banner of liberating the Greeks from Persian subjugation (Diod. 19.91.1, 17.24.1). This propaganda was a useful rallying cry for some Ionians, but Mace-

---

1. John Buckler, *Aegean Greece in the Fourth Century BC* (Leiden: Brill, 2003), 519–20. For recent discussions of Philip's diplomacy, see Stephen Ruzicka, "The 'Pixodarus Affair' Reconsidered Again," in *Philip II and Alexander the Great: Father and Son, Lives and Afterlives*, ed. Elizabeth Carney and Daniel Ogden (Oxford: Oxford University Press, 2010), 3–11; Ian Worthington, *By the Spear: Philip II, Alexander the Great, and the Rise and Fall of the Macedonian Empire* (Oxford: Oxford University Press, 2014), 110, with bibliography.

2. Pixodarus remained dynast, but his daughter's husband Orontobantes inherited control of the region when he died in 336/5; see Pierre Briant, "The Empire of Darius III in Perspective," in *Alexander the Great: A New History*, ed. Waldemar Heckel and Lawrence A. Tritle (Malden, MA: Blackwell, 2009), 156–60; Waldemar Heckel, *Who's Who in the Age of Alexander the Great* (New York: Routledge, 2005), 186; Simon Hornblower, *Mausolus* (Oxford: Oxford University Press, 1982), 49–50; Stephen Ruzicka, *Politics of a Persian Dynasty: The Hecatomnids in the Fourth Century* (Norman: University of Oklahoma Press, 1992), 135; A. B. Bosworth, *A Historical Commentary on Arrian's History of Alexander*, vol. 1 (Oxford: Oxford University Press, 1980), 153. Pierre Briant, *From Cyrus to Alexander: A History of the Persian Empire*, trans. Peter T. Daniels (Winona Lake, IN: Eisenbrauns, 2002), 783, notes that the appointment allowed Darius to exert his influence while preserving continuity.

3. Worthington, *By the Spear*, 111.

donian freedom was not markedly different from either Athenian freedom or Persian subjugation. This chapter examines the transition from the opportunities and risks presented by an unstable and divided imperial system in the last days of the Persian Empire to the domestic challenges of a unipolar Macedonian system that lasted less than a decade.

Pressures on Ionia

The Macedonian invasion of 336, the first sustained military incursion from Europe in more than half a century, destabilized the strategic situation in the eastern Aegean. Philip's vanguard troops crossed into Anatolia with the mandate to secure the freedom of the Greek poleis (προστάξας ἐλευθεροῦν τὰς Ἑλληνίδας πόλεις) before Philip would follow with the main expedition later that summer (Diod. 16.91.2).[4] Philip had already been negotiating with the Greeks in Asia Minor, so there must have been the expectation that the Macedonians would receive them as liberators. In time, this assumption would be proven false.

The campaign began in northern Anatolia near Abydus, and its primary theater of operations was Aeolis to the north of Ionia. Nominally, Philip ordered the advance force to liberate the Greek communities in Anatolia. In practice, this meant encouraging factions to enact coups and join the Panhellenic crusade against Persia or taking them by force if they did not. "Liberation" from Persia was not optional.[5] Diodorus records that the Macedonian general Parmenion undertook two sieges in Aeolis, a successful one against Grynium, where he sold the inhabitants into slavery, and one against Pitane that Memnon, a Rhodian mercenary commander in Persian service, relieved (Diod. 17.7.9).[6] Memnon then defeated the Macedonians in a pitched battle

---

4. Briant, *From Cyrus to Alexander*, 817–18. On Philip's Panhellenic agenda, see Polybius 3.6.12–13; M. Faraguna, "Alexander and the Greeks," in *Brill's Companion to Alexander the Great*, ed. J. Roisman (Leiden: Brill, 2003), 107; Ian Worthington, *Philip II of Macedonia* (New Haven, CT: Yale University Press, 2008), 166–69; Worthington, *By the Spear*, 104–5.

5. Ernst Badian, "Alexander the Great and the Greeks of Asia," in *Collected Papers on Alexander the Great* (New York: Routledge, 2012), 126 (= "Alexander the Great and the Greeks of Asia," in *Ancient Society and Institutions: Studies Presented to Victor Ehrenberg*, ed. Ernst Badian [Oxford: Oxford University Press, 1966], 37–69), highlights the grim irony of a mission of liberation selling the population of a Greek community into slavery and is certainly correct in the implication that Philip's declaration was a matter of propaganda rather than policy.

6. Badian, "Alexander the Great," 126–27; A. B. Bosworth, *Conquest and Empire: The Reign of Alexander the Great* (Cambridge: Cambridge University Press 1993), 250; Worthington, *Philip II*, 180. The Greek sources tend to overemphasize Memnon's role in leading the Persian resistance, glossing over the actions of Persian commanders such as Arsites, the satrap of Hellespontine Phrygia; see Briant, *From Cyrus to Alexander*, 817–18.

near Magnesia on the Sipylus (Polyaenus 5.44.4) and retook Grynium, forcing the Macedonians back toward the Troad.[7] In July 335, Memnon attacked Cyzicus, probably because it had sided with the Macedonians, but settled for ravaging its territory after he failed to take the city (Diod. 17.7.8; Polyaenus 5.44.5).

The Persian leadership met the Macedonian invasion head-on with a counteroffensive in Aeolis and the Troad.[8] Led by Memnon and other Persian commanders, this strategy was successful, but it also meant that they did not spend time shoring up the loyalty of anywhere not directly threatened by Macedonian forces. Although the Macedonian expedition never reached Ionia, it nevertheless led to upheaval in the region.

Evidence for the domestic situation in the Ionian poleis in 336 is fragmentary. Complicating matters is that Alexander's campaign in 334 exerts a powerful magnetic force on circumstantially dated evidence. Take, the so-called Philites Stele, probably from Erythrae, which records two decrees regarding care and upkeep of the statue of the tyrannicide Philites (*SIG*[3] 284). The actual stele was inscribed in the third century, but clearly refers to an earlier episode where first Philites received an honorary statue for killing a tyrant and then the civic aristocracy removed its sword because they saw the statue as targeting their position.[9] It was originally held that the tyrannicide that precipitated the chain of events recorded in the decrees coincided with the Macedonian expedition and thus that the tyrant was a Persian puppet.[10] Despite loose parallels with events in Ephesus in the 330s, there is nothing in either decree that mentions Alexander, Persia, or democracy, which Heisserer rightly argues should appear, and so he dates the decree to the early Hellenistic period.[11]

Somewhat more is known about the situation in Ephesus, where deep factional divides erupted into open conflict. No historical source records an embassy between Philip and Ephesus, but there is good reason to believe that some sort of negotiations took place. Probably in 336, the Ephesians commissioned a statue to be erected in the sanctuary of Artemis (ἐν τῷ ἱερῷ, Arr.

---

7. There are multiple sites named Magnesia, but Briant, *From Cyrus to Alexander*, 817, and Badian, "Alexander the Great," 127 n. 20, are correct that the site of this battle was the Magnesia on the Sipylus river in Aeolia, rather than Magnesia on the Maeander to the east of Ionia. Buckler, *Aegean Greece*, 519–20 n. 31, doubts the existence of the battle on the grounds that the campaign was mostly limited to the Troad.

8. Briant, *From Cyrus to Alexander*, 818.

9. The most recent treatment of the Philites stele is Matthew Simonton, "The Local History of Hippias of Erythrai: Politics, Place, Memory, and Monumentality," *Hesperia* 87, no. 3 (2018): 497–54, who interprets the removal of the statue as the product of an oligarchic coup.

10. See A. J. Heisserer, "The Philites Stele (*SIG*[3] 284 = *IEK* 503)," *Hesperia* 48, no. 3 (1979): 281–82, on the early interpretations. Some modern scholars maintain a dating during the 330s, e.g., David A. Teegarden, *Death to Tyrants! Ancient Greek Democracy and the Struggle against Tyranny* (Princeton, NJ: Princeton University Press, 2014), 157–62.

11. Heisserer, "Philites Stele," 281–93.

1.17.11). This statue is sometimes considered to be Philip's supposed divine pretensions playing out in an Anatolian milieu, but this is misleading. The statue is
attested as a likeness (*eikon*) rather than cult statue (*agalma*) and was an honor
afforded Lysander, Timotheus, and others in the fifth century.[12] The contexts
for the earlier offerings of honorific statues varied. Lysander used Ephesus as
his base of operations and as a connection to Cyrus the Younger, but, despite
expanding Athenian power in the eastern Aegean, Timotheus did not. Moreover, excavations at Ephesus have revealed a veritable topography of urban
dedications in the Hellenistic and Roman periods, but Archaic and Classical
honors, including grants of citizenship, were limited to the Artemisium.[13] The
statue probably also included a dedicatory inscription. The inscription did not
survive its *damnatio*, but, paradoxically, there is reason to believe that it would
have been no more enlightening, since a comparable Milesian dedication for
Ada and Idreius at Delphi offers no insight other than the origin of the monument and the names of the honorands (*Tod* 2 161B = *SIG*³ 225).[14] John Ma has
demonstrated that such dedications were part of the world of Hellenistic politics, and Philip's diplomacy in the eastern Aegean is evident from as early as 337
in his negotiations with Pixodarus, so there is no reason to attribute this statue
to extraordinary circumstances of divine pretentions, the presence of Macedonian soldiers, or premature honors in expectation of Philip's victory.[15]

   But what does this mean for Ephesian domestic politics? Scholars frequently
assume that the appearance of Macedonian forces in Asia was the catalyst for a
political coup that brought to power the demos.[16] Indeed, the supposed revolution offers a neat explanation for the dedication to Philip, but the evidence for
it is a house of cards built on three pylons, all of which emerge from Arrian's

----

12. Worthington, *By the Spear*, 151; Worthington, *Philip II*, 180, 201, and examined at greater
length in his Appendix 5, 228–33, particularly at 231; Bosworth, *Historical Commentary*, 133; contra Badian, "Alexander the Great," 127; Ernst Badian, "The Death of Philip II," in *Collected Papers
on Alexander the Great* (New York: Routledge, 2012), 108 (= "The Death of Philip II," *Phoenix* 17,
no. 4 [1963]: 244–50); Peter Green, *Alexander of Macedon* (Berkeley: University of California Press,
1992), 81, 98. Margaret Bieber, "The Portraits of Alexander the Great," *TAPhA* 93 (1949): 378, and
Margaret Bieber, *Alexander the Great in Greek and Roman Art* (Chicago: Argonaut, 1964), 20–21,
argues implausibly that Alexander commissioned the statue as a posthumous honor for Philip.
13. On the citizenship grants, see Lene Rubinstein, "Ionia," in *An Inventory of Archaic and Classical Poleis*, ed. Mogens Herman Hansen and Thomas Heine Nielsen (Oxford: Oxford University
Press, 2004), 1073.
14. John Ma, *Statues and Cities: Honorific Portraits and Civic Identity in the Hellenistic World*
(Oxford: Oxford University Press, 2013), 26–27, describes the variations on dedicatory formulae.
15. On the diplomacy of honorific dedications, see Ma, *Statues and Cities*.
16. This coup is generally taken for granted; see Badian, "Alexander the Great," 127; Bosworth,
Conquest and Empire, 34–35; J. R. Ellis, *Philip II and Macedonian Imperialism* (London: Thames
and Hudson, 1976), 221–22; N. G. L. Hammond and G. T. Griffith, *A History of Macedonia*, vol. 2
(Oxford: Oxford University Press, 1979), 691; Waldemar Heckel, *The Conquests of Alexander the
Great* (Cambridge: Cambridge University Press, 2008), 43; Worthington, *By the Spear*, 111, 151.

account of the upheaval surrounding Alexander's capture of Ephesus in 334, at which point a Persian-backed junta controlled the city (1.17.9–12). Arrian describes how people dragged Syrphax and his family from the temple of Artemis, lynching them because they invited in Memnon. In the fighting that ensued after the Persians arrived, they destroyed the *eikon* of Philip in the sanctuary of Artemis and tore up the tomb of Heropythos in the agora. Heropythos is a shadowy figure in fourth-century Ephesian history but receiving a tomb in the agora is an unusual honor. Arrian calls him the liberator of the polis (ἐλευθερώσαντος τὴν πόλιν), which frequently leads to the assumption that he was a leader of the imagined democratic coup, died in the fighting, and was thus honored.[17] Heropythos, however, has also been identified with a military and political leader from the middle of the fourth century who oversaw the restoration of Ephesian prominence and may have fought against Mausolus of Caria (Polyaenus 7.23.2).[18] In this context, then, reading Arrian's declaration that Heropythos liberated Ephesus as a reference to 336 is an overly literal interpretation of the evidence. His role in making Ephesus great again could easily be remembered as liberation.

Although the evidence for Ephesus at this critical juncture is particularly fragmentary, several observations can be made about its domestic situation. First, Arrian does not indicate that the men calling for Memnon's support were in exile. Nor is there an increase in the number of published decrees until after 334, which Krzysztof Nawotka reasonably argues reflects a political change from oligarchy to democracy.[19] Thus, I believe that there was no coup in 336. Rather, the lax Persian oversight that had allowed the Ephesians to assert their regional power in the middle of the fourth century also presented an opportunity for them to receive Philip's entreaties. Heropythos' death left the leading Ephesians in a precarious position, particularly when they opted to let their bet on the Macedonians ride, dispatching an orator, Delius, to advocate on behalf of the expedition (Plut. *Mor.* 1126d). Alexander needed no persuading, but this was a piece of political theater designed to demonstrate that the Greeks in Asia

17. E.g., Badian, "Alexander the Great," 127; Hans-Joachim Gehrke, *Stasis: Untersuchungen zu den inneren Kriegen in den grieschen Staaten des 5. und 4. Jahrhunderts v. Chr.* (Munich: Hans Beck, 1985), 59.

18. Polyaenus records the name as "Herophytus," which is probably a corruption of Heropythos; see T. Corsten, *Lexicon of Greek Personal Names,* vol. 5A (Oxford: Oxford University Press, 2010), 261.

19. Krzysztof Nawotka, "Freedom of Greek Cities in Asia Minor in the Age of Alexander the Great," *Klio* 85, no. 1 (2003): 18–24. What democracy meant at this point in the fourth century is a fraught issue because it could refer to any type of constitution that was not a tyranny; see Jeremy LaBuff, *Polis Expansion and Elite Power in Hellenistic Caria* (Lanham, MD: Lexington Books, 2015), 8–11, but see Matthew Simonton, *Classical Greek Oligarchy: A Political History* (Princeton, NJ: Princeton University Press, 2017), for the characteristics of oligarchic regimes.

were primed to rise up against their barbarian overlords as Isocrates had predicted (4.135).

At the same time, an opposition party that included Syrphax disapproved of the alliance with Macedonia and exploited the situation to call for support from Memnon, who was then securing the Persian hold over Asia Minor. This coup resulted in the exile of the Ephesians who had negotiated the Macedonian alliance, but probably should not be seen as the outgrowth of a particular loyalty to Persia. Syrphax and his associates orchestrated a power grab that, if the retributive purges in 334 are any indication, was bloody and brutal.

There is a dearth of evidence from elsewhere in Ionia, but there is no reason to assume that Ephesus was unique. The upheaval that followed the appearance of the Macedonian army in Asia stoked the flames of domestic conflict, both as a debate over the future of each community and as an opportunity to strike at political opponents, using imperial forces as a bludgeon to expel or kill them. Between 336 and 334, Memnon restored Persian control over Ionia, temporarily smothering the possibility of revolt and exacerbating domestic conflicts even though much of the region remained only lightly garrisoned.

Alexander in Ionia

In 334, Alexander III led his army across the Bosporus and into the Troad. After defeating the Persian satrapal armies at the Granicus River, he led his army to Sardis and from there along the royal road to Ephesus (Arr. 1.17.9–12).[20] The small Persian garrison seized two Ephesian ships and fled, allowing the citizens to open the gates to Alexander (Arr. 1.17.9). The king restored Ephesian exiles and declared Ephesus a democracy, thereby demonstrating that his was a campaign to liberate the Greeks. Arrian concludes, "Never did Alexander achieve such acclaim as for what he did at Ephesus" (καὶ εἰ δή τῳ ἄλλῳ, καὶ τοῖς ἐν Ἐφέσῳ πραχθεῖσιν Ἀλέξανδρος ἐν τῷ τότε εὐδοκίμει, 1.17.12), but the situation was not so simple.

Around the time of Alexander's entrance to Ephesus the citizen population dissolved into an orgy of retributive violence against the people who had invited in Memnon. The family of Syrphax had sought asylum at a sanctuary, but the citizens dragged them from the temple to stone them to death and looked poised to kill others until Alexander ordered an end to the violence.

---

20. Bosworth, *Conquest and Empire*, 44–45; Donald W. Engels, *Alexander the Great and the Logistics of the Macedonian Army* (Berkeley: University of California Press, 1980), 30–33.

While this violence was clearly political in nature, the connection to Persia is incidental. The Persian-backed coup had forced prominent Ephesians into exile, stolen from the temple of Artemis, and desecrated public monuments, meaning that in this context they were simply receiving their just deserts. We are told, however, that Alexander ordered an end to both inquiry and punishment (ἐπιζητεῖν καὶ τιμωρεῖσθαι) to prevent the Ephesians from exploiting the situation to punish private enemies (Arr. *Anab.* 1.17.11–12).

While at Ephesus, Alexander led his army in a procession before the temple of Artemis, made the appropriate dedications, and, according to Arrian, ordered the Ephesians to pay their *phoros* to the sanctuary. This simple statement has elicited consternation for several reasons. First, Alexander relieved the *phoros* from the rest of Ionia and replaced it with a *syntaxis* to pay for the campaign (see below, "A Macedonian World") and, second, because a later ancient tradition records that the Ephesians rebuffed an offer from Alexander to pay for construction and upkeep of the sanctuary. The combination of these two issues led Ernst Badian to argue that the fickle king turned hostile to the prideful Ephesians, refusing to relieve the *phoros* and levying a *syntaxis* in addition.[21]

Although the temple of Artemis had allegedly burned on the day of his birth (Plut. *Alex.* 3.3), there is nothing in Arrian's account of Alexander at Ephesus that marks the sanctuary as special to the king. The first extant connection between the birth and the conflagration comes from the work of Hegesias of Magnesia, a third-century rhetorician whose work was accounted perverse and puerile in antiquity (e.g., Cic. *Brut.* 83.286–87).[22] Similarly, the evidence for Alexander's offer to pay for the construction and upkeep in perpetuity appears only in a comment attributed to the first century BCE geographer Artemidorus of Ephesus, who praised his predecessors for not accepting a dedication from one god to another (Strabo 14.1.22).[23] While this rationale would be a good way of flattering Alexander, it reads like a later invention. The Ephesians had already

---

21. Badian, "Alexander the Great," 131, and A. J. Heisserer, *Alexander and the Greeks: The Epigraphic Evidence* (Norman: University of Oklahoma Press, 1980), 157–58, suggest pride and wealth respectively; Helga Botermann, "Wer Baute das Neue Priene? Zur Interpretation der Inschriften von Priene Nr. 1 und 156," *Hermes* 122, no. 2 (1994): 181–82, dismisses it as a fiction modeled after Alexander's dedication at Priene.

22. See Lionel Pearson, *The Lost Historians of Alexander the Great* (Oxford: Oxford University Press, 1960), 246–47.

23. Strabo 14.1.26 records that Artemidorus was awarded a golden *eikon* in the sanctuary after a successful embassy to Rome in 104; see Guy Maclean Rogers, *The Mysteries of Artemis of Ephesos: Cult, Polis, and Change in the Graeco-Roman World* (New Haven, CT: Yale University Press, 2012), 93. If the Ephesian response is genuine, then Alexander's offer must have come later than 334, but I am skeptical of its historicity; see Boris Dreyer, "Heroes, Cults, and Divinity," in *Alexander the Great: A New History*, ed. Waldemar Heckel and Lawrence A. Tritle (Malden, MA: Blackwell, 2009), 225–26; cf. Bosworth, *Historical Commentary*, 132–33.

raised money for the construction by selling the columns from the old temple and dedicating private jewelry, as well as allegedly stealing Persian gold, the last of which I believe was the *phoros* that Alexander retroactively directed to the sanctuary (see Chapter 9).

Ephesus nevertheless played a pivotal role in Alexander's campaign. It was the first large Greek polis that he came to in Asia Minor and thus an opportunity to put into action his declarations of Panhellenic liberation. But Arrian records two additional strategic decisions. First, embassies from Magnesia and Tralles approached Alexander while he was at Ephesus. Although Ernst Badian took these embassies as evidence for Greek uprisings against Persia,[24] it is more likely that this was yet another example of internal divisions and political exiles making an appeal for political support. Alexander indulged their requests and dispatched two forces to liberate the rest of the region (Arr. 1.18.1).[25] Second, Alexander formally abolished the *phoros* payments, installing instead a *syntaxis* (contribution).[26] By replacing tribute with a contribution, he symbolically liberated the Greeks of Asia in a stroke. The change may have carried some weight among the Ionian audiences given that it implied that the payments would last only as long as the campaign against Persia, but, in practice, it was a semantic distinction for propaganda purposes.

Arrian records these decisions at Ephesus with customary surety, but behind his words are questions with few clear answers. First is the question of

---

24. Badian, "Alexander the Great," 131.

25. Bosworth, *Historical Commentary*, 133–36; Bosworth, *Conquest and Empire*, 45–46, 256. Richard A. Billows, *Antigonus the One-Eyed and the Creation of the Hellenistic State* (Berkeley: University of California Press, 1985), 39, argues for the existence of a third force, with Antigonus going to Priene. This is unlikely since Priene lay on Alexander's route from Ephesus to Miletus. Scholars like Benjamin D. Meritt, "Inscriptions of Colophon," *AJPh* 56, no. 4 (1935): 371, use the invocation of Alexander and Antigonus in Ionian inscriptions to date them to 334 with undue confidence. Early Hellenistic inscriptions frequently recall Alexander, in conscious dialogue with royal propaganda; see Chapter 8.

26. One might compare this changed terminology as akin to the change from δασμός to φόρος in the fifth century. Alexander was not doing anything new with this change. The Second Athenian League had also assessed a *syntaxis* rather than a *phoros* to avoid associations with the fifth century; see Patrice Brun, *Eisphora, Syntaxis, Stratioke* (Paris: Les Belles Lettres, 1983), 114–16; Oswyn Murray, "Ο ΑΡΧΑΙΟΣ ΔΑΣΜΟΣ," *Historia* 15, no. 2 (1966): 150; cf. David Whitehead, "Ο ΝΕΟΣ ΔΑΣΜΟΣ: 'Tribute' in Classical Athens," *Hermes* 126, no. 2 (1998): 176–81. On issues of *phoros* and *syntaxis*, see recently Maxim M. Kholod, "On the Financial Relations of Alexander the Great and the Greek Cities in Asia Minor," in *Ruthenia Classica Aetatis Novae*, ed. Andreas Mehr, Alexander V. Makhlayuk, and Oleg Gabelko (Stuttgart: Franz Steiner Verlag, 2013), 83–92, and Maxim M. Kholod, "The Financial Administration of Asia Minor under Alexander the Great," in *Ancient Historiography on War and Empire*, ed. Tim Howe, Sabine Müller, and Richard Stoneman (Oxford: Oxford University Press 2017), 136–48, with bibliography. Michele Faraguna, "Alexander the Great and Asia Minor: Conquest and Strategies of Legitimation," in *The Legitimation of Conquest*, ed. Kai Trampedach and Alexander Meeus (Stuttgart: Franz Steiner Verlag, 2020), 243–61, emphasizes the continuity of Achaemenid administration.

Alexander's intentions toward the Greeks of Asia. Despite the presentation of the campaign as a crusade for Panhellenic liberty against the barbarian oppressor, Alexander did not have a predetermined strategy for managing conquered territories but responded to issues as they arose.[27]

Priene, which lay close by the route from Ephesus to Miletus on the north side of the Gulf of Latmus, poses additional complications for understanding Alexander's passage through Ionia. The problems arise, ironically, because there is an unusually rich epigraphical record for Alexander's interactions with Priene. One inscription records that "King Alexander dedicated the temple to Athena Polias" (*SIG*[3] 277),[28] a second inscription indicates both the introduction of a garrison and the remission of their financial obligations (*RO* 86B = *I.Priene*[2] 149), and the original editor of the inscriptions from Priene, Friedrich Hiller von Gaertringen, assigned an additional seven inscriptions to Alexander's reign (*I.Priene*[2] 15, 16, 17, 18, 19, 20, 107). However, recent scholarship has liberated these inscriptions from Alexander's gravitational pull, down-dating many of them to the early Hellenistic period, leaving only the dedication at the temple of Athena Polias and the remission of the *phoros*.[29] Neither of these two decrees can be positively dated on their own grounds, in no small part because they were reinscribed as part of a Hellenistic archive,[30] and thus the dates are subject to controversy based on circumstantial evidence. Some scholars maintain that Alexander would not have used the royal title in dealing with the Greeks before the battle of Gaugamela in 331, while others argue that either it was part of the Macedonian royal stylings or that he assumed it while in Asia.[31] Another debate puts Priene's apparent willingness to accept

---

27. Badian, "Alexander the Great," 131; Faraguna, "Alexander and the Greeks," 109–10.

28. Βασιλεὺς Ἀλέξανδρος | ἀνέθηκε τὸν ναὸν | Ἀθηναίηι Πολιάδι. Joseph C. Carter, *The Sculpture of the Sanctuary of Athena Polias at Priene* (London: Thames and Hudson, 1983), 30, notes that this is the same dedicatory formula used by Croesus at the temple of Ephesus, but this may be more the result of formula than conscious imitation.

29. C. V. Crowther, "I.Priene 8 and the History of Priene in the Early Hellenistic Period," *Chiron* 26 (1996): 195–238.

30. On this archive, see S. M. Sherwin-White, "Ancient Archives: The Edict of Alexander to Priene, a Reappraisal," *JHS* 105 (1985): 69–89.

31. Orthodox position: Emiliano Arena, "Alessandro 'Basileus' nella documentazione epigrafica: La dedica del Tempio di Atena a Priene ('I.Priene' 156)," *Historia* 62, no. 1 (2013): 48–79; Ernst Badian, "History from 'Square Brackets,'" *ZPE* 79 (1989): 64–68; Ernst Badian, "A Reply to Professor Hammond's Article," *ZPE* 97 (1994): 388–90; Ernst Badian, "Alexander the Great between Two Thrones and Heaven: Variations on an Old Theme," in *Subject and Ruler: The Cult of Ruling Power in Classical Antiquity*, ed. Alastair Small (Ann Arbor: University of Michigan Press, 1996), 11–26; R. Malcolm Errington, "Macedonian Royal Style and Its Historical Significance," *JHS* 94 (1974): 20–37; Paul Goukowsky, *Essai sur les origines du mythe d'Alexandre*, vol. 1, *Les origines politiques* (Nancy: University of Nancy, 1978), 182; Anna Maria Prestianni Giallombardo, "Philippos o Basileus: Nota a Favorin 'Corinth' 41," *QUCC*[2] 49 (1985): 19–27. For the revisionist argument that

Alexander's largesse in direct contrast to Ephesus, suggesting that Priene's compliance won the king's favor where the Ephesian intransigence won his enmity.[32] Although Alexander would have passed near Priene on his way to Miletus, he probably never visited the polis. Without a Persian garrison, the people of Priene probably did not resist the Macedonian expedition, but these inscriptions likely belong to a later period in Alexander's reign after the conclusion of the war in the Aegean in 332, and so I treat them below ("A Macedonian World").

When Alexander arrived at Miletus, the southernmost Ionian polis, he had every reason to expect it to capitulate without a fight. The rest of the region had accepted Macedonian liberation and, moreover, the garrison commander, Hegistratus, had promised to surrender (Arr. *Anab.* 1.18.4). The imminent arrival of the Persian fleet caused Hegistratus to have a change of heart, however, so Alexander found the gates closed to him. With his characteristic impatience and decisiveness, Alexander had his fleet seize the island of Lade, which controlled the harbor of Miletus, and forced the Persian fleet to anchor on the opposite side of the bay near Mount Mycale, where it was vulnerable to the Macedonian army (Arr. *Anab.* 1.18.7–11). He then launched an immediate attack but failed to take the walls (Diod. 17.22); once the siege train arrived, Miletus fell in just one day (Arr. *Anab.* 1.19.2; cf. Diod. 17.22.4–5).[33]

On the day before the final assault, a Milesian named Glaucippus approached Alexander on behalf of the citizens and the mercenary garrison, suggesting that Miletus would be open to both Persians and Macedonians (τά τε τείχη ἔφη ἐθέλειν τοὺς Μιλησίους καὶ τοὺς λιμένας παρέχειν κοινοὺς Ἀλεξάνδρῳ καὶ Πέρσαις, Arr. *Anab.* 1.19.1).[34] Bosworth plausibly argues that Glaucippus was a senior member

---

the title *basileus* was part of Macedonian practice: N. G. L. Hammond, "The King and the Land in the Macedonian Kingdom," CQ^2 38, no. 2 (1988): 382–91; N. G. L. Hammond, "Inscriptions Concerning Philippi and Calindoea in the Reign of Alexander the Great," *ZPE* 92 (1990): 167–75; N. G. L. Hammond, "A Note on Badian 'Alexander and Philippi,' *ZPE* 95 (1993) 131–9," *ZPE* 97 (1995): 385–87; Miltiades B. Hatzopoulos, "The Olveni Inscription and the Date of Philip II's Reign," in *Philip II, Alexander the Great and the Macedonian Heritage*, ed. W. Lindsay Adams and Eugene N. Borza (Lanham, MD: University Press of America, 1982), 21–42; Miltiades B. Hatzopoulos, "Épigraphie et villages en Grèce du Nord: Ethnos, polis et kome en Macédoine," in *L'epigrafia del villaggio*, ed. Alda Calbi, Angela Donati, and Gabriella Poma (Faenza: Fratelli Lega, 1993), 151–71; Miltiades B. Hatzopoulos, "La letter royale d'Olévéne," *Chiron* 25 (1995): 163–85. For the idea that Alexander was creating a new kingship: Teresa Alfieri Tonini, "Basileus Alexandros," in λόγιος ἀνήρ: *Studi di Antichità in memoria di Mario Attilio Levi*, ed. Pier Giuseppe Michelotto (Milan: Cisalpino Instituto, 2002), 3; and for the argument that Greeks in Asia were treated differently from those in Europe: W. E. Higgins, "Aspects of Alexander's Imperial Administration: Some Modern Methods and Views Reviewed," *Athenaeum* 68 (1980): 135.

32. Badian, "Alexander the Great," 132.

33. Bosworth, *Historical Commentary*, 138–39; Bosworth, *Conquest and Empire*, 46; Worthington, *By the Spear*, 153. Engels, *Alexander the Great*, 33–34, suggests that Alexander initially left behind the siege train because the promontory where Miletus sat could not support a large force.

34. Bosworth, *Historical Commentary*, 138; Bosworth, *Conquest and Empire*, 46. Glaucippus

of the ruling faction and hoped to find a workable solution for the polis,[35] but it is hard to imagine that he thought that Alexander would agree to his proposal. The king told the Milesians to prepare for battle. A bloody slaughter ensued, with only a small part of the garrison escaping the sword (Arr. *Anab.* 1.19.4–6; Diod. 17.22.4–5).[36] In his account of the assault, however, Arrian draws a distinction between the Persian garrison at Miletus and the Milesian soldiers and indicates that both groups resisted the Macedonian onslaught. Some Milesians were killed in the initial clash, but Alexander spared the rest because they surrendered once the walls were breached (Arr. *Anab.* 1.19.6; cf. Strabo 14.1.7).

Much as with Ephesus, Alexander's attitude toward Miletus is a subject of some uncertainty. The crux of the matter is whether the fact that this polis, alone to this point in the campaign, had to be taken by storm nullified the general grant of the freedom for the Ionians. Brian Bosworth rightly points out that Arrian refers to freedom of the specific prisoners captured during the assault and not to Miletus as a whole.[37] The second stele of the list of annual eponymous officials contains a dedication thanking Antigonus Monophthalmus for establishing the democracy and granting Miletus freedom and autonomy (*Milet* I.3, no. 123, ll. 2–4; see Chapter 8). These inscriptions are, however, an imperfect record. The praise for Antigonus heads a second stele that likely begins with the year 313/2, while Alexander's entry appears on the first stele that was probably erected in 332 at the conclusion of the war in the Aegean.[38] This distinction has several consequences. As we shall see, declarations of freedom and autonomy were a regular feature of Hellenistic propaganda, and these reciprocal thanks given to Antigonus belong in that Hellenistic context. However, the absence of a comparable inscription for Alexander should be regarded as a performed respect for Milesian liberty. There is thus nothing about the circumstances in Miletus to indicate different treatment after its capture.

After settling affairs in Miletus, Alexander went on to Caria. Before leav-

was probably the father of Leucippus and Chrysippus, who were the eponymous magistrates in 340/39 and 336/5, respectively (*Milet* I.3, no. 122 II, l. 75 and 78).

35. Bosworth, *Historical Commentary*, 138.

36. Bosworth, *Historical Commentary*, 139 notes that Alexander distinguished between the garrison and the Milesian soldiers.

37. Bosworth, *Historical Commentary*, 140; Bosworth, *Conquest and Empire*, 250.

38. The monument and Alexander's appointment are sometimes dated to 334/3, but more appropriately belong in 333/2 as part of an outpouring of offerings for Alexander; see P. J. Rhodes, Milesian "'Stephanephoroi': Applying Cavaignac Correctly," *ZPE* 157 (2006): 116, following the dating proposed by E. Cavaignac, "Les dékarchies de Lysandre," *REH* 90 (1924): 285–316. The list of names down to Alexander's were probably the work of a single stonecutter, while the ones that follow are in different hands; see Robert K. Sherk, "The Eponymous Officials of Greek Cities IV: The Register: Part III: Thrace, Black Sea Area, Asia Minor (Continued)," *ZPE* 93 (1992): 229–31. Eric W. Driscoll, "The Milesian Eponym List and the Revolt of 412 B.C.," *The Journal of Epigraphic Studies* 2 (2019): 11–32 argues that this version of the list represents a reinscription of an annual list.

ing Miletus, though, Alexander disbanded the Hellenic fleet (Arr. *Anab.* 1.20.1; Diod. 17.22.5–23.3). This action has been subject to scrutiny in terms of Alexander's strategic planning,[39] but more relevant for Ionia than contrafactual armchair generalship is what that fleet had done in the first year of the campaign.

The Macedonian Naval Campaign in Ionia

There is scant mention of the Hellenic fleet until it arrived off Miletus (Arr. *Anab.* 1.18.5–6). To this point it had been conducting a campaign among the Aegean islands, parallel to that of the army. The best evidence for their activities comes from inscriptions recording Alexander's letters to the island communities. Most importantly for Ionia are the so-called First and Second Letters to the Chians (*RO* 84 A and B = *SIG*³ 283 and *SEG* XXVII 506).[40] Both documents, as well as a third fragmentary decree that Maxim Kholod dates to the same period, primarily concern the relationship between the citizens and returning exiles.[41] The "First Letter" declares that the Chians are to be autonomous and be governed according to their democracy, probably referring to the constitution created in the late 390s, but also requires the Chians appoint men to write new laws and stipulates that they be approved by the king (*RO* 84 A = *SIG*³ 283, ll. 3–7). However, its principal provision, being both the first (l. 3) and last (ll. 17–19) point addressed, is the return of the exiles.[42] This inscription shows an awareness of the potential for domestic disruption with the return by establishing a garrison to preempt conflict (ll. 17–18). However, the uncertain date of these documents introduces problems for the interpretation.[43]

There are two proposed dates for the First Letter: 332, at the conclusion of the war in the Aegean, or 334, between the capture of Chios and the dismissal

---

39. Scholars have traditionally deferred to Arrian who says that Alexander was short money, e.g., Ulrich Wilcken, *Alexander the Great* (New York: Norton, 1967), 92; J. R. Hamilton, *Plutarch, Alexander: A Commentary* (Oxford: Oxford University Press, 1969), 37; W. W. Tarn, *Alexander the Great*, vol. 1 (Cambridge: Cambridge University Press, 1948), 18, but Bosworth, *Historical Commentary*, 141–43, and *Conquest and Empire*, 46–47, argues that Alexander simply made a mistake.

40. On the text of the first decree, see Heisserer, *Alexander and the Greeks*, 80–81.

41. Maxim M. Kholod, "On the Dating of a New Chian Inscription concerning the Property of Returned Exiles," in *Das imperiale Rom und der hellenistische Osten*, ed. Linda-Marie Günther and Volker Grieb (Stuttgart: Franz Steiner Verlag, 2012), 21–34.

42. Gustav Adolf Lehmann, *Alexander der Große und die "Freiheit der Hellenen"* (Berlin: de Gruyter, 2015), 93. Heisserer, *Alexander and the Greeks*, 92–93, though, declares that the section regarding the betrayers is the most important.

43. Two subsequent decrees belong later; see Kholod, "New Chian Inscription," 21–32; Lehmann, *Alexander der Große*, 97–99. *RO* 84 B = *SEG* XXVII 506, in particular, should be read as a response to the questions of an embassy in 331.

of the league fleet at Miletus. The orthodox date for the inscription is 332, after Hegelochus captured Chios again from the Persian fleet (Arr. *Anab.* 3.2.3).[44] This date is reached based on the interpretation of two points, the installation of a garrison (ll. 17–20) and the return of the exiles (ll. 5–6). The decree refers to individuals who betrayed Chios, so, in this thesis, these are the same men whom Hegelochus took to Elephantine in Egypt (Arr. *Anab.* 3.2.3–4; Curt. 4.5.14–17), while the triremes to be provided are those conscripted for the siege of Mytilene (Curt. 4.8.12). In contrast, Heisserer argues that the decree belongs in 334, envisioning the situation on Chios as parallel to that of Ephesus (Arr. *Anab.* 1.17.11).[45] The strongest point in favor of this view is that the decree specifies that the people who betrayed the population were to be tried by the league *synedrion* and those who fled were banned from entering those communities (ll. 10–15).[46] Heisserer rightly, I believe, argues that the constitutional reorganization of Chios is more likely to have taken place in 334 since the restoration of the constitution in 332 would have been a continuation of this process rather than a new revision.

While I agree in principle with Heisserer's early dating of the First Letter, I believe that his reading is flawed. Both dates for the inscription assume that the order to supply triremes "so long as the rest of the Greek fleet sails with us" (ταότας δὲ πλεῖν μέχρι ἄν καὶ τὸ ἄλλο ναοτικὸν τὸ τῶν Ἑλλήνων μεθ᾽ ἡμῶν συμπλῇ, l. 9–10) indicates that the decree came near the end of the campaign.[47] In Heisserer's interpretation, the decree was issued after Alexander had decided to dismiss the fleet at Miletus (Arr. 1.20.1), with the instructions providing a limit for the term of service. However, the inscription does not specify when the ships will be dismissed, and thus likely indicates an open-ended mandate. A date for the inscription between 334 and 332 is usually excluded because it is often assumed that Alexander did not order the reconstitution of the fleet until he was in Gordium, when Arrian first mentions Hegelochus' command (2.2.3).[48] This evidence comes after Arrian narrates Memnon's capture of Chios (2.1.1) and Curtius introduces the new fleet by describing Amphoterus'

---

44. Most recently argued by Lehmann, *Alexander der Große*, 90–97; Kholod, "New Chian Inscription," 26–27.

45. Heisserer, *Alexander and the Greeks*, 83–95, followed by P. J. Rhodes and Robin Osborne, *Greek Historical Inscriptions, 404–323* (Oxford: Oxford University Press, 2007), 422.

46. Heisserer, *Alexander and the Greeks*, 83–95; Rhodes and Osborne, *Greek Historical Inscriptions*, 422–43.

47. Heisserer, *Alexander and the Greeks*, 86–87; Lehmann, *Alexander der Große*, 97. Thomas Lenschau, "Alexander der Grosse und Chios," *Klio* 33 (1940): 205–6, argues that the first-person plural referred to the Chians rather than Alexander and his fleet.

48. Heisserer, *Alexander and the Greeks*, 87–88; Stephen Ruzicka, "War in the Aegean, 333–331 B.C.: A Reconsideration," *Phoenix* 42, no. 2 (1988): 132; Bosworth, *Historical Commentary*, 184.

charge to liberate the island from Memnon (Curt. 3.1.19). However, two points indicate that Alexander had already ordered the reassembly of the Macedonian fleet before Chios fell to the Persians.[49] First, Arrian uses the pluperfect (προσετέτακτο), which suggests that the order had come earlier than where it appears in the narrative, and second, he says that the assembly of the fleet was already underway. Further, Curtius records that the new fleet included Greek ships, not just Macedonian (Curt. 3.1.19). I believe, therefore, that the letter to the Chians should be dated to the very end of 334 or start of 333, at the outset of Hegelochus' command rather than at the end of it, but before Chios had fallen.

During his march south through Ionia, Alexander offered two competing but not contradictory visions for the region. First, the official message delivered by the campaign was that he was liberating the Greeks from Persia.[50] Henceforth the Ionians were to be autonomous (e.g., RO 84B = SEG XXVII 506, ll. 3–4), they would have liberal governments under their ancestral, democratic, constitutions, and exiles would return and have property restored to them. Underlying this propaganda was a second message: that the Ionians were now Alexander's subjects. Despite the measures taken at Chios and Ephesus to ensure that the returning exiles did not disrupt domestic stability, the Macedonian conquest led to considerable turmoil amid a situation ripe to be exploited.

War in the Aegean

While Alexander's relentless assault east continued through 333 and 332, Persian operations continued in the Aegean.[51] In Caria, the Macedonian forces faced prolonged resistance from Orontobates, while a Persian fleet threatened coastal and island communities and the remnants of Darius' army retreated into Anatolia from the east after their defeat at Issus in a pass linking Cilicia and Syria in November 333.[52] Far from ending the Persian threat, Alexander's

---

49. Heisserer, *Alexander and the Greeks*, 87–89, argues implausibly that Hegelochus' fleet was categorically different from Alexander's fleet.

50. On this message, see A. B. Bosworth, "Alexander the Great Part 2: Greece and the Conquered Territories," in *Cambridge Ancient History*², vol. 6, ed. David M. Lewis, John Boardman, Simon Hornblower, and Martin Ostwald (Cambridge: Cambridge University Press 1994), 868–70; Sviatoslav Dmitriev, *The Greek Slogan of Freedom and Early Roman Politics in Greece* (Oxford: Oxford University Press, 2011), 102–3, 111.

51. Ruzicka, "War in the Aegean," 133–34.

52. On the battle, see Diod. 17.32.2–35; Arr. 2.8–11; Curt. 3.9–11; Plut. *Alex.* 20; Bosworth, *Conquest and Empire*, 55–64; Worthington, *By the Spear*, 165–71. For the subsequent Persian retreat, Curt. 4.1.34–35, Billows, *Antigonus*, 41–45.

victory intensified the war in Anatolia until defections crippled the Persian fleet in early 332.[53]

Despite the general impression of Alexander's headlong rush to the east, he was not wholly neglectful of this threat. He had disbanded the league fleet after capturing Miletus (Diod. 17.22.5–23.3; Arr. *Anab.* 1.20.1), but probably soon recognized the strategic error and ordered its reconstitution before the spring of 333 (Arr. *Anab.* 2.2.3; Curt. 3.1.19–20), and had garrisoned much of western Anatolia, including Priene.[54] Until the new Macedonian fleet arrived, however, the Persian forces, consisting of the ships that had failed to prevent the fall of Miletus and a sizable army under the command of Memnon of Rhodes dominated the eastern Aegean (Arr. *Anab.* 2.2.1).[55] Greek sources for this campaign attest to fears that the Persians were preparing to cross the Aegean, but these proved unfounded (Diod. 17.29.3, 30.1; Arr. *Anab.* 2.2.4–5). The Persians instead continued to threaten the Bosporus and worked to secure control of the Anatolian coast, which placed Ionia front and center.

Early in 333, Memnon recaptured Chios, which Arrian says was given over to him by treason (προδοσία, *Anab.* 2.1.1; cf. Diod. 17.29.2, 31.2, Curt. 3.1.19).[56] He turned Chios over to those who had opened the gates, but probably refrained from installing a garrison since we hear of a later date when the Persians did garrison the island (Arr. *Anab.* 2.13.4–5),[57] instead relying on the proximity of the Persian fleet at Mytilene to dissuade a counterrevolution. After the Macedonian fleet captured Tenedos in the Hellespont the Persian commanders Autophradates and Pharnabazus established a garrison of fifteen

---

53. For this phase of Alexander's campaign, see Bosworth, *Conquest and Empire*, 64–65; Worthington, *By the Spear*, 172–78.

54. Alexander had forces in Caria where the region was split between the Hecatomnid Ada, who turned over her fortresses to Alexander and adopted him as her son in return for his support (Arr. *Anab.* 1.23.6; Strabo 14.2.17; Diod 17.24.2–3; Plut. *Alex.* 22.4), and the citadel of Halicarnassus, which held out until the defeat of Orontobates about a year later (Arr. *Anab.* 2.5.7). On events in Caria, see Maxim M. Kholod, "The Garrisons of Alexander the Great in the Greek Cities of Asia Minor," *Eos* 97 (2010): 252; Ruzicka, "War in the Aegean," 135; Matthew A. Sears, "Alexander and Ada Reconsidered," *CPh* 109, no. 3 (2014): 211–21.

55. Greek sources probably overstate Memnon's importance in the Persian command structure; see Ruzicka, "War in the Aegean," 133–34, 138; and Briant, *From Cyrus to Alexander*, 826–27, who independently reach the conclusion that there is an overemphasis on Memnon in the Greek sources. However, Diodorus' declaration that Darius gave him overall command of the Persian defense of Asia Minor may be accurate given the death of the satrap Spithridates at Granicus and his family connections to the Persian aristocracy. His nephew Pharnabazus took up the command after Memnon died in 333 (Arr. *Anab.* 2.2.1; Curt. 3.3.1).

56. Heisserer, *Alexander and the Greeks*, 92–93, suggests that there were individuals who would have been seen as traitors both before and after this time, so this episode need not correlate to Alexander's First Letter to the Chians. There is reason to suspect bribery; see Diod. 17.29.4.

57. See Bosworth, *Historical Commentary*, 223–24.

hundred mercenaries on Chios that was later reinforced (Arr. *Anab.* 2.13.5; Curt. 4.1.37).[58] Even less is known about the Persian capture of Miletus, where Pharnabazus exacted money (Curt. 4.1.37). There is no evidence for a garrison, but Miletus's long-standing ties to Caria ensured that it did not revert to Macedonian control until after the defeat of a Persian force near the city in 332 (Curt. 4.5.13). About the same time, the new Macedonian fleet arrived at Chios and laid siege (Curt. 4.5.14). The Persian garrison initially prevented Chios from surrendering, but with the writing on the wall the citizens sided with the Macedonians, slaughtered the garrison, and turned over the commanders, mercenaries, and pirates (Arr. *Anab.* 3.2.3–5; Curt. 4.5.17–18). Curtius and Arrian share a general outline for the events on Chios but differ in key details. Where Curtius says that the citizens waited until the gate was breached to join the Macedonians, Arrian records that they opened the gates for them. Macedonian operations against Persian forces in the Aegean continued after the capture of Chios, but Ionia itself was spared from those conflicts.[59]

There is no evidence to indicate that the Persians had recaptured any poleis other than Chios and Miletus, but it strains credulity to believe that the rest of the region was simply passed over, regardless of whether they had Macedonian garrisons.[60] But neither is there evidence for Persian garrisons in Ionia. Peter Green advances the argument that some of this was because the Ionians harbored latent hostility toward Alexander's impositions and therefore welcomed the Persian fleet as their true liberators.[61] Certainly, the Ionians did not universally adore Alexander, but the Persians were the other side of the same coin, and Memnon's intrigues Ephesus in 336 had resulted in bloody purges.[62] Most likely, every polis in the region was subject to extortion or raids from Persian forces and opportunistic neighbors that are attested as pirates, depending on which side of the fence it chose to sit (Arr. *Anab.* 3.2.5; Curt. 4.5.18).[63] The war opened the door again to domestic infighting that Alexander had curtailed in

---

58. Ruzicka, "War in the Aegean," 141, rightly notes that the passages recorded in Curtius and Arrian must refer to the same events despite a discrepancy in chronology.

59. On the conclusion of the conflict, see Ruzicka, "War in the Aegean," 145–51.

60. On Macedonian garrisons, see Kholod, "Garrisons of Alexander," 252.

61. Green, *Alexander of Macedon*, 211–12.

62. Elsewhere in the eastern Aegean, Mytilene put up stiff resistance to the Persian siege in 333/2 and negotiated with the Persians for the Macedonian garrison to leave unmolested. See Maxim M. Kholod, "Mytilene under Alexander the Great: A Way to a Democracy under the Monarchic Aegis," *Bulletin of St. Petersburg State University*[2] 55, no. 4 (2010): 36–39. My thanks to Dr. Hana Akselrod for translating this article from Russian.

63. J. E. Atkinson, *A Commentary on Q. Curtius Rufus' Historiae Alexandri Magni, Books 3 and 4* (Leiden: Brill, 1980), 330, sees the reference to pirates in these sources as indicative of increased activity after the Social War. The Ionians had a particular reputation for "painting both sides of the walls" (τοὺς τοίχους τοὺς δύο ἐπαλείφοντες, Paus. 6.3.15); see Chapter 4.

Ephesus and is attested in Chios, but in many places any change of allegiance was easily reversed as the Macedonian forces regained the upper hand.[64]

When the dust settled in 332, Ionia was again firmly under Macedonian control. Those deemed traitors were sent to Alexander in Egypt for trial, accompanied by embassies from Ionia. Nevertheless, the creation of a new unipolar Macedonian world only managed to paper over domestic fault lines that would begin to rupture again before the end of Alexander's life.

A Macedonian World

The conclusion to the war in the Aegean took place a year later across the Mediterranean in Egypt (Arr. *Anab.* 3.5.1; Curt. 4.8.12–13; Strabo 17.1.43). The overall outcome of the embassies unclear. Arrian concludes that Alexander left no one unsatisfied (καὶ οὐκ ἔστιν ὅντινα ἀτυχήσαντα ὧν ἐδεῖτο ἀπέπεμψε) and Curtius largely matches this declaration. He says that embassies from Chios, Rhodes, and Athens brought before Alexander concerns about the fate of the prisoners and complaints about the imposition of Macedonian garrisons. Alexander, he says, found the requests reasonable.

By contrast, the first-century geographer Strabo preserved a record of embassies from Miletus and Erythrae described by Callisthenes in conjunction with Alexander's visit to Siwah. Not interested in the social and political consequences of these embassies, Callisthenes includes them as additional prodigies that supported Alexander's divinity, a confluence of interests that frequently leads scholars to suggest Alexander solicited favorable oracles.[65]

The suspect nature of both oracles lends plausibility to this thesis. Didyma, the oracle at Miletus, had been silent from the time of the Persian Wars, when the Branchidae, its hereditary priestly clan, allegedly betrayed the sanctuary to the Persians and had subsequently been deported to central Asia (Hdt. 6.19.2–20).[66] According to Strabo/Callisthenes, the Milesians declared that

---

64. As noted by Briant, *From Cyrus to Alexander*, 855.

65. Alan M. Greaves, *Miletos: A History* (New York: Routledge, 2002), 134–36; Alan M. Greaves, "Divination at Archaic Branchidai-Didyma," *Hesperia* 81, no. 2 (2012): 179; H. W. Parke, *The Oracles of Apollo in Asia Minor* (New York: Routledge: 1985), 36; Worthington, *By the Spear*, 266–67. Tim Howe, "The Diadochi, Invented Tradition, and Alexander's Expedition to Siwah," in *After Alexander*, ed. Victor A. Tronscoso and Edward M. Anson (Oxford: Oxford University Press, 2013), 62, describes Didyma as Alexander's "tame oracle."

66. Alexander's interaction with the Branchidae is an impossible historiographical problem. N. G. L. Hammond, *Three Historians of Alexander the Great: The So-Called Vulgate Authors, Diodorus, Justin, and Curtius* (Cambridge: Cambridge University Press, 1983), 141; Pearson, *Lost Historians*, 240; and W. W. Tarn, "The Massacre of the Branchidae," *CR* 36, nos. 3–4 (1922): 63–65, argue that it was introduced to contextualize the punishment of Greek traitors, while other scholars believe that

the sacred spring miraculously reappeared after Alexander liberated them and with it returned the gift of prophecy, complete with utterances about his divinity, a revolt stewing in Greece, and the final victory over Persia. The prophecies that appear in Strabo are not recorded verbatim and the specific events such as the battle at Gaugamela were likely later amendments to general pronouncements.

But what about this alleged connection between Alexander and the foundation of the oracle? There is no evidence that Alexander patronized Didyma, either in the guise of Panhellenic piety or as a reward for declaring him divine, so another explanation is needed for this series of events. Much as elsewhere in Ionia, there had been a new wave of public construction in Miletus in the 340s and 330s that was disrupted by the wars before, during, and in the wake of Alexander's expedition. Work had not progressed on restoration of the new temple of Apollo, probably on account of its exceptionally steep cost, but plans for it were likely formulated in this same period. The miraculous rebirth of and alleged responses from the oracle therefore developed in a milieu where the restoration was already in the works but was accelerated through its capacity for political exploitation. The oracular responses allowed the embassy to simultaneously offer a performance of loyalty to Alexander as recompense for lapses during the war and to deliver a not-so-subtle petition for funds to restore the temple (see Chapter 9).[67]

A similar picture appears when looking at the Erythraean Athenais. Strabo describes her as like another Erythraean prophetess, the Sibyl (Strabo 17.1.43), which served to legitimize this largely unknown woman. And yet, in his study of north Ionian cults, Fritz Graf concluded that, in the fourth century, prophetess of the Erythraeid was a contested position with multiple communities claiming to have the heir of the Erythraean Sibyl.[68] Moreover, Erythrae was another community whose loyalty to Alexander during the months of the war in the Aegean was suspect. In this context, then, the declaration of Alexander's divinity again served double duty, demonstrating that Erythrae was loyal to Alexander while, if accepted, also staking a claim to legitimacy as the genuine heir to the Sibyl.

---

a massacre of some sort did take place; see Greaves, "Divination," 179–80; N. G. L. Hammond, "The Branchidae at Didyma and in Sogdiana," CQ^2 48, no. 2 (1998): 339–44; Heckel, *Conquests*, 95–96; H. W. Parke, "The Massacre of the Branchidae," *JHS* 105 (1985): 59–68.

67. For how Alexander became associated with the restoration of Didyma, see Joshua P. Nudell, "Oracular Politics: Propaganda and Myth in the Restoration of Didyma," *AHB* 32 (2018): 44–60.

68. Fritz Graf, *Nordionische Kulte: Religionsgeschichtliche und epigraphische Untersuchungen zu den Kulten von Chios, Erythrai, Klazomenai und Phokaia* (Rome: Schweizerisches Institut in Rom, 1985), 342–43.

Alexander's decision regarding Ionia that invites the most questions is regarding the fate of the Ionian *phoros*. Alexander officially relieved the region of its tributary obligations in 334, changing it into a *syntaxis* (contribution). What this looked like in practice is more opaque but, given that the new payments were contributions for a collective war, the contribution was likely released upon the symbolic end of the war against Persia in 330. An inscription from Priene offers additional insight as to this change (*RO* 86B = *I.Priene²* 1).[69] The inscription, which addressed Priene and its port, Naulochon, drew a distinction between the presumably Greek citizens of Priene in both locations and the Myrseloi, Pedieis, and land that belonged to noncitizens, which Alexander claimed for himself (ll. 8–13).[70] The former received autonomy and relief from their contributions, while the latter continued to owe their *phoros*. The explicit removal of the *syntaxis* leads scholars to regard this as a special grant to Priene, perhaps, in contrast to the "non-Greeks" in Naulochon.[71] It is this sort of leap that leads to the conclusion that this edict was a unique grant for Priene. The citizens of Priene also received a favorable ruling from Alexander regarding a long-running border dispute over the Samian *peraea* that they referred to as evidence when the case came up again in the third century (*I.Priene²* 132), but there is nothing that marks Priene as uniquely important and this edict could have been repeated throughout the region after 330 to formally record the autonomy of Ionia and to remit the *syntaxis*.

The evidence for Ionia during Alexander's reign after 331 is particularly fragmentary, which makes it difficult to evaluate Macedonian rule. It is clear, however, that Alexander remained involved in decisions that affected Ionia. Plutarch, for instance, says that Alexander wrote a letter to Megabyzus about how to handle a situation where a servant staged a sit-in in the temple, encouraging him to lure the protester out of the sanctuary to avoid impurity (Plut. *Alex.* 42.1).[72] Alexander's specific correspondent here is unknown, but the name resembles the title held by the priest at the temple of Artemis in Ephesus, mak-

---

69. On this inscription, see Badian, "Alexander the Great," 133–36; Heisserer, *Alexander and the Greeks*, 145–68; Lehmann, *Alexander der Große*, 109–14; Peter Thonemann, "Alexander, Priene, and Naulochon," in *Epigraphical Approaches to the Post-Classical Polis*, ed. Paraskevi Martzavou and Nikolaos Papazarkadas (Oxford: Oxford University Press, 2013), 23–36; cf. Appendix 2.

70. Bosworth, *Historical Commentary*, 280–82; Kholod, "Financial Relations," 85, contra Sherwin-White, "Ancient Archives," 85. Thonemann, "Alexander, Priene, and Naulochon," 23–36, suggests that Alexander's decision to distinguish between different populations increased the pressures for non-Greeks to adopt Greek culture, but see Appendix 2.

71. See particularly, Rhodes and Osborne, *Greek Historical Inscriptions*, 435.

72. The status of the person is unclear. Plutarch uses θεράπων, which usually refers to an attendant or worshipper, but was also a word used for enslaved people.

ing this connection likely. At the same time, Alexander largely left the preexisting administration intact, but limited its power by appointing his own financial and military officers. In the case of western Anatolia, Philoxenus received the position of *hyparch* that appears to be roughly synonymous with the position held by Cyrus the Younger some four score years earlier.[73] Philoxenus was first responsible for collecting tribute in the region and later imposed a garrison in Ephesus when officials there refused to arrest Anaxagoras, Codrus, and Diodorus, three brothers who assassinated Hegesias (Polyaenus 6.49). There is no clear date for these events, but the fact that when Alexander died Diodorus was awaiting trial after an injury thwarted his escape attempt suggests that it took place in the 320s. Nor is there much information about any of these four men, and Hegesias is variously identified as either one of the men pardoned by Alexander in 334 or a leading member of the pro-Macedonian junta that governed Ephesus on the basis that Polyaneus refers to him as the tyrant of Ephesus (6.49).[74] The importance of this episode is clear because it escalated until Philoxenus became involved, but there is insufficient evidence to say more. While Polyaenus' account points to internal conflict in Ephesus, it says nothing about on whose order the brothers were supposed to be arrested. He implies that first the brothers and then the Ephesians flouted Macedonian rule, but it is equally possible that that the assassination had nothing to do with Macedonia since Perdiccas ultimately returned Diodorus to Ephesus for trial.

Despite the lack of evidence about the political situation in Ionia during the 320s, it is nevertheless possible to trace the broad strokes of cultural change in the region. Perhaps the biggest development was the influx of money, which would only accelerate in the early Hellenistic period. The infusion of capital came from several sources, all of them linked to individuals. In addition to the inscription for Alexander's dedication of the temple of Athena Polias at Priene, he is said to have commissioned a massive portrait of himself wielding lightning bolts at the cost of twenty talents (Pliny *H.N.* 35.36).[75] Apelles, the artist of that portrait, offers a common Ionian story of this period. He was born in

---

73. Philoxenus likely accumulated powers as the years passed. Heckel, *Who's Who*, 220, follows Bosworth, *Historical Commentary*, 280–82, in distinguishing this Philoxenus from the one who inherited the satrapy of Caria after the death of Ada ([Arist.] *Oec.* 2.31, 1351b), on the grounds that former was too eminent an individual to be considered "some Macedonian" (τις Μακεδών). This argument is not wholly convincing given how little we know about Philoxenus. Arrian *Anab.* 7.23.1 mentions Menander as the satrap of Lydia and Philoxenus in Caria, but this could have been the result of an administrative shuffle after Alexander returned from India.

74. A pardoned tyrant: Badian, "Alexander the Great," 142 n. 36; junta: Bosworth, *Historical Commentary*, 132.

75. Heckel, *Who's Who*, 39–40. Bosworth, *Historical Commentary*, 133; Bosworth, *Conquest and Empire*, 45; Nawotka, "Freedom of Greek Cities," 29–30.

Colophon but moved to Ephesus and even before Alexander's reign had taken commissions to paint portraits at the Macedonian court in Pella (Pliny *H.N.* 35.86).[76] Prior interaction may have contributed to Alexander's special patronage, but Apelles was hardly alone in following financial opportunities presented by Alexander's conquest. Andron of Teos was appointed trierarch on the Indus in 326 (Arr. *Ind.* 18.4–8), and his brother Hagnon was a member of Alexander's inner circle who was said to have particularly indulged in the luxuries of the east, such as by wearing gold studs in his footwear (Plut. *Alex.* 22, 40; Athen. 12.55 [539c]).[77] And yet, where Alexander's campaigns opened lucrative opportunities for individuals that caused money to flow back to Ionia in some places, his regime on balance extracted resources. In one extreme request, Alexander demanded that the Ionians send him purple dye, prompting the acid-tongued Theocritus to quip that he had seized purple death and mighty fate.[78]

Exiles in Ionia

One consequence of the new unipolar Macedonian world that deserves broader consideration is the relationship between the Ionian poleis and political exiles. Political exiles had been an endemic problem throughout the Classical period, and frequently a subject of negotiation between the Ionians and the cycle of imperial powers in the region. Thus, while Alexander only made a general ruling about exiles in 324 with the Exiles Decree (Diod. 18.8.4–6), he had been arbitrating this issue in Ionia since the outset of his campaign in ways that established the framework out of which developed his general policy.

---

76. There is an anecdote that Alexander's gave Apelles a commission to paint Pancaste (see Heckel, *Who's Who*, 189), his favorite courtesan, nude and then gave her to him (Ael. *VH* 12.34; Pliny *H.N.* 35.36). If this episode is not apocryphal, it likely took place in Pella, not later in Alexander's reign.

77. Martine Cuypers, "Andron of Teos (802)," *BNJ* T 1, commentary; Heckel, *Who's Who*, 128; Billows, *Antigonus*, 286–88. Heckel argues that the two men are the same, but it is equally possible that they were brothers; see Cuypers, "Andron of Teos (802)." After Alexander's reign, Andron wrote histories, including a *Periplus* of the Black Sea, though Cuypers' biographical essay suggests that the surviving fragments indicate "time spent in the library more than a navy career." Hagnon received Ephesian citizenship in 322/1 for petitioning Craterus on behalf of the community (*I.Eph.* 1437) and by 316 was a navarch under Antigonus Monophthalmus (*IG* II² 682).

78. ἔλαβε πορφύρεος | θάνατος καὶ μοῖρα | κραταιή, Athen. 12.55 [539c]. This was probably a Homeric reference where there is an association between purple and death. Theocritus was known for his biting wit, which ultimately cost him his life when, told he would have to plead for his life before the Antigonus Monophthalmus' eyes, he quipped that that was impossible to do with a one-eyed king ([Plut.] *Mor.* 633c). Duane W. Roller, "Theokritos of Chios (760)," *BNJ*, biographical essay, dates this exchange to 319/8, when Antigonus came into possession of the island, but if it is appropriate to refer to Antigonus as king, then it belongs in 306–301.

The Exiles Decree was formally announced at the Olympic Games in 324, where, Diodorus says, tens of thousands of Greek exiles had assembled (Diod. 18.8.4–6). The decree declared the repatriation of all exiles, excepting only those who were exiled on religious grounds. In other words, Alexander was issuing a general amnesty and mandating the end to all domestic political conflicts in the Greek world, and, importantly, giving Antipater, his representative in Europe, authority to enforce the decision. Diodorus says that most Greeks approved of the decree. The primary exceptions, he says, were the Athenians and Aetolians, who resented Alexander's interference with their domestic affairs and prepared to resist.[79] However, Alexander's death less than a year later makes most interpretations of how the decree affected the relationship between the king and the Greeks speculative, and the revolts against Macedonian control came during the turbulent years after 323.[80]

There is no evidence for how the Exiles Decree affected Ionia. This silence leads to multiple speculative interpretations. First and most directly, Diodorus' naming of Athens and Aetolia as particular malcontents may serve as a framing device to foreshadow the Lamian War. Indeed, he concludes by saying that fortune soon provided them an opportunity, namely after Alexander died. Further, Diodorus provides this information in a passage in Book 18, among the events surrounding Alexander's death. His focus on Athens and Aetolia causes further problems for considering the reception of the Exiles Decree but does suggest that opposition elsewhere was muted or nonexistent.

A second possible interpretation is that the Exiles Decree simply did not apply to Ionia. This position is not supported by the ancient evidence but is built from assumptions about the relative political statuses of different communities. This argument would hold that Alexander observed a qualitative difference between the members of the League of Corinth, which were formally autonomous, and the Greek poleis he captured from Persia, which were formally his subjects.[81] If the Exiles Decree applied to the former and not the lat-

---

79. The Athenians may have resented the Exiles' Decree, but the explanation Diodorus gives for their preparations for war is Samos, which was a separate decision.

80. Sviatoslav Dmitriev, "Alexander's Exiles Decree," *Klio* 86, no. 2 (2004): 348–81, goes further, arguing that the Exiles Decree allowed Greek poleis to enact its mandate through local legislative processes and therefore was not as much of an imposition as is sometimes assumed.

81. I do not believe that Alexander used the league as an administrative mechanism in Asia, but whether Alexander enrolled the Greeks of Asia into it is a question without a clear answer. Recently Miltiades B. Hatzopoulos, "Perception of the Self and the Other: The Case of Macedonia," in *Ancient Macedonia*, vol. 7 (Thessaloniki: Institute for Balkan Studies, 2007), 51–66, tried to draw new conclusions based on the description of Alexander's *trierarchs* in India (Arr. *Ind.* 18.3–8), but his argument is refuted by Maxim M. Kholod, "Arr. *Ind.* 18.3–8 and the Question of the Enrollment of the Greek Cities of Asia Minor in the Corinthian League," in *Koinon Doron: Studies and Essays in Honour of Valery P. Nikonorov*, ed. Alexander A. Sinitsyn and Maxim M. Kholod (St. Petersburg:

ter, this would provide an explanation for why there is no evidence that it had any effect in the region. And yet the problems with this position are manifold. First, the ancient evidence for the decree suggests that it was a blanket pronouncement that applied to *all* Greek poleis, without indicating that Alexander distinguished between those he had power over such as Athens and those he did not, such as Syracuse, let alone between European and Asian Greece, which were both artificial categories. Second, while Alexander did exert more authority over the Ionians than over his "allies," I believe it was a distinction without a difference.

If there was no distinction made between Ionia and the other Greeks in the text of the Exiles Decree, why is there no evidence that it was enacted on the region? The answer lies in Alexander's earlier rulings regarding Ionian exiles. Ionia had served Alexander as a laboratory for policies regarding exiles since 334. At Ephesus near the start of the campaign he restored people who had been exiled on his account (δι' αὐτὸν, Arr. 1.17.10), thereby claiming responsibility for them and making clear that their loyalty to him would be repaid as a form of reciprocal obligation. As with the assembled throngs at Olympia in 324, this declaration curried goodwill with the exiles being restored, but also made loyalty a precondition for repatriation. This situation had probably continued through much of 334 when Alexander received supplication from other exiles in and around Ionia and agreed to restore them to their communities.

When Alexander's considerations ceased to be primarily given to exiles already loyal to him and expanded to include people who would be loyal on account of their restoration is unknown, but there is evidence that it also dates to the early part of his reign. The first sign of this change comes in Alexander's First Letter to the Chians from 334/3, which created a new category of exiles (those who betrayed the polis to the barbarians, *RO* 84A = *SIG*³ 283, ll. 10–12) and otherwise instructed the Chians to restore all other exiles along with its constitutional transition to a democracy.[82] Together with the so-called Second Letter, these inscriptions from Chios indicate extensive interference in an autonomous community.

The immediate restoration of exiles threatened domestic stability, as is evi-

---

St. Petersburg University, 2013), 479–82. Cf. recent discussions in Faraguna, "Alexander and the Greeks," 99–130, and Elisabetta Poddighe, "Alexander and the Greeks," in *Alexander the Great: A New History*, ed. Waldemar Heckel and Lawrence A. Tritle (Malden, MA: Blackwell, 2009), 99–120.

82. The Second Letter makes a specific exception for Alcimachus, who it says was Alexander's friend and was not working for Persia of his own volition. This man is probably a Chian, rather than the Macedonian officer in charge of capturing Aeolis in 334; see Francis Piejko, "The 'Second Letter' of Alexander the Great to Chios," *Phoenix* 39, no. 3 (1985): 245–47; contra Heisserer, *Alexander and the Greeks*, 108–11.

denced by the bloody purges that took place at Ephesus, and the broader the amnesty, the more issues threatened to crop up. A third inscription from Chios, plausibly from c.332/1, addressed the return of property and made the state liable for damages if it could not be returned to the original owner (*SEG* 51, 1075 ll. 3–7).[83] The decree established a board of ten judges to resolve disagreements between the returning exiles and those who remained (ll. 9–11),[84] but the exact composition of this tribunal is unknown. At around the same time at Mytilene, though, Alexander established a local board of arbitrators composed of equal numbers of men who returned and men who had stayed to resolve property disputes (*RO* 85B = *IG* XII^2 6, ll. 21–34).

Although the provisions on Chios demonstrate an awareness of the complications that accompanied the return of exiles, conflicts did not only arise from legal disputes over property. The case of Theopompus provides an illustrative example. Perhaps the most famous repatriated exile in Ionia, Theopompus was a prolific writer and historian whose father had been exiled from Chios on the charge of laconism, probably in the 390s.[85] He had been familiar with the Macedonian court in his adult life but did not receive preferential treatment and only returned after the general amnesty in 332/1. Theopompus became involved in politics upon repatriation and the surviving fragments of his letters to Alexander reveal that he resumed what might be called the family grudge against Theocritus, whose relatives had led Chios into an alliance with Athens in the 390s.[86] In particular, he accused Theocritus of having amassed a great deal of wealth to the detriment of the state and perhaps at the expense of the returned exiles (*BNJ* 115 T 9, F 252; Strabo 14.1.35). The veracity of these accusations is unknown, but they are likely libel meant to denigrate his rival and enhance his position on Chios. At the same time, the best lies contain a kernel of truth. Theocritus may well have used his prominent position and the opportunity presented by returning exiles to make money, but the mechanics of this and whether it was as corrupt as Theopompus implies is unknown. What is

---

83. I have followed the text in Kholod, "New Chian Inscription," 22–23.

84. None of the fragments mention Alexander, but the decree is missing the first line, which is where Alexander's name most likely would occur; see Kholod, "New Chian Inscription," 22–32.

85. Theopompus' exile has been variously dated; see Chapter 5.

86. These letters were said to have enhanced his position on the island and flattered Alexander (*BNJ* 115 T 8, T 20a, F 251). Five fragments survive, *BNJ* 115 T 8–9, F 250–54, with commentary. See also Robin Lane Fox, "Theopompus of Chios and the Greek World," in *Chios: A Conference at the Homerion in Chios*, ed. John Boardman and C. E. Vaphopoulou-Richardson (Oxford: Oxford University Press, 1986), 117–20; Michael A. Flower, *Theopompus of Chios: History and Rhetoric in the Fourth Century BC* (Oxford: Oxford University Press, 1994), 23–25; Gordon S. Shrimpton, *Theopompus the Historian* (Montreal: McGill University Press, 1991), 7–9, 21–23. On Theocritus' allegedly impoverished background, see Roller, "Theokritos of Chios (760)," biographical essay.

clear, however, is that Theompompus' complaints came to naught, and, after Alexander's death, he was again exiled, was refused entry to Egypt allegedly on the charge of being a meddlesome busybody (πολυπράγμων), and only just avoided execution (*BNJ* 115 T 2).[87]

Specific evidence for exiles in Ionia beyond Chios is frustratingly absent, but there is no reason to assume that comparable processes were not at work. There were few crimes (sacrilege and sedition on behalf of Persia) that kept a person in exile, while Alexander offered everyone else an amnesty that heralded an era. In propagating the Exiles Decree of 324 the principal change was the absence of reference to those who collaborated with Persia, but otherwise formalized and extended an ad hoc policy that had developed in Asia Minor nearly a decade earlier. Although the Exiles Decree did not have immediate consequences for Ionia, it indirectly led to war in the region, ironically over an issue that it did not address: ownership of Samos.

Samos

The elephant in Ionia in the last years of Alexander's reign was Samos, which had been occupied by Athens in the 360s. In his compressed account, Diodorus Siculus states that the principal Athenian grievance with Alexander over the Exiles Decree was that they had to give up Samos, which they had divided into cleruchies (18.8.7). Despite this evidence, Diodorus is mistaken, though perhaps preserving the Athenian interpretation of events. From Alexander's perspective, however, these were probably two unconnected issues. Nevertheless, in a near-contemporaneous decision to the Exiles Decree, Alexander demanded that the Athenians cede Samos to the displaced Samians.[88]

These Samians held an anomalous position. They considered themselves to be exiles (ἐν τῆι φυγῆι, *RO* 90B = *SIG*³ 312, l. 6), but there was no polis to return to at that time, and any restoration required extricating thousands of

---

87. This biographical detail is revelatory for the outcome of his political career, but factually suspect; see Flower, *Theopompus*, 17; William S. Morison, "Theopompus of Chios (115)," *BNJ* T 2, commentary. Cf. Shrimpton, *Theopompus*, 8–9.

88. The separate ruling is attested by Ephippus, *BNJ* 126 F 5; see Graham Shipley, *A History of Samos, 800–188 BC* (Oxford: Oxford University Press, 1987), 165. The precise date of this decision is controversial. For a date in 324, see Heisserer, *Alexander and the Greeks*, 184; Ernst Badian, "Harpalus," *JHS* 81 (1961): 30; Christopher W. Blackwell, *In the Absence of Alexander: Harpalus and the Failure of Macedonian Authority* (Bern: Peter Lang, 1999), 14, 145; for the clarification in 323, see Shipley, *Samos*, 297.

Athenians from the island.[89] The Samians had also probably petitioned Alexander unsuccessfully in 334 when he passed areas where many of the refugees settled, only to witness him confirm Athenian possession of the island.[90] The situation at Alexander's court had changed by 324, when the Samian cause found advocates, particularly in the person of Gorgus of Iasus.[91] Gorgus' motivations are hard to reconstruct. Ancient sources present him as a particularly implacable enemy of Athens to the point that he pledged ten thousand suits of armor and an equal number of catapults for an attack (Ephippus, *BNJ* 126 F 5), and the loss of Samos constituted a significant blow to Athens. Lurking behind this immediate political concern, however, may be an additional motivation. Iasus was a Greek polis in Hecatomnid Caria, making it a likely destination for Samian refugees after their expulsion. It is likely, therefore, that Gorgus had long familiarity with their plight, which led him not only to champion their cause in Alexander's court, but also to offer his own money to finance their restoration (*RO* 90B = *SIG*³ 312). Samians began to return to the island late in 324 or early 323, and more gathered at Anaea, where some had likely lived since 365. To dissuade emulators, the Athenian assembly responded by ordering the strategos on Samos to arrest any persons making the crossing and to send them to Athens as hostages, where they were ultimately condemned to death until Antileon of Chalcis paid their ransoms.[92]

Alexander's conquests temporarily created a unipolar Macedonian world that lasted only about a decade. But this reset in the imperial playing field only created new problems in both the regional and domestic spheres that were

---

89. Christian Habicht, "Athens, Samos, and Alexander the Great," *PAPS* 140, no. 3 (1996): 397–405, estimates that almost a third of the adult male Athenian citizens lived on Samos. *RO* 90B = *SIG*³ 312 mentions the goodwill toward the Samians in exile (l. 6) and Alexander's goodwill toward the Samian people (l. 9), but this decree belongs after the Samians had returned to the island. This language helped legitimize the new regime; see Joshua P. Nudell, "Remembering Injustice as the Perpetrator? Athenian Orators, Cultural Memory, and the Athenian Conquest of Samos," in *The Orators and Their Treatment of the Recent Past*, ed. Aggelos Kapellos (Berlin: de Gruyter, 2022), 447–63.

90. Plutarch (28.1) quotes from a letter from Alexander to the Athenians, probably in response to a letter protesting the demand to cede the island, in which he passes credit to Philip to distance himself from having previously confirmed Athenian ownership of the island (cf. Diod. 16.56.7). This was not likely the first such letter but has received scholarly attention on grounds of chronology and whether the letter does, as Plutarch suggests, demonstrate Alexander's divine pretensions; see particularly J. R. Hamilton, "Alexander and His 'So-Called' Father," *CQ*² 3, nos. 3–4 (1953): 151–57; N. G. L. Hammond, "Alexander's Letter Concerning Samos in Plut. 'Alex.' 28.2," *Historia* 42, no. 3 (1993): 379–82; Klaus Rosen, "Der 'göttliche' Alexander, Athen und Samos," *Historia* 27, no. 1 (1978): 20–25.

91. Heisserer, *Alexander and the Greeks*, 189; Heckel, *Who's Who*, 127.

92. R. Malcolm Errington, "Samos and the Lamian War," *Chiron* 5 (1975): 56; Bosworth, *Conquest and Empire*, 226. Christian Habicht, "Samische Volksbeschlüsse der hellenistischen Zeit," *MDAI(A)* 72 (1957): 159–69, no. 2, dates these events to early 321.

ready to boil over when Alexander suddenly died. The fissures in the Aegean at the end of Alexander's life are most visible in the dispute over Samos, but this was not an isolated incident. All was not well, and the Ionians were forced to adapt to a new geopolitical dynamic that once again threatened to expose old fault lines. And yet with the upheavals in the political landscape also came new opportunities.

CHAPTER 8

ॐ

Facing a New Hellenistic World

323–294

Ancient historians suggest that the world waited for Alexander's death with bated breath and careful preparation, and that the news was met with a flurry of activity. In Europe Athens instigated the Lamian War, in Asia Minor Rhodes expelled its Macedonian garrison (Diod. 18.8.1), and in central Asia colonists settled by Alexander refused to stay in place (Diod. 18.7.1–5). In Ionia, there was no revolt against Macedonian rule and, with the notable exception of refugee Samians returning to their island in the face of Athenian resistance, the Hellenistic period began with a conspicuous calm at the eye of the storm overtaking the eastern Mediterranean. That calm did not last, and Ionia was soon caught up in the conflicts and rivalries that defined the end of the fourth century.

Richard Billows has characterized this period in Ionia as a time of rebirth, in which the rulers considered the region to be of central importance and therefore planted the seeds of prosperity with favorable policies.[1] As is typical of recent scholarship, Billows here challenged a tradition that treated the early Hellenistic period as a destructive time in Ionia. Mikhail Rostovtzeff, for instance, described the wars of this period as an unstoppable force that "stunted and then gradually atrophied" the economic capacity of the Greek poleis, and Michael Austin described the Diadochoi as pirates who used wars to gather money to pay soldiers and legitimize their rule as "spear-won territory" in emulation of Alexander.[2] On one level it is hard to disagree with Billows: Hellenistic rulers offered tax exemptions, favorable statuses, and donations to gain influ-

---

1. Richard A. Billows, "Rebirth of a Region: Ionia in the Early Hellenistic Period," in *Regionalism in Hellenistic and Roman Asia Minor*, ed. Hugh Elton and Gary Reger (Pessac: Ausonius, 2007), 33–44.

2. Mikhail Rostovtzeff, *Social and Economic History of the Hellenistic World*, vol. 1 (Oxford: Oxford University Press, 1941), 4; M. M. Austin, "Hellenistic Kings, War, and the Economy," *CQ*[2] 36, no. 2 (1986): 464–65.

ence with the Ionians that laid a solid foundation for renewed prosperity, while also allowing some of the tribute payments to stay in the community. Even the outlay of resources for urban walls proved invaluable during the Galatian wars of the 270s (*I.Priene* 17; *I.Ery.* 24). However, the dissolution of the Macedonian empire after Alexander's death made for an unstable situation, and the same central geographic location that made the Ionians worth courting put them firmly in the middle of the early wars of the successors. This environment of competition allowed the Ionians to manipulate the imperial contenders, but in its own way this perpetuated the situation that the Ionians had been living under for two centuries. Only after the wars moved away from Ionia in the 290s did the Ionian renaissance begin in earnest.

Samians Restored

After the Athenian conquest of Samos in 365, refugees had scattered across the Mediterranean. Most found a new home nearby through the patronage of the Hecatomnid dynasts and existing networks of relationships, but a few found themselves as far away as Sicily.[3] Some individuals may have received citizenship where they settled, but most would have lived as metics.[4] Despite lacking a polis, the Samians appear to have maintained something of a coherent identity after their displacement, and even competed in and won events in Panhellenic festivals.[5] This situation where the Samians preserved their identity and never gained full protections of citizenship elsewhere explains why when Alexander reversed his ruling on Athenian ownership of Samos in 324, the refugees began to flock to Anaia on the mainland across from the island.

Refugees began to return to Samos late in 324 or early 323, and an Athenian decree issued instructions for the strategos on the island to arrest those who made the crossing and send them to Athens as hostages.[6] Despite the official ruling in their favor and support from foreign patrons, including two ships provided to them by Nausinicus of Sestus,[7] the short voyage to Samos was a dan-

---

3. Christian Habicht, "Samische Volksbeschlüsse der hellenistischen Zeit," *MDAI(A)* 72 (1957): nos. 25 and 30 dated to 306/5, probably recording honors for Syracusans. Another inscription (no. 23) records honors for a man from Heraclea, but it is unknown whether this was the polis of that name in Sicily or Heraclea under Latmus; see Graham Shipley, *A History of Samos, 800–188 BC* (Oxford: Oxford University Press, 1987), 164 n. 52, who prefers the latter identification.

4. On the consequences, see Shipley, *Samos*, 165–66.

5. *BNJ* 76 T 4; Robert B. Kebric, *In the Shadow of Macedon, Duris of Samos* (Wiesbaden: Franz Steiner, 1977), 7. There are complications in this evidence for a coherent polis-in-exile.

6. Habicht, "Samische Volksbeschlüsse," no. 1.

7. Habicht, "Samische Volksbeschlüsse," no. 2.

gerous proposition. Athens enjoyed temporary naval supremacy in the Aegean at the outset of the Lamian War,[8] but Samos was just one of its concerns, and the Samian position was enhanced when the Athenian fleet suffered defeats near Amorgus in 323/2, and then near Abydus (*IG* II² 398; II² 493) and off the Lichades islands in 322.[9] When the war turned against the Athenians, they condemned the Samian hostages to death but relented after Antileon of Chalcis stepped in to pay their ransoms.

Antipater, the governor of Macedon, referred the issue of Samos to the kings Philip III Arrhidaeus and Alexander IV after the conclusion of the Lamian War, and the regent Perdiccas issued a decree on their behalf that confirmed Alexander's decision to return the island to the Samians (Diod. 18.18.69). In return, the Samians established a new festival, the *basilica*, in honor of the kings, but official support did not return the island to them. The Samians still had to kill or physically expel the cleruchs, and the Athenians, impelled by the influx of displaced citizens, continued to regard the return as illegal. Several inscriptions may testify to additional Athenian attacks in the years after 321 (*IG* XII 6 51–52),[10] but Samos never again fell to Athens.

However, physical security was just one of the difficulties facing the new community. A series of honorific decrees reveal the extent to which the new polis relied on foreign aid. In addition to the decree for Gorgos of Iasus, who financed the return of some Samians (*RO* 90B = *SIG*³ 312), and Antileon of Chalcis, who paid the ransom for those captured by Athens (*IG* XII 6 1:42),[11] there are inscriptions detailing honors for citizens of Ephesus, Erythrae, Magnesia, Priene, and Heraclea, as well as the tyrant of Syracuse and Gela.[12] The Spartans reportedly underwent a one-day fast, with the savings going to Samos (Arist. *Oec.* 2.1347b 16–20), and Sosistratus of Miletus offered a three-talent loan to the new community (*IG* XII 37).[13]

---

8. The Athenians had access to around 410 ships in the 320s, *IG* II² 1631, ll. 167–74. See N. G. Ashton, "The Naumachia near Amorgos in 322 B.C.," *ABSA* 72 (1977): 1–11; A. B. Bosworth, "Why Did Athens Lose the Lamian War?," in *The Macedonians in Athens, 322–229 B.C.*, ed. Olga Palagia and Stephen V. Tracy (Oxford: Oxford University Press, 2003), 14–15.

9. Ashton, "Naumachia Near Amorgos," 1–11; Waldemar Heckel, *Who's Who in the Age of Alexander the Great* (New York: Routledge, 2005), 87–88. Bosworth, "Why Did Athens Lose?," 19–22 argues that there were additional, unrecorded naval battles in 323/2. The arrival of Cleitus the White's massive fleet in 322 drove the Athenians from the eastern Aegean.

10. Lara O'Sullivan, *The Regime of Demetrius of Phalerum in Athens, 317–307 BCE* (Leiden: Brill, 2009), 261–63; Lara O'Sullivan, "Asander, Athens, and 'IG' II² 450: A New Interpretation," *ZPE* 119 (1997): 107–8.

11. Habicht, "Samische Volksbeschlüsse," 156–64, no. 1.

12. Christian Habicht, "Hellenistische Inscriften aus dem Heraion von Samos," *MDAI(A)* 87 (1972): nos. 2, 4; Habicht, "Samische Volksbeschlüsse," nos. 2, 18, 23, 30; Shipley, *Samos*, 161–63. On the honorific inscriptions cf. below, "Samos and Diadochic Politics."

13. On long-term loans for the Samian state, see Habicht, "Hellenistische Inscriften," 201–2.

The Samian need is easily explained. The refugees were long absent from their land, which was the primary source of wealth in ancient Greece, and what little they had in the way of liquid assets was probably needed to equip and pay soldiers to defend against Athenian attacks. Moreover, once returned to Samos, they faced agricultural start-up costs for tools and seed at the same time as needing to purchase grain to feed the community because it is unlikely that the departing Athenians left much behind. A widespread grain shortage around the Aegean in these years complicated matters further (*RO* 96 = *SEG* IX 2; Dem. 56),[14] and Samian inscriptions reveal the lengths that the community went to encourage merchants to bring grain. One decree from c.322/1 (*SEG* I 361),[15] for instance, records honors for Gyges of Torone for bringing three thousand medimnoi of grain to Samos and offers him citizenship, either in accordance with a law that honored grain traders or in a bid to persuade Gyges to sell them even larger quantities.

In contrast, the motivations for the honorands are less clear. They might have sympathized with the refugees, but neither spite for Athens nor human rights considerations explain the outpouring of support. Priene, Ephesus, and Miletus, despite disputes with Samos that spanned generations, also had regional connections through institutions like the Panionion and local trade that would have encouraged investment in the new community.[16] Likewise,

Christian Habicht, "Der Beitrag zur Restitution von Samos während des lamischen Krieges (Ps. Aristoteles, Ökonomik II, 2.9)," *Chiron* 5 (1975): 45–50, connects the Spartan fast to their refusal to assist Athens in the Lamian War, but Shipley, *Samos,* 168, also points out that Samos and Sparta had a history of close relationships dating back to the Archaic period; cf. L. H. Jeffrey and Paul Cartledge, "Sparta and Samos: A Special Relationship?," *CQ*² 32, no. 2 (1982): 243–65.

14. The inscription records the purchase of grain from Cyrene for many communities in the Aegean and for Olympia and Cleopatra. Rhodes and Osborne also provide a map showing sale distribution, but Ionia is conspicuously absent from the list. This fact could be interpreted to mean that Ionia was self-sufficient in grain, but it is more likely that Ionian imports came from the north. Dominic Rathbone, "The Grain Trade and Grain Shortages in the Hellenistic East," in *Trade and Famine in Classical Antiquity,* ed. P. D. A. Garnsey and C. R. Whittaker (Cambridge: Cambridge University Press 1983), 45–55, posits that though war could have disrupted the flow of grain, many of the crises were the result of price gouging rather than limited supply. By the end of the third century there were regular grain distributions at the temple of Hera; see Habicht, "Samische Volksbeschlüsse," no. 63, with the dating. Daniel J. Gargola, "Grain Distributions and the Revenue of the Temple of Hera on Samos," *Phoenix* 46, no. 1 (1992): 12–28, points out that the law was a form of social control rather than a humanitarian venture. See Errietta M. A. Bissa, *Governmental Intervention in Foreign Trade in Archaic and Classical Greece* (Leiden: Brill, 2009), 169–203, on Ionian grain imports, which were a regular part of Greek legislation; cf. Wim Broekaert and Arjan Zuiderhoek, "Food and Politics in Classical Antiquity," in *A Cultural History of Food in Antiquity,* ed. Paul Erdkamp (London: Bloomsbury, 2012), 75–94.

15. Habicht, "Samische Volksbeschlüsse," no. 6. One *medimnos* in the Attic measurement system was 51.84 liters.

16. An Athenian inscription from 387/6 regulating trade at Clazomenae lists poleis that Clazomenaeans purchased grain from, including Phocaea, Chios, and Smyrna, demonstrating the robust regional trade in Ionia (*RO* 18 = *IG* II² 28, ll. 17–18).

honors are not mutually exclusive from straightforward economic motiva-tions. Men like Gyges and Sosistratus undoubtedly saw in Samos an investment opportunity, which would reap dividends through straightforward monetary repayment and through an outpouring of honors.[17]

The leaders of Samos in the years after the restoration were the wealthy citi-zens who led the exiles back to the island. Notable among these was the family of Duris of Samos. Pausanias describes a statue at Olympia dedicated to Caius, Duris' father, for his victory during the period of exile (νικῆσαι Σκαῖον ἡνίκα ὁ Σαμίων δῆμος ἔφευγεν ἐκ τῆς νήσου, 6.13.5 = BNJ 76 T 4).[18] The text continues, revealing that in due time Caius had something to do with the return of the Samians (τὸν δὲ καιρὸν [. . .] ἐπὶ τὰ οἰκεῖα τὸν δῆμον), but there is a critical lacuna that includes the verb of the clause. Modern scholars restore the text that he both led the exiles back and infer that he became a tyrant soon thereafter (BNJ 76 T 4).[19] Graham Shipley has, however, called into question the source tradition about the early days of the new Samian state. He contends that Pau-sanias' source for the importance of Caius in 322/1 is Duris himself, who had a reputation for exaggeration and a vested interested in burnishing his father's reputation (BNJ 76 T 8 = Plut. Per. 28.1–3).[20] The monument may record an authentic victory, but the inscription probably dates to after the restoration of Samos, which makes it impossible to know whether Caius represented himself as a member of a Samian community at Olympic games or, as I believe, this is an embellishment meant to show his dedication to his homeland.

The incipient state was heavily dependent on its wealthy citizens to func-tion, for many of the same reasons that it was dependent on foreign aid. Robert Kebric argues that it was this dependence that led to a peaceful emergence of Caius' tyranny out of what had been a de facto plutocracy.[21] The question is what to make of this position called "tyranny." If Duris is an unreliable narra-

17. For honors being a regular aim of commerce, see Darel Tai Engen, Honor and Profit: Athe-nian Trade Policy and the Economy and Society of Greece, 415–307 BCE (Ann Arbor: University of Michigan Press, 2010), 8–12.

18. The name Caius is remarkable for its parallel to the Latin praenomen, which is taken to buttress the case that his family spent the period of their exile in Sicily; see Kebric, In the Shadow of Macedon, 4; Frances Pownall, "Duris of Samos (76)," BNJ T 4, commentary, but this is a particu-larly tenuous connection so long before the First Punic War that established Roman control of the island.

19. Pownall, "Duris of Samos (76)," T 4 commentary; J. P. Barron, "The Tyranny of Duris at Samos," CR 12, no. 3 (1962): 191; Helen S. Lund, Lysimachus: A Study in Early Hellenistic Kingship (New York: Routledge, 1992), 124; Kebric, In the Shadow of Macedon, 7–8.

20. Shipley, Samos, 178. On Duris, see Pownall, "Duris of Samos (76)," T 8, commentary, fol-lowing W. E. Sweet, "Sources of Plutarch's Demetrius," Classical Weekly 44 (1951): 177–81.

21. Kebric, In the Shadow of Macedon, 8. See Pownall, "Duris of Samos (76)," T 4 commentary and biographical commentary, for arguments on the dates of Caius' tyranny and the proposal that Duris' reign should not be tied to the hegemony of a single Hellenistic king.

tor presenting an official account of this period, it is more difficult to reconstruct the political divisions on Samos. On the one hand, Caius and his sons
undoubtedly held a dominant position in Samian politics. Duris' name appears
on Samian coins dating to c.310–300, which indicates that he held a monetary
office during that period, and a brother Lysagoras introduced the honorific
decree for Heraclea c.300.[22] This confluence suggests that the family held a
tight grip on the reins of power, but it is also possible that their position was
not unlike that of Pericles in fifth-century Athens in that he was able to dominate the polis and be characterized as a tyrant without actually being one.[23]
This family's prominence on Samos clearly existed under the leadership of their
patriarch Caius, but its role in the restoration of Samos was expanded in memory through Duris' writing and strategically erected monuments.

Samos and Diadochic Politics

The contested status of Samos made it particularly vulnerable to the political
disputes of the early Hellenistic period. In 319 the new regent for Alexander IV
and Philip III Arrhidaeus, Polyperchon, tried to win Athenian support for his
war against Cassander by offering among other things to recognize Athenian
ownership of the island in the name of the kings (Diod. 18.56.7). This scheme
came to naught when Demetrius of Phalerum seized Athens with Cassander's
support in 317, but this did not mean that the Athenians abandoned their
insular ambitions. In 313, the Athenian assembly voted to award honors to the
satrap Asander in return for warships (*IG* II² 450, ll. 19–20). The purpose of the
gifts to Athens is unknown, but Lara O'Sullivan argues that Asander provided
the ships with the understanding that they would be used against Samos and
connects this with two inscriptions from the island that record a siege (*IG* XII
6, ll. 51–52).[24]

These continuing threats against Samos had the effect of strengthening its

---

22. Habicht, "Samische Volksbeschlüsse," no. 23; Stephen V. Tracy, "Hands in Samian Inscriptions of the Hellenistic Period," *Chiron* 20 (1990): 62; Shipley, *Samos*, 178; J. P. Barron, *The Silver
Coins of Samos* (London: Athlone, 1966), 124–40.

23. Cf. Thuc. 2.65 for Pericles' power over Athens.

24. O'Sullivan, *Regime of Demetrius*, 261–63. Edward M. Anson, "The Chronology of the Third
Diadoch War," *Phoenix* 60, nos. 3–4 (2006): 230–31, finds O'Sullivan's chronology problematic and
concludes that while her reconstruction is the most attractive thus far, the purpose can only be
guessed. Cf. Richard A. Billows, *Antigonus the One-Eyed and the Creation of the Hellenistic State*
(Berkeley: University of California Press, 1985), 116–17 n. 43. Shipley, *Samos*, 172, connects the
attack to the campaign waged by Myrmidon of Athens, a mercenary who commanded Cassander's
Carian campaign. Most likely, Cassander and Demetrius coordinated their attacks.

relationship with Antigonus Monophthalmus. Despite Perdiccas' support for the restoration of Samos, Antigonus was likely building his relationships there as early as 322/1. Certainly, after Triparadeisus, Antigonus' sphere of influence as strategos of Asia was expanded to include Ionia, and his position as the protector of Samos was strengthened by Polyperchon's support for the Athenian claim. Antigonus' aid allowed the Samians to triumph against the attacks in 313, which cemented Samos within the Antigonid sphere of influence until 294.

The relationship between Samos and Antigonus is most clearly demonstrated in stone. Surviving inscriptions record numerous honors granted to members of Antigonus' retinue, including a statue for Nicomedes of Cos.[25] There is likewise evidence of Samian soldiers serving with Antigonus' forces in various capacities. At the upper levels, Themison of Samos brought Antigonus forty ships at Tyre in 314 (Diod. 19.62.7) and served as a naval commander at the battle of Salamis in 306 (Diod. 20.50.4). But more indicative of this relationship than a single highly placed individual is that the Samians inscribed their thanks for Hipparchus of Cyrene for his support for Samos and, in particular, his treatment of Samian soldiers in Caria.[26] On the island itself, there are the remains of towers on the western side that were probably constructed under the Antigonid aegis.[27] These towers plausibly indicate the presence of a garrison, but the threat of force was probably not overtly coercive because the unique situation meant that the Samians also stood to gain time to restore their community.

The Wars of the Diadochoi and Ionia

While the Samians were occupied with the restoration of their polis, the rest of Ionia was buffeted by the currents that swept across the Macedonian empire. The first Macedonian settlement, which took place at Babylon in the immediate aftermath of Alexander's death in 323, confirmed the existing political structure of Asia Minor. Antigonus Monophthalmus received an expanded satrapy that included Pamphylia, Lycia, and Greater Phrygia, while Menander and Asander had their commands in Lydia and Caria confirmed (Diod. 18.3.1).[28]

---

25. Habicht, "Samische Volksbeschlüsse," no. 3. Shipley, *Samos*, 171, modifies Habicht's dating of the inscription from 320 to 319 in responses to Polycheron's edict granting Samos to Athens, but Billows, *Antigonus*, 411–12, Appendix 3 no. 82 dates the inscription to 312–310.

26. Habicht, "Samische Volksbeschlüsse," no. 22.

27. Shipley, *Samos*, 246–47.

28. On the power struggle among the Macedonian ruling class, see Edward M. Anson, *Alexander's Heirs: The Age of the Successors* (Malden, MA: Wiley-Blackwell, 2014), 47–49; Richard A.

The settlement at Babylon did not have a significant impact on Ionia at face value, but it laid the groundwork for a showdown between Antigonus and the regent Perdiccas, who was bringing him up on charges.

Antigonus fled from his province in 322, seeking protection from Antipater and Craterus in Macedon (Diod. 18.23.3–4). When Perdiccas left Anatolia to invade Egypt in 321, Antigonus crossed the Aegean again, this time with three thousand soldiers and ten Athenian ships. It was at this point that Ionia joined the story. According to Arrian in his fragmentary history of this period, Ephesus and the other Ionian poleis followed the lead of the Menander and Asander in throwing their support behind Antigonus (*Succ.* F 1.2). Antigonus' rapid success leads Richard Billows to speculate that he had struck a deal with the two satraps in advance of crossing back to Asia.[29] Irrespective of when Menander and Asander committed to war against Perdiccas, diplomatic communication between them and Antigonus is all but certain. The same cannot be said with confidence about the cities of Ionia. Antigonus had accepted the surrender of Priene on Alexander's behalf in 331, but then the evidence for continuing communication disappears. Nevertheless, there is reason to suggest that Antigonus laid the diplomatic groundwork to quickly gain their support. It is certainly possible that Asander and Menander served as proxies for him in their respective spheres, but, more directly, Antigonus' satrapal retinue included at least one Ionian, Aristodemus of Miletus, and the Macedonian Theotimides, whom the Samians awarded honors.[30]

Billows, *Kings and Colonists: Aspects of Macedonian Imperialism* (Leiden: Brill, 1995), 90–92; Billows, *Antigonus*, 402–3; R. Malcolm Errington, "From Babylon to Triparadeisos: 323–320 B.C.," *JHS* 90 (1970): 49–59; Alexander Meeus, "The Power Struggle of the Diadochoi in Babylon, 323 BC," *Anc.Soc.* 38 (2008): 39–83; Robin Waterfield, *Dividing the Spoils: The War for Alexander the Great's Empire* (Oxford: Oxford University Press, 2011), 16–29. Menander had been satrap of Lydia since 331; see Heckel, *Who's Who*, 163. The decision at Babylon with the greatest significance for Ionia was Lysimachus receiving Thrace, but the consequences of that appointments would not be seen for nearly two decades.

29. The chronology for the first Diadoch War is contested. Pierre Briant, *Antigone le Borgne: Les débuts de sa carrière et les problèmes de l'Assemblée macédonienne* (Paris: Les Belles Lettres, 1973), 208, suggests that Asander and Menander only joined with Antigonus after Craterus and Antipater declared war. On the issues of chronology, cf. Anson, *Alexander's Heirs*, 57–58; Hans Hauben, "The First War of the Successors (321 B.C.): Chronological and Historical Problems," *Anc. Soc.* 8 (1977): 85–119; Waterfield, *Dividing the Spoils*, 57–60. Supposedly it was news of Perdiccas' courtship of Alexander's sister Cleopatra, which Antigonus learned after he crossed into Asia, that swayed the other two Macedonians (Diod. 18.25.3). Anson, *Alexander's Heirs*, 56; James Romm, *Ghost on the Throne: The Death of Alexander the Great and the Bloody Fight for His Empire* (New York: Vintage Books, 2011), 147–48; Waterfield, *Dividing the Spoils*, 57–60. Asander and Antigonus may have been kinsmen; see Heckel, *Who's Who*, 57. Menander supposedly resented Perdiccas because the regent had made Cleopatra his superior at Sardis: Arr. *Succ.* 1.2.6; Waldemar Heckel, *Marshals of Alexander's Empire* (New York: Routledge, 1992), 54; Heckel, *Who's Who*, 57, 163.

30. Antigonus dispatched Aristodemus to the Peloponnese to recruit mercenaries. Diodorus (19.57.4–5) refers to him as strategos; Plutarch *Demet.* (17.2), calls him "first in flattery"

Yet it is worth asking how the Ionians received these entreaties. Samos and Ephesus had known grounds for sympathy for Perdiccas because the regent had rendered judgments in their favor. For the Samians, he had confirmed Alexander's ruling against Athens (Diod. 18.18.6–9). They had appropriately decreed honors for the kings in whose name he issued the ruling but were unlikely to be ignorant of who stood as their benefactor. The situation at Ephesus was more complicated. Under uncertain circumstances in the last years of Alexander's reign Philoxenus had arrested the three sons of Echeanax and taken them to Sardis (Polyaneus 6.49; see Chapter 7). The brothers planned a daring jailbreak, filing their chains and escaping over the walls dressed as slaves, but one, Diodorus, fell and was left behind, and so was sent to Alexander in Babylon for punishment. Perdiccas, however, returned Diodorus to Ephesus to stand trial, thereby demonstrating a deference to the local Ephesian institutions, particularly if, as I suggested in the last chapter, the root cause of this incident lay in local factionalism. This decision was just a small part of Perdiccas' courtship of Ephesus, where his brother Alcetas, Cleitus the White, and another Ionian with ties to the Macedonian court, Hagnon of Teos, all received citizenship.[31] Ephesian inscriptions in these years reflect a community in turmoil, and Andreas Walser describes the outpouring of honors as the result of fearful maneuvering,[32] and with good reason. Polyaenus only provides the narrowest glimpse into domestic divisions in the city but concludes his anecdote by saying that Anaxagoras and Codrus returned to Ephesus to rescue their brother, almost certainly with the support of Antigonus.

The political map of the Macedonian world shifted again in 320 when Antipater, Antigonus, and the survivors of Perdiccas' invasion of Egypt convened a meeting at Triparadeisus (Diod. 18.39.2–6).[33] Asander was con-

---

(πρωτεύοντα κολακείᾳ); Billows, *Antigonus*, for Aristodemos: 372, for Theotimides: 437–38; Jeff Champion, *Antigonus the One-Eyed: Greatest of the Successors* (Malden, MA: Blackwell, 2014), 23; Shipley, *Samos*, 166.

31. *I.Eph.* 1435, 1438, 1437; Andrew J. Bayliss, "Antigonos the One-Eyed's Return to Asia in 322," *ZPE* 155 (2006): 108–26; Attilio Mastrocinque, *La Caria e la Ionia méridionale in epoca ellenistica* (Rome: L'Erma di Bretschneider, 1979), 17.

32. Andreas Victor Walser, *Bauern und Zinsnehmer: Politik, Recht und Wirthschaft im frühhellenistischen Ephesos* (Munich: C.H. Beck, 2008), 49–55.

33. The chronology of this period is disputed between the so-called high chronology and the low, which holds that events took place one year later; I follow the low chronology. For the low, see Errington, "From Babylon to Triparadeisos," 75–77; R. Malcolm Errington, "Diodorus Siculus and the Chronology of the Early Diadochoi, 320–311 B.C.," *Hermes* 105, no. 4 (1977): 478–504; Edward M. Anson, "Diodorus and the Date of Triparadeisus," *AJPh* 107, no. 2 (1986): 208–17; Edward M. Anson, "The Dating of Perdiccas' Death and the Assembly at Triparadeisus," *GRBS* 43, no. 4 (2003): 373–90; Anson, *Alexander's Heirs*, 58–59; Billows, *Antigonus*, 64–80; Joseph Roisman, *Alexander's Veterans and the Early Wars of the Successors* (Austin: University of Texas Press, 2012), 136–44; high: A. B. Bosworth, "Philip III Arrhidaeus and the Chronology of the Successors," *Chiron* 22

firmed in his position as satrap of Caria, but Cleitus the White replaced
Menander in Lydia (Diod. 18.39.6; Arr. *Succ.* F 1.41) and while Antipater
formally became the new regent, Antigonus became strategos of Asia.[34] The
new arrangement lasted about year before Antipater died in 319, leaving the
regency to Polyperchon (Diod. 18.48.4). The following year Cleitus prepared
for war by installing garrisons in poleis in his territory, including at Ephesus,
before crossing the Aegean to denounce Antigonus to Polyperchon. Antigonus promptly marched on and captured Ephesus with ease because a faction
inside the walls opened the gates to his army (Diod. 18.52.7). Diodorus says
that Antigonus seized six hundred talents of silver being carried from Cilicia
to Macedon when the ship put into the harbor at Ephesus, thereby formally
renouncing his allegiance to the kings. However, this episode is generally not
considered for what it meant for Ephesus. Antigonus' presumption marked a
new phase in the unfolding Macedonian drama, but the appearance of rival
factions who exploited that same drama for their own local ends remained
business as usual in Ionia.

After Antigonus left Ephesus to chase Eumenes into the interior of Asia,
there was a period of respite for Ionia until 315 when the Third Diadochic War
returned the fighting to the eastern Aegean. This war set Antigonus and his son
Demetrius Poliorcetes against Ptolemy in Egypt, Cassander in Macedonia, and
Lysimachus in Thrace, and the fighting extended from the European side of the
Aegean to Gaza and Babylon.[35] Ionia was not a stronghold for any of the principal warlords, but nevertheless was exposed to attack by virtue of being in the
middle of this wide-ranging war. One campaign in particular brought the war
to the region. In the autumn of 315 Seleucus, having fled Babylon after arousing
Antigonus' ire earlier that year, led a Ptolemaic fleet to the Aegean and laid siege
to Erythrae (Diod. 19.60.3–4).[36] Antigonus responded by sending his nephew

---

(1992): 55–81; A. B. Bosworth, "Perdiccas and the Kings," *CQ²* 43, no. 2 (1993): 420–27. Tom Boiy,
Between High and Low: A Chronology of the Early Hellenistic Period (Mainz: Verlag Antike, 2007)
offers a compromise between the two.

34. Anson, *Alexander's Heirs*, 70–74; Errington, "From Babylon to Triparadeisos," 67–71;
Heckel, *Who's Who*, for Asander 57, for Menander 163, for Cleitus, 87–88; Heckel, *Marshals*, 58–
64; Waterfield, *Dividing the Spoils*, 66–68. The two other appointments at Triparadeisus with rami-
fications for Ionia later in the Hellenistic period were Ptolemy in Egypt and Seleucus in Babylon.

35. For studies of the Third Diadochic War, see particularly Anson, "Chronology," 226–35;
Alexander Meeus, "Diodorus and the Chronology of the Third Diadoch War," *Phoenix* 66, nos. 1–2
(2012): 74–96; Roisman, *Alexander's Veterans*, 130–44; Pat Wheatley, "The Chronology of the Third
Diadoch War, 315–311 B.C.," *Phoenix* 52, nos. 3–4 (1998): 257–81.

36. Billows, *Antigonus*, 113; Champion, *Antigonus*, 80. John D. Grainger, *Seleukos Nikator:
Constructing a Hellenistic Kingdom* (New York: Routledge, 1990), 58–59, speculates that Seleucus'
siege of Erythrae was a distraction to give his troops something to do while he negotiated with
Asander.

Polemaeus to the region to deter Ionian communities from capitulating, and Seleucus quickly abandoned the siege (Diod. 19.86.6).

Polemaeus' campaign put additional pressure on Asander, the satrap of Caria, who concluded an alliance with Ptolemy in 314/3 and subsequently sailed to Athens seeking support from Cassander and Demetrius of Phalerum (*IG* II² 450). Both Ptolemy and Cassander offered him military assistance, but both expeditions suffered disastrous defeats (Diod. 19.68.2–7), and Asander agreed to surrender his armies to Antigonus (Diod. 19.75).[37] When he reneged on this deal and called for support from the Ptolemaic fleet still under the command of Seleucus, Antigonus recalled his forces from their winter quarters, divided them into four columns, and conquered the region in a matter of weeks (Diod. 19.75).

The nature of the sources for the Third Diadochic War make it difficult to reconstruct its effects on Ionia. For instance, Diodorus records that Seleucus besieged Erythrae in 315, but offers scant detail about the polis other than that it held out against Ptolemy's fleet. Diodorus also paints a simplistic picture of the situation at Erythrae where the resistance was more likely an Antigonid garrison than general opposition from the citizens. The exception to the general dearth of sources for Ionia during these years is at Miletus, which, although particular to the conditions there, also helps to shed light on the relationship between Ionia and the Macedonian warlords.

There is limited evidence for Miletus after 334, when Alexander captured it, but, at some point, the walls punctured by Alexander's siege weapons were repaired and reinforced. Like the other Greek poleis in Asia Minor, Miletus slipped into limbo after Alexander's death, but it remained deeply connected to Caria, which Asander received in the Macedonian settlements. In the wake of his agreement with Antigonus in 313, Asander installed a garrison in Miletus, allowing Antigonus' forces to encourage the Milesians to assert their freedom (τούς τε πολίτας ἐκάλουν ἐπὶ τὴν ἐλευθερίαν, Diod. 18.75.4).

Yet there are signs that the Milesians were not passive victims of Hellenistic predation. Two years earlier, in 315, leading Milesians probably opened negotiations with Seleucus, then besieging Erythrae. The details of these negotiations are unknown, but in later years Seleucus would claim to have received a favorable oracle in the exchange. The problem, though, is that the oracle at Didyma had fallen silent when its hereditary priests were deported to central Asia a century and a half earlier. The Milesians had delivered alleged oracles

---

37. For analyses of the relationship between Asander and Antigonus at this juncture, see Richard A. Billows, "Anatolian Dynasts: The Case of the Macedonian Eupolemos in Karia," *CA* 8, no. 2 (1989): 173–206; Billows, *Antigonus*, 120; Waterfield, *Dividing the Spoils*, 116–17.

to Alexander in Egypt in 331 as a veiled request for money (Strabo 17.43) and may have done so again with Seleucus.[38] These negotiations therefore reveal a community trying to recover its lost prominence in this new world. The political and diplomatic activity was mirrored by a renewed spate of monumental construction that included the Delphinium and plans to restore the sanctuary of Apollo at Didyma. But there are signs of discontent and difficulty beneath the surface. One of the smaller pieces of monumental construction was the publication of inscriptions that record the list of *aesymnetes* (the eponymous officials; cf. Chapter 2). The second list begins after Antigonus' capture of Miletus in 313/2 with the declaration that, in the term of Hippomachus, Antigonus restored autonomy and democracy to the polis (Ἱππόμαχος Θήρωνος, ἐπὶ τούτου ἡ πόλις | ἐλευθέρα καὶ αὐτόνομος ἐγένετο ὑπὸ | Ἀντιγόνου καὶ ἡ δημοκρατία ἀπεδόθη, *Milet* I.3, no. 123, ll. 2–4).[39]

The credulous reading of this inscription would accept that this was indeed how the Milesians thought of Antigonus, even though it invokes loaded terms such as "freedom" that became increasingly impotent missiles to be launched at opponents in the verbal wars of the Diadochoi. Further, the first entry to follow this declaration was Ἀπόλλων Διός, meaning that in the very next year the eponymous official was the god Apollo. Apollo appeared only twice on the list before this date, both in the tumult that followed Alexander's conquest, but became a common occurrence in the early Hellenistic period, including four consecutive years in the 260s (*Milet* I.3, no. 123 ll. 53–56). The most common explanation for why the Milesians formally recorded Apollo as *aesynmnetes* is that these were years in which Miletus was in a state of financial emergency,[40] but it is equally possible that it records a moment of social strife when the typical mechanisms for selecting the eponymous official broke down. In both scenarios, it holds that the reference to Antigonus was representative of the warlord's demands and not a celebration of liberty.

The inscription on the Milesian *aesynmnetes* list was a local manifestation of Antigonus' imperial policy. In 314, Antigonus had made a proclamation at Tyre that all Greek poleis were to be free, autonomous, and ungarrisoned, which

38. See Joshua P. Nudell, "Oracular Politics: Propaganda and Myth in the Restoration of Didyma," *AHB* 32 (2018): 49–53, on the nature and date of this interaction.

39. Anson, "Chronology," 230; Lund, *Lysimachus*, 115; R. H. Simpson, "Antigonus the One-Eyed and the Greeks," *Historia* 8, no.4 (1959): 392. Robin Seager, "The Freedom of the Greeks of Asia: From Alexander to Antiochus," *CQ²* 31, no. 1 (1981): 107, notes that Diodorus says this campaign is how the Greeks became subject to Antigonus.

40. Stanley M. Burstein, *The Hellenistic Age from the Battle of Ipsos to the Death of Kleopatra VII* (Cambridge: Cambridge University Press, 1985), 33 n. 3; Robert K. Sherk, "The Eponymous Officials of Greek Cities IV: The Register: Part III: Thrace, Black Sea Area, Asia Minor (Continued)," *ZPE* 93 (1992): 229–32.

was followed in short order by a decree from Ptolemy to the same effect (Diod. 19.61.3–5).[41] Richard Billows puts the proclamation in the context of Antigonus facing four hostile dynasts and thus argues that "the primary motive . . . was clearly to incite mainland Greeks to rebel against Kassandros [and] one may conclude that it was purely a politico-military maneuver, devoid of any broader policy or idealistic content."[42] Likewise, Sviatoslav Dmitriev sees the policy in light of Antigonus' urgent need to "break down a military alliance that had been forged against him."[43] He further declares: "All these words and deeds had nothing to do with the actual status of individual cities."[44] The autonomy of the Greeks, including the Ionians, was a cornerstone of Antigonus' policy between 315 and 301. What set him apart from his rivals with reference to Ionia was that he was in position to act upon his words.

Antigonus' actions toward Ionia between 318 and 315 were opportunistic, driving Cleitus the White's garrison from Ephesus (Diod. 18.52.5–8), but also supporting Cassander against Polyperchon, the latter of whom had promised the Greeks that he would remove Antipater's garrisons installed after the Lamian War (Diod. 18.53.2–57.1; Plut. Phocion 31.1).[45] In 318, Antigonus had a sphere of influence that was nominally limited to Anatolia, where he supported the Greeks against Cleitus. Since Polyperchon had already issued a declaration of freedom of the other Greek poleis, Antigonus gained little by following suit. This was also a period in which Antigonus had only minimal contact with Ionia since he was in the interior of Asia in pursuit of Eumenes until 316.[46] Antigonus probably saw more value in independent allied cities than in expending his own forces to secure their allegiance. His forces therefore "liberated" the rest of Anatolia, and he ensured that a clause guaranteeing Greek autonomy appeared in the treaty of 311 (Diod. 20.19.3–4).[47] These actions gave Antigonus a reputa-

41. On these proclamations, see Claude Wehrli, Antigone et Démétrios (Geneva: Librairie Droz, 1968), 110–11; Billows, Antigonus, 116, 199–200; Sviatoslav Dmitriev, The Greek Slogan of Freedom and Early Roman Politics in Greece (Oxford: Oxford University Press, 2011), 117–19; Simpson, "Antigonus the One-Eyed," 390; Ian Worthington, Ptolemy I: King and Pharaoh of Egypt (Oxford: Oxford University Press 2016), 118–19.
42. Billows, Antigonus, 199.
43. Dmitriev, Greek Slogan of Freedom, 118.
44. Dmitriev, Greek Slogan of Freedom, 119.
45. Billows, Antigonus, 199; Heckel, Who's Who, 227. Cornelius Nepos, Phocion, 3, says that Cassander had supporters in Athens, but that the popular party in Athens had the support of Polyperchon.
46. Billows, Antigonus, 198.
47. Billows, Antigonus, 200 n. 29; Mastrocinque, La Caria, 26, describes the Peace of 311 as a temporary truce along the lines of the status quo, while R. H. Simpson, "The Historical Circumstances of the Peace of 311," JHS 74 (1954): 25–31, posits strategic gain for Antigonus through diplomacy in that he conducted negotiations with Lysimachus and Cassander that forced Ptolemy to exclude Seleucus from of the settlement. Cf. Simpson, "Antigonus the One-Eyed," 393–94.

tion for defending autonomy that Ionian poleis made reference to later in the third century when seeking royal benefactions,[48] but he was also not opposed to creating garrisons when necessary (e.g., Diod. 20.111.3).[49] Autonomy for Ionia served Antigonus' purposes, but it was autonomy on his terms and always backed by the threat of force. The result was an upheaval in the human geography, as we will see at the end of this chapter.

The wars of the Diadochoi between the Peace of 311 and the Ipsus campaign of 302/1 largely bypassed Ionia. Ptolemy sent a fleet to the southern coast of Caria, capturing Phaselis, Xanthus, Caunus, Myndus and Iasus, but Demetrius prevented the fall of Halicarnassus, so the campaign stalled before reaching Miletus (Diod. 20.27.1–2). Ptolemy spent the winter of 309/8 at Cos, where he proposed marriage to Alexander the Great's sister Cleopatra, but after her murder he sailed on to Europe without attacking Ionia (Diod. 20.37).[50] At the same time, Ionians participated in these wars on all sides. Much like the Samian soldiers discussed above and individual *philoi*, there is scattered evidence for Ionian mercenaries serving abroad, including a list of 150 mercenaries at Athens c.300 that records at least seven Ionians from five different poleis (*IG* II², 1956).[51] However, only in 302, when Lysimachus' and Cassander's general Prepelaus crossed the Hellespont as part of the final campaign against Antigonus, did war return to Ionia.

Prepelaus led his forces south through Aetolia to Ionia, where, according to Diodorus, his siege struck fear into the Ephesians and they surrendered without a fight (τὴν δ᾿Ἔφεσον πολιορκήσας καὶ καταπληξάμενος τοὺς ἔνδον παρέλαβε τὴν πόλιν, 20.107.4). Prepelaus made a show of liberating Ephesus, confirming the tax exemption for the sanctuary of Artemis, freeing Rhodian hostages Demetrius had sent there, and declaring its freedom. At the same time, he burned warships in the harbor and, in a more galling move, installed his own garrison that either he or the garrison commander quartered in land belonging to the sanctuary of Artemis, from which they also requisitioned supplies (Diod. 20.107.4–5).[52] Moreover, despite Diodorus' mild language, Prepelaus enacted

---

48. E.g., C. Bradford Welles, *Royal Correspondence in the Hellenistic Period* (New Haven, CT: Yale University Press, 1934), no. 15.

49. Seager, "Freedom of the Greeks," 107; Lund, *Lysimachus*, 116–17. Lund's list of garrisons is exaggerated, and includes one dated after Antigonus' death and those in Cilicia.

50. On the marriage proposal, see recently Worthington, *Ptolemy*, 152–54, with bibliography.

51. There were one each from Ephesus and Priene, two from Colophon, three from Miletus, and an indeterminate number of Erythraeans. This is a small, but not insignificant, percentage of the total.

52. On the capture of Ephesus, see Billows, *Antigonus*, 176; Lund, *Lysimachus*, 72, 118; Guy Maclean Rogers, *The Mysteries of Artemis of Ephesos: Cult, Polis, and Change in the Graeco-Roman World* (New Haven, CT: Yale University Press, 2012), 44–46; Walser, *Bauern und Zinsnehmer*, 67.

a domestic revolution within the ruling elite that rewarded the groups who opened the gates to him and toppled those that had been supported by Antigonus. When Demetrius recaptured Ephesus in 302, he replaced the garrison with one of his own and forced it back to its earlier condition (ἠνάγκασε τὴν πόλιν εἰς τὴν προϋπάρχουσαν ἀποκαταστῆναι, Diod. 20.111.3).[53]

There is a frustrating lack of information regarding what the Ionians thought about these shifting tides of war. Much as at the end of the fifth century, when Pausanias described the Ionians "painting both sides of the walls" (6.3.15; see Chapter 4), they seem to have fostered ties with both sides such that they were always victorious—or, at least, always in a position to minimize property damage.[54] Certainly, the Hellenistic kings went to lengths to present their conquests as liberations, but their armies still needed to be fed, which placed strains on the Ionian economies.[55] It is therefore not a surprise that the most common type of honorific decrees from early Hellenistic Ionia were those given to men who helped supply food, such as the Samian grant of citizenship for Gyges of Torone in 322/1 (SEG I 361)[56] and the Ephesian decree for Archestratus of Macedonia in 302 (OGIS 9).[57] Although the necessity of supplying grain to the Ionian poleis had governed the relationship with imperial powers in the past, the ubiquity of these honors reflects both the changing epigraphic habits in the early Hellenistic period and an evolution in how these negotiations took place. Where before Clazomenae might have received exemptions from regulation to ensure the grain supply (see Chapter 5), poleis now offered honors to individuals who might procure food for the community. Pausanias' proverb about the Ionian flip-flopping represents a whitewashed memory of a divisive period in Ionian history when the contests over control of the region required poleis to court anyone able to help.

53. Lund, Lysimachus, 125–26.
54. J. K. Davies, "The Well-Balanced Polis: Ephesos," in The Economies of Hellenistic Societies, Third to First Centuries BC, ed. Vincent Gabrielsen, J. K. Davies, and Zosia Archibald (Oxford: Oxford University Press, 2011), 193–94, suggests that Ephesus was particularly adept at this practice.
55. Angelos Chaniotis, "The Impact of War on the Economy of Hellenistic Poleis: Demand Creation, Short-Term Influence, Long-Term Impacts," in The Economies of Hellenistic Societies, Third to First Centuries BC, ed. Vincent Gabrielsen, J. K. Davies, and Zosia Archibald (Oxford: Oxford University Press, 2011), 126–27; A. Chaniotis, War in the Hellenistic World (Malden, MA: Blackwell, 2005), 122–28. Gary Reger, "The Economy," in Companion to the Hellenistic World, ed. Andrew Erskine (Malden, MA: Blackwell, 2003), 337–38, also notes that expanding populations challenged the food supply of Hellenistic poleis.
56. Habicht, "Samische Volksbeschlüsse," no. 6.
57. On the grain supply to Ionian poleis, see Richard A. Billows, "Cities," in Companion to the Hellenistic World, ed. Andrew Erskine (Malden, MA: Blackwell: 2003), 212; Chaniotis, War in the Hellenistic World, 129; Léopold Migeotte, "Le pain quotidian dans les cités hellénistiques: À propos des fonds permanents pour l'approvisionnement en grain," Cahiers du Centre G. Glotz 2 (1991): 19–41; Rathbone, "Grain Trade and Grain Shortages," 45–55.

Prepelaus concluded his campaign in northern Ionia by accepting the surrender of Teos and Colophon but had to settle for raiding the territory of Clazomenae and Erythrae when they were reinforced by Antigonid soldiers. Such was the situation in Ionia in 301 when a coalition army under the command of Seleucus and Lysimachus defeated Antigonus and Demetrius at the battle of Ipsus.

After Ipsus

According to Plutarch, the victors of Ipsus carved up Antigonus' kingdom as though it was a slaughtered animal (*Demet.* 30.1).[58] Ionia nominally fell into the haunch claimed by Lysimachus north of the Taurus Mountains, but the situation on the ground was less certain. Immediately following the battle, Demetrius led nine thousand soldiers from the interior of Asia Minor to Ephesus (Plut. *Demet.* 30). He did not remain there long, but took steps to ensure its loyalty, including that he prohibited his soldiers from desecrating the sanctuary of Artemis. There is also evidence from Ephesus that Lysimachus encroached on Ionian territory, resulting in a low-intensity war after which the Ephesians gave citizenship to Thras[—] of Magnesia because he paid ransom for their captured citizens (*I.Eph.* 1450). (The final letters of his name are unfortunately lost.) Another inscription from after 299 records honors granted to Nicagoras of Rhodes, who relayed a joint declaration from Demetrius and Seleucus reaffirming their commitment to the freedom of the Greeks against Lysimachus—and gives Demetrius pride of place despite then being a political prisoner of Seleucus (*OGIS* 10).[59]

Concurrent with this apparently positive relationship between Demetrius and Ionia was the reality that the key to control of the region was Demetrius' garrisons. According to Polyaenus, Lysimachus sought to claim Ephesus by bribing Diodorus the commander garrison in 301/0, but Demetrius ended this threat by luring him onto a boat in the harbor and killing him along with his supporters (4.7).[60] Nor was Ephesus unique, and another decree granted honors to Archestratus, Demetrius' strategos in Clazomenae, for protecting the ships carrying grain (*OGIS* 9).

---

58. For broader fallout from the battle of Ipsus, see Grainger, *Seleukos*, 121–22; R. Malcolm Errington, *A History of the Hellenistic World* (Malden, MA: Blackwell, 2008), 51–52; Waterfield, *Dividing the Spoils*, 172–74.

59. A. B. Bosworth, *The Legacy of Alexander: Politics, Warfare and Propaganda under the Successors* (Oxford: Oxford University Press, 2002), 268, observes the order of the honors.

60. Lund, *Lysimachus*, 84 n. 14 points out that the dearth of evidence makes it equally possible that Lysimachus' attack could be dated to 301 in the immediate aftermath of Ipsus or to 298. Cf. Rogers, *Mysteries of Artemis*, 53–54.

Lysimachus was not the only king with ambitions toward Ionia. Ptolemy's forces captured Miletus in c.299/8, though Demetrius appeared on the *aesymnetes* list for 295/4, indicating that he continued to wield influence there (*Milet I.3, no.* 123 l. 22).[61] It was in this same period that Seleucus' relationship with Miletus flourished. Seleucid propaganda promoted the story that the oracle at Didyma had foretold his rise and backed up this claim with a set of massive offerings to adorn the new temple (*I.Didyma* 479), as well as with dedications from his son Antiochus and wife Apame that defrayed the construction costs (*SEG* 4 470 and *SEG* 34 1075).[62] The Milesians duly offered honors for the royal family, but these benefactions did not prevent the reappearance of Apollo on the *aesymnetes* list for 299/8 (*Milet* I.3, no. 123, l. 18).

Demetrius sailed to Athens in 296/5, and Lysimachus took the opportunity to seize Ionia. Although Demetrius temporarily regained control of the region in 286/5, Lysimachus' campaign in 294 was the denouement of the war in Ionia that reached its bloody climax at Ipsus.

Ionia and the Kings: Euergetism and Human Geography

The early Hellenistic period in Ionia was defined by its relationship with the kings, both for good and for ill. On one side of the ledger, Richard Billows has argued that royal favor in the form of tax exemptions and donations laid the foundation for a renaissance in Ionia.[63] On the other side, though, the wars of the successors imposed economic costs that stunted growth. Apollo appears with increasing regularity on the Milesian *aesymnetes* list in this period, for instance, and there is an Ephesian debt law of c.297 that was likely directed at ameliorating the consequences of property destruction. Nor were taxes the only financial demand made on Ionia. Poleis were expected to contribute to the upkeep of the garrisons, and while they benefited from royal building programs, they were also frequently expected to both leave alone sacred funds and pick up the tab for civic projects.

The toll war took on Ionia is taken as a truism in scholarship, with the question then being which of the kings is to blame for impoverishing the region, because that might give some indication of political sympathies. Lysimachus is

---

61. Stanley M. Burstein, "Lysimachus and the Greek Cities of Asia: The Case of Miletus," *AncW* 3, nos. 3–4 (1980): 78–79, argues that Demetrius received Miletus as a condition of his peace with Ptolemy in 297/6.

62. On the relationship between these gifts and the restoration of the oracle at Didyma, see Nudell, "Oracular Politics." Cf. Chapter 9.

63. Billows, "Rebirth of a Region," 33–44.

the traditional villain because he demanded new taxes after he captured Ionia in 294. Moreover, Lysimachus was uncommonly honest about his taxation, leading to the assumption of his miserliness that exposed him to denunciations from the other kings about how he deprived the Greeks of their freedom. Helen Lund has persuasively argued that Lysimachus' impositions were neither novel nor excessively harsh and therefore blames Antigonus and Demetrius instead.[64] Stanley Burstein likewise relieves Lysimachus of sole blame but more plausibly accuses all the Diadochoi of extorting the Ionians.[65] There are also examples of euergetism from kings courting Ionian poleis while they were subject to a rival. These donations were symbols that marked out an ideological claim to space, while simultaneously performing elaborate courtship rituals that paid homage to the fiction of the autonomous polis.[66]

The reciprocal relationship of taxation and benefaction only tells one part of the story. Ionian poleis offered the kings a variety of honors, including festivals and grants of *ateleia* (tax exemption). These awards went out to a king for his euergetism on behalf of the community. Samos founded a religious festival for Antigonus and Demetrius after 306 and renamed one of its existing tribes *Demetrieis* to proclaim its allegiance to Antigonus and his son. Similarly, the Samians voted honors for an associate of Demeterius' wife Phila, whom they petitioned about an unknown issue in 306 (*SIG*[3] 333, ll. 8–9).[67] On the mainland, Ephesus awarded the traditional founder cult honors to Lysimachus when he moved its location in c.294 and by 289/8, Seleucus asked for libations from the temple of Apollo at Didyma for his continued good health (*OGIS* 214, ll. 11–12).

The politics of reciprocity demanded that the kings exchange something in return even if the privileges were frequently more symbolic than practical. In rare instances the benefits included tax exemptions such as Antigonus granted to Erythrae (*I.Ery.* 31 and 32) and Ephesus,[68] but these were the exception. In other cases, the kings prescribed new civic building projects, such as walls at Colophon, Erythrae, and Ephesus, but left a significant portion of the expenses to the

---

64. Lund, *Lysimachus*, 128–52. Ptolemy is excused for the purposes of this discussion because his interaction with Ionia came later in the Hellenistic period.

65. Burstein, "Lysimachus and the Greek Cities," 73–75.

66. The clearest example of this was Seleucus' interactions with Miletus, which Paul J. Kosmin, *The Land of the Elephant Kings: Space, Territory, and Ideology in the Seleucid Empire* (Cambridge, MA: Harvard University Press, 2014), 61–67, has shown marked the far northwestern bound of his territory.

67. Shipley, *Samos*, 173.

68. Dieter Knibbe and Bülent Iplikçioglu, "Neue Inscriften au Ephesos VIII," *JÖAI* 53 (1982): 130–32.

citizens.[69] There was a proliferation of increasingly expensive defensive fortifications, including circuit walls, forts, and watchtowers, built in nearly every Ionian polis, which marked a departure from the fifth and early fourth centuries, when Ionia was famously unwalled. The impressive circuit walls of Ephesus and Colophon dated to the early Hellenistic period, and Anthony McNicoll characterizes the technical details as a response to the increasing sophistication of Macedonian siege warfare, but these structures were part of a longer continuum of Ionian history. At Priene, for instance, the fortifications that Rostovtzeff characterized as "unsurpassed in technical efficiency and sober beauty" show clear parallels with contemporary Carian examples, suggesting that they were established earlier in the century.[70] Inscriptions also record the appointment of civic officials to oversee maintenance on the walls (e.g., *I.Ery.* 23).[71] More importantly, though, are inscriptions recording private donations for wall construction, with fragments from Erythrae revealing contributions of more than sixteen thousand drachmae for one part of the construction (two and half talents; *I.Ery.* 22A and B) and an inscription at Colophon recording contributions of more than two hundred thousand drachmae (thirty-five talents).[72]

The human geography of Ionia also changed in the early Hellenistic period. Either Antigonus or Lysimachus refounded Smyrna by combining four small towns, though tradition gave credit to Alexander (Pausanias 7.5.1–3; Aelius

---

69. Benjamin D. Meritt, "Inscriptions of Colophon," *AJPh* 56, no. 4 (1935): nos. 1 and 2. The inscription for the walls of Colophon does include an entry for allied contribution; John Ma, "Fighting Poleis of the Hellenistic World," in *War and Violence in Ancient Greece*, ed. Hans van Wees (London: Duckworth, 2000), 340–41; Lund, *Lysimachus*, 128–29; for a study of Hellenistic walls, see Anthony W. McNicoll, *Hellenistic Fortifications From the Aegean to the Euphrates*, rev. N. P. Milner (Oxford: Oxford University Press, 1997), 46–48, with table 7 and 69–70.

70. Rostovtzeff, *Social and Economic History*, 179. On the comparison with other fortifications in the time of Mausolus, see Andreas L. Konecny and Peter Ruggendorfer, "Alinda in Karia: The Fortifications," *Hesperia* 83, no. 4 (2014): 739. The fortifications at Ephesus are confidently dated to the early third century; see Thomas Marksteiner, "Bemerkungen zum hellenistischen Stadtmauerring von Ephesos," in *100 Jahre österreichische Forschungen in Ephesos*, ed. Herwig Freisinger and Fritz Krinzinger (Vienna: Verlag der Österreichischen Akademie der Wissenschaften, 1999), 413–20, while recent archaeological research at Priene, e.g., Uli Ruppe, "Neue Forschungen an der Stadtmauer von Priene—Erste Ergebnisse," *MDAI(I)* 57 (2007): 271–322, has shown the evolution of the fortifications there.

71. This inscription from Erythrae specifically deals with the official designated with protecting the walls against moisture damage, a process called ἀντιπλάδη. The name of this office varied by polis, being τειχοποιοί at Miletus and Priene, ἐπίσταται τεῖχον at Teos and Erythrae; cf. Chaniotis, *War in the Hellenistic World*, 32.

72. For the estimated amount for Erythrae, see Léopold Migeotte, *Les souscriptions publiques dans les cités grecques* (Paris: Editions du Sphinx, 1992), 336. The contributions range from as little as twenty drachmae (l. 125) to as many as five hundred (ll. 38 and 40), and one entry that might have been more than a thousand (l. 48). For Colophon, see Migeotte, *Les souscriptions publiques*, 337.

Aristides 10.7, 20.20), and it was likely at this time that it received admission to the Panionion.[73] Although local identities proved an intractable problem in some of these *synoikisms*, the reshuffling made sense for the kings. The patchwork of small towns made each community vulnerable, while consolidation made control over the region easier.[74] The nucleated settlement at Colophon moved between 315 and 306, which is attested by a new set of walls built by Antigonus that enclosed both the new and old settlements.[75] What makes this civic project notable beyond that the community soon relocated is a partial list of donors who contributed funds for construction. In addition to many citizens, the list includes four men identified as Macedonians. One Stephanus offered one of the largest single donations: three hundred gold staters.[76] Although there is no information about these people outside this list, other Ionian poleis offered the Macedonians citizenship,[77] so the listed individuals likely had close connections to the community, perhaps even living there. In c.303, there was also a proposed *synoikism* of Teos and Lebedus that, if it was not the brainchild of Antigonus, was pursued under his direction (*Ager* 13, ll. 5–15).[78] An earthquake in 304/3 had caused considerable damage in Ionia, so Billows posits that both poleis suffered damage and sought Antigonus' help, perhaps unaware that the king would instruct them to merge and to send joint representatives to the Panionion.[79] In contrast, the citizens of Myus voluntarily relocated to Miletus because the gnats in the surrounding marshes became unbearable (Pausanias 7.2.11; Strabo 14.1.10).[80] The story that insects defeated the polis is probably hyperbolic, but the silting up of the Gulf of Latmus likely

---

73. Billows, "Rebirth of a Region," 34; Billows, *Antigonus*, 213; Lund, *Lysimachus*, 175–76. The site of the new community was likely the suburb Ephesian Smyrna; see Lene Rubinstein, "Ionia," in *An Inventory of Archaic and Classical Poleis*, ed. Mogens Herman Hansen and Thomas Heine Nielsen (Oxford: Oxford University Press, 2004), 1071. Ryan Boehm, *City and Empire in the Age of the Successors* (Berkeley: University of California Press, 2018), continues to credit Alexander.

74. Boehm, *City and Empire*, 29–87. Smyrna would come to rival Ephesus in time but it was far enough away that the immediate impact was minor since most conflicts between Ionians involved borders.

75. Billows, "Rebirth of a Region," 35; Billows, *Antigonus*, 213; *I.Ery.* 22.

76. Argyro B. Tataki, *Macedonians Abroad: A Contribution to the Prosopography of Ancient Macedonia* (Paris: Diffusion de Boccard, 1998), 56, 61, 191, 238.

77. For instance, Leucippus, son of Ermogenous, and one Calladas at Ephesus; see Tataki, *Macedonians Abroad*, 140, 335. Rogers, *Mysteries of Artemis*, 56, notes that Ephesus sold citizenship to raise money.

78. Billows, "Rebirth of a Region," 36.

79. Billows, *Antigonus*, 213–14, 217; Welles, *Royal Correspondence*, no. 3; Sheila L. Ager, *Interstate Arbitrations in the Greek World, 337–90 B.C.* (Berkeley: University of California Press, 1997), 61–64.

80. Alan M. Greaves, *Miletos: A History* (New York: Routledge, 2002), 137.

caused the farmland at Myus to turn to marsh and provides a salient reminder that the Ionian communities faced natural as well as human challenges in the early Hellenistic period.[81]

The largest Ionian polis to undergo a transformation was Ephesus, which moved to a new site shortly before 294 because the original location ceased to have access to the sea due to the silting of the Cayster River (Paus. 1.9.7).[82] According to Strabo, the Ephesians found the idea of moving distasteful, but Lysimachus literally flushed them from their homes by blocking the sewers in advance of a torrential downpour, thereby flooding the original settlement (Strabo 14.1.21). Strabo's story is far-fetched, but the flooding was most likely real. The contemporary poet Duris of Elaia composed an epigram about a deluge sweeping all into the sea (Stephanus, *Greek Anthology* 9.424) and Ephesus had long been combating the rivers, including a project to dam the Silenous in order to prevent it from flooding the sanctuary.[83] Guy Rogers therefore convincingly argues that Ephesus moved location before Lysimachus captured the region and that blaming him for the deluge was a story started by Demetrius' allies in the polis.[84]

In addition to renaming Ephesus "Arsinoeia" after his third wife, Lysimachus added to it the populations of Colophon, Lebedus, and probably Pygela (Paus. 1.9.7, 7.3.4–6).[85] The capture of Colophon prompted the iambic poet Phoenix to compose a lament (Paus. 1.9.7), and Pausanias cryptically adds that the Colophonians were the only people to fight against the new foundation of Arsinoeia (7.3.4). How the evidence for the sack of Colophon and temporary relocation of the citizens to Ephesus correlates with the earlier *synoikism* of the

---

81. Ronald T. Marchese, *The Lower Maeander Flood Plain: A Regional Settlement Study* (Oxford: Oxford University Press, 1986), 117–19, 166–68; Peter Thonemann, *The Maeander Valley: A Historical Geography* (Cambridge: Cambridge University Press, 2011), 295–338.

82. Billows, "Rebirth of a Region," 35; Billows, *Antigonus*, 217; Lund, *Lysimachus*, 120, 175–76; Burstein, "Lysimachus and the Greek Cities," 75; Rogers, *Mysteries of Artemis*, 62–67.

83. On the silting of the Cayster River, see Anton Bammer and Ulrike Muss, "Water Problems in the Artemision of Ephesus," in *Cura Aquarum in Ephesus*, vol. 1, ed. Gilbert Wiplinger (Leuven: Peeters, 2006), 61–64; Rogers, *Mysteries of Artemis*, 65.

84. Rogers, *Mysteries of Artemis*, 64–67.

85. Pygela largely escapes mention in the ancient accounts of the refoundation, which focus on the more prominent Ionian poleis to the north, but was likely included without having been physically relocated, as suggested by Louis Robert, "Sur les inscriptions d'Éphèse: Fêtes, athletes, empereurs, épigrammes," *RPh* 41 (1967): 40, and followed by Boehm, *City and Empire*, 147; François Kirbihler, "Territoire civique et population d'Éphèse (Vᵉ siècle av. J.-C.-IIIᵉ siècle apr. J.-C.)," in *L'Asie Mineure dans l'Antiquité: Échanges, populations et territoires: Regards actuels sur une péninsule*, ed. Hadrien Bru, François Kirbihler, and Stéphane Lebreton (Rennes: Presses Universitaires de Rennes, 2009), 309; Gabrièle Larguinat-Turbatte, "Les premiers temps d'Arsinoeia-Éphèse: Étude d'une composition urbaine royale (début du IIIᵉ S.)," *REA* 116, no. 2 (2014): 470–73; Giuseppe Ragone, "Pygela/Phygela: Fra Paretimologia e storia," *Athenaeum* 84, no. 1 (1996): 371–74.

old and new settlements in the reign of Antigonus is unknown.[86] The Lebedians maintained a coherent identity at Ephesus, though, and refounded their polis in c.266 with the blessing of Ptolemy II Philadelphus in exchange for naming it "Ptolemais," once again using imperial politics for local ends.[87] Arsinoeia (Ephesus) flourished at the new location even though some of its new populations left after Lysimachus' death, but it reverted to its traditional name and continued to struggle with the silting of the Cayster River (Strabo 14.1.21, 25).[88]

Although the traditions surrounding Lysimachus' refoundation of Ephesus are suspect, he did have a lasting impact on Ephesus by neutering the power of the Artemisium, perhaps because it was closely associated with Demetrius. The sanctuary itself was untouchable, so Lysimachus instead underwrote the costs of a new temple complex at Ortygia for Artemis Soter. The cult was multidimensional. Ortygia, near the boundary between Ephesus and Pygela, was one of the traditional birthplaces for Artemis, and this martial avatar commemorated Lysimachus' victory and alluded to his protection of Ephesus, while calling to mind the Ephesian claim to Pygela even if the community was in the process of being incorporated into Arsinoeia. But the most important feature of the cult was that Lysimachus took for himself some of the religious authority and delegated to the Arsinoeian Gerousia the right to oversee the festivals and mediate between the two sanctuaries of Artemis, which gave Ephesus unprecedented control over its sanctuary.[89]

The kings also intervened in the Ionian poleis through arbitrations.[90] When Antigonus presided over the proposed *synoikism* between Teos and Lebedos, he appointed Mytilene as an arbitrator in cases that dealt with the special agreement he instructed the two states to develop, but both the new laws and unforeseen disputes were to be referred to Antigonus himself, following the model established by Alexander, which in turn, followed the example of the

---

86. Billows, "Rebirth of a Region," 36–37.

87. Billows, *Antigonus*, 217; Billows, "Rebirth of a Region," 36–37. Strabo 14.29 records that the citizens of Lebedus fled to Ephesus from civil strife in Teos.

88. Strabo refers to Ephesus as the largest emporium east of the Taurus Mountains and writes about the construction of a mole to narrow the harbor entrance with the idea that it would keep the harbor deep enough to accommodate large merchant ships. Engineers working for Attalus Philadelphus (r. 160–138) only succeeded in trapping the silt in the harbor (Strabo 14.1.25).

89. As argued by Rogers, *Mysteries of Artemis*, 81–88. It was in this same period that the Milesians subordinated Didyma to the polis, but there the process accompanied the restoration of the cult; see Nudell, "Oracular Politics," 53–56.

90. Lysimachus continued to arbitrate between Ionian poleis beyond the scope of this inquiry, including between Magnesia and Priene in 287/6 and Samos and Priene in 283/2; see Ager, *Interstate Arbitrations*, 87–93; Sheila L. Ager, "Keeping the Peace in Ionia: Kings and Poleis," in *Regionalism in Hellenistic and Roman Asia Minor*, ed. Hugh Elton and Gary Reger (Pessac: Ausonius, 2007), 45–52.

Persian satraps.[91] The king framed his decision in the language of a neutral arbitrator, but royal suggestions carried the force of commands. Antigonus also likely established regulations for the arbitration of a border dispute between Clazomenae and Teos c.302 (*SEG* XXVIII 697). Though the inscription is heavily reconstructed and both the name Antigonus and the regulations open to debate, Clazomenae and Teos shared a small peninsula, and Sheila Ager reasonably argues that population growth from the result of the inchoate *synoikism* between Teos and Lebedos prompted the Teians to expand their territory and thus ran into conflict with the Clazomenaeans.[92]

Finally, the kings supported the Ionian League, which took on a new political importance (see Appendix 1). The league served the kings by providing a system of organization. When Lysimachus conquered Ionia he appointed strategoi to oversee the league, perhaps in parallel to Philoxenus during the reign of Alexander, but there is no evidence for a comparable appointee under Antigonus.[93] The relationship between strategos and league is largely unattested; Helen Lund speculates that he had the authority to intervene in the judicial and financial affairs, but she also posits that the absence of evidence for strategoi later in Lysimachus' reign indicates that the position was an extra security measure for an important region that was neither routine nor entirely unique.[94]

The question remains what can be said about the state of the Ionian poleis between 323 and 294. They were clearly subordinate to and, in many respects, at the mercy of the Diadochoi, even while they maintained some level of autonomy. In other words, whereas the early Hellenistic period saw a radical reorientation on the imperial playing field, there was a great deal of continuity in Ionia. The replacement of satraps and imperial poleis with kings increased the asymmetrical power relationships, but it did not stop the Ionian poleis from negotiating their existence within this sphere. Characterizing the Ionian poleis as simply subordinate to the Diadochoi also obscures the local and regional political activity taking place, as Jeremy LaBuff has recently shown for Hellenistic Caria.[95] Likewise, in addition to circuit walls around the nucleated settlements, the *chorae* of Hellenistic Ionia contained forts garrisoned by citizen-soldiers, which John Ma has demonstrated indicates an ongoing militarism.[96] In Ionia,

---

91. Ager, *Interstate Arbitrations*, 61–64; Ager, "Keeping the Peace," 46; Billows, *Antigonus*, 213–14; Welles, *Royal Correspondence*, no. 3, ll. 24–40, 43–52.

92. On this arbitration, see Ager, *Interstate Arbitrations*, 67–69; Sheila L. Ager, "A Royal Arbitration between Klazomenae and Teos?," *ZPE* 85 (1991): 87–97.

93. Lund, *Lysimachus*, 143–44.

94. On Lysimachus' other administrative measures, see Lund, *Lysimachus*, 144–46.

95. Jeremy LaBuff, *Polis Expansion and Elite Power in Hellenistic Caria* (Lanham, MD: Lexington Books, 2015).

96. Ma, "Fighting Poleis," 341–44; cf. John Ma, "Une culture militaire en Asie Mineure hellé-

Miletus and Teos were two of the earliest poleis outside Athens to institute formal *ephebeia*, and an inscription found at Smyrna records regulations and pay for the Teian garrison in the citadel of Cyrbissus, a nearby town whose inhabitants gained citizenship at Teos in the third century (*SEG* XXVI 1306).[97] Likewise, a late fourth-century inscription records a treaty of *isopolity* between Pygela and Miletus (*Milet* I.3, no. 142), giving Pygelans rights in Miletus, but equally important, offering protection against the ongoing encroachment of Ephesus that culminated in Pygela being absorbed by Arsinoeia. Even as the Ionians were subject to the demands of the Hellenistic kings, they continued to play out regional competitions that had existed for as long as their cities had.

nistique?," in *Les cités grecques en Asie Mineure à l'époque hellénistique*, ed. Jean-Christophe Couvenhes and Henri-Louis Fernoux (Tours: Presses universitaires François-Rabelais, 2004), 199–220; Thibaut Boulay, *Ares dans la cite: Les poleis et la guerre dans l'Asie Mineure hellénistique* (Pisa: Fabrizio Serra Editore, 2014); Chaniotis, "The Impact of War," 122–41.

97. On this inscription, see Louis Robert and Jeanne Robert, "Une inscription grecque de Téos en Ionie: L'union de Téos et de Kyrbissos," *JS* (1976): 188–228; Jean-Christophe Couvenhes, "Les cités grecques d'Asie Mineure et le mercenariat à l'époque hellénistique," in *Les cités grecques en Asie Mineure à l'époque hellénistique*, ed. Jean-Christophe Couvenhes and Henri-Louis Fernoux (Tours: Presses universitaires François-Rabelais, 2004), 92–93. Although this inscription is often seen as coercive, William Mack, "Communal Interests and Polis Identity under Negotiation: Documents Depicting Sympolities between Cities Great and Small," *Topoi* 18, no. 1 (2013): 105–6, characterizes it as the product of a negotiation between the two sides and notes that such treaties established protections for the weaker party.

CHAPTER 9

The Ornaments of Ionia

Temple Construction and Commercial Prosperity

The monumental temple came to define ancient Ionia in popular memory.[1] A poem attributed to Antipater of Thessalonica in the Palatine Anthology compares the temple of Artemis at Ephesus to other man-made wonders (9.58):

> The rocky walls of Babylon on which carts can drive
> And the statue of Zeus by Alpheus, I have gazed upon,
> And the hanging gardens and the Colossus of Helios,
> And the tall pyramids piled with great toil,
> And the mighty memorial for Mausolus, but when I looked upon
> The house of the goddess Artemis that reached even into the clouds
> Those others dimmed, and I thought: excepting only Olympus,
> Helios has never illuminated anything such as this!

> καὶ κραναᾶς Βαβυλῶνος ἐπίδρομον ἅρμασι τεῖχος
> καὶ τὸν ἐπ᾽ Ἀλφειῷ Ζᾶνα κατηυγασάμην,
> κάπων τ᾽ αἰώρημα, καὶ Ἡελίοιο κολοσσόν,

---

1. Most cults had small temples or rural shrines like the ones detailed in the Molpoi Decree at Miletus (*Milet* I.3, no. 133). The Molpoi Decree is preserved in a Hellenistic inscription erected in the late third or early second century BCE professing to detail the annual procession from the intramural Delphinion to the sanctuary at Didyma. Although scholars have long assumed that the inscription celebrated and preserved archaic rituals, Anja Slawisch has recently suggested instead that the inscription belongs in the set of invented traditions about Didyma that legitimized new ideas by casting them into the Archaic past. On the decree, see, particularly, Alexander Herda, *Der Apollon-Delphinios-Kult in Milet und die Neujahrsprozession nach Didyma* (Darmstadt: Verlag Philipp von Zabern, 2006); Alexander Herda, "How to Run a State Cult," in *Current approaches to religion in ancient Greece*, ed. Matthew Haysom and Jenny Wallensten (Stockholm: Stockholm Universitet, 2011), 57–93; Anja Slawisch, "Epigraphy versus Archaeology: Conflicting Evidence for Cult Continuity in Ionia during the Fifth Century BC," in *Sacred Landscapes in Anatolia and Neighboring Regions*, ed. Charles Gates, Jacques Morin, and Thomas Zimmermann (Oxford: Archaeopress, 2009), 29–34.

καὶ μέγαν αἰπεινᾶν πυραμίδων κάματον,
μνᾶμά τε Μαυσώλοιο πελώριον· ἀλλ' ὅτ' ἐσεῖδον
Ἀρτέμιδος νεφέων ἄχρι θέοντα δόμον,
κεῖνα μὲν ἠμαύρωτο †δεκηνιδε νόσφιν Ὀλύμπου
ἅλιος οὐδέν πω τοῖον ἐπηυγάσατο.

Despite Antipater's extravagant praise that put the temple of Artemis at Ephesus at the pinnacle of the seven wonders of the ancient world, it was neither the oldest nor the largest such structure in Ionia,[2] where commercial interaction with Egypt may have contributed to the early development of the colonnaded temple.[3]

But if Ionian culture was shaped by interaction with the eastern Mediterranean, how did the inhabitants afford these monumental structures? Scholars often suppose that Ionian commerce begat prosperity, which created a surplus that they invested in temples.[4] Auditing the books of modern sports stadiums

2. Ionian monumental temples underwent multiple phases of construction and reconstruction in what Robin Osborne, "Cult and Ritual: The Greek World," in *Classical Archaeology*, ed. Susan E. Alcock and Robin Osborne (Malden, MA: Blackwell, 2007), 256, characterizes as a process of local competition; see below, "Classical Ionia and Temple Construction." The Heraion on Samos was probably the earliest of the monumental temples, though the cult of Artemis may have predated it, and the Heraion's fourth iteration just surpassed the temple of Artemis (6,038 m^2 to 6,017 m^2). The Hellenistic temple of Apollo at Didyma surpassed both at 7,115.78 m^2. Nevertheless, the sanctuary of Artemis was particularly famous, as indicated by the silversmith Demetrius in the biblical book of Acts, who boasts: "Who among men does not know that the polis of Ephesus is the custodian of this temple for the great goddess Artemis?" (Ἄνδρες Ἐφέσιοι, τίς γάρ ἐστιν ἀνθρώπων ὃς οὐ γινώσκει τὴν Ἐφεσίων πόλιν νεωκόρον οὖσαν τῆς μεγάλης Ἀρτέμιδος, 19.35).

3. This connection was identified already by the nineteenth century, e.g., A. Marquand, "Reminiscences of Egypt in Doric Architecture," *AJA* 6, nos. 1–2 (1890): 47–58, and has largely persisted since. L. H. Jeffery, *The Local Scripts of Archaic Greece*, rev. ed. (Oxford: Oxford University Press, 1990), 30, who also sees overseas trade as the vector for the "archaic style" of sculpture, though see Whitney M. Davis, "Egypt, Samos, and the Archaic Style in Greek Sculpture," *JEA* 67 (1981): 69 n. 31. J. J. Coulton, "Towards Understanding Greek Temple Design: General Considerations," *ABSA* 70 (1975): 77–82, and J. J. Coulton, *Ancient Greek Architects at Work: Problems of Structure and Design* (Ithaca, NY: Cornell University Press, 1982), 31–50, caution that the Egyptian influence may have been to "accelerate" developments already underway in the Aegean. On the intersection of Ionian temples and the Mediterranean world, see Kenan Eran, "Ionian Sanctuaries and the Mediterranean World in the 7th Century B.C.," in *SOMA 2011*, vol. 1, ed. Pietro Maria Militello and Hakan Öniz (Oxford: Archaeopress, 2015), 321–27.

4. See Jack Martin Balcer, *Sparda by the Bitter Sea: Imperial Interaction in Western Anatolia* (Providence, RI: Brown University Press, 1984), 365; Pericles Georges, "Persian Ionia under Darius: The Revolt Reconsidered," *Historia* 49, no. 1 (2000): 3–4; Alan M. Greaves, *Miletos: A History* (New York: Routledge, 2002), 126; Carl Roebuck, "The Economic Development of Ionia," *CPh* 48, no. 1 (1953): 9–16. Slawisch, "Epigraphy versus Archaeology," and Anja Slawisch and Toby Christopher Wilkinson, "Processions, Propaganda, and Pixels: Reconstructing the Sacred Way between Miletos and Didyma," *AJA* 122, no. 1 (2018): 102, implicitly accept this connection. Brian Rutishauser, *Athens and the Cyclades: Economic Strategies, 510–314 BC* (Oxford: Oxford University Press, 2012), 229–35, reverses the causation by arguing that the fiscal demands of construction monetized Aegean economies.

would reveal the extent to which they are paid for taxpayer-funded programs, but comparable accounts for Greek temples are rare.[5] The connection between commerce and temple construction is a logical inference, reinforced by the supposition that Ionia suffered from a deep financial depression throughout the Classical period, the sign of which being that the temples destroyed at the close of the Ionian revolt in 494/3 were not rebuilt, while Pericles decorated Athens with their money.[6] Since the remaining evidence for the relative prosperity of Ionia is circumstantial, the resulting argument is a closed loop that depends entirely on the record of temple construction.

Commerce, then as now, could make individuals wealthy enough to make lavish displays of piety, and a unified citizen body with ample resources of stone, workers, skilled artisans, and draft animals was necessary for erecting large, monumental temples. Polycrates (c.538–522), we are told, paid for a series of engineering projects on Samos, including the final phase of construction at the Heraion, through piracy (e.g., Hdt. 3.39; Thuc. 1.13.6), but this is also a testament to his ability to centralize resources and manipulate foreign relationships.[7] By contrast, the fact that Chios, a polis with a history of commercial prosperity that extended into the Classical period, never built a temple on a scale comparable to those of its peer polities should give us pause. Commercial prosperity was an important part of the story of temple construction, but the economic hypothesis both overstates and misunderstands Ionian wealth in the Archaic period and poverty in the Classical.

Interstate diplomacy of the Hellenistic world often involved royal euergetism, but reverence for Classical Greece as the age of the autonomous city-state obscures that the same held true during the earlier periods in Ionia. Indeed, John Boardman declares, "The great Ionian building programmes owed no little to Lydian gold," but scholars tend to overlook the implications of this

---

5. Inscriptions recording temple inventories are rare before the Classical period; see David M. Lewis, "Temple Inventories in Ancient Greece," in *Pots and Pans*, ed. Michael Vickers (Oxford: Oxford University Press, 1986), 71–81. The only one from Ionia comes from a series of stelae at Didyma dated to 177/6; see Beate Dignas, *Economy of the Sacred in Hellenistic and Roman Asia Minor* (Oxford: Oxford University Press, 2002), 238, with n. 37.

6. J. M. Cook, "The Problem of Classical Ionia," *PCPhS* 187, no. 7 (1961): 9–18; repeated in *The Greeks in Ionia and the East* (London: Thames and Hudson 1962), 122. Isocrates 4.156 praises the Ionians for leaving the destroyed temples as memorials to barbarian impiety, which offers an oblique, if likely fictional, commentary about the economic state of Ionia in the fifth century. On the Periclean building program, see below, "Classical Ionia and Temple Construction."

7. Jens David Baumbach, *The Significance of Votive Offerings in Selected Hera Sanctuaries in the Peloponnese, Ionia, and Western Greece* (Oxford: Archeopress, 2004), 152. Some Egyptian dedications found at the sanctuary date to this period; see Philip Kaplan, "Dedications to Greek Sanctuaries by Foreign Kings in the Eighth through Sixth Centuries BCE," *Historia* 55, no. 2 (2006): 134; Sarah P. Morris, "The View from East Greece: Miletus, Samos and Ephesus," in *Debating Orientalization*, ed. Corinna Riva and Nicholas C. Vella (Sheffield: Equinox, 2006), 72–74. Only two small new temples went up at the sanctuary in the fifth and fourth centuries.

observation for Classical Ionia.[8] Locating Ionian temple construction in the Classical period within a network of interstate relations reveals that the story of these monuments is not primarily one of commercial prosperity, but rather the intersection of local initiative and external investment.

Monumental Temples in Archaic Ionia

Already in the Archaic period the largest temples in Ionia had a series of reconstructions that represented a form of peer-polity competition, with communities leapfrogging one another in a race to construct the largest and most magnificent edifice. Thus Robin Osborne observes, "It is hard to believe that it is a mere coincidence that the fourth temple of Hera at Samos just surpasses the first temple of Artemis at Ephesos in ground area (6,038 m^2 compared to 6,017)."[9] The temple of Apollo at Didyma also went through multiple phases, including two stone temples in the seventh and sixth centuries, and the intramural temples of Aphrodite and Athena at Miletus were both rebuilt shortly before the sack in 494.[10] Competition did not result in a uniform style. While the earliest known Greek peripteral temple was the eighth-century Artemisium at Ephesus, that form was not used at the site on Mount Mycale identified as the Panionion.[11] Likewise, instead of the simple fluted columns that were later associated with the "Ionic" order, the Panionion had smooth columns, while the column bases at the temples of Artemis at Ephesus and of Apollo at Didyma were decorated with human figures.[12]

---

8. *Persia and the West: An Archaeological Investigation of the Genesis of Achaemenid Persian Art* (London: Thames and Hudson, 2000), 37.

9. Osborne, "Cult and Ritual," 256; cf. Robin Osborne, "Archaeology and the Athenian Empire," *TAPhA* 129 (1999): 328. Peer-polity competition in this context was first articulated in Anthony M. Snodgrass, "Interaction by Design: The Greek City-State," in *Peer Polity Interaction and Socio-political Change*, ed. Colin Renfrew and John F. Cherry (Cambridge: Cambridge University Press, 1986), 47–58.

10. On the Archaic temple of Apollo, see Joseph Fontenrose, *Didyma: Apollo's Oracle, Cult, and Companions* (Berkeley: University of California Press: 1988), 31–34. On the temples of Aphrodite and Athena, see Volkmar von Graeve, "Funde aus Milet XVII: Fragmente von Bauskulptur aus dem archaischen Aphrodite-Heiligtum," *AA*, no. 2 (2005): 41–48; Alan M. Greaves, *The Land of Ionia: Society and Economy in the Archaic Period* (Malden, MA: Wiley-Blackwell, 2010), 175, with n. 30, and Greaves, *Miletos*, 84; Winifried Held, "Zur Datierung des klassischen Athenatempels in Milet," *AA*, no. 1 (2004): 123–27.

11. Greaves, *Land of Ionia*, 176; Hans Lohmann, "The Discovery and Excavation of the Archaic Panionion in the Mycale (Dilek Daglari)," *Kazı Sonuçları Toplantısı* 28 (2007): 575–90. In addition to the controversies about the identification of the Panionian sanctuary, analyzing construction of a regional cult site introduces additional difficulties. On the Panionion and Ionian League generally, see Appendix 1.

12. J. M. Cook, *The Greeks in Ionia and the East* (London: Thames and Hudson 1962), 81–82; Greaves, *Land of Ionia*, 175–76. However, the Ionic volute capital does appear; see, e.g., Aenne Ohnesorg, and Mustafa Büyükkolanci, "Ein ionisches Kapitell mit glatten Voluten in Ephesos," *MDAI(I)* 57 (2007): 209–33.

In addition to developing in a milieu of regional competition, Ionian sanctuaries were inextricably linked with their Anatolian setting (e.g., Paus. 4.31.8; 7.2.7–8). Some sanctuaries, including Didyma at Miletus, were set near to sites that show evidence of "Phrygian" cult activity,[13] while excavations at the Archaic sanctuary at Kato Phano on Chios have turned up numerous Bronze Age finds.[14] More directly, the use of amber at the temple of Artemis at Ephesus and in votive offerings at the sanctuary of Hera at Samos are linked to the continuity of cult practice.[15] The deities themselves also show evidence of being Anatolian. The image of Artemis Ephesia, for instance, was a "many breasted" deity that Christian authors condemned and modern scholars see as a representation of fertility. But these iconic bulbs likely were not breasts. Comparable iconography is found on the images of other Anatolian deities such as a Carian Zeus, leading to skepticism about connecting them simply with gender.[16] The

13. Greaves, *Land of Ionia*, 174, 195–96. On the Phrygian connection at Didyma, see Walter Burkert, "Olbia and Apollo of Didyma: A New Oracle Text," in *Apollo: Origins and Influence*, ed. Jon Solomon (Tucson: University of Arizona Press, 1994), 51. The earliest archaeological find, a Mycenaean pottery fragment, dates to the fourteenth century; see Alan M. Greaves, "Divination at Archaic Branchidai-Didyma," *Hesperia* 81, no. 2 (2012): 178. Excavations at the Heraion on Samos show multiple phases of occupation as early as c.2650 BCE, when this community served as a node in commercial networks that connected Anatolia, Crete, and the Cyclades; see Ourania Kouka and Sergios Menelaou, "Settlement and Society in Early Bronze Age Heraion: Exploring Stratigraphy, Architecture and Ceramic Innovation after Mid-3rd Millennium BC," in *Pottery Technologies and Sociocultural Connections between the Aegean and Anatolia during the 3rd Millennium BC*, ed. Eva Alram-Stern and Barbara Horejs (Vienna: Austrian Academy of Sciences Press, 2018), 119–42. Recently, Abdulkadir Baran, "The Role of Carians in the Development of Greek Architecture," in *Listening to the Stones: Essays on Architecture and Function in Ancient Greek Sanctuaries in Honour of Richard Alan Tomlinson*, ed. Elena C. Partida and Barbara Schmidt-Dounas (Oxford: Archaeopress, 2019), 233–44, has argued that Caria influenced the trajectory of Greek architecture, both through its own contact with the eastern Mediterranean and with Carian craftsmen working on Greek projects; cf. Alexander Herda, "Greek (and Our) Views on the Karians," in *Luwian Identities: Culture, Language and Religion between Anatolia and the Aegean*, ed. Alice Mouton, Ian Rutherford, and Ilya Yakubovich (Leiden: Brill, 2013), 452–60, who recalls a story from Vitruvius (10.2.15) where a shepherd with the Carian name Pixodarus received honors at Ephesus for locating the marble quarry for the sanctuary of Artemis of Ephesus.

14. Excavators have suggested, though, that the location may have been a lookout rather than a site of ritual significance; see Lesley Beaumont et al., "Excavations at Kato Phano, Chios: 1999, 2000, and 2001," *ABSA* 99 (2004): 201–55. This sanctuary also had extensive retaining walls that protected it from flooding and created a monumental sacred space; see Lesley Beaumont, "Shaping the Ancient Religious Landscape at Kato Phana, Chios," in *Listening to the Stones: Essays on Architecture and Function in Ancient Greek Sanctuaries in Honour of Richard Alan Tomlinson*, ed. Elena C. Partida and Barbara Schmidt-Dounas (Oxford: Archaeopress, 2019), 182–90.

15. Ulrike Muss, "Amber from the Artemision from Ephesus and in the museums of Istanbul and Selçuk Ephesos," *Araştirma Sonuçları Toplantısı* 25 (2008): 13–26; Baumbach, *Significance of Votive Offerings*, 149–50.

16. On the history of interpretation of these images, see Morris, "View from East Greece," 70–71; Sarah P. Morris, "Artemis Ephesia: A New Solution to the Enigma of Her 'Breasts'?," in *Das Kosmos der Artemis von Ephesus*, ed. Ulrike Muss (Vienna: Österreiches Archäologisches Institut, 2001), 135–51; Lynn R. LiDonnici, "The Images of Artemis Ephesia and Greco-Roman Worship: A Reconsideration," *HThR* 85, no. 4 (1992): 389–415. Elspeth R. M. Dusinberre, *Empire, Authority, and Autonomy in Ach-*

local epithets for Apollo and Artemis also identified them as Anatolian-born, Lycian and Ortygian, respectively, and scholars have speculated since the nineteenth century that the Greek deity Apollo originated as an Anatolian sun god homonymous with the Trojan Appaliŭnas.[17]

This Anatolian context for the extramural sanctuaries complicated the relationship with their associated polis. Take Didyma and Miletus. Both the sanctuary and the oracle predated their later Greek identity (Paus. 7.2.6) and, unique among the sanctuaries in the Greek world, were administered by a single family, the Branchidae. This family became so associated with the sanctuary that in Roman times it was designated by their patronymic even though their relationship with the site had ended in the Archaic period.[18] It is only possible to speculate about the origins of the Branchidae. Joseph Fontenrose proposes that a mixed Hellenic and Carian population calling itself "Ionian" founded Didyma as a sanctuary of Apollo, but Greek genealogies that identify the eponymous Branchus as the beloved of the god only develop in the Hellenistic period.[19] Moreover, the name does not have clear Hellenic parallels, making the most probable suggestion that the name derives from a non-Hellenic Anatolian language and therefore that the family was not Greek. Didyma's location in the *chora* also meant that it was ideally suited to unify the Milesia, serving as a common ritual space for the Greek and non-Greek populations, as well as between Miletus and the other urban settlements such as Teichoussa.[20] Around

---

aemenid Anatolia (Cambridge: Cambridge University Press, 2013), 213–15, notes that the Artemis Ephesia also might have syncretized with other Anatolian mother goddess cults.

17. Speculation takes Apollo all the way to Çatal Hüyük. Michel Mazoyer, "Télipinu et Apollon fondateurs," *Hethitica* 14 (1999): 55–62, and Michel Mazoyer, "Apollon à Troie," in *Homère et l'Anatolie*, ed. Michel Mazoyer (Paris: L'Harmattan, 2008), 151–60, identified cultic links between the Trojan Apollo of the *Iliad* and the Hittite divinity Telipinu, an idea that met with resistance on methodological and evidential grounds; see Hatice Gonnet, J. D. Hawkins, and Jean-Pierre Grélois, "Remarques sur un article recent relative a Telibinu et a Apollon Fondateurs," *Anatolica* 27 (2001): 191–97. For a recent survey of the scholarship and evidence that the name Artemis also has Anatolian roots, see Edwin L. Brown, "In Search of Anatolian Apollo," in ΧΑΡΙΣ: *Essays in Honor of Sara A. Immerwahr*, Hesperia Supp. 33, ed. Anne P. Chapin (Athens: American School of Classical Studies, 2004), 243–57, who follows Walter Burkert, *Griechische Religion der archaischen und klassischen Epoche* (Stuttgart: Kohlhammer, 1977), 225–33, in seeing multiple strands coming together to form the Greek deity, but emphasizes that the Anatolian contribution is not merely iconographic.

18. A disconnect noted by H. W. Parke, "The Massacre of the Branchidae," *JHS* 105 (1985): 59.

19. Fontenrose, *Didyma*, 8; cf. Parke, "Massacre of the Branchidae," 60, with n. 7. In the Hellenistic iteration of the myth, Branchus was the son of Smikros, the son of a Delphian man and a Milesian woman who, while pregnant, dreamed of the sun entering through her mouth and exiting through her genitals. Branchus was so named for her throat (Conon *FGrH* 26 F 133). Conon's version represents a manufactured genealogy for the new Hellenistic oracle to derive legitimacy through a link to Delphi; see Greaves, "Divination," 181–83.

20. The accounts of the Ionian Migration at Miletus are particularly violent and preserve memories of rape that link the conquerors to the land, though I believe "Greek" and "non-Greek" are not useful categories of analysis in Ionia (see Appendix 2). On Didyma as a locus of ritual unification, see Greaves, *Miletos*, 122–23.

the same time that the earliest stone buildings went up in the late seventh or early sixth century Miletus formally took control of the sanctuary, and Apollo Delphinius became the patron god of the polis. However, the subordinated sanctuary still exerted a measure of autonomy even as the oracle began to be a tool in Miletus' diplomatic toolbox.[21] Construction continued into the Achaemenid period, possibly continuing until the Ionian revolt, leading Elspeth Dusinberre to suggest that the Achaemenids had taken over patronage of the cult.[22] The oracle fell silent with the deportation of the Branchidae in the late 490s,[23] but the unrestored sanctuary continued to fulfill its local political and symbolic roles and was the destination in an annual procession involving the Molpoi.[24] The relationship between city and sanctuary was thus not straightforward, once again complicating the economic thesis that draws a causal connection between prosperity and the construction of temples.

Sacred ways between the poleis and the extramural sanctuaries completed the religious topography. The purpose here is not to review the religious and ceremonial functions of the sacred ways or to review their construction and upkeep, but to identify the panorama of features connected to the sanctuaries that contributed to the overall cost and note what can be said about the sources of funding.[25] Each route took the procession to rural shrines, tombs, natural sanctuaries, and statues that marked them as monumental arrangements in and of themselves. The route from Miletus to Didyma included two additional sanctuaries from the Archaic period that fell into disuse about the same time

---

21. Herodotus links Didyma to Miletus, but also specifies the Branchidae (1.46, 1.92, 2.156, 6.19). One of the goals of the Hellenistic revisions to the foundation myths was to bind the sanctuary more clearly to the city; see below, "Kings and Cities." The extent to which the polis managed the sanctuary in the Archaic period is a matter of some debate. Klaus Tuchelt, "Die Perserzerstörung von Branchidai-Didyma und ihre Folgen-archäologisch bettrachtet," *AA*, no. 3 (1988): 427–38, argues that while Didyma belonged to Miletus in name it fell under its administrative diktat only after its reconstruction in the fourth century, while Norbert Ehrhardt, "Didyma und Milet in archaischer Zeit," *Chiron* 28 (1998): 11–20, argues for a closer connection. I side with Tuchelt. On the oracle's importance to Miletus' relationships with other states, see Greaves, *Miletos*, 124–27; Catherine Morgan, "Divination and Society at Delphi and Didyma," *Hermathena* 147 (1989): 17–42; H. W. Parke, *The Oracles of Apollo in Asia Minor* (New York: Routledge: 1985), 14–19.

22. Dusinberre, *Empire, Authority, and Autonomy*, 220–21.

23. The date at which the Branchidae "betrayed" Miletus is a matter of debate. The *communis opinio* places it at the close of the Ionian revolt (e.g., Greaves, "Divination," 179; Parke, *Oracles of Apollo*, 21), but N. G. L. Hammond, "The Branchidae at Didyma and in Sogdiana," *CQ*[2] 48, no. 2 (1998): 339–41, proposes a date of 479.

24. See Chapter 2.

25. For a survey of the sacred ways in Ionia, see Greaves, *Land of Ionia*, 180–88. We have little evidence for either the road surfaces, which leads Slawisch and Wilkinson, "Processions, Propaganda, and Pixels," to propose that the term "the sacred way" is a misleadingly anachronistic. They deconstruct the sacred way between Miletus and Didyma into its component parts, revealing an assemblage with discrete chronological and spatial clusters that suggests an absence of a fixed processional route until perhaps as late as the Roman period.

as did Didyma.[26] Unlike the temple proper, but quite like other aspects of the sanctuary, monuments along the sacred ways did not adhere to a central plan but went up as piecemeal dedications by the community and prominent individuals. The most famous statue from the route to Didyma, the Chares group, proclaims in an inscription "I am Chares, son of Kleisis, archon of Teichioussa. This statue is for Apollo."[27]

In short, the operation of a sanctuary and its adjacent features, including upkeep for the staff, constituted an enormous outlay of resources from the Archaic period onward. Before turning to the revenue streams available to a sanctuary, there is one more expense to examine: the temple itself.

The Costs of Temple Construction

The most detailed accounts of temple construction in the Greek world come from the fourth-century Asclepium at Epidaurus.[28] The cult had been founded at the end of the sixth century and came into prominence in the 430s or shortly thereafter, but construction at the site did not begin until the 370s.[29] Intermittent warfare and limited funding hampered construction, but Alison Burford points to a scarcity of skilled labor during a period of economic depression that resulted in few public works anywhere in the Greek world.[30] It is unknown how widely skilled workers traveled, but warfare and recession must have reduced mobility, and surviving ethnonyms for the workers at Epidaurus came overwhelming from elsewhere in the Greek world.[31] Since much of the cost of building temples was bound up in human and animal labor, it

---

26. On the archaeological evidence for these sanctuaries falling into disuse, see Slawisch, "Epigraphy versus Archaeology."

27. Χαρῆς εἰμι ὁ Κλέσιος Τειχιόσης ἀρχὸς, | ἄγαλμα το Ἀπόλλονος (*I.Didyma* 6). John Boardman, *Greek Sculpture: The Archaic Period* (London: Thames and Hudson, 1978), 96; Fontenrose, *Didyma*, 166; Greaves, *Land of Ionia*, 186–87; Herda, *Der Apollon-Delphinios-Kult*, 332–50; Slawisch and Wilkinson, "Processions, Propaganda, and Pixels," 125–27. On comparable statue groups in Ionia, see Cook, *Greeks in Ionia*, 103–6.

28. In this section I follow Alison Burford, *The Greek Temple Builders at Epidaurus* (Liverpool: Liverpool University Press, 1969), who analyzes the phases of construction at the Asclepium at Epidaurus.

29. Burford, *Greek Temple Builders*, 32, connects the international prominence to the plague at Athens, but a date in the 430s puts it somewhat earlier.

30. Burford, *Greek Temple Builders*, 33–35, also noting that the lack of evidence for an uptick in offerings in the 370s.

31. John Salmon, "Temples the Measures of Men: Public Building in the Greek Economy," in *Economies beyond Agriculture in the Classical World*, ed. David J. Mattingly and John Salmon (New York: Routledge, 2001), 204, contra Coulton, *Ancient Greek Architects*, 26–27, who argues that architects and workers largely stayed within their regions under ordinary circumstances.

varied widely depending on the distance from the source of the stone to the sanctuary.[32]

Despite the accounts at Epidaurus, estimating the cost of construction is an inexact science owing to factors that ranged from the variable costs of materials and labor to fluctuation in currency values to interruptions in the work. At the Asclepium, Burford estimates the total cost between 240 and 290 talents spent over more than a century.[33] The temple went up first, with the contracts showing straightforward payments for services rendered, while later contracts frequently show payments in installments, indicating that project had depleted the initial appropriation.[34] The cost of the Asclepium was not exceptional; construction on the sixth-century temple of Apollo at Delphi cost c.300 talents, and the fifth-century Parthenon at Athens, which was larger than the temple at Delphi but less than half the size of the temples in Ionia, between 460 and 500 talents.[35]

The circumstances for construction at each Greek temple were idiosyncratic and dependent on the relationship with between temple and polis, but interstate politics frequently contributed both positively and negatively to the pace of construction. The Asclepium was famed as a center of healing, which meant that it could count on a stream of offerings.[36] The case of the temples at Panhellenic sanctuaries is equally telling. The temple of Apollo at Delphi collapsed in an earthquake in 373/2 and construction needed to begin before the oracle could be active (Xen. Hell. 7.1.27).[37] The Amphictyonic commission for the project met annually between 370 and 356 to approve special taxes, and the sanctuary possessed a large amount of collected wealth from oracular consultations and dedicated plunder (e.g., Xen. Hell. 4.3.21; Plut. Ages. 19.3),

---

32. On the labor costs, see Salmon, "Temples the Measures of Men," 200–201. Ionia had few local sources of stone, and a late-Hellenistic shipwreck carrying a column drum that matches those of the temple of Apollo at Clarus suggests the need to move building materials by sea; see Deborah N. Carlson and William Aylward, "The Kizilburun Shipwreck and the Temple of Apollo at Claros," AJA 114, no. 1 (2010): 145–59.

33. Burford, Greek Temple Builders, 35; cf. Salmon, "Temples the Measures of Men," 100–101.

34. Burford, Greek Temple Builders, 109–18, discusses the differences in the inscriptions.

35. The accounts for the construction of the Propylaea and Parthenon together totaled about two thousand talents; see RO 145 = IG I³ 449 and ML 60 = IG I² 366. IG I³ 449 is a well-preserved example of inscriptions (IG I³ 433–97) that record accounts for public works in the fifth century, so the total expenditure could have been higher. For the temple at Delphi: Michael Scott, Delphi: A History of the Center of the Ancient World (Princeton, NJ: Princeton University Press, 2014), 145–62; the Parthenon: Burford, Greek Temple Builders, 81–85. The Parthenon was 2,147.55 m², with columns rising just over 10 meters, compared to 6,038 m² and 18.3 m at the Artemisium and 7,115.78 m² and 19.71 m at Didyma.

36. Burford, Greek Temple Builders, 18–39.

37. Scott, Delphi, 147–48; John K. Davies, "Rebuilding a Temple: The Economic Effects of Piety," in Economies beyond Agriculture in the Classical World, ed. David J. Mattingly and John Salmon (New York: Routledge, 2001), 214.

but the project progressed slowly.[38] The picture at Delphi is a consensus that the temple needed to be reconstructed, but since the temple lacked fungible assets, the members of the Amphictyonic Council exploited the crisis for political maneuvering. The pace of construction only picked up after the end of the Third Sacred War in 346, when the Phocian indemnity payments began to arrive.[39] The Amphictyonic Council imposed unique conditions on the sanctuary of Apollo that did not exist at sanctuaries that belonged to a single polis, but this case is nevertheless instructive: reconstruction offered an opportunity to articulate or rearticulate the history of the sanctuary.[40]

The Wealth of Sanctuaries

Operating sanctuaries was expensive in ancient Greece, with costs that included maintenance and pay for priestly personnel in addition to the initial outlay for construction. And yet prominent sanctuaries also concentrated wealth such that they served as banks whose resources a polis might draw on in times of need.[41] Beyond civic appropriations, sanctuaries frequently owned land, both in their immediate vicinity and in the *chora*, from which they received a portion of the profits. Land around the Ionian sanctuaries was often marginal, though likely suitable for animal husbandry and collecting timber.[42] Gifts from wealthy individuals expanded these holdings, as evidenced by Xenophon's purchase of land in the Peloponnese, where he created a temple modeled on the cult of

---

38. The largest contribution, just over three talents, came from the Dorians of the Peloponnese; see Davies, "Rebuilding a Temple," 219. The commission included delegates from Athens, which was then boycotting the Pythian games.

39. The Phocians plundered the temple to pay for the war; see Diod. 16.23.1. Davies, "Rebuilding a Temple," 219, notes the increased speed of construction, though Scott, *Delphi*, 156–57, argues that the influx of funds caused a corresponding growth of ambitions for the magnificence of the sanctuary. The sanctuary of Apollo prominently features an altar dedicated by the Chians that was already a reference point for Herodotus (2.135), but that was rebuilt in the later Classical and Hellenistic periods.

40. Scott, *Delphi*, 162; cf. Joshua P. Nudell, "Oracular Politics: Propaganda and Myth in the Restoration of Didyma," *AHB* 32 (2018): 44–60.

41. The treasury of Athena, for instance, funded the Athenian expedition against Samos in 440/39; see *IG* I³ 363, 454, with G. Marginesu and A. A. Themos, "Ἀνέλοσαν ἐς τὸν πρὸς Σαμίος πόλεμον: A New Fragment of the Samian War Expenses (*IG* I³ 363 + 454)," in ΑΘΗΝΑΙΩΝ ΕΠΙΣΚΟΠΟΣ: *Studies in Honour of Harold B. Mattingly*, ed. Angelos P. Matthaiou and Robert K. Pitt (Athens: Greek Epigraphical Society, 2014), 171–84. On that expedition, cf. Chapter 3.

42. Though the details varied from case to case, the use of sacred land was subject to regulation. A fourth-century inscription from Chios, for instance, records a prohibition against sheep and pigs from entering the sanctuary to prevent them from defecating there, while a first-century one from Samos prohibits collecting timber in the vicinity of the sanctuary. See Franciszek Sokolowksi, *Lois sacrées des cités grecques* (Paris: De Boccard, 1969), 116.5–6, 11–12; Matthew P. J. Dillon, "The Ecology of the Greek Sanctuary," *ZPE* 118 (1997): 120–22, 125.

Artemis at Ephesus (*Anab*. 5.3.7–13). Endowed properties, while increasing the holdings of the sanctuary in the long run, also hid taxable assets from the dedicator since there were laws against taxing farmers on sacred land, and sanctuaries frequently leased the land back to the original owner at reduced rates.[43]

Sale of votive offerings, *aparche* (first-fruit offerings), and fees from visitors provided additional revenue streams. One stream was the *thesauros* (offering box). By the Hellenistic period it was common practice for visitors to a sanctuary to make a preliminary offering by dropping coins into the box. Traditionally, this practice was interpreted as a cult fee imposed to make up for budget shortfalls and therefore either repealed when the endowment was restored or kept in place simply to maximize profit.[44] More recently, however, Isabelle Pafford convincingly has argued that the inscriptions regulating the deposit, storage, and use of the coins drew a distinction between money that would be used for the priestly sustenance and salaries and the income used for religious purposes.[45] The *thesauroi* offerings in the Hellenistic period, she argues, standardized the purchase of sacrifices and other religious items such as clothing for the cult statue.

Inscriptions also demonstrate how sanctuaries had broad economic purview to collect and manage their resources. At Delos and in the Acarnanian League in the third century there were specific taxes on luxury items such as enslaved people and on harbor commerce for sanctuary use, and a decree from the Acarnanian League specifies that harbor dues were charged during the festival at Anactorium in order to help rebuild the temple.[46] There is no comparable decree where an Ionian sanctuary received a portion of harbor fees, but it is reasonable to assume that the method of funding sanctuaries nonetheless existed. At early third-century Miletus, Antiochus dedicated a stoa and instructed that the profits be given to Apollo at Didyma (*I.Didyma* 479; see below, "Kings and Cities").

The last and, in my opinion, most important source of Ionian temple revenue came from prominent noncitizens. I separate these from private votives as far as the evidence allows for several reasons. First, conspicuous offerings

---

43. Dignas, *Economy of the Sacred*, 39; Dillon, "Ecology of the Greek Sanctuary," 117. On the relationship between endowments and taxation, see Joshua D. Sosin, "Endowments and Taxation in the Hellenistic Period," *Anc. Soc.* 44 (2014): 43–89.

44. Franciszek Sokolowski, "Fees and Taxes in the Greek Cults," *HThR* 47, no. 3 (1954): 153–64.

45. Isabelle Pafford, "Priestly Portion vs. Cult Fees—the Finances of Greek Sanctuaries," in *Cities and Priests: Cult Personnel in Asia Minor and the Aegean Islands from the Hellenistic to the Imperial Period*, ed. Marietta Horster and Anja Klöckner (Berlin: de Gruyter, 2013), 51.

46. Tulia Linders, "Sacred Finances: Some Observations," in *Economics of Cult in the Ancient World*, ed. Tulia Linders and Brita Alroth (Stockholm: Almquist and Wicksell, 1992), 9–12; cf. Davies, "Rebuilding a Temple," 218–19.

were large enough that ancient authors and Hellenistic inscriptions made note of them. Ionian temples had particularly close ties with the kings of Lydia and Phrygia, for instance, where kings were proverbially wealthy on account of their unusually ready access to gold.[47] Second, these gifts were not strictly signals of piety, but also demonstrations of power that give some indication of the prominence of that sanctuary in the world.

According to Herodotus, Midas of Phrygia made the first foreign donation to a Greek sanctuary when he dedicated his throne to Delphi (1.14.2–3). Herodotus likely did see Phrygian offerings at Delphi, which, as a prominent oracle, had particular appeal to non-Greeks, but attempts to identify specific material remains with the semimythical donations of Midas are quixotic.[48] However, the most famous—and likely more historical—offerings at Delphi were those of the Mermnad kings of Lydia. Gyges (c.699–c.644) dedicated heaps of silver and six kraters made from thirty talents' worth of gold in the seventh century (Hdt. 1.14; Athen. 6.20 [231e–f]), which Strabo says were melted down during the Third Sacred War of 356–346 (9.3.7–8).[49] The fourth Mermnad king, Alyattes (c.619–c.560), dedicated a magnificent krater made by the Chian craftsman Glaucus (Hdt. 1.25; Athen. 5.45 [210b]) and his son Croesus dedicated a silver krater made by Theodoros of Samos (Hdt. 1.51.2–3).[50] But Delphi was not the exclusive recipient of the largesse of the Lydian kings. Alyattes obeyed an oracle to rebuild the temple of Athena at Assessus in Miletus, which he had plundered (see Chapter 1). Croesus offered two golden cows and columns at the Artemisium at Ephesus (Hdt. 1.92) and, more infamously, made offerings at Didyma to purchase favorable oracles (Hdt. 1.46–56). Some of these dedications were ornamental, and Hecataeus proposed melting down the ones at Didyma to pay

---

47. Boardman, *Persia and the West*, 37. On the gold of Lydia and Phrygia, see Strabo 14.5.28; Ovid *Met.* 11.85–90. The proverb "wealthy as Croesus" appears at Archilochus F 22; Plato *Rep.* 2.359c–360b. The traditional thesis that gold and silver coinage entered the Greek world from Lydia has been supported by finds that firmly situate the coins before the Persian conquest: Nicholas Cahill and John H. Kroll, "New Archaic Coin Finds at Sardis," *AJA* 109, no. 4 (2005): 589–617, and an analysis of the facilities for minting coins: Andrew Ramage, "King Croesus' Gold and the Coinage of Lydia," in *Licia e Lidia prima dell'ellenizzazione*, ed. Mauro Giorgieri (Rome: Consiglio nazionale Della Richerche, 2003), 285–90.

48. On the development of the Midas myth, see Lynn E. Roller, "The Legend of Midas," *CA* 2, no. 2 (1983): 299–313; Kaplan, "Dedications to Greek Sanctuaries," 130.

49. For discussion of these offerings, see Kaplan, "Dedications to Greek Sanctuaries," 130; Jon D. Mikalson, *Herodotus and Religion in the Persian Wars* (Chapel Hill: University of North Carolina Press, 2003), 115–16. All dates for the Mermnad kings are rife with problems; see Anthony J. Spalinger, "The Date of the Death of Gyges and Its Historical Implications," *JAOS* 98, no. 4 (1978): 400–409. I accept Spalinger's argument that the date of Gyges' death in the Classical sources is too early but have left the dates as approximates because they do not change my argument.

50. Kaplan, "Dedications to Greek Sanctuaries," 139; H. W. Parke, "Croesus and Delphi," *GRBS* 25, no. 3 (1984): 209–12.

for a fleet during the Ionian revolt of 499–494 (Hdt. 5.36), but others were more functional. Excavations at the Artemisium at Ephesus, for instance, have turned up column drums with Lydian inscriptions that speak to the monarch underwriting the costs of construction of the enormous building.[51] Likewise, Elspeth Dusinberre recently suggested that the Achaemenid administration took up the patronage of these cults in the second half of the sixth century based on the intensity of work at both Didyma at the Artemision.[52]

There is no reason to doubt the evidence for Ionian commerce with Egypt, Lydia, and beyond during the Archaic period, but I am skeptical that individual, private prosperity would have resulted in the concentrated expenditure necessary to create monumental temples, particularly in the absence of inscriptions that show as much. Indeed, sanctuaries were powerful foci for diplomatic activity and royal euergetism during the early phase of Ionian temple construction, even if the vocabulary for these relationships was not as developed as it became in the Hellenistic period. The critical question, however, is whether analyzing temple construction in the Classical period along these same lines changes how we should think about Ionia.

Classical Ionia and Temple Construction: The Artemisium

The prominence of Ionia's Archaic temples is accentuated by Persia's violent suppression of the revolt in 494 and an acute absence of new monumental construction throughout the fifth century. J. M. Cook explained this pattern by positing that Ionian "city life" went into eclipse after the Persian wars because the poleis were impoverished on account of paying tribute to both Athens and Persia.[53] In a review of Cook's *Greeks in Ionia and the East*, John Boardman offered a single-sentence rebuttal, saying, "Cook suggests that there was no substantial new building in Ionia . . . but there seems to be evidence for new temples or significant reconstruction in Chios, Samos, and Didyma,"[54] but Robin

---

51. See L. H. Jeffrey, *The Local Scripts of Archaic Greece*, rev. ed. (Oxford: Oxford University Press, 1990), 339, for discussion of these inscriptions.

52. Dusinberre, *Empire, Authority, and Autonomy*, 218–21.

53. Cook, "Problem of Classical Ionia," 9–18; cf. Balcer, *Sparda*, 414–17. Rutishauser, *Athens and the Cyclades*: 233, likewise identifies Athenian tribute demands behind the absence of Cycladic temple construction in the fifth century. Without dismissing the stress that Athenian tribute imposed on Ionia, this alone is insufficient explanation. Construction projects began to appear in the fourth century at a time when they still owed tribute first to Persia and then to Alexander. If tribute were the limiting factor, then the absence of construction at Chios, which was never a tributary ally, once again stands out.

54. John Boardman, "Eastern Greeks," *CR* 14, no. 1 (1964): 83.

Osborne subsequently observed that if the field at large shared Boardman's reservations of Cook's thesis based on archaeological evidence, it did so quietly.[55] Indeed, while there is evidence of continued construction at some sanctuaries, there were no new colossal temples and only a few stone temples of any sort constructed in Ionia during the fifth century. But monumental temples were rare even in the sixth century, and thus Osborne argues that Cook misinterpreted the contrast between the sixth and fifth centuries and that the decision not to construct or reconstruct monumental temples indicates overall satisfaction with the Athenian empire because the Ionians willingly patronized Delian League cults at the expense of their own.[56]

Osborne is likely correct that "both sixth- and fifth-century patterns of building make more sense in terms of competition within and between communities, of neighborly rivalry and 'peer polity interaction,' than in term of economic boom and slump."[57] But the Delian League did not eliminate peer-polity competition. Further, the refoundation of Miletus had explicit provisions for the construction of new monumental buildings such as the sanctuary of Dionysus and the intramural Delphinion,[58] and yet the temple of Apollo at Didyma allegedly lay in ruins.[59] Closer inspection of Ionian temple construction in the Classical period reveals both the orthodox economic thesis and Osborne's revision inadequate on their own.

The Artemisium at Ephesus offers a counterpoint to Didyma (Strabo 14.1.5). The Artemisium's relationship with non-Greeks was among the strongest in Ionia, and the cult itself shows signs of Persianization. In addition to the Persian items that appear as votives, mirroring the Egyptian goods at the Heraeum on Samos, one of the temple officials took the Persian title *Megabyxos* (Xen. *Anab.* 5.3.6), and friezes show figures in Persian garb participating in ritual activity.[60] Non-Greek clothing is not unusual for figures in temple friezes,

---

55. Osborne, "Archaeology and the Athenian Empire," 320.

56. Osborne, "Archaeology and the Athenian Empire," 329–31.

57. Osborne, "Archaeology and the Athenian Empire," 328.

58. See Alexander Herda, "Copy and Paste? Miletos before and after the Persian Wars," in *Reconstruire les villes: Modes, motifs et récits*, ed. Emmanuelle Capet, C. Dogniez, M. Gorea, R. Koch Piettre, F. Mass, and H. Rouillard-Bonraisin (Turnhout: Brepols, 2019), 100; Sotiris G. Patronos, "Public Architecture and Civic Identity in Classical and Hellenistic Ionia" (PhD diss., Oxford University, 2002), 58–60, 103–4. Similarly, the refoundation of Priene in the fourth century made provisions for the construction of new temples.

59. Herda, "Copy and Paste?," 101, with n. 62, recently challenged the literary orthodoxy that the temple was destroyed by pointing out the absence of evidence for fire from the Archaic level of the temple and instead suggests that the temple was only demolished to clear the space for the Hellenistic temple.

60. Margaret C. Miller, "Clothes and Identity: The Case of Greeks in Ionia c.400 BC," in *Culture, Identity and Politics in the Ancient Mediterranean World*, ed. Paul J. Burton (Canberra: Australasian Society for Classical Studies, 2013), 29–30. Cf. Elspeth R. M. Dusinberre, *Aspects of*

but their participation in the rituals is. Moreover, there is evidence that this scene reflects common practice at the sanctuary. There is a record of non-Greek potentates offering sacrifices at Ephesus, including the satrap Tissaphernes (Thuc. 8.109), who also used Artemis as a rallying cry (Xen. *Hell.* 1.2.5–6), and Cyrus the Younger (Xen. *Anab.* 1.6.7). Further, the so-called Sacrilege Decree, a late fourth-century inscription from Ephesus that sentenced to death a large number of Lydians for having assaulted emissaries delivering sacred objects to branch of the cult at Sardis, demonstrates its reach (*I.Eph.* 2).[61] Beyond showing that the Ephesians were empowered to adjudicate the case, the names of the condemned hint at local connections, with the name "Ephesus" coming up in at least two patronymics (ll. 38 and 45) and the name Miletus appearing in one (l. 17). This regional prominence, along with the Ephesian ambivalence toward the Ionian revolt, helped the temple avoid destruction in 494, and its prominence was in turn redoubled by its survival, becoming the home to the Ephesia,

---

Empire in Achaemenid Sardis (Cambridge: Cambridge University Press, 2003), 59–79, on the syncretism of Achaemenid rituals with the worship of Artemis. Despite Xenophon's implication to the contrary, Megabyxos is not a name, but a title given to wardens at the sanctuary who oversaw financial management. The earliest reference to the Megabyxos may be Craterus' comedy *Tolmai* F 37, while inscriptions from after Priene 334 offer honors to the Megabyxos of Ephesus for his support of the construction of the temple of the temple of Athena and name him "Megabyxos son of Megabyxos" (*I.Priene* 3 and 231). Jan Bremmer, "Priestly Personnel of the Ephesian Artemision: Anatolian, Persian, Greek, and Roman Aspects," in *Practitioners of the Divine: Greek Priests and Religious Figures from Homer to Heliodorus*, ed. Beate Dignas and Kai Trapedach (Washington, DC: Center for Hellenic Studies, 2008) plausibly suggests that the Ephesians adopted the name Megabyxos because of the Persian conquest, though he attaches the nebulous date of c.500 BCE. The early adoption, perhaps even several decades earlier, helps explain the apparent lack of controversy around acculturation at this cult, where a fourth-century frieze includes figures in Persian court dress participating in the procession; see Miller, "Clothes in Ionia," 29–33. Evidence from the Roman period suggests that the Ephesians sought Megabyxoi from abroad because men in the position were castrated (Strabo 14.1.23). Artemis Ephesia had a distinctly Anatolian flavor (see especially Morris, "View from the East Greece," 70–71), but the lack of early evidence for castrated Megabyxoi makes it difficult to determine whether this was part of the cult already in the Classical period, as Bremmer argues, or a development of the Hellenistic period, perhaps in tandem with the rising prominence of the cult of Magna Mater. Dusinberre, *Empire, Authority, and Autonomy*, 218–19, suggests that the Megabyxos was a Persian.

    61. Franciszek Sokolowski, "A New Testimony on the Cult of Artemis of Ephesus," *HThR* 58, no. 4 (1965): 427–31; Guy Maclean Rogers, *The Mysteries of Artemis of Ephesos: Cult, Polis, and Change in the Graeco-Roman World* (New Haven, CT: Yale University Press, 2012), 6. On the implications of this inscription for Sardis in the Persian Empire, see Pierre Briant, *From Cyrus to Alexander: A History of the Persian Empire*, trans. Peter T. Daniels (Winona Lake, IN: Eisenbrauns, 2002), 702. The cult of Artemis at Sardis has long been thought to date to Croesus because of the king's patronage of the sanctuary of Artemis at Ephesus, but, despite a Lydian phase of activity in and around the so-called Lydian Altar, which Dusinberre, *Empire, Authority, and Autonomy*, 226–30, posits belongs to the Achaemenid period, there is little evidence for a temple before the Hellenistic period; see Nicholas Cahill and Crawford H. Greenewalt Jr., "The Sanctuary of Artemis at Sardis: Preliminary Report, 2002–2012," *AJA* 120, no. 3 (2016): 492–98. Its prominence at the end of the fifth century is revealed in Xen. *Anab.* 1.6.7 when Cyrus mentions it as a place where Orontas allegedly repented while quizzing this man who had again betrayed him.

an athletic competition that drew contestants from around Ionia (Thuc. 3.104; Dionysius *Ant. Rom.* 4.25).[62]

Outside the few references testifying to the continued prominence of the sanctuary of Artemis, there is little evidence for construction from the fifth century. In the fourth century, however, it underwent two building phases. A column drum contemporary to the first phase of construction in the 390s bears an inscription saying that it was dedicated by "Agesilaus"—probably the Spartan king who campaigned in Asia Minor in 397/6.[63] This identification is, ultimately, speculative, but accounts of the campaign indicate that Agesilaus paid particular attention to the sanctuary in his diplomatic efforts in the region (Xen. *Ages.* 1.27; *Hell.* 3.4.18). Dedications to subsidize repairs already begun plausibly fits into this setting where Agesilaus' political needs matched the local project.

The evidence for the second phase of construction is clearer, but more controversial. The temple burned in 356, reputedly on the same day that Alexander the Great was born, with the goddess gone to oversee the momentous birth (Plut. *Alex.* 3.3).[64] Herostratus took the blame for burning the temple, but the cause of the fire is a matter of debate, with suggestions ranging from a lightning strike (following Aristotle *Meteorology* 3.1) to deliberate sabotage by the temple administration because the they want to move the sanctuary from the Cayster River floodplain to more solid ground.[65] The next reference to the construction came in 334 when Alexander the Great allegedly offered to pay all costs for the temple in perpetuity, only to be rebuffed by the Ephesians (Strabo 1.41.22). The king responded by ordering the Ephesians to pay their *phoros* to the sanctuary (Arr. 1.17.10–12; see Chapter 7).

Scholars have traditionally placed too much weight on this sentence in Arrian. Since Arrian also explicitly says that Alexander relieved the other cities

62. P. J. Stylianou, "Thucydides, the Panionian Festival, and the Ephesia (III 104), Again," *Historia* 32, no. 2 (1983): 245–49, contra Simon Hornblower, "Thucydides, the Panionian Festival, and the Ephesia (III 104)," *Historia* 31, no. 2 (1982): 241–45, who argues that Thucydides' mention of the Ephesia meant a temporary relocation of the Panionion festival, and Irene Ringwood Arnold, "Festivals of Ephesus," *AJA* 76, no. 1 (1972): 17–18, who sees a permanent relocation of the Panionion to Ephesus. Cf. Chapter 6 and Appendix 1.

63. The context of the inscription is disputed, with Christoph Börker, "König Agesilaos von Sparta und der Artemis-Tempel in Ephesus," *ZPE* 37 (1980): 69–70, arguing for an otherwise unattested building phase. Burkhardt Wesenberg, "Agesilaos im Artemision," *ZPE* 41 (1981): 175–80, challenges that interpretation, though not the identification of the name. The repairs need not have been to the columns, despite the location of the inscription. On Agesilaus' expedition, see Chapter 5.

64. In point of fact, the two events did not coincide.

65. See Dieter Knibbe, *Ephesos-Ephesus: Geschichte einer bedeutenden antiken Stadt und Portrait einer modern Großgrabung* (Bern: Peter Lang, 1998), 88–89; Muss, "Amber from the Artemision," 51; Rogers, *Mysteries of Artemis*, 33 n. 6.

of their *phoros* (tribute) payments and began to collect a *syntaxis* (contribution), the specific provisions for Ephesus seem pregnant with meaning for the interpretation of both Alexander and Alexander's policy in the first years of his campaign. Ernst Badian, for instance, maintained that when the Ephesians turned away Alexander's generosity, the fickle king turned hostile, not relieving the *phoros* and levying a *syntaxis* in addition.[66] This thesis resolves the contradiction inherent in allowing the Ephesians to keep their tribute local while requiring the rest of the Ionians to help pay for the campaign, but it rests on shaky foundations.

Badian's formulation is based on triangulating Arrian's narrative with a passage in Strabo that paraphrases the first century BCE geographer Artemidorus of Ephesus (14.1.22):[67]

> Alexander [he adds] offered to the Ephesians to undertake all costs that had occurred and all those yet to come, in return for an inscription thereupon, but they were unwilling, just as they were unwilling to acquire renown for temple robbery. [Artemidorus] praises the Ephesian who said to the king that it was unseemly for a god to make dedications to gods.

> Ἀλέξανδρον δὴ τοῖς Ἐφεσίοις ὑποσχέσθαι τὰ γεγονότα καὶ τὰ μέλλοντα ἀναλώματα, ἐφ᾽ ᾧ τε τὴν ἐπιγραφὴν αὐτὸν ἔχειν, τοὺς δὲ μὴ ἐθελῆσαι, πολὺ μᾶλλον οὐκ ἂν ἐθελήσαντας ἐξ ἱεροσυλίας καὶ ἀποστερήσεως φιλοδοξεῖν· ἐπαινεῖ τε τὸν εἰπόντα τῶν Ἐφεσίων πρὸς τὸν βασιλέα, ὡς οὐ πρέποι θεῷ θεοῖς ἀναθήματα κατασκευάζειν.

Despite its apparent simplicity, this bold declaration hides a murky history. For instance, he rebuts a claim put forward by Timaeus of Tauromenium that the Ephesians had stolen Persian treasures kept at the temple:

> Artemidorus says that Timaeus of Tauromenium, being ignorant of these and generally being a slanderous sycophant, . . . says that they achieved the restoration of the temple through the [gold] the Persians deposited there. But in the first place there was nothing deposited there

66. Ernst Badian "Alexander the Great and the Greeks of Asia," in *Collected Papers on Alexander the Great* (New York: Routledge, 2012), 127–31 (= "Alexander the Great and the Greeks of Asia," in *Ancient Society and Institutions: Studies Presented to Victor Ehrenberg*, ed. Ernst Badian [Oxford: Oxford University Press, 1966], 37–69).

67. The quoted Artemidorus fragment is criticizing Timaeus. Translation adapted after H. L. Jones in volume 6 of the Loeb edition of *Strabo's Geography*.

then, and if it had been, it would have burned together with the temple. After the conflagration it was missing a roof, and who would want to deposit such things lying in an open-air enclosure?

ἅπερ ἀγνοοῦντά φησιν ὁ Ἀρτεμίδωρος τὸν Ταυρομενίτην Τίμαιον καὶ ἄλλως βάσκανον ὄντα καὶ συκοφάντην . . . λέγειν ὡς ἐκ τῶν Περσικῶν παρακαταθηκῶν ἐποιήσαντο τοῦ ἱεροῦ τὴν ἐπισκευήν· οὔτε δὲ ὑπάρξαι παρακαταθήκας τότε, εἴ τε ὑπῆρξαν, συνεμπεπρῆσθαι τῷ ναῷ· μετὰ δὲ τὴν ἔμπρησιν τῆς ὀροφῆς ἠφανισμένης, ἐν ὑπαίθρῳ τῷ σηκῷ τίνα ἂν ἐθελῆσαι παρακαταθήκην κειμένην ἔχειν;

Strabo seems inclined to accept Artemidorus' claim even though he opens the section by detailing how the Ephesians paid for construction:

When one Herostratus set it aflame they furnished another, better, one, gathering the women's jewelry and private offerings, and disposing of the earlier columns. Contemporary decrees bear witness to this.

ὡς δὲ τοῦτον Ἡρόστρατός τις ἐνέπρησεν, ἄλλον ἀμείνω κατεσκεύασαν συνενέγκαντες τὸν τῶν γυναικῶν κόσμον καὶ τὰς ἰδίας οὐσίας, διαθέμενοι δὲ καὶ τοὺς προτέρους κίονας· τούτων δὲ μαρτύριά ἐστι τὰ γενηθέντα τότε ψηφίσματα

Timaeus was a historian with a particularly poor reputation in antiquity,[68] but there is no reason to put any more faith in Artemidorus. Artemidorus was concerned with relieving his forebearers of any hint of sacrilege that might have been associated with taking gold at the temple, but παρακαταθήκη, the word Timaeus uses, can mean either dedication or deposit. Artemidorus clearly applied the former definition, but what if Timaeus intended the latter? It is plausible that the gold stored at the temple seized by the Ephesians to pay for repairs was the *phoros* payment owed to Persia. Taking the passage in Strabo altogether, the Ephesians paid for repairs to the temple through private donations, the sale of old column drums, and redirecting tribute payments at a time when Persian power in the region had waned.[69] This interpretation also offers

---

68. Polybius dedicated an extended portion of his twelfth book to an extended ad hominem attack against Timaeus where he tears down the latter's qualifications as a historian. Christopher A. Baron, *Timaeus of Tauromenium and Hellenistic Historiography* (Cambridge: Cambridge University Press, 2013), 58–88, offers a thorough assessment.

69. On the ebb tide of Persian power, see Chapter 6.

a new resolution for Arrian's apparent contradiction. Rather than punishing a prideful community or curiously rewarding a polis he had little other connection to, Alexander's decision to direct the *phoros* to Artemis retroactively approved the local initiative that appropriated the tribute in the first place.

Material poverty must have contributed to the pace of temple construction in Classical Ionia, but it was not *the* defining factor. The sanctuary of Artemis demonstrates that the Ionian temples continued to play an important role in mediating the position of the polis in the larger political arena. Stabilizing southern Ionia might have brought enough prosperity that the Milesians began planning new construction projects, but more important than the hand of market forces in the new construction projects at poleis like Priene was the Hecatomnid dynasty.[70]

Kings and Cities: Hellenistic Reconstructions

The Hellenistic period in Ionia is often presented as a new spring that followed a long, fallow Classical period, with Alexander's liberation heralding a period of economic revitalization and thus new construction projects up and down the coast.[71] The second half of the fourth century did witness an architectural renaissance in Ionia, but this traditional account buys into propaganda about the oppressive burden of Persian tribute now released by Alexander's "liberation." Alexander did formally abolish the *phoros*, though he soon replaced it with the more generously named, but equally onerous, *syntaxis*. Even more damning to this thesis than the flawed distinction between Persian and Macedonian rule is that the start of this Ionian construction boom began in the 340s, well before Alexander conquered the region. At Miletus, renovation in the city Delphinium began in the early 330s, and the plans for restoring the oracle at Didyma plausibly formed at the same time.[72] Similarly, the temple to Apollo that Alexander dedicated at Priene was likely commissioned by Artemisia of Caria (Pliny *H.N.* 36.30–31; Vitruv. *De arch.* 1.1.12),[73] and the Hellenistic sanc-

---

70. For Mausolus and Caria, see Chapter 6.

71. E.g., Parke, *Oracles of Apollo*, 129, "a burst of prosperity."

72. Walter Voigtländer, *Der jüngste Apollotempel von Didyma: Geschichte seine Baudekors* (Tübingen: Wasmuth, 1975), 14–28, argues that the plans dated to the 340s, based on a stylistic analysis of the decorations and the alleged careers of the architects who worked on the project, but J. M. Cook, "Review: *Der jüngste Apollotempel von Didyma*," *JHS* 96 (1976): 243–44, rightly notes that this chronology relies on evidence for the interrelationship of monumental construction that is speculative at best. For the dating of the Delphinium, see Patronos, "Public Architecture and Civic Identity," 65.

73. I follow an earlier chronology for the "refoundation" of Priene that places it during the

tuary of Apollo at Claros appears to have been begun at about this time.[74] The Ionian renaissance began before Alexander's conquest, but it flourished after his death by taking full advantage of the competition between the Diadochoi.[75]

The most notable Hellenistic temple-building project in Ionia was the temple of Apollo at Didyma. The new temple would be the largest building in Ionia at 7,115.78 square meters, with monumental steps that served as grand-stands overlooking the processional way and a double row of columns rising to the height of 19.7 meters.[76] The new temple outstripped the famed temple of Artemis in size, and its interior was unique. The *prodomos* (entry chamber) led visitors to a wall nearly a meter and half in height, topped by an enormous win-dow through which the *naiskos* (inner sanctuary) was just visible. The visitor entered the inner courtyard by first going down to an interior room at ground level and from there down a monumental staircase into the heart of the tem-ple. The *adyton* (the inner chamber of the *naiskos*) was nearly 5 meters below ground and the inner courtyard, surrounded by solid walls that rose between 22 and 25 meters, contained a grove of bay trees. Although it has been thought that the general appearance was completed in the third century, construction continued for nearly six hundred years until the third century CE.[77]

Oracles in antiquity had enormous financial potential. Archaic Didyma had a reputation on par with any in the Greek world, but by the late fourth century it

reign of Mausolus (c.377–353). Architectural genealogies are as problematic as literary and mythi-cal ones in the ancient world, but the architect for the temple of Athena, Pytheus, the primary architect on the project, was said to have also worked on the Mausoleum in Halicarnassus. Other scholars have suggested that Alexander refounded the polis. The date of the inscription at Priene is controversial; the inscription reads Βασιλεὺς Ἀλέξανδρος, and it is commonly thought that he did not adopt the royal titulature in his correspondence with the Greeks until taking the mantle of the King of Asia after the battle of Gaugamela in 331. For a recent reevaluation argues against the pos-sibility of the early dating in 334, see Emiliano Arena, "Alessandro 'Basileus' nella Documentazione Epigrafica: La Dedica del Tempio di Atena a Priene ('I.Priene' 156)," *Historia* 62, no. 1 (2013): 48–79. S. M. Sherwin-White, "Ancient Archives: The Edict of Alexander to Priene, a Reappraisal," *JHS* 105 (1985): 69–89, argues that Lysimachus made the dedication in honor of Alexander. While it was common for the Diadochoi to compete in making performative dedications to Alexander, the placement of this one in a location that hid its visibility does not quite fit the bill. I believe the inscription attests to an actual donation in the first years of Alexander's campaign.

74. Jean-Charles Moretti, "Le Temple D'Apollon à Claros: État des Recherches en 2007," *RA*[2] 1 (2009): 172.

75. Pierre Debord, *L'Asie Mineure au IVe Siècle (412–323 a.C.)* (Pessac: Ausonius, 1999) shows how the Hellenistic period accelerated political changes in Ionia that had begun in the fourth century.

76. On the monumental steps, see Mary B. Hollinshead, *Shaping Ceremony: Monumental Steps and Greek Architecture* (Madison: University of Wisconsin Press, 2014), 69.

77. Parke, *Oracles of Apollo*, 53. Greaves, *Miletos*, 136, offers a parallel between Hellenistic Miletus and Didyma in terms of shared visions of grandeur that never came to pass. Slawisch and Wilkinson, "Processions, Propaganda, and Pixels," 130–31, associate the first series of inscriptions that mention a sacred way at the end of the third or start of the second century BCE, with the near-completion of the temple and complete recovery of Miletus from its destruction in 494.

had been dormant for nearly a century and a half. This set of circumstances lay behind their delivery of an oracle to Alexander in 331 proclaiming his divinity, but while the king's propagandist Callisthenes recorded the message in a list of favorable utterances, there was no financial reward, and plans for construction languished for decades.[78] Although the oracle had officially been restored by 331, inscriptions recording the offerings at the sanctuary reveal that the new oracle was neither popular nor prosperous. The first signs of a change appear in the last decade of the fourth century. As early as 311 on his return to Babylon, Seleucus reputedly told his soldiers that the oracle at Didyma had predicted his eventual victory, probably in an imitation of Alexander (Diod. 19.90.4).[79] Seleucus then declared that he found the Archaic cult statue in the Persian palace at Ecbatana and, starting in c.300, he and his family made a series of offerings, which both provided the sanctuary with funds to begin construction in earnest and, equally important, gave public support for the legitimacy of the new oracle. The Milesians took full advantage of this collaboration with Seleucus to rewrite the mythical genealogy of the oracle and cult procedures to bring them in line with the more familiar Delphic practice while simultaneously employing archaizing elements such as an old-style blood altar that made it look like the new oracle was the old one reborn.[80]

Work on the temple at Didyma and the Seleucid relationship with Miletus flowered in the years after the battle of Ipsus in 301. Although Seleucus promoted the royal cult of Zeus in imitation of Alexander's divine parentage early in his reign, Apollo served a similar political purpose by c.305 when the god began to appear on Seleucid coins from Babylonia.[81] In time stories made Seleucus Apollo's son. When Seleucus founded the sanctuary of Apollo at Daphne near Antioch in 300 he said it was at the urging of the oracle at Didyma.[82] The years that followed saw a series of gifts from the royal family to the sanctuary. Antiochus donated a stoa and stipulated its revenues were to

---

78. For how Alexander became inextricably linked with the restoration of Didyma, see Nudell, "Oracular Politics."

79. E.g., the "prophecy" came in a mistaken address, like one Alexander received at Siwah; see Nudell, "Oracular Politics," 51–52. On the legend of Seleucus, see Daniel Ogden, *The Legend of Seleucus: Kingship, Narrative, and Mythmaking in the Ancient World* (Cambridge: Cambridge University Press, 2017), 70–84.

80. Ulf Weber, "Der Altar des Apollon von Didyma," *MDAI(I)* 65 (2015): 5–61.

81. On early Seleucid religious iconography, see particularly Kyle Erickson, "Seleucus I, Zeus and Alexander," in *Every Inch a King: Comparative Studies on Kings and Kingship in the Ancient and Medieval Worlds*, ed. Lynette G. Mitchell and Charles Melville (Leiden: Brill, 2013), 113–18.

82. On Didyma and Daphne, see Andrea De Giorgi, *Ancient Antioch: From the Seleucid Era to the Islamic Conquest* (Cambridge: Cambridge University Press, 2016), 150–54; Ogden, *Legend of Seleucus*, 57, 138–51, 272.

go to furnishing the sanctuary (McCabe, *Didyma* 7 = *I.Didyma* 479, ll. 7–11) and Queen Apame dedicated funds for the construction of the *naos* (McCabe, *Didyma* 8 = *I.Didyma* 480, ll. 8–9).[83] Seleucus himself made a lavish offering of sacrificial animals, ornately wrought bowls, and tons of precious spices such as cinnamon, frankincense, and myrrh (McCabe, *Didyma* 19 = *I.Didyma* 424). These gifts, which present a cohesive dynastic image, were an established part of Hellenistic diplomacy between kings and cities. The Milesians reciprocated with honors for Apame and Antiochus, including right to consult at the oracle (McCabe, *Didyma* 7 = *I.Didyma* 479, ll. 38–41) and an equestrian statue of Antiochus at Didyma (l. 30).[84] The inscription honoring Apame thanked her for intervening on behalf of Milesian mercenaries (McCabe, *Didyma* 8 = *I.Didyma* 480, l. 6), and Demodamas, the proposer of both decrees, entered into Seleucid service, dedicating an altar to Didymaean Apollo in central Asia sometime after 294 (Pliny *H.N.* 6.49).[85] Thus, as Paul Kosmin has recently argued, Didymaean

---

83. The inscription for Apame appeared at the sanctuary of Artemis at Didyma, rather than at the one for Apollo, where a second inscription testifies to honors made on her behalf (McCabe, *Didyma* 182 = *OGIS* 745), as well as for Seleucus' second wife, Phila (McCabe, *Didyma* 183 = *I.Didyma* 114), and Ptolemy I's daughter Philotera (McCabe, *Didyma* 186 = *I.Didyma* 115).

84. For the diplomatic function of sanctuaries, see particularly Hugh Bowden, "The Argeads and Greek Sanctuaries," in *The History of the Argeads: New Perspectives*, ed. Sabine Müller, Tim Howe, Hugh Bowden, and Robert Rollinger (Wiesbaden: Harrassowitz, 2017), 163–82.

85. The traditional date for the altar aligns it with Seleucus' failed expedition to the Indus in 306–303 (App. *Syr.* 55); see Elias Bikerman, *Institutions des Séleucides* (Paris: Librairie Orientaliste Paul Geuthner, 1938), 73; Bernard Hausoullier, *Études sur l'histoire de Milet et du Didymeion* (Paris: Librairie Emile Bouillon, 1902), 48–49; Andreas Mehl, *Seleukos Nikator und sein Reich*, part 1, *Seleukos' Leben und die Entwicklung seiner Machposition* (Leuven: Peeters, 1986), 166–81; Louis Robert, "Documents d'Asie Mineure," *BCH* 108, no. 1 (1984): 471–72; Ivana Savalli-Lestrade, *Les philoi dans l'Asie Hellénistique* (Paris: Librairie Droz: 1998), 5; Gillian Ramsay, "The Diplomacy of Seleukid Women: Apama and Stratonike," in *Seleukid Royal Women: Creation, Representation and Distortion of Hellenistic Queenship in the Seleukid Empire*, ed. Altay Coskun and Alex McAuley (Stuttgart: Franz Steiner, 2016), 89–90, but this date is unsatisfactory because of the reference to the two kings; see Nudell, "Oracular Politics," 54–55, with citations. Demodamas became a *philos* in the Seleucid court, but his role there is unknown. Hausoullier, 36, argues that he had relatives in the Seleucid court, but he is often thought to have been a mercenary general. Marie Widmer, "Apamè: Une reine au coer de la construction d'un royaume," in *Femmes influents dans le monde hellénistique et à Rome*, ed. Anne Bielman Sánchez, Isabelle Cogitore, and Anne Kolb (Grenoble: UGA Éditions, 2016), 25–27, rightly notes he could have served to build relationships with local aristocracy; cf. Ramsay, 95–96, but these are not mutually exclusive. Jeffrey Rop, *Greek Military Service in the Ancient Near East, 401–330 BCE* (Cambridge: Cambridge University Press, 2019), has shown how recruitment and service were inextricably linked to patronage networks. Recent work has seen a more expansive role for Demodamas, including the transition from Zeus to Apollo as a tutelary deity; see Krzysztof Nawotka, "Seleukos I and the Origin of the Seleukid Dynastic Ideology," *SCI* 36 (2017): 31–43, and Krzysztof Nawotka, "Apollo, the Tutelary God of the Seleucids, and Demodamas of Miletus," in *The Power of the Individual and Community in Ancient Athens and Beyond*, ed. Z. Archibald (London: Bloomsbury, 2018), 261–84. Cynzia Bearzot, "Demodamante di Mileto e l'identità ionica," *Erga-Logoi* 5, no. 2 (2017): 143–54, takes a different approach to a similar end in suggesting that Demodamas worked to promote Ionian identity in the early Hellenistic world.

Apollo symbolically came to represent the far northwestern and northeastern limits of Seleucid territory.[86]

Evidence for contemporary construction at Claros near Colophon is more problematic. Archaic poetry associates Claros with Apollo from an early date, and its prophets claimed lineage from Teirisias through Mopsus, the son of his daughter Manto, which gave the site both legitimacy and antiquity.[87] Throughout most the Classical period, however, the site is rarely mentioned and never associated with Colophon.[88] In fact, H. W. Parke suggests that Claros' mythic genealogy to an Aeolic prophetic tradition points to an Aeolian rather than Ionian foundation, in turn tying it to Notium rather than Colophon. Notion and Colophon had a strained relationship in the Classical period, with the former generally subordinate to the latter, but also with significant numbers of Colophonians living in Notium. By the middle of the fourth century, likely around the time when its coins began to feature Apollo's tripod, Colophon annexed both Notium and Claros.[89]

Colophon's changed relationship with Claros coincided with the wave of monumental construction up and down the coast of Anatolia. It should be of little surprise, then, that the site shows a surge in activity that culminated in the construction of a new Doric temple of a size with contemporary Doric structures elsewhere, if still a fraction of the size of its colossal neighbors.[90] The only Ionian polis without direct access to the sea, Colophon was not wealthy compared to most of its peers, so the decision to renovate the temple on a monumental scale requires explanation. Parke, for instance, proposes that its genesis belonged in "some burst of prosperity" that followed liberation from Persia, but that the wars of the Diadochoi meant that all available funds were redirected to the construction of a new set of fortifications.[91] Circumstantial

---

86. Paul J. Kosmin, *The Land of the Elephant Kings: Space, Territory, and Ideology in the Seleucid Empire* (Cambridge, MA: Harvard University Press, 2014), 61–67, while Bearzot, "Demodamante," 151, suggests that the altar might have been in service of a Milesian community in the region.

87. There is only one, likely apocryphal, prophecy attributed to Claros in the fourth century, associated with the founding of Smyrna, but Parke, *Oracles of Apollo*, 125–26, rejects the notion that the oracle only developed in the Hellenistic period on the strength of the legendary material that associated the site with Mopsus and Manto. This does not mean that the oracle was active. Recent finds have revealed Bronze Age material; see Nuran Şahin and Pierre Debord, "Découvertes récentes et installation du culte d'Apollon pythien à Claros," *Pallas* 87 (2011): 169–204.

88. Herodotus mentions Colophon on five occasions, but never Claros. Thucydides (3.33.1–2) says that the Spartan fleet put in at Claros in 427 but uses the name only as a landmark.

89. Parke, *Oracles of Apollo*, 123.

90. Claros had a footprint of 1,027.68 m², which was roughly the size of the temple for Zeus at Nemea and the temple of Asclepius at Epidaurus and half the size of the Parthenon; see Moretti, "Le Temple d'Apollon à Claros," 172. The footprint of the Hellenistic temple was adjusted during the Augustan period; see Parke, *Oracles of Apollo*, 128–29.

91. Parke, *Oracles of Apollo*, 129.

evidence at Claros again seems to support thesis of early-Hellenistic prosperity. An inscription dated to 307/6 records a list of contributions to build Colophon's walls and the late-Hellenistic column drums found at the Kızılburun shipwreck indicate that construction progressed slowly.[92] Once again, though, chronology intrudes. Much as at Didyma, the plans for new construction at Claros predated Alexander and thus cannot be attributed to a sudden economic swing in his wake. Moreover, Parke undersells Colophon's poverty in 307. The inscription in question records a long list of contributors to the construction of the wall (McCabe, *Kolophon* 6 = *SEG* 19, 698). The largest number of entries are for small donations of twenty or thirty drachmae, and the strain these sums posed is demonstrated by entries that list the donor as an individual and his son or brother (e.g., ll. 375, 393), but these donations are dwarfed by the entries at the top of the list that include large individual contributions of tens of thousands of drachmae, mostly from Macedonians (ll. 134–60). Construction at Claros was not a small project, and Lysimachus' attempt to incorporate Colophon into Arsinoeia in c.294 temporarily halted construction. When it resumed, the plans were scaled back, probably for lack of funds, and ultimately never completed.[93]

The sanctuary of Artemis at Ephesus again provides a telling counterpoint to the other Ionian sanctuaries. It had served as a locus of diplomatic activity throughout the Classical period, and Ephesian honorific inscriptions were traditionally posted in the sanctuary. However, its continued operation and regional clout meant not only that the sanctuary did not require foreign patronage, but also that the sanctuary resisted subordination to Ephesus the way that the revisions to the mythic genealogy of Didyma changed the relationship between that sanctuary and Miletus. But even famous Artemisium could not maintain its autonomy for long under the new pressures of the Hellenistic period. Guy Rogers has recently shown that coercion worked where flattery and bribes failed. When Lysimachus refounded Ephesus as Arsinoeia in the 290s, he changed the status of the Artemisium, in part because its supporters had sided with Demetrius in 301 (see Chapter 8). Lysimachus could not be seen to commit sacrilege against such a prominent sanctuary, so he instead underwrote the costs of a new temple complex for Artemis Soter at Ortygia, near the border with Pygela.[94] Patronizing a new cult of Artemis also gave Lysimachus an opening to oversee the Artemisium. He took the final authority for

92. For Colophon inscription, see Benjamin D. Merrit, "Inscriptions of Colophon," *AJPh* 56, no. 4 (1935): 358–97, and Léopold Migeotte, *Les souscriptions publiques dans les cités grecques* (Paris: Editions du Sphinx, 1992), 337. On this shipwreck and the identification of the drums with Claros, see Carlson and Aylward, "Kizilburun Shipwreck."

93. Moretti, "Le Temple d'Apollon à Claros," 173.

94. On the contentious relationship between Ephesus and Pygela, see Chapter 3 and Chapter 6.

himself but granted the Arsinoeian Gerousia the right to mediate between the two sanctuaries and therefore to oversee the management of the mysteries of Artemis.[95]

Conclusion

In the introduction to his history of the Peloponnesian War, Thucydides compared what future commentators might think of Sparta and Athens if only ruins remained (1.10.2):

> If the city of the Lacedaemonians should be laid to ruin, leaving only the foundations of its temples and permanent fixtures, I think there would be much disbelief in its power compared to its fame among those in the distant future. For, although it has two of the five parts of the Peloponnese, and leads all the rest and has many allies, all the same the city is not united and is furnished with neither temples nor expensive buildings but arranged in unwalled villages after the fashion of ancient Greece, making it seem deficient. But if Athens were to suffer the same, one would conclude from the visible appearance that the city's power was twice what it was.

> Λακεδαιμονίων γὰρ εἰ ἡ πόλις ἐρημωθείη, λειφθείη δὲ τά τε ἱερὰ καὶ τῆς κατασκευῆς τὰ ἐδάφη, πολλὴν ἂν οἶμαι ἀπιστίαν τῆς δυνάμεως προελθόντος πολλοῦ χρόνου τοῖς ἔπειτα πρὸς τὸ κλέος αὐτῶν εἶναι καίτοι Πελοποννήσου τῶν πέντε τὰς δύο μοίρας νέμονται, τῆς τε ξυμπάσης ἡγοῦνται καὶ τῶν ἔξω ξυμμάχων πολλῶν· ὅμως δὲ οὔτε ξυνοικισθείσης πόλεως οὔτε ἱεροῖς καὶ κατασκευαῖς πολυτελέσι χρησαμένης, κατὰ κώμας δὲ τῷ παλαιῷ τῆς Ἑλλάδος τρόπῳ οἰκισθείσης, φαίνοιτ' ἂν ὑποδεεστέρα, Ἀθηναίων δὲ τὸ αὐτὸ τοῦτο παθόντων

---

95. For the development of the cult of Artemis in this period, see particularly Rogers, *Mysteries of Artemis*, 61–67, 80–88. The hypothesis of a cult reorganization in the early third century comes from a second century CE inscription (*I.Eph.* 26) that says as much (ll. 1–3), though Kevin Clinton, "Mysteria at Ephesus," *ZPE* 191 (2014): 117–19, cautions that the identification of Lysimachus with the changes is an uncertain reconstruction. Clinton also distinguishes between the two aspects of Artemis, calling into question Rogers' thesis that competing cults gave an opening for oversight. In a review of Rogers' book, Jennifer Larson, "Review: *The Mysteries of Artemis of Ephesos,*" *AHR* 120, no. 2 (2015): 692, expressed skepticism that the Artemisium ever had the autonomy that Rogers imagines, comparing it to the sanctuary at Eleusis. It is necessary to consider the sanctuary and the city as having a symbiotic relationship, but Didyma is a more apt parallel than is Eleusis, despite the rites in question being mysteries.

διπλασίαν ἂν τὴν δύναμιν εἰκάζεσθαι ἀπὸ τῆς φανερᾶς ὄψεως τῆς πόλεως ἢ ἔστιν.

Thucydides was commenting on the crude power of political and military force, but his warning to not judge a city by its ruined temples is instructive: we would do well not to judge the power or, in this case, wealth, of a city from its ruins alone.

Every Ionian polis constructed temples and sanctuaries, but only three, Ephesus, Miletus, and Samos, erected the enormous temples for which the region was known. These were among the largest and wealthiest Ionian poleis, but Erythrae and Teos regularly paid as much in *phoros* as Miletus and Ephesus on the Athenian Tribute Lists and Chios was arguably as wealthy as Samos. And yet, excepting only the Panionion, the most prominent sanctuary outside the big three was the oracle of Colophon's Apollo at Claros. Peer-polity competition drove the successive phases of temple construction, and commercial prosperity shaped the landscape of religious offerings in each polis, but neither adequately explains the record of Ionian temple construction.

Taken in a broader perspective, the Ionian sanctuaries were not Greek in an isolated sense at least until the Hellenistic period, when there was a conscious effort to link Didyma to Delphi. Instead, these sanctuaries were part of Anatolian religious networks that included Caria, Lydia, and Phrygia, and were absorbed by the Persian administration. Viewed in this light, foreign gifts and regional influence that extended up the river valleys facilitated temple construction. The political environment that encouraged donations from foreign kings dried up during the fifth century but returned in earnest in the second half of the fourth century when the sanctuaries took on renewed importance as a locus of political interaction. Negotiating a balance between dependence and autonomy, the sanctuaries were a microcosm of Ionia itself.

CHAPTER 10

Epilogue

When the funeral games for Alexander ended more than two decades after his death, three large kingdoms and numerous small contenders had replaced his ephemeral empire. In some ways nothing had changed; in others, everything had. The Ionian poleis remained a keystone in the Aegean system and therefore continued to be courted by the kings and dynasts. However, rather than a contested zone conceived of as holding the "barbarian" world at bay, Ionia became a link in the chain connecting the new Hellenistic kingdoms to the world of "old" Greece.[1] The new world of kingdoms did not precisely replicate the situation that had preceded Alexander, where local and regional developments took place under the watchful eye of a Persian king who sought to manage conflicts on his imperial frontier, but neither was it wholly new. The following century may be characterized as a period of relative political stability, but Ionia remained contested between the kings and dynasts who jockeyed to performatively defend their autonomy while otherwise engaging in coercive practices.[2] The bands of Gauls that swept into Anatolia in early 270s gave kings new opportunities to build influence by touting their victories in defense of the Greeks (Justin 26.2).[3]

Ionia's location connecting the Aegean world to the new kingdoms enabled

---

1. As Richard A. Billows, "Rebirth of a Region: Ionia in the Early Hellenistic Period," in *Regionalism in Hellenistic and Roman Asia Minor*, ed. Hugh Elton and Gary Reger (Pessac: Ausonius Éditions, 2007), 41–42, for instance, has observed.

2. Billows, "Rebirth of a Region," 39, characterizes this autonomy as "a relatively painless favor for a king to bestow," but the actual relationships were more complicated; see Angelos Chaniotis, *Age of Conquests: The Greek World from Alexander to Hadrian* (Cambridge, MA: Harvard University Press, 2018), 100–105; Sviatoslav Dmitriev, *The Greek Slogan of Freedom and Early Roman Politics in Greece* (Oxford: Oxford University Press, 2011).

3. Most notable was Antiochus I, who allegedly achieved an "Elephant Victory" over the Gauls that won him the epithet "Soter" (App. *Syr.* 11; Lucian *Zeuxis*), but see Altay Coşkun, "Deconstructing a Myth of Seleucid History: The So-Called 'Elephant Victory,'" *Phoenix* 66, nos. 1–2 (2012): 57–73. Victory over the Gauls was also a foundational story for the creation of the Attalid dynasty at Pergamum (see Strabo 13.4.2) and again in the 160s; see Peter Thonemann, *The Maeander Valley: A Historical Geography* (Cambridge: Cambridge University Press, 2011), 170–77.

it to flourish until Strabo, writing at the dawn of the Roman Empire, could characterize Ephesus as the foremost emporium in Asia (12.8.15). Richard Billows makes an important point in noting that specific actions also planted the seeds of these developments, but it would be a mistake to simply characterize this success as the product of "brute geographic fact" of location.[4] In his formulation, location gave the Hellenistic rulers incentive to court the Ionian poleis through refoundations, donations, and tax breaks (e.g., *I.Ery.* 31 and 32). Billows is not wrong that the prosperity that emerged later in the Hellenistic period can be traced to the settlements and privileges first conferred by the Diadochoi, but his argument requires modification in several important ways.

Billows characterizes the early Hellenistic period as a time of rebirth, but change is not the same as rebirth, for rebirth necessarily requires death. It has long been assumed that after the vibrant Archaic period, the Ionian poleis experienced economic and cultural stagnation that lasted for nearly two centuries, when, in truth, the Classical period was a complicated time of continuity and persistence during which the developments usually thought of as Hellenistic had already begun to sprout.[5] Further, the rebirth that Billows identifies largely bypasses the Ionians except in their service to the Hellenistic kings. Simply put, the argument of this book has been that the Ionian poleis were active agents in negotiating their position within the changing political landscape of the Classical Aegean. To neglect that fact is to overlook how local and regional issues intersected with these imperial projects. Thus, the restoration of the sanctuary at Didyma engaged not only the local community, but also Demodamas, a Milesian in the service of the Seleucid court, and the Seleucid kings who used Didymaean Apollo as a symbolic marker of territory (see Chapter 9).

When the king Antiochus III declared that the Ionians were accustomed to obedience to barbarian kings more than a century into the Hellenistic period, he appealed to a discourse about freedom (ἐλευθερία) and autonomy (αὐτονομία) in a bid to retain a part of his kingdom (App. *Syr.* 12.1). These ideals went to the heart of what it meant to be a polis, and, Antiochus claimed, the Ionians had forfeited them because of their tradition of servitude. Antiochus' appeals fell on deaf Roman ears, but it should not be overlooked that his historical evidence in this moment is deeply flawed. Freedom and autonomy were characteristics of the ideal polis that have subsequently been picked up because they appeal to the Enlightenment values espoused by European and American commentators. But autonomy was not one-half of a binary that toggled on and off. Rather, it

---

4. Billow, "Rebirth of a Region."
5. As Pierre Debord, *L'Asie Mineure au IVᵉ Siècle (412–323 a.C.)* (Pessac: Ausonius, 1999), 497.

was an ideal that was not incompatible with the imperial systems of the Classical period—except when it was turned into a political slogan—and it is in this context that Ionian actions need to be interpreted. Although not always incorporated into a formal imperial apparatus, the Ionians were partners in the imperial endeavor, abetting or resisting the external powers for political, rather than ideological, reasons.

Throughout this book I have argued that Ionia offers a prism through which we might better understand Classical Greece. The tendency for many histories of ancient Greece to be centered on Athens sometimes leads to the unfortunate implication that the two are synonymous when the historical reality is much more diverse and heterogeneous. Ionia offers a cross section of these complexities that in many ways allows it to be metonymic for thinking about ancient Greece as a whole. It was a region with poleis of various sizes that possessed a common identity that did little to blunt conflict, and its location meant that it interacted with both Greek poleis like Athens and Persian administrative centers like Sardis. Focusing on Ionia thus illuminates not only regional interaction between the local poleis but also the interplay between regional relationships and the Aegean and Mediterranean worlds. The confluence of these levels of interaction in Ionia make it particularly useful for this sort of study, but its story at the confluence of obedience, exploitation, and resistance was common in its time.

Appendix 1

Whither the Ionian League?

Perhaps the single most intractable challenge to understanding Ionia in the Archaic and Classical periods is the nature of the Ionian *koinon*, usually referred to as the Ionian League. The early history of the *koinon* is almost entirely speculative and inferred from later sources.[1] Meetings took place at the Panionion on the Mycale Peninsula, which housed the sanctuary of Poseidon Heliconius (Hdt. 1.148).[2] The sanctuary was established on the site of Melie, which was either an Ionian or Carian community against which the Ionians waged a common war (Vitr. *De arch.* 4.1.3–5).[3]

---

1. Alan M. Greaves, *The Land of Ionia: Society and Economy in the Archaic Period* (Hoboken, NJ: Wiley-Blackwell, 2010), 220; Naoíse Mac Sweeney, *Foundation Myths and Politics in Ancient Ionia* (Cambridge: Cambridge University Press, 2013), 173–77, with references. Cf. Marietta Horster, "Priene: Civic Priests and Koinon-Priesthoods in the Hellenistic Period," in *Cities and Priests in Asia Minor and the Aegean Islands from the Hellenistic to the Imperial Period*, ed. Marietta Horster and Andreas Klöckner (Berlin: De Gruyter, 2013), 177, with n. 2.

2. Two locations on the Mycale Peninsula have received attention as potential sites of the Panionion. Excavations from the 1950s revealed ruins at the top of Otomatik Tepe, on the north side of the Mycale promontory. Hans Lohmann, "The Discovery and Excavation of the Archaic Panionion in the Mycale (Dilek Daglari)," *Kazı Sonuçları Toplantısı* 28 (2007): 575–90, and "Ionians and Carians in the Mycale: The Discovery of Carian Melia and the Archaic Panionion in the Mycale," in *Landscape, Ethnicity and Identity in the Archaic Mediterranean Area*, ed. Gabriele Cigani and Simon Stoddart (Oxford: Oxford University Press, 2011), 32–50, rejects this identification on the grounds that it shows no evidence of occupation in the Archaic period, instead associating it with the Hellenistic refoundation. Lohmann's identification of another site on Çatallar Tepe, higher up the slope, has not received universal acceptance, however, on the grounds that this sanctuary shows no evidence of association with Poseidon and that it had fallen out of use too early; see the recent survey of evidence in Nicholas Cross, "The Panionia: The Ritual Context for Identity Construction in Archaic Ionia," *Mediterranean Studies* 28, no. 1 (2020): 9–10; Michael J. Metcalfe, "Reaffirming Regional Identity: Cohesive Institutions and Local Interactions in Ionia 386–129 BC" (PhD diss., University College London, 2005), 48–51.

3. The date of this event if, indeed, it is historical, is unknown. Recently, Lohmann, "Ionians and Carians," and Jan Paul Crielaard, "The Ionians in the Archaic Period: Shifting Identities in a Changing World," in *Ethnic Constructs in Antiquity: The Role of Power and Tradition*, ed. Ton Derks and Nico Roymans (Amsterdam: Amsterdam University Press, 2009), 57–60, both posit a date close to 600, though a date in the dimmer past is still more commonly applied. On the issue of Ionian ethnicity in the Classical period, see Appendix 2.

The two traditional lines of scholarship about the organization represent a chicken-and-egg problem. One treats the Ionian League anachronistically by envisioning it as a political organization along the lines of Hellenistic federal leagues that served to resolve debates and organize collective action against encroachment from foreign powers. Despite the irrepressible myth of the Ionian Migration, Ionian identity developed in situ in Anatolia.[4] Although Wilamowitz-Moellendorff followed Vitruvius in seeing the original purpose of the league being a common war against Melie, the more commonly accepted position on this side of the ledger is the one proposed by M. O. B. Caspari, which suggests that the league formed for common defense against Lydian aggression.[5] However, since they established the sanctuary on the site of Melie and held the common festival there as a commemoration of victory, the festival had to have followed from some sense of unity.

On the other end of the spectrum, some scholars hold that the league began as a religious network that had little or no political activity.[6] While some adherents of this theory, such as Naoíse Mac Sweeney, suggest that the *koinon* bound its members only to a loose sense of communal identity,[7] others, including Barbara Kowalzig and Nicholas Cross, have recently revived the argument that the Panionion laid the groundwork for a common Ionian identity and therefore that the *koinon* of the Ionians took on an incipiently political function by the end of the Archaic period.[8]

---

4. While the now-lost fragment of the Marmor Parium (*FGrH* 239 A1 27) places the foundation of the common festival as coterminous with the migration, these accounts are looking to the mythological past to explain the present and in so doing are projecting the current situation into the mythological past. In this case, the Marmor Parium dates to after 264/3 BCE, which marked a new era that Andrea Rotstein, *Literary History in the Parian Marble* (Washington, DC: Center for Hellenic Studies, 2016), suggests corresponds to the activity of Ptolemy II in the Aegean. The inscription's particular attention on literary activity likely explains the entry that dates the foundation of the Panionia.

5. M. O. B. Caspari, "The Ionian Confederacy," *JHS* 35 (1915): 173–78; M. O. B. Caspari, "The Ionian Confederacy—Addendum," *JHS* 36 (1916): 102; cf. Ulrich von Wilamowitz-Moellendorff, *Panionion* (Berlin: Reichsdruckerei, 1906).

6. See Giovanni Fogazza, "Per una storia della lega ionica," *La parola del passato* 28 (1973): 157–69; C. J. Emlyn-Jones, *The Ionians and Hellenism: A Study of the Cultural Achievement of Early Greek Inhabitants of Asia Minor* (New York: Routledge, 1980), 17; Cinzia Bearzot, "La guerra lelantina e il koinon degli Ioni d'Asia," *Contributi dell'Instituto di storia antica* 9 (1983): 57–81; Klaus Tausend, *Amphiktyonie und Symmachie: Formen zwischenstaatlicher Beziehungen im archaischen Griechenland* (Stuttgart: Franz Steiner Verlag, 1992), 55–57 and 70–95.

7. Mac Sweeney, *Foundation Myths and Politics*, 196, characterizes the Ionian League as a "fight club" to monitor conflict between member states since "inter-Ionian competition became not just a sideshow—it was the fundamental principle underlying the Ionian League." Cf. Crielaard, "Ionians in the Archaic Period," 70.

8. Cross, "The Panionia"; Barbara Kowalzig, "Mapping Out *Communitas*: Performances of *Theoria* in Their Sacred and Political Context," in *Pilgrimage in Graeco-Roman and Early Christian Antiquity: Seeing the Gods*, ed. Jas Elsner and Ian Rutherford (Oxford: Oxford University Press, 2005), 52. This thesis was already present in C. Roebuck, "Tribal Organization in Ionia," *TAPhA* 92

Indeed, the textual evidence for the early Ionian League appears to support the second interpretation. Herodotus records at least four assemblies of the Ionian *koinon* that took place between c.550 and 494 (1.141.4, 1.170, 5.108, 6.7). Each meeting had a distinctly political flavor. In c.550, they met to discuss their options for collective action. Several years later, they met for a second meeting in which Bias of Priene, one of the legendary sages of ancient Greece, proposed that the Ionians sail away to form a common city in Sardo (perhaps Sardinia), while Thales, the Phoenician sage living in Miletus, proposed that the Ionians establish a single political seat (1.170, βουλευτήριον) located at Teos on the grounds that it was the center of the region.[9] Although neither plan came to fruition, the Panionion remained an important locus for collective action such that leaders gathered there again decades later in order to coordinate the Ionian revolt. Thus, despite the "Ionian revolt" itself being a misnomer,[10] scholars have nevertheless suggested that the revolt took place because of this developing sense of common identity.[11]

Proponents of a political Ionian league in the Archaic period explain the absence of political institutions in the Classical period by arguing that the Persians dissolved the organization in 492.[12] After the "liberation" of Ionia, they continue, Athens had little interest in reviving a rival *koinon* to the new Athenian League. While this argument follows in part from the undeniable geopolitical reality of the relative positions of the Ionian poleis and the succession of hegemons, it is based in part on a circular logic: the *koinon*'s political function in the Archaic period is confirmed because imperial powers saw fit to suppress it, while the suppression in the Classical period was made necessary because of its political function.

Reexamining the textual evidence for the political function also introduces serious issues for this interpretation. First, as we have seen, pressure from the

---

(1961): 507, who saw the political function developing near the end of the period. A sense of Pan-Ionianism also underpins the generally compelling argument for "the invention of the 'Barbarian'" in the sixth century found in Hyun Jin Kim, "The Invention of the 'Barbarian' in Late Sixth-Century BC Ionia," in *Ancient Ethnography*, ed. Eran Almagor and Joseph Skinner (London: Bloomsbury, 2013), 25–48; cf. Appendix 2.

9. W. W. How and J. Wells, *A Commentary on Herodotus*, vol. 1 (Oxford: Oxford University Press, 1989), 130, suggest that Herodotus believed Thales' suggestion to be a genuine political unification because of the similarity between his language and Thucydides' description of the unification of Attica (2.15.2–3). However, this parallel need not vouch for the historicity of the proposal.

10. See Chapter 1.

11. E.g., Donald Lateiner, "The Failure of the Ionian Revolt," *Historia* 31, no. 2 (1982): 131–35, though he believes the league was not originally political. The Ionian revolt extended beyond Ionia and did not include every member the *koinon*; see Mac Sweeney, *Foundation Myths and Politics*, 175; J. Neville, "Was There an Ionian Revolt?," *CQ*² 29, no. 2 (1979): 268–75.

12. Cross, "The Panionia"; Caspari, "Ionian Confederacy," 181–82.

Delian League was anything but even. Not only did the Athenians tolerate regional hegemonies throughout their space, so too did its imperial institutions grow with time, and even in the mid-470s there is no evidence for a move to revive a political organization that was the Ionian League. Second, and even more telling, are the notable absences from the assemblies of the Ionian *koinon*. In c.550, Herodotus says, the Milesians did not attend because they had already agreed to a treaty with Cyrus (1.41.4). Likewise, in 499, the Ephesians appear to have stood apart from the revolt. The raid on Sardis employed Ephesian guides (5.100), but when the Persian counterattack caught up with the rebels in the Ephesian *chora*, the polis suffered no reprisals, and the Ephesians even attacked some of the survivors of the battle of Lade (6.16). In each of these cases the assembly of the Ionian *koinon* takes on a much more fluid composition, and thus it is more accurate to describe these meetings as taking place at the Panionion as a common space rather than being meetings of an inherently political Ionian League.

However, common identity is not easily unmade. The scant evidence for the Panionia in the Classical period introduces additional complications for understanding both the Ionian League and the Ionians during this period.[13] Thucydides introduces an annual pan-Ionian festival at Ephesus, comparing it to a common Ionian festival on Delos (3.104.3–4). Simon Hornblower correctly distinguished this Ephesia from the Artemisia but proceeded to identify this festival as the Panionia on the grounds that Diodorus Siculus claims that at some point the festival had moved there because of war in the vicinity of Mycale (15.49.1).[14] P. J. Stylianou responded to Hornblower, vehemently rejecting this interpretation and more plausibly dating the change in location to around 400, during the period of the Spartan expeditions to Ionia based at Ephesus (see Chapter 5).[15] He therefore connects this reference in Diodorus to a decision to move the festival back to Mycale in c.373.[16] While Stylianou's

---

13. The best survey of evidence is Metcalfe, "Reaffirming Regional Identity," 70–85. He notes that the festival permanently moved from the sanctuary in the Hellenistic period.

14. ὕστερον δὲ πολέμων γενομένων περὶ τούτους τοὺς τόπους οὐ δυνάμενοι ποιεῖν τὰ Πανιώνια, μετέθεσαν τὴν πανήγυριν εἰς ἀσφαλῆ τόπον, ὃς ἦν πλησίον τῆς Ἐφέσου. Simon Hornblower, "Thucydides, the Panionion Festival, and the Ephesia (III 104)," *Historia* 31, no. 2 (1982): 241–45, with a clarification in Metcalfe, "Reaffirming Regional Identity," 80 n. 147, that this was a temporary fusion of festivals. Cf. Irene Ringwood Arnold, "Festivals of Ephesus," *AJA* 76, no. 1 (1972): 17–18, who identifies the Ephesia as a pan-Ionian festival and the Artemisia as a festival celebrated throughout the Greek world, albeit with particular verve at Ephesus. Which outbreak of war Diodorus is alluding to is unknown. Eloisa Paganoni, "Priene, il *Panionion* e gli Ecatomnidi," *Aevum* 88 (2014): 49, created a partial list of four possible dates before the King's Peace.

15. P. J. Stylianou, "Thucydides, the Panionion Festival, and the Ephesia (III 104), Again," *Historia* 32, no. 2 (1983): 245–49.

16. "Stylianou, Thucydides, the Panionian Festival, and the Ephesia," followed by Metcalfe,

argument for the date and length of time of the Panionian festivities at Ephesus is sound, he regards it as a revival of the *koinon*,[17] even though Diodorus indicated a transfer. This sort of error is not beyond Diodorus given his propensity to project his contemporary context into his history, but the positive evidence for the interpretation is lacking.

There is only one datable inscription that suggests a revival of the Ionian *koinon* around 400, the record of an arbitration between Myus and Miletus. In either 392 or 388, the Persian satrap, Struthas, ordered jurors of the Ionians (οἱ τῶν Ἰώνων δικασταί) to resolve this dispute, and the surviving fragments include lists of jurors from Erythrae, Chios, Clazomenae, Lebedus, and Ephesus (*RO* 16 = *I.Priene* 458; see Chapter 5). The specification of *Ionian* jurors has led scholars to argue that he delegated the arbitration to the Ionian *koinon*, but nothing in the text of the inscription supports this conclusion.[18] Struthas likely used membership in the *koinon* to choose the arbitrators, but this followed Persian practice in the region going back to the sixth century (Hdt. 6.42).[19]

Other evidence is no more illuminating. The remaining inscriptions are only tenuously dated to this period,[20] and surviving ancient histories offer no evidence for collective action. However, the absence of evidence for the existence of the Panionion in this period need not be evidence of absence if the *koinon* remained as it had been for much of its existence: a loose organization with limited substance—that is, if it lacked a political function.

The dearth of solid evidence for the Ionia in this period frustratingly makes any hypothesis little more than speculation, but treating the Panionion as a loose, largely symbolic organization rather than one that fostered strong ties in the region offers intriguing possibilities. In discussing the temporary relo-

---

"Reaffirming Regional Identity," 80–82. Maxim M. Kholod, "On the Ionian League in the Fourth Century BC," *Studia Antiqua et Archaeologica* 26, no. 2 (2020): 199–211, argues for the complete restoration of the cult. The date 373 is supported by an earthquake that swamped Helice in that year after its citizens allegedly mistreated Ionian ambassadors. I agree with Kholod that the revived league was primarily a religious network.

17. Dating the revival to c.400 broadly follows Caspari, "Ionian Confederacy," 182–83, who held that the league was again dissolved by the King's Peace.

18. For the delegation thesis, see Frank Adcock and D. J. Mosley, *Diplomacy in Ancient Greece* (London: Thames and Hudson, 1975), 213; Luigi Piccirilli, *Gli arbitrati interstatali Greci: Dalle origini al 338 A.C.* (Pisa: Marlin, 1973), 158.

19. Pierre Briant, *From Cyrus to Alexander: A History of the Persian Empire*, trans. Peter T. Daniels (Winona Lake, IN: Eisenbrauns, 2002), 495. Metcalfe, "Reaffirming Regional Identity," 88–89, notes that the Myesians addressed the poleis, rather than the *koinon, when they* withdrew the suit, as one would expect if that were the adjudicating body. No other known case in Ionia used arbitrators from Ionia.

20. *I.Ery* 16; *I.Priene* 139. *I.Priene* 139 plausibly belongs before 335/4, when the eponymous magistrate changed from prytanis to *stephanephoros*, but the other two are undated. For a survey of these inscriptions, see Metcalfe, "Reaffirming Regional Identity," 89–91.

cation of the Panionia to Ephesus, Diodorus says, "Nine cities in Ionia were accustomed to making a common assembly of all of the Ionians" (κατὰ τὴν Ἰωνίαν ἐννέα πόλεις εἰώθεισαν κοινὴν ποιεῖσθαι σύνοδον τὴν τῶν Πανιωνίων, 15.49.1). The confident declaration that nine poleis did this has caused no small amount of consternation on the grounds that twelve is the more common number associated with the sanctuary (e.g., Hdt. 1.145; Strabo 14.1.4). Scholars have offered various explanations for the discrepancy, whether as an error introduced by either Diodorus or his source (probably Ephorus) or looking for explanations for why some of the members would not have been included. The most common explanation is to strike Chios and Samos from the list on the grounds that they were formally independent of Persia and to suggest that Priene did not exist at the time of the transition, leaving nine poleis. Stylianou goes a step further, plausibly suggesting that the revival of the festival on Mycale corresponded with the refoundation of Priene with the support of Mausolus. However, while he is correct to suggest that Diodorus' implication that the Panionion always had twelve members was an "injudicious epitome of Ephorus," bringing Priene back into the picture for the restoration ticks the number back up to ten viable members outside of Chios and Samos. If Stylianou is right in identifying the return to Mycale as the result of Hecatomnid influence in the region, then *Ephesus* would be the more likely exclusion. This proposal is, admittedly, speculative, but it fits the geopolitical context of a showdown between Ephesus and Mausolus over their respective positions in the region in the late 370s and early 360s (see Chapter 6).

The relationship between the Ionians and Alexander in the 330s further supports the interpretation of a largely symbolic league. Much as Struthas and Agesilaus both treated the Ionian poleis individually rather than collectively, Alexander continued in the same vein.[21] Further, while he made a procession at the Artemisium at Ephesus and contributed to the building of the Temple of Athena at Priene (see Chapter 7), he made no comparable offer to the common Ionian sanctuary at any point during his reign. Once again, the absence of evidence does not positively confirm the nonexistence of a political league, but the preponderance of evidence points to the *koinon* of the Ionians remaining a religious network that created a loose sense of common identity among disparate poleis.[22]

---

21. Kholod, "On the Ionian League," 206–7, speculates that Alexander's cult in Ionia was celebrated at the Panionion, holding that the Alexandreia was created during his reign rather than by one of his successors. His argument is plausible, but by no means certain.

22. Richard A. Billows, "Rebirth of a Region: Ionia in the Early Hellenistic Period," in *Regionalism in Hellenistic and Roman Asia Minor*, ed. Hugh Elton and Gary Reger (Pessac: Ausonius, 2007), 40–41, suggests that Antigonus reestablished Panionion, in part based on his provision in the syn-

The changed political landscape of the early Hellenistic period breathed new relevance into the old cultic network. The earliest evidence for this change comes from an inscription dated to 289/8 that reads (*SIG³* 368):

Resolved by the *koinon* of the Ionians. Whereas Hippostratos, son of Hippodamos of Miletus, a friend of King Lysimachus and strategos over the poleis of Ionia, continues to treat the cities generously, both each individually and the Ionians as a whole, with good fortune, [he receives] from the *koinon* of the Ionians praise for Hippostratos son of Hippodamus on account of his virtue and *eunoia*
that he continues to have toward the *koinon* of the Ionians, and a tax exemption among all of the Ionian poleis and that these provisions apply to him and his descendants. And [it is resolved] to erect a bronze *eikon*
of this man on horseback in the Panionion . . .

ἔδοξε Ἰώνων τῶι κοινῶι· ἐπειδὴ Ἱππόστρατος Ἱπποδήμου Μιλήσιος φίλος ὢν τοῦ βασιλέως Λυσι-
μάχου καὶ στρατηγὸς ἐπὶ τῶν πόλεων τῶν Ἰώνων
κατασταθεὶς οἰκείως καὶ φιλανθρώπως καὶ ἰδίαι ἑ-
κάστηι τῶμ πόλεων καὶ κοινῆι Ἰωσι χρωμενος διατελεῖ, ἀγαθῆι τύχηι, δεδόχθαι τῶι κοινῶι τῶι Ἰώνων, ἐπαινέσαι Ἱππόσταρτον Ἱπποδήμου ἀρε-
τῆς ἕνεκε καὶ εὐνοίας ἣν ἔχων διατελεῖ πρὸς
τὸ κοινὸν τὸ Ἰώνων, καὶ εἶναι αὐτὸν ἀτελῆ πάντων ἐν <ταῖς>
πόλεσι ταῖς Ἰώνων· τὰ αὐτὰ δὲ ὑπάρχειν Ἱπποστρά-
τωι αὐτῶι καὶ ἐκγόνοις· στῆσαι δὲ αὐτοῦ καὶ εἰκόνα
χαλκῆν ἐφ᾽ ἵππου ἐμ Πανιωνίωι·

The decree concludes with instructions that each city inscribe and publicize it, as well as for a copy to appear beside the equestrian statue in the Panionion. The extant copy from Miletus also included two additional decrees related to Hippostratos and his honors, both of which speak to the ratification in the Pan-

oecism of Teos and Lebedus in c.304/3 (Welles *RC* 3 1–3), but this inscription only testifies to the existence of the koinon. As Sheila L. Ager, "Civic Identity in the Hellenistic World: The Case of Lebedos," *GRBS* 39, no. 1 (1998): 14, notes, Antigonus' orders do not seem to have materially changed the Ionian League since the Smyrnean copy of *SIG³* 368 (*I.Smyrna* II 577) from 289/8 refers to *thirteen*-member poleis. This count requires the full roster of the original dodecapolis plus Smyrna.

ionion. Unlike the earlier evidence for a political function at the *koinon*, this inscription suggests that decisions made at the Panionion, at least in the case of certain exceptional honors, were binding for league members.

It would still be a bridge too far to say that the Ionian League had finally molted into a fully fledged federal league. Despite his position as strategos for Ionia and intermediary to the king, the decree presents Hippostratos as separate from the *koinon*, and as liable to treat the Ionian poleis individually as to treat them as a coherent group. Nevertheless, this regional network served as a point of contact for Hellenistic kings, issuing a decree in honor of the Seleucid king Antiochus I between 267 and 262 (*I.Ery.* 504)[23] and receiving an inscription from the Pergamene king Eumenes II in 167/6 (*RC* 52 = *OGIS* 763). In other words, the political function often identified in the late-Archaic Ionian League finally came into being in the Hellenistic period.

23. For a detailed study of this inscription, see Francis Piejko, "Decree of the Ionian League in Honor of Antiochus I, CA 267–262 B.C.," *Phoenix* 45, no. 2 (1991): 126–47.

Appendix 2

Greeks and Non-Greeks in Classical Ionia

[The Ionian poleis] were, so to speak, fragments of the western world on
the fringe of the eastern, serving as connecting links between the two.
—Mikhail Rostovtzeff[1]

If the Ionian Migration was not the seed that gave root to collective Ionian
identity, it gave the inhabitants of the region an unimpeachable claim to Greekness. By the time of Hadrian's Panhellenion in the second century CE, it was
precisely this lineage that justified the inclusion of Ephesus, Miletus, and
Samos.[2] There is also no evidence that the numerous Ionian athletes participating in the Olympic Games ever had their Greekness challenged by the *hellenodikai*, whose task it was to certify that the athletes met the qualifications
for competition.[3] In terms of the Ionian self-identity, a similar process was at
work where the charter myth for the Panionion was a collective war against the
Carian community of Melie (see Appendix 1). With such a basis for collective

---

1. Mikhail Rostovtzeff, *Social and Economic History of the Hellenistic World*, vol. 1 (Oxford:
Oxford University Press, 1941), 81.

2. The Roman-era Panhellenion founded in 131/2 CE created a network of Greek cities with a
capital at Athens and linked by (notional) common descent from the "original" Greeks. New members had to trace their ancestry to the charter members; see Panagiotis N. Doukellis, "Hadrian's
Panhellenion: A Network of Cities?," *Mediterranean Historical Review* 22, no. 2 (2007): 295–308;
Ilaria Romeo, "The Panhellenion and Ethnic Identity in Hadrianic Greece," *CPh* 97, no. 1 (2002):
21–40; A. W. Spawforth and Susan Walker, "The World of the Panhellenion. I. Athens and Eleusis,"
JRS 75 (1985): 78–104.

3. One of the qualifications, at least nominally, was Greekness, which led to a famous showdown between the judges and Alexander I of Macedonia until the *hellenodikai* ruled that he was
in fact Greek (Hdt. 5.22). Cf. W. Lindsay Adams, "Other People's Games: The Olympics, Macedonia and Greek Athletics," *Journal of Sport History* 30 (2003): 205–17, though a curious story in
Xenophon (*Hell.* 4.1.39–40) suggests that these rules were not absolute; see James Roy, "The Son
of Pharnabazos and Parapita, a Persian Competing in the Olympic Games: Xenophon *Hellenica*
4.1.39–40," *C&M* 68 (2020): 119–34.

identity, one might expect a robust delineation between the Greek Ionian poleis on the one hand and the barbarians on the other.[4] Indeed, Hyun Jin Kim has recently argued that the divide between Greeks and barbarians developed first in sixth-century Ionia.[5]

Classical Ionia *was* Greek—in culture, in language, and in identity—but recent scholarship has clearly demonstrated that any assumption that it was purely so is untenable.[6] Indeed, recent developments in postcolonial theory have shown that culture and identity are not static because they are constantly being negotiated.[7] Whereas ancient authors offer trace evidence of violent expulsion or subjugation of the indigenous inhabitants (e.g., Philip of Theangela, *BNJ* 741 F 2), others explain that the newcomers and existing inhabitants mixed together to form Ionians.[8] Herodotus declares that Milesian women

4. "Identity through alterity," as Jonathan Hall, "Ancient Greek Ethnicities: Towards a Reassessment," *BICS* 58, no. 2 (2015): 28, calls this process, has become a common way of understanding Greek ethnic consciousness; see, e.g., Walter Burkert, *The Orientalizing Revolution: Near Eastern Influences on Greek Culture in the Early Archaic Period*, trans. Margaret E. Pinder and Walter Burkert (Cambridge, MA: Harvard University Press, 1992), 1; Paul Cartledge, *The Greeks: A Portrait of Self and Others* (Oxford: Oxford University Press, 2002), 12–13; Jan Paul Crielaard; "The Ionians in the Archaic Period: Shifting Identities in a Changing World," in *Ethnic Constructs in Antiquity: The Role of Power and Tradition*, ed. Ton Derks and Nico Roymans (Amsterdam: Amsterdam University Press, 2009), 63–64, 73; Edith Hall, *Inventing the Barbarian: Greek Self-Definition through Tragedy* (Oxford: Oxford University Press, 1989). Rebecca Futo Kennedy, "A Tale of Two Kings: Competing Aspects of Power in Aeschylus' Persians," *Ramus* 42, nos. 1–2 (2013): 64–88, has rightly cautioned that even the Athenians did not treat Persia as a universal other, even ideologically.

5. Hyun Jin Kim, "The Invention of the 'Barbarian' in Late Sixth-Century BC Ionia," in *Ancient Ethnography*, ed. Eran Almagor and Joseph Skinner (London: Bloomsbury, 2013), 25–48, principally building on the work of Hall, *Inventing the Barbarian*, backdates the creation of "barbarian" as a category from fifth-century Athens to sixth-century Ionia.

6. E.g., Yasar E. Ersoy, "Pottery Production and Mechanism of Workshops in Archaic Clazomenae," in *Greichische Keramik im kulturellen Kontext*, ed. Bernard Schmaltz and Magdalene Söldner (Muenster: Scriptorium, 2003), 254–57; Alan M. Greaves, *The Land of Ionia: Society and Economy in the Archaic Period* (Malden, MA: Wiley-Blackwell, 2010); David Hill, "Conceptualising Interregional Relations in Ionia and Central-West Anatolia from the Archaic to the Hellenistic Period," in *Bordered Places, Bounded Times: Cross-Disciplinary Perspectives on Turkey*, ed. Emma L. Baysal and Leonidas Karakatsanis (Ankara: British Institute at Ankara, 2017), 85–96; Naoíse Mac Sweeney, *Foundation Myths and Politics in Ancient Ionia* (Cambridge: Cambridge University Press, 2013).

7. Particularly "Third Space" theory articulated by Homi K. Bhabha, "The Third Space," in *Identity: Community, Culture, Difference*, ed. Jonathan Rutherford (London: Lawrence and Wishart, 1990), 207–21, and *The Location of Culture* (New York: Routledge, 1994); cf. Fetson Kalua, "Homi Bhabha's Third Space and African Identity," *Journal of African Cultural Studies* 21, no. 1 (2009): 23–32, on African identity, and Vivien Xiaowei Zhou and Nick Pilcher, "Revisiting the 'Third Space' in Language and Intercultural Studies," *Language and Intercultural Communication* 19, no. 1 (2019): 1–8, on the development of third-space theory. This theory is based on modern colonial power relationships that are an imperfect analogue for the ancient world, but its insight into culture as the product of interactions is valuable for understanding identity in Ionia, as Greaves, *Land of Ionia*, recognizes.

8. On the development of the foundation myths, see Mac Sweeney, *Foundation Myths and Politics* and Naoíse Mac Sweeney, "Separating Fact from Fiction in the Ionian Migration," *Hesperia* 86, no. 3 (2017): 379–421, with Rosalind Thomas, *Polis Histories, Collective Memories and the Greek World* (Cambridge: Cambridge University Press, 2019), 177–226. Miletus and Ephesus had both

neither dined with their husbands nor referred to them by name because the Ionians forced them into marriage after slaughtering their fathers, husbands, and sons (Hdt. 1.146.2–3), while Pausanias offers examples of more peaceful coexistence at Ephesus (7.2.7–8) and Teos (7.3.6).[9] Moreover, the name Sadyattes appears three times on the Milesian *aesymnetes* list well into the Classical period, indicating that men with this name shared with a Lydian king operated in the upper echelons of Milesian society.[10]

Material culture, too, reveals the inadequacy of considering Greek and barbarian as binary, oppositional categories in Ionia. Both the Apollo of Didyma and the Artemis of Ephesus were deities of Anatolian extraction that imbued their primary sanctuaries with a non-Greek flavor.[11] These sanctuaries thus preserved traces of earlier practice, while also providing a locus of interaction

been occupied since the second millennium BCE and show no unambiguous signs of violent displacement; see Jana Mokrišová, "On the Move: Mobility in Southwest Anatolia and the Southeast Aegean during the Late Bronze to Early Iron Age Transition" (PhD diss., University of Michigan, 2017), 230–67, 284–87, who characterizes the process as mobility rather than migration and suggests that bilingualism was common. The narratives of violent subjugation of the Leleges (e.g., Hdt. 1.171) likely took on a new political valence under Mausolus; see Raymond Descat, "Les traditions grecques sur les Lélèges," in *Origines Gentium*, ed. Valérie Fromentin and Sophie Gotteland (Paris: Ausonius, 2001), 169–77. John Michael Kearns, "Greek and Lydian Evidence of Diversity, Erasure, and Convergence in Western Asia Minor," *Syllecta Classica* 14 (2003): 23–36, argues for a convergence between Greek and Lydian cultures in Ionia.

9. J. N. Coldstream, "Mixed Marriages at the Frontiers of the Early Greek World," *Oxford Journal of Archaeology* 12, no. 1 (1993): 93–96, reads the Herodotus passage as a critique of Milesian pretensions to racial purity, while Naoíse Mac Sweeney, "Violence and the Ionian Migration: Representation and Reality," in *Nostoi: Indigenous Culture, Migration and Integration in the Aegean Islands and Western Anatolia during the Late Bronze Age and Early Iron Age*, ed. Çiğdem Maner, Konstantinos Kopanias, and Nicholas Stampolidis (Istanbul: Koç University Press, 2013), 221, interprets the passage as evidence that every Ionian family was of mixed Anatolian and Ionian heritage.

10. *Milet* I.3 no. 122, ll. 1.55, 1.108, 2.55. Onomastic evidence is an imperfect barometer of cultural fusion. The name could have entered the family through political relationships, as Nicholas V. Sekunda, "Iphicrates the Athenian and the Menestheid Family of Miletus," *ABSA* 89 (1994): 303–6, argues, but marriages were likely common; see Coldstream, "Mixed Marriages."

11. Jens David Baumbach, *The Significance of Votive Offerings in Selected Hera Sanctuaries in the Peloponnese, Ionia, and Western Greece* (Oxford: Archeopress, 2004), 149–50; Edwin L. Brown, "In Search of Anatolian Apollo," in ΧΑΡΙΣ: *Essays in Honor of Sara A. Immerwahr*, ed. Anne P. Chapin (Athens: American School of Classical Studies, 2004), 243–57; Maria Brosius, "Artemis Persike and Artemis Anaitis," in *Studies in Persian History: Essays in Memory of David M. Lewis*, ed. Maria Brosius and Amelie Kuhrt (Leiden: Brill, 1998), 227–38; Walter Burkert, *Griechische Religion der archaischen und klassischen Epoche* (Stuttgart: Kohlhammer, 1977), 225–33; Greaves, *Land of Ionia*, 174, 195–96. Lynn R. LiDonnici, "The Images of Artemis Ephesia and Greco-Roman Worship: A Reconsideration," *HThR* 85, no. 4 (1992): 389–415; Sarah P. Morris, "The View from East Greece: Miletus, Samos and Ephesus," in *Debating Orientalization*, ed. Corinna Riva and Nicholas C. Vella (Sheffield: Equinox, 2006), 70–71; Sarah P. Morris, "Artemis Ephesia: A New Solution to the Enigma of Her 'Breasts'?," in *Das Kosmos der Artemis von Ephesus*, ed. Ulrike Muss (Vienna: Österreiches Archäologisches Institut, 2001), 135–51; Ulrike Muss, "Amber from the Artemision from Ephesus and in the Museums of Istanbul and Selçuk Ephesos," *Araştirma Sonuçları Toplantısı* 25 (2008): 13–26.

that was not limited to the citizen body.[12] The Carian Branchidae family operated the sanctuary of Didyma, which served as a space of reconciliation for the
diverse populations that lived in throughout the Milesia.[13] Similarly, the temple
of Artemis at Ephesus showed distinctly Anatolian characteristics such as its
famous "breasted" cult statue, even before considering that its priests took on
the Persian title *Megabyxos* (Xen. *Anab.* 5.3.6; Pliny *H.N.* 35.36, 40; see Chapter
9). Fragments from a Classical frieze from the temple of Artemis show both
people in Greek clothes and a figure in Persian shoes taking part in a procession.[14] While the temples show perhaps the clearest evidence of this intermix-
ing, it also appeared elsewhere in Ionia, such as in both the pottery production
at Clazomenae and a series of decorated sarcophagi dated c.500–470 that display images where the horsemen in Persian clothing fight alongside the hoplites, rather than against them.[15]

And yet other evidence has been used to posit the existence of a stratum
of "non-Greeks" in and around Ionia. Several inscriptions from Priene dated
to the final third of the fourth century and first half of the third century testify to the presence of *pedieis* (πεδιεῖς) in and around the polis.[16] But just who
were these *pedieis*? The subsequent inscriptions, all of which likely date to the
early third century, testify to increasing conflict between the two groups and
intervention from Lysimachus (*I.Priene* 14, ll. 5–6; with the response *I.Priene*
15). Likewise, *I.Priene²* 16, which granted the Ephesian Megabyxos the right
to purchase property, reveals the presence of *pedieis* who owned property in

---

12. Thomas, *Polis Histories*, 212–26.

13. Alan M. Greaves, *Miletos: A History* (New York: Routledge, 2002), 122–23.

14. Margaret C. Miller, "Clothes and Identity: The Case of Greeks in Ionia c.400 BC," in *Culture, Identity and Politics in the Ancient Mediterranean World*, ed. Paul J. Burton (Canberra: Australasian Society for Classical Studies, 2013), 29–30. Elspeth R. M. Dusinberre, *Aspects of Empire in
Achaemenid Sardis* (Cambridge: Cambridge University Press, 2003), 59–79, and *Empire, Authority,
and Autonomy in Achaemenid Anatolia* (Cambridge: Cambridge University Press, 2013), 216–19,
evaluates the syncretism of Achaemenid rituals with the worship of Artemis, which runs against
earlier belief that there was little Achaemenid influence in, e.g., Jack Martin Balcer, "The Greeks
and the Persians: Processes of Acculturation," *Historia* 32, no. 3 (1983): 257–67; David M. Lewis,
Sparta and Persia (Leiden: Brill, 1977), 115; H. D. Westlake, "Ionians in the Ionian War," *CQ²* 29,
no. 1 (1979): 40–41. On the Artemisium, see Chapter 9.

15. Pottery: Ersoy, "Pottery Production"; sarcophagi: R. M. Cook, *Clazomenian Sarcophagi*
(Mainz: von Zabern, 1981); Dusinberre, *Empire, Authority, and Autonomy*, 169.

16. *I.Priene²* 2, 4, 16 = McCabe, *Priene* 60, 139, 63, with different restorations. McCabe, *Priene*
132 and some other epigraphers restore π[εδίων to *IK Priene* 1, l. 12; cf. A. J. Heisserer, *Alexander
and the Greeks: The Epigraphic Evidence* (Norman: University of Oklahoma Press, 1980), 142–68;
S. M. Sherwin-White, "Ancient Archives: The Edict of Alexander to Priene, a Reappraisal," *JHS*
105 (1985): 79–82, but Peter Thonemann, "Alexander, Priene, and Naulochon," in *Epigraphical
Approaches to the Post-Classical Polis*, ed. Paraskevi Martzavou and Nikolaos Papazarkadas (Oxford:
Oxford University Press, 2013), 23–36, has convincingly argued against this interpretation in favor
of identifying it as the name of an unknown village rather than the general descriptor *pedieis*.

Priene. However, these inscriptions offer no insight into the ethnic makeup of these people. While it might be tempting to regard these *pedieis* as necessarily non-Greek, this interpretation requires a clear binary between those two categories that is not supported by these inscriptions.[17] In this context, *pedieis* was general term for the people who lived in the Maeander plain, as distinct from the people of Priene who occupied a raised position on the slopes of Mount Mycale, leading Peter Thonemann to suggest that the word held a connotation akin to the English "hillbilly."[18] Priene's honors to Lysimachus because of his action against the *pedieis*, for instance, specifically mention "the Magnesians and the other *pedieis*" (τοὺς Μάγνη]- | [τας] καὶ τοὺς ἄλλους Πεδιεῖς, *I.Priene* 14, ll. 5–6). Magnesia might have been a polis outside of the circle of the Ionian *koinon*, but it had every bit as much of a claim as Priene to being Greek.[19]

In fact, the only evidence of a distinction between Greek and barbarian in Ionia comes from Thonemann's recent reconstruction of *I.Priene* 1.[20] This heavily reconstructed inscription records an edict of Alexander that established aspects of fiscal policy and land rights for the people of Priene. The inscription's first clause referred to some group of people living in the port of Naulochon whose identity is entirely lost except for a final sigma (l. 3). The original editor, E. L. Hicks, reconstructed the name as [Πριηνεῖ]ς, indicating that the edict governed the Prienians living in Naulochon. However, Thonemann is correct that A. J. Heisserer's subsequent reconstruction of line 7 as ὥ[σπερ οἱ] Πριηνε[ῖς leads to a potential tautology that the Prienians at Naulochon had the same privileges as the Prienians, at least without some additional contortions.[21] Thonemann's solution is to replace [Πριηνεῖ]ς in line 3 with [Ἕλληνε]ς—"of those living at Naulochon, as many as are [Greek]s."[22] The demarcation of "Greeks" is unusual in Classical Ionia but makes sense if understood as an outside imposition that presaged similar restrictive policies established in the Hellenistic kingdoms.

17. Contra Sherwin-White, "Ancient Archives," 77, "the (probably) non-Greek dependent cultivators of royal land," and Noel Robertson, "Government and Society at Miletus, 525–442 B.C.," *Phoenix* 41, no. 4 (1987): 375. On the development of this binary, see Hill, "Conceptualising Interregional Relations." Recent studies have begun to reject the automatic interpretation of the *pedieis* as non-Greek; see, e.g., Peter Thonemann, *The Maeander Valley: A Historical Geography* (Cambridge: Cambridge University Press, 2011), 15–16 with n. 34; Thonemann, "Alexander, Priene, and Naulochon," 23–36.

18. Thonemann, *Maeander Valley*, 15–16; cf. Thonemann, "Alexander, Priene, and Naulochon."

19. Lene Rubinstein, "Ionia," in *An Inventory of Archaic and Classical Poleis*, ed. Mogens Herman Hansen and Thomas Heine Nielsen (Oxford: Oxford University Press, 2004), 1081–82.

20. Thonemann, "Alexander, Priene, and Naulochon."

21. Heisserer, *Alexander and the Greeks*, 142–68; Thonemann, "Alexander, Priene, and Naulochon."

22. Thonemann, "Alexander, Priene, and Naulochon."

"Greek" and "barbarian" are on balance not useful categories for understanding local relationships in and around Classical Ionia except perhaps when referring to the Persian king and his deputies.[23] Rather, these statuses ought to be interpreted as fluid legal categories. In his recent study of Hellenistic Caria, Jeremy LaBuff argued that "the distinction between *polis* and *koinon* may in fact depend more on discursive context than settlement reality."[24] Much the same held true in Ionia with respect to this terminology. The *pedieis* in these inscriptions referred to all the people of the plain who were not Prienian citizens, regardless of their background.

The very ambiguity of Ionian identity set the ideological stakes of defining Ionia as Greek, which imbued the categories with new significance in the writing of Ionian history.[25] When local circumstances gave way to abstractions, it became possible to imagine a clear delineation between the Ionian Greeks beset by a tide of barbarity in Anatolia. Thus, Plutarch says, Ephesus was in a sad state when Lysander arrived to take control of the Spartan fleet in 408 (*Lys.* 3.2). In his telling, Lysander found the Ephesians enthusiastic for the Spartan cause, but in a wretched state on account of the poverty and "in danger of becoming barbarized" (κινδυνεύουσαν ἐκβαρβαρωθῆναι) by close contact with Persian and Lydian customs.[26] What "saved" Ephesus from this grim fate was an economic stimulus package. Lysander immediately ordered merchant ships to Ephesus and gave contracts for trireme construction, which revived the economic prospects of the city and allowed it to achieve the grandeur that it had in Plutarch's day (*Lys.* 3.3). Plutarch thus fully realizes the Greek-Barbarian antithesis in a way that elides that Greek, Anatolian, and Persian cultures were inextricably intertwined in Ionian identity.

---

23. I.e., how Kim, "Invention of the Barbarian," characterizes the term's development.

24. Jeremy LaBuff, *Polis Expansion and Elite Power in Hellenistic Caria* (Lanham, MD: Lexington Books, 2015), 4. In this context, *koina* were villages clustered around a sanctuary, often with an urban center. Similarly, Dominique Lenfant, "Les designations des Grecs d'Asie à l'époque Classique, entre ethnicité et jeux politiques," *Erga-Logoi* 2, no. 2 (2017): 15–33, has argued that references to "the Greeks of Asia" in Classical literature served political ends.

25. Hill, "Conceptualising Interregional Relations"; Mac Sweeney, *Foundation Myths and Politics*, 24.

26. Plutarch's account of Lysander at Ephesus may have been drawn from Theopompus, see Westlake, "Ionians in the Ionian War," 40. Theopompus wrote a *Hellenica* that picked up Thucydides' narrative and included a long passage on Ionian history in his *Philippica*; see William S. Morison, "Theopompus of Chios (115)," *BNJ*, biographical commentary. Plutarch's interest in connecting his biographical subject to the contemporary city of Ephesus led him to embellish the consequences of Lysander's activities.

Appendix 3

Long Ago the Milesians Were Powerful

What about luxurious and sumptuous Ionia,
Tell me how it fares.

τί γὰρ ἡ τρυφερὰ καὶ
καλλιτράπεζος Ἰωνία εἴφ᾽ τι πράσσει[1]

The Ionian migration was not, strictly speaking, a military campaign. Yet, as early as the late Archaic period, it, combined with the Meliac War, was taken for proof of Ionian superiority over the aboriginal Carian population (Mimnermus F 10; Hdt. 1.146.2–3; Diod. 5.84).[2] One infamous version of the foundation of Miletus explained that Milesian women refused to eat or speak with their husbands because the invaders had slaughtered their families and forcibly took them as wives (1.46).[3] In time, the power of Ionia became proverbial. "He put Colophon to it," meant "to put an end to an affair," according to Strabo, because of the quality of their cavalry (τὸν Κολοφῶνα ἐπέθηκεν, 14.1.28). Another saying, "Long ago the Milesians were powerful," meant "Times have changed" (πάλαι ποτ᾽ ἦσαν ἄλκιμοι Μιλήσιοι, Athen. 12.26 [523f]).

Times did indeed change. Although the central thesis of this book complicates the straightforward relationship between Ionia and the imperial states

---

1. Athenaeus 12.28 [524f], citing the Cyclopes of the comic playwright Callias.
2. On the formation of Ionian collective identity, see Appendix 1.
3. Alan M. Greaves, *Miletos: A History* (New York: Routledge, 2002), 77. This story was repeated and adopted by Pausanias for the foundation of Miletus (7.2.1–3) and Dionysius of Halicarnassus' version of the foundation of Rome (2.30). Cf. Alan M. Greaves, "Dionysius of Halicarnassus, *Antiquitates Romane* 2.30 and Herodotus 1.146," *CQ*[2] 48, no. 2 (1998): 20–22; Naoíse Mac Sweeney, *Foundation Myths and Politics in Ancient Ionia* (Cambridge: Cambridge University Press, 2013), 228.

of the Classical period, that does not change the reality that the Ionian poleis remained in a subordinate position within the power structure of the Aegean world. By the start of the second century BCE the Seleucid king Antiochus III even denied the Ionians the language of freedom and autonomy that had been granted to Greek cities in the Aegean for centuries. They were, he claimed, accustomed to obedience to barbarian kings (App. *Syr.* 3.12.1).[4] Antiochus did not deny Ionia a glorious past, but he suggested that its long interaction with barbarian kings made Ionia incapable of self-sufficiency.

The appearance that Ionian power at the end of the Archaic period faded both implicitly and explicitly informs much modern scholarship on the region.[5] Less well understood is how these attitudes toward Ionian impotence developed. The traditional approach to these Ionian memories suggests that Ionian wealth and power grew together until they reached a tipping point when wealth gave way to decadence and luxury that corrupted the society and led to its downfall. Certainly, through both local advantages and long serving as an intermediary with wealthy non-Greek communities, Ionia became associated with luxurious commodities. Herodotus also invokes Sybaris, which itself came to be a byword for excessive luxury, when recounting the fall of Miletus, using the verb ξενόω (enter a treaty of hospitality with) and saying that no two cities had ever been closer (6.21.1). Robert and Vanessa Gorman have recently demonstrated that the connection between luxury (τρυφή) and corruption, long thought to be a foundational principle in Greek literature, actually developed in the Hellenistic and Roman periods.[6] Thus, where Athenaeus' sources might present economic inequality as a cause of social strife at Miletus, he declares that "when they were yoked by pleasure and luxury, all the valiant character of the polis disappeared" (ὡς δὲ ὑπήχθησαν ἡδονῇ καὶ τρυφῇ, κατερρύη τὸ τῆς πόλεως ἀνδρεῖον, 12.26 [523f]).[7]

<hr />

4. Αἰολέας δὲ καὶ Ἴωνας οὐ συνεχώρει ὡς ἐκ πολλοῦ καὶ τοῖς βαρβάροις βασιλεῦσι τῆς Ἀσίας εἰθισμένους ὑπακούειν.

5. For an overview of the treatment of Ionians in modern scholarship since 1750, see Rik Vaessen, "Cultural Dynamics in Ionia at the End of the Second Millennium BCE: New Archaeological Perspectives and Prospects" (PhD diss., University of Sheffield, 2014), 43–97.

6. Robert J. Gorman and Vanessa B. Gorman, *Corrupting Luxury in Ancient Greek Literature* (Ann Arbor: University of Michigan Press, 2014). See Rebecca Futo Kennedy, "Airs, Waters, Metals, Earth: People and Environment in Archaic and Classical Greek Thought," in *The Routledge Handbook of Identity and the Environment in the Classical and Medieval Worlds*, ed. Rebecca Futo Kennedy and Molly Jones-Lewis (New York: Routledge, 2015), 9–28, on the variety of ways that the Greeks interpreted the relationship between the identity of people and their environment. These tropes are persistent, including recently in Eduardo Federico, "Ioni senza *malakie*: Chio, Erodoto e la rivolta ionica," *Erga-Logoi* 5, no. 2 (2017): 95–112, who argues for a strain of Chian propaganda in Herodotus' account of the Ionian revolt. Such an influence is certainly possible but the form he proposes overstates the negative reputation of the rest of Ionia in the fifth century.

7. See Chapter 2 for the economic explanation for stasis in Miletus. On the preoccupation with

Throughout the Classical period, Ionia *was* dominated by more powerful neighbors, which forced the inhabitants of the region to adapt to this imperial reality. Contemporary commentators were frequently dismissive of their fighting capacity. Thucydides, for instance, concludes that the Athenian allies enabled the development of the empire by their own unwillingness to protect themselves (1.98–99), while Xenophon narrates both how a force of Athenian peltasts decisively defeated Milesian hoplites (*Hell.* 1.2.2) and how the Ionians under Dercylidas' command simply dropped their weapons and fled in the face of a larger Persian army (*Hell.* 3.2.17). However, both authors frame these conditions in terms of preparation and training rather than indolence and weakness.[8] It is also not as though the Ionians themselves were unaware of these factors, which led Miletus and Teos to be among the earliest poleis to institute ephebic educational programs.[9]

The notion that different cultures have differing martial capabilities has a long and toxic history that was and is often intertwined with gender constructs.[10] Ionia was no exception: it was there that King Agesilaus reportedly stripped Persian captives naked so that his soldiers would see that their enemies were fat and lazy (πίονας δὲ καὶ ἀπόνους) and therefore think that going to war against them would be like fighting women (εἰ γυναιξὶ δέοι μάχεσθαι, Xen. *Ages.* 1.28). However, when explaining the Ionian inability to defend themselves, commentators of the Classical period looked to the lack of training, civil stasis, and political fragmentation. Any explanation that looked to indolence would have flown in the face of the reality that Ionian soldiers fought alongside their own. In time, the two strands of historical memory merged to offer a new interpretation about the decline and fall of Ionia that could serve as a warning for subsequent generations. Ionian power led to prosperity that gave way to decadence and indolence and, finally, irrelevance.

---

internal changes in Greek political thought, see Peter T. Manicas, "War, Stasis, and Greek Political Thought," *Comparative Studies in Society and History* 24, no. 4 (1982): 673–88.

8. Cf. Herodotus 6.11–12 on the battle of Lade, which Gorman and Gorman, *Corrupting Luxury*, 135–39, have convincingly demonstrated is a commentary about excessive last-minute training.

9. Teos: *SEG* II (1925) 640; Miletus: *Milet* I.3, no. 139; Nigel M. Kennell, *Ephebeia: A Register of Geek Cities with Citizen Training Systems in the Hellenistic and Roman Periods* (Zurich: Hildesheim, 2006), xi. On the military activities of Hellenistic poleis, see John Ma, "Fighting Poleis of the Hellenistic World," in *War and Violence in Ancient Greece*, ed. Hans van Wees (London: Duckworth, 2000), 337–76.

10. These ideas reached their pinnacle in the nineteenth century, concurrent with the development of race science. See particularly Heather Streets, *Martial Races: The Military, Race and Masculinity in British Imperial Culture, 1857–1914* (Manchester: Manchester University Press, 2004).

Bibliography

Abbott, Evelyn. "The Early History of the Delian League." *CR* 3 (1889): 387–90.

Accame, Silvio. *La lega Ateniese del secolo IV a.C.* Rome: Angelo Signorelli, 1941.

Adams, W. Lindsay. "Other People's Games: The Olympics, Macedonia and Greek Athletics." *Journal of Sport History* 30 (2003): 205–17.

Adcock, Frank and D. J. Mosley. *Diplomacy in Ancient Greece.* London: Thames and Hudson, 1975.

Ager, Sheila L. "4th Century Thera and the Second Athenian Sea League." *AncW* 32, no. 1 (2001): 99–119.

Ager, Sheila L. "A Royal Arbitration between Klazomenae and Teos?" *ZPE* 85 (1991): 87–97.

Ager, Sheila L. "Civic Identity in the Hellenistic World: The Case of Lebedos." *GRBS* 39, no. 1 (1998): 5–21.

Ager, Sheila L. *Interstate Arbitrations in the Greek World, 337–90 B.C.* Berkeley: University of California Press, 1997.

Ager, Sheila L. "Interstate Governance: Arbitration and Peacekeeping." In *A Companion to Ancient Greek Government*, edited by Hans Beck, 497–511. Malden, MA: Wiley-Blackwell, 2013.

Ager, Sheila L. "Keeping the Peace in Ionia: Kings and *Poleis*." In *Regionalism in Hellenistic and Roman Asia Minor*, edited by Hugh Elton and Gary Reger, 45–52. Pessac: Ausonius, 2007.

Aikyo, Kunihiro. "Clazomene, Eritre ed Atene prima della Pace di Antalcida (385 A.C.)." *ACME* 41 (1988): 17–33.

Alfieri Tonini, Teresa. "Basileus Alexandros." In λόγιος ἀνήρ: *Studi di Antichità in memoria di Mario Attilio Levi*, edited by Pier Giuseppe Michelotto, 1–13. Milan: Cisalpino Instituto, 2002.

Aloni, Antonio. "The Politics of Composition and Performance of the Homeric 'Hymn to Apollo.'" In *Apolline Politics and Poetics*, edited by Lucia Athanassaki, Richard P. Martin, and John F. Miller, 55–65. Athens: Hellenic Ministry of Culture, 2009.

Ameling, Walter. "Komoedie und Politik zwischen Kratinos und Aristophanes: Das Beispiel Perikles." *QC* 3, no. 6 (1981): 383–424.

Ameling, Walter. "Plutarch, *Perikles* 12–14." *Historia* 34, no. 1 (1985): 47–63.

Anderson, Benedict. *Imagined Communities: Reflections on the Origins and Spread of Nationalism.* New York: Verso Books, 1983.

Anderson, J. K. "The Battle of Sardis in 395 B.C." *California Studies in Classical Antiquity* 7 (1974): 27–53.

Andrewes, A. "The Opposition to Perikles." *JHS* 98 (1978): 1–8.

Andrewes, A. "Two Notes on Lysander." *Phoenix* 25, no. 3 (1971): 206–26.

Anson, Edward M. *Alexander's Heirs: The Age of the Successors.* Malden, MA: Wiley-Blackwell, 2014.

Anson, Edward M. "The Chronology of the Third Diadoch War." *Phoenix* 60, nos. 3–4 (2006): 226–35.

Anson, Edward M. "The Dating of Perdiccas' Death and the Assembly at Triparadeisus." *GRBS* 43, no. 4 (2003): 373–90.

Anson, Edward M. "Diodorus and the Date of Triparadeisus." *AJPh* 107, no. 2 (1986): 208–17.

Arena, Emiliano. "Alessandro 'Basileus' nella documentazione epigrafica: La dedica del Tempio di Atena a Priene ('I.Priene' 156)." *Historia* 62, no. 1 (2013): 48–79.

Armayor, O. Kimball. "Herodotus' Catalogues of the Persian Empire in the Light of the Monuments and the Greek Literary Tradition." *TAPhA* 108 (1978): 1–9.

Ashton, N. G. "The Naumachia near Amorgos in 322 B.C." *ABSA* 72 (1977): 1–11.

Atkinson, J. E. *A Commentary on Q. Curtius Rufus' Historiae Alexandri Magni, Books 3 and 4.* Leiden: Brill, 1980.

Austin, M. M. "Hellenistic Kings, War, and the Economy." *CQ²* 36, no. 2 (1986): 450–66.

Azoulay, Vincent. *Pericles of Athens.* Translated by Janet Lloyd. Princeton, NJ: Princeton University Press, 2014.

Bachvarova, Mary. *From Hittite to Homer: The Anatolian Background of Greek Epic.* Cambridge: Cambridge University Press, 2016.

Backman, Clifford R. "Piracy." In *A Companion to Mediterranean History*, edited by Peregrine Horden and Susan Kinoshita, 170–83. Malden, MA: Wiley, 2014.

Badian, Ernst. "Alexander the Great and the Greeks of Asia." In *Collected Papers on Alexander the Great*, 124–52. New York: Routledge, 2012 [= "Alexander the Great and the Greeks of Asia." In *Ancient Society and Institutions: Studies Presented to Victor Ehrenberg*, edited by Ernst Badian, 37–69. Oxford: Oxford University Press, 1966].

Badian, Ernst. "Alexander the Great between Two Thrones and Heaven: Variations on an Old Theme." In *Subject and Ruler: The Cult of Ruling Power in Classical Antiquity*, edited by Alastair Small, 11–26. Ann Arbor: University of Michigan Press, 1996.

Badian, Ernst. "The Death of Philip II." In *Collected Papers on Alexander the Great*, 106–12. New York: Routledge, 2012 [= "The Death of Philip II." *Phoenix* 17, no. 4 (1963): 244–50].

Badian, Ernst. "A document of Artaxerxes IV?" In *Greece and the Eastern Mediterranean in ancient history and prehistory: Studies presented to Fritz Schachermeyr on the occasion of his 80. birthday*, ed. Konrad H. Kinzel, 40–50. Berlin: De Gruyter, 1977.

Badian, Ernst. "The Ghost of Empire: Reflections on Athenian Foreign Policy in the Fourth Century." In *Die athenische Demokratie im 4. Jahrhundert v. Chr.*, edited by Walter Eder and Christoph Auffarth, 79–106. Stuttgart: Franz Steiner Verlag, 1995.

Badian, Ernst. "Harpalus." *JHS* 81 (1961): 16–43.

Badian, Ernst. "History from 'Square Brackets.'" *ZPE* 79 (1989): 59–70.

Badian, Ernst. "The Peace of Callias." *JHS* 107 (1987): 1–39.

Badian, Ernst. "A Reply to Professor Hammond's Article." *ZPE* 97 (1994): 388–90.

Balcer, Jack Martin. "The Ancient Persian Satrapies and Satraps in Western Anatolia." *AMI* 26 (1993): 81–90.

Balcer, Jack Martin. "Fifth Century B.C. Ionia: A Frontier Redefined." *REA* 87, nos. 1–2 (1985): 31–42.

Balcer, Jack Martin. "The Greeks and the Persians: Processes of Acculturation." *Historia* 32, no. 3 (1983): 257–67.

Balcer, Jack Martin. "The Liberation of Ionia: 478 B.C." *Historia* 46, no. 3 (1997): 374–77.

Balcer, Jack Martin. *The Persian Conquest of the Greeks, 545–450 B.C.* Konstanz: Universitätsverlag Konstanz, 1995.

Balcer, Jack Martin. "Separatism and Anti-separatism in the Athenian Empire (478–433 B.C.)." *Historia* 23, no. 1 (1974): 21–39.

Balcer, Jack Martin. *Sparda by the Bitter Sea: Imperial Interaction in Western Anatolia.* Providence, RI: Brown University Press, 1984.

Bammer, Anton and Ulrike Muss. "Water Problems in the Artemision of Ephesus." In *Cura Aquarum in Ephesus*, vol. 1, edited by Gilbert Wiplinger, 61–64. Leuven: Peeters, 2006.

Baran, Abdulkadir. "The Role of Carians in the Development of Greek Architecture." In *Listening to the Stones: Essays on Architecture and Function in Ancient Greek Sanctuaries in Honour of Richard Alan Tomlinson*, edited by Elena C. Partida and Barbara Schmidt-Dounas, 233–44. Oxford: Archaeopress, 2019.

Baron, Christopher A. "The Aristoteles Decree and the Expansion of the Second Athenian League." *Hesperia* 75, no. 3 (2006): 379–95.

Baron, Christopher A. *Timaeus of Tauromenium and Hellenistic Historiography.* Cambridge: Cambridge University Press, 2013.

Barron, John P. "Chios in the Athenian Empire." In *Chios: A Conference at the Homereion in Chios*, edited by John Boardman and C. E. Vaphopoulou-Richardson, 89–104. Oxford: Oxford University Press, 1986.

Barron, John P. "Milesian Politics and Athenian Propaganda, c.460–440 B.C." *JHS* 82 (1962): 1–6.

Barron, John P. *The Silver Coins of Samos.* London: Athlone, 1966.

Barron, John P. "The Tyranny of Duris at Samos." *CR* 12, no. 3 (1962): 189–92.

Baumbach, Jens David. *The Significance of Votive Offerings in Selected Hera Sanctuaries in the Peloponnese, Ionia, and Western Greece.* Oxford: Archeopress, 2004.

Bayliss, Andrew J. "Antigonos the One-Eyed's Return to Asia in 322." *ZPE* 155 (2006): 108–26.

Bean, G. E. "Gerga in Caria." *Anatolian Studies* 19 (1969): 179–82.

Bean, G. E. and J. M. Cook. "The Carian Coast III." *ABSA* 52 (1957): 58–146.

Bearzot, Cinzia. "Demodamante di Mileto e l'identità ionica." *Erga-Logoi* 5, no. 2 (2017): 143–54.

Bearzot, Cinzia. "La Guerra lelantina e il koinon degli Ioni d'Asia." *Contributi dell'Instituto di storia antica* 9 (1983): 57–81.

Bearzot, Cinzia. "L'impero del mare come egemonia subaltern nel IV secolo (Diodoro, Libri XIV–XV)." *Aevum* 89 (2015): 83–91.

Beaumont, Lesley. "Shaping the Ancient Religious Landscape at Kato Phana, Chios." In

Listening to the Stones: Essays on Architecture and Function in Ancient Greek Sanctuaries in Honour of Richard Alan Tomlinson, edited by Elena C. Partida and Barbara Schmidt-Dounas, 182–90. Oxford: Archaeopress, 2019.

Beaumont, Lesley, Aglaia Archontidou-Argyri, Hugh Beames, Angeliki Tsigkou, and Nicola Wardle. "Excavations at Kato Phano, Chios: 1999, 2000, and 2001." *ABSA* 99 (2004): 201–55.

Berthold, Richard M. "A Historical Fiction in Vitruvius." *CPh* 73, no. 2 (1978): 129–34.

Berthold, Richard M. *Rhodes in the Hellenistic Age*. Ithaca, NY: Cornell University Press, 1984.

Bhabha, Homi K. *The Location of Culture*. New York: Routledge, 1994.

Bhabha, Homi K. "The Third Space." In *Identity: Community, Culture, Difference*, edited by Jonathan Rutherford, 207–21. London: Lawrence and Wishart, 1990.

Bicknell, Peter J. "Axiochos Alkibiadou, Aspasia and Aspasios." *L'Antiquité Classique* 51 (1982): 240–50.

Bieber, Margaret. *Alexander the Great in Greek and Roman Art*. Chicago: Argonaut, 1964.

Bieber, Margaret. "The Portraits of Alexander the Great." *TAPhA* 93 (1949): 373–421, 423–27.

Bikerman, Elias. *Institutions des Séleucides*. Paris: Librairie Orientaliste Paul Geuthner, 1938.

Billows, Richard A. "Anatolian Dynasts: The Case of the Macedonian Eupolemos in Karia." *CA* 8, no. 2 (1989): 173–206.

Billows, Richard A. *Antigonus the One-Eyed and the Creation of the Hellenistic State*. Berkeley: University of California Press, 1985.

Billows, Richard A. "Cities." In *Companion to the Hellenistic World*, edited by Andrew Erskine, 44–55. Malden, MA: Blackwell, 2003.

Billows, Richard A. *Kings and Colonists: Aspects of Macedonian Imperialism*. Leiden: Brill, 1995.

Billows, Richard A. "Rebirth of a Region: Ionia in the Early Hellenistic Period." In *Regionalism in Hellenistic and Roman Asia Minor*, edited by Hugh Elton and Gary Reger, 33–44. Pessac: Ausonius, 2007.

Bissa, Errietta M. A. *Governmental Intervention in Foreign Trade in Archaic and Classical Greece*. Leiden: Brill, 2009.

Blackwell, Christopher W. *In the Absence of Alexander: Harpalus and the Failure of Macedonian Authority*. Bern: Peter Lang, 1999.

Blamire, Alec. "Athenian Finance, 454–404 B.C." *Hesperia* 70, no. 1 (2001): 99–126.

Blanshard, Alastair. "The Problem with Honouring Samos: An Athenian Documentary Relief and Its Interpretation." In *Art and Inscriptions in the Ancient World*, edited by Zahra Newby and Ruth Leader-Newby, 19–37. Cambridge: Cambridge University Press, 2007.

Blanshard, Alastair. "Trapped between Athens and Chios: A Relationship in Fragments." In *The World of Ion of Chios*, edited by Victoria Jennings and Andrea Katsaros, 155–75. Leiden: Brill, 2007.

Blok, Josine H. "Perikles' Citizenship Law: A New Perspective." *Historia* 58, no. 2 (2009): 141–70.

Boardman, John. "Eastern Greeks." *CR* 14, no. 1 (1964): 83.

Boardman, John. *Greek Sculpture: The Archaic Period*. London: Thames and Hudson, 1978.

Boardman, John. *Persia and the West: An Archaeological Investigation of the Genesis of Achaemenid Persian Art*. London: Thames and Hudson, 2000.

Bodzek, Jarosław. "On the Dating of the Bronze Issues of Tissaphernes." *Studies in Ancient Art and Civilization* 16 (2012): 105–18.

Boehm, Ryan. *City and Empire in the Age of the Successors*. Berkeley: University of California Press, 2018.

Boiy, Tom. *Between High and Low: A Chronology of the Early Hellenistic Period*. Mainz: Verlag Antike, 2007.

Bolmarcich, Sarah. "The Athenian Regulations for Samos (IG I³ 48) Again." *Chiron* 39 (2009): 45–64.

Börker, Christoph. "König Agesilaos von Sparta und der Artemis-Tempel in Ephesus." *ZPE* 37 (1980): 69–70.

Bosworth, A. B. "Alexander the Great Part 2: Greece and the Conquered Territories." In *Cambridge Ancient History*², vol. 6, edited by David M. Lewis, John Boardman, Simon Hornblower, and Martin Ostwald, 846–75. Cambridge: Cambridge University Press, 1994.

Bosworth, A. B. *Conquest and Empire: The Reign of Alexander the Great*. Cambridge: Cambridge University Press, 1993.

Bosworth, A. B. *A Historical Commentary on Arrian's History of Alexander*. Vol. 1. Oxford: Oxford University Press, 1980.

Bosworth, A. B. *The Legacy of Alexander: Politics, Warfare and Propaganda under the Successors*. Oxford: Oxford University Press, 2002.

Bosworth, A. B. "Perdiccas and the Kings." *CQ*² 43, no. 2 (1993): 420–27.

Bosworth, A. B. "Philip III Arrhidaeus and the Chronology of the Successors." *Chiron* 22 (1992): 55–81.

Bosworth, A. B. "Why Did Athens Lose the Lamian War?" In *The Macedonians in Athens, 322–229 B.C.*, edited by Olga Palagia and Stephen V. Tracy, 14–22. Oxford: Oxford University Press, 2003.

Botermann, Helga. "Wer Baute das Neue Priene? Zur Interpretation der Inschriften von Priene Nr. 1 und 156." *Hermes* 122, no. 2 (1994): 162–87.

Bouley, Thibaut. *Arès dans la cité: Les poleis et la guerre dans l'Asie Mineure hellénistique*. Pisa: Fabrizio Serra Editore, 2014.

Bourke, Graeme. *Elis: Internal Politics and External Policy in Ancient Greece*. New York: Routledge, 2017.

Bowden, Hugh. "The Argeads and Greek Sanctuaries." In *The History of the Argeads: New Perspectives*, edited by Sabine Müller, Tim Howe, Hugh Bowden, and Robert Rollinger, 163–82. Wiesbaden: Harrassowitz, 2017.

Bradeen, Donald W. "The Popularity of the Athenian Empire." *Historia* 9, no. 3 (1960): 257–69.

Braund, D. C. and G. R. Tsetzkhladze. "The Export of Slaves from Colchis." *CQ*² 39, no. 1 (1989): 114–25.

Bremmer, Jan. "Priestly Personnel of the Ephesian Artemision: Anatolian, Persian,

Greek, and Roman Aspects." In *Practitioners of the Divine: Greek Priests and Religious Figures from Homer to Heliodorus*, edited by Beate Dignas and Kai Trapedach. Washington D.C.: Center for Hellenic Studies, 2008. http://nrs.harvard.edu/urn-3:hul.ebook:CHS_DignasB_and_TrampedachK_eds.Practitioners_of_the_Divine.2008

Briant, Pierre. *Antigone le Borgne: Les debuts de sa carriere et les problemes de l'Assemblée macedonienne*. Paris: Les Belles Lettres, 1973.

Briant, Pierre. "The Empire of Darius III in Perspective." In *Alexander the Great: A New History*, edited by Waldemar Heckel and Lawrence A. Tritle, 141–70. Malden, MA: Blackwell, 2009.

Briant, Pierre. *From Cyrus to Alexander: A History of the Persian Empire*. Translated by Peter T. Daniels. Winona Lake, IN: Eisenbrauns, 2002.

Briant, Pierre. "From the Indus to the Mediterranean: The Administrative Organization and Logistics of the Great Roads of the Achaemenid Empire." In *Highways, Byways, and Road Systems in the Pre-modern World*, edited by Susan E. Alcock, John Bodel, and Richard J. A. Talbert, 185–201. Malden, MA: Wiley-Blackwell, 2012.

Brodersen, Kai. "Aegean Greece." In *A Companion to the Classical World*, edited by Konrad H. Kinzl, 99–114. Malden, MA: Wiley-Blackwell, 2006.

Broekaert, Wim and Arjan Zuiderhoek. "Food and Politics in Classical Antiquity." In *A Cultural History of Food in Antiquity*, edited by Paul Erdkamp, 75–94. London: Bloomsbury, 2012.

Brosius, Maria. "Artemis Persike and Artemis Anaitis." In *Studies in Persian History: Essays in Memory of David M. Lewis*, edited by Maria Brosius and Amelie Kuhrt, 227–38. Leiden: Brill, 1998.

Brosius, Maria. "Persian Diplomacy between 'Pax Persica' and 'Zero Tolerance.'" In *Maintaining Peace and Interstate Stability in Archaic and Classical Greece*, edited by Julia Wilker, 150–64. Mainz: Verlag Antike, 2012.

Brown, Edwin L. "In Search of Anatolian Apollo." In ΧΑΡΙΣ: *Essays in Honor of Sara A. Immerwahr*, edited by Anne P. Chapin, 243–57. Athens: American School of Classical Studies, 2004.

Bruce, I. A. F. "The Alliance between Athens and Chios in 384 B.C." *Phoenix* 19, no. 4 (1965): 281–84.

Brückner, Helmut. "Delta Evolution and Culture: Aspects of Geoarchaeological Research in Miletos and Priene." In *Troia and the Troad: Scientific Approaches*, edited by Günther A. Wagner, Ernst Pernicka, and Hans-Peter Uerpmann, 121–42. Berlin: Springer, 2003.

Brun, Patrice. *Eisphora, Syntaxis, Stratioke*. Paris: Les Belles Lettres, 1983.

Buckler, John. *Aegean Greece in the Fourth Century BC*. Leiden: Brill, 2003.

Burford, A. *The Greek Temple Builders at Epidaurus*. Liverpool: Liverpool University Press, 1969.

Burkert, Walter. *Griechische Religion der archaischen und klassischen Epoche*. Stuttgart: Kohlhammer, 1977.

Burkert, Walter. "Gyges to Croesus: Historiography between Herodotus and Cuneiform." In *Schools of Oriental Studies and the Development of Modern Historiography*, edited by Antonio Panaino, Andrea Piras, and Gian Pietro Basello, 41–52. Milan: Mimesis, 2004.

Burkert, Walter. "Kynaithos, Polycrates, and the Homeric Hymn to Apollo." In *Arktouros*, edited by Glen W. Bowersock, Walter Burkert, and Michael C. J. Putnam, 53–62. Berlin: de Gruyter, 1979.

Burkert, Walter. "Olbia and Apollo of Didyma: A New Oracle Text." In *Apollo: Origins and Influence*, edited by Jon Solomon, 49–60. Tucson: University of Arizona Press, 1994.

Burkert, Walter. *The Orientalizing Revolution: Near Eastern Influences on Greek Culture in the Early Archaic Period.* Translated by Margaret E. Pinder and Walter Burkert. Cambridge, MA: Harvard University Press, 1992.

Burn, A. R. *Persia and the Greeks: The Defence of the West, c.546–478 B.C.* London: Edward Arnold, 1962.

Burstein, Stanley M. *The Hellenistic Age from the Battle of Ipsos to the Death of Kleopatra VII.* Cambridge: Cambridge University Press, 1985.

Burstein, Stanley M. "Lysimachus and the Greek Cities of Asia: The Case of Miletus." *AncW* 3, nos. 3–4 (1980): 73–79.

Buxton, Richard. "The Northern Syria 2007 Hoard of Athenian Owls: Behavioral Aspects." *AJN*[2] 21 (2009): 1–27.

Bylkova, Valeria P. "The Chronology of Settlements in the Lower Dnieper Region (400–100 BC)." In *Chronologies of the Black Sea Area, c. 400–100 BC*, edited by Lise Hannestad and Vladimir F. Stolba, 217–47. Aarhus: Aarhus University Press, 2006.

Cahill, Nicholas and Crawford H. Greenewalt Jr. "The Sanctuary of Artemis at Sardis: Preliminary Report, 2002–2012." *AJA* 120, no. 3 (2016): 473–509.

Cahill, Nicholas and John H. Kroll. "New Archaic Coin Finds at Sardis." *AJA* 109, no. 4 (2005): 589–617.

Cahn, Herbert. "Tisaphernes in Astyra." *AA* 4 (1985): 587–94.

Campbell, Peter B. and George Koutsouflakis. "Aegean Navigation and the Shipwrecks of Fourni: The Archipelago in Context." In *Under the Mediterranean*, vol. 1, edited by S. Demesticha and L. Blue, 279–98. Leiden: Sidestone Press, 2021.

Carey, Chris, Mike Edwards, Zoltán Farkas, Judson Herrman, László Horváth, Gyula Mayer, Tamás Mészárow, P. J. Rhodes, and Natalie Tchernetska. "Fragments of Hyperides' 'Against Diondas' from the Archimedes Palimpsest." *ZPE* 165 (2008): 1–19.

Cargill, Jack. *Athenian Settlements of the Fourth Century B.C.* Leiden: Brill, 1995.

Cargill, Jack. "The Decree of Aristoteles: Some Epigraphical Details." *AncW* 27, no. 1 (1996): 39–51.

Cargill, Jack. "Hegemony Not Empire: The Second Athenian League." *AncW* 5, nos. 3–4 (1982): 91–102.

Cargill, Jack. "*IG* II[2] 1 and the Athenian Kleruchy on Samos." *GRBS* 23, no. 4 (1983): 321–32.

Cargill, Jack. *The Second Athenian League: Empire or Free Alliance.* Berkeley: University of California Press, 1981.

Carlson, Deborah N. and William Aylward. "The Kizilburun Shipwreck and the Temple of Apollo at Claros." *AJA* 114, no. 1 (2010): 145–59.

Carradice, Ian. "The Regal Coinage of the Persian Empire." In *Coinage and Administration in the Athenian and Persian Empires*, edited by Ian. Carradice, 73–95. Oxford: Oxford University Press, 1987.

Carter, Joseph C. *The Sculpture of the Sanctuary of Athena Polias at Priene*. London: Thames and Hudson, 1983.

Cartledge, Paul. *Agesilaos and the Crisis of Sparta*. London: Duckworth, 2000.

Cartledge, Paul. *The Greeks: A Portrait of Self and Others*. Oxford: Oxford University Press, 2002.

Caspari, M. O. B. "The Ionian Confederacy." *JHS* 35 (1915): 173–88.

Caspari, M. O. B. "The Ionian Confederacy—Addendum." *JHS* 36 (1916): 102.

Catling, R. W. V. "Sparta's Friends at Ephesos: The Onomastic Evidence." In *Onomatologos: Studies in Greek Personal Names Presented to Elaine Matthews*, edited by R. W. V. Catling and Fabienne Marchand, 195–237. Oxford: Oxford University Press, 2010.

Cavaignac, E. "Les dékarchies de Lysandre." *REH* 90 (1924): 285–316.

Cawkwell, George L. "The Foundation of the Second Athenian Confederacy." *CQ*² 23, no. 1 (1973): 47–60.

Cawkwell, George L. *The Greek Wars: The Failure of Persia*. Oxford: Oxford University Press, 2005.

Cawkwell, George L. "The Imperialism of Thrasybulus." *CQ*² 26, no. 2 (1976): 270–77.

Cawkwell, George L. "A Note on the Heracles Coinage Alliance of 394 B.C." *NC* 16 (1956): 69–75.

Cawkwell, George L. "Notes on the Failure of the Second Athenian Confederacy." *JHS* 101 (1981): 40–55.

Cawkwell, George L. "Notes on the Social War." *C&M* 23 (1962): 34–49.

Cawkwell, George L. "The ΣΥΝ Coins Again." *JHS* 83 (1963): 152–54.

Champion, Jeff. *Antigonus the One-Eyed: Greatest of the Successors*. Malden, MA: Blackwell, 2014.

Chaniotis, Angelos. *Age of Conquests: The Greek World from Alexander to Hadrian*. Cambridge, MA: Harvard University Press, 2018.

Chaniotis, Angelos. "The Impact of War on the Economy of Hellenistic *Poleis*: Demand Creation, Short-Term Influence, Long-Term Impacts." In *The Economies of Hellenistic Societies, Third to First Centuries BC*, edited by Vincent Gabrielsen, J. K. Davies, and Zosia Archibald, 122–43. Oxford: Oxford University Press, 2011.

Chaniotis, Angelos. *War in the Hellenistic World*. Malden, MA: Blackwell, 2005.

Chryssanthaki, Katerina. "Les trois fondations d'Abdère." *REG* 114 (2001): 383–406.

Clinton, Kevin. "Mysteria at Ephesus." *ZPE* 191 (2014): 117–28.

Cobet, Justus. "Wann wurde Herodots Darstellung der Perserkriege publiziert?" *Hermes* 105, no. 1 (1977): 2–27.

Cohen, Getzel. *The Hellenistic Settlements in Europe, the Islands, and Asia Minor*. Berkeley: University of California Press, 1996.

Coldstream, J. N. "Mixed Marriages at the Frontiers of the Early Greek World." *Oxford Journal of Archaeology* 12, no. 1 (1993): 89–107.

Constantakopoulou, Christy. *The Dance of the Islands: Insularity, Networks, the Athenian Empire, and the Aegean World*. Oxford: Oxford University Press, 2007.

Connor, W. Robert. *Theopompus and Fifth-Century Athens*. Washington, DC: Center for Hellenic Studies, 1968.

Cook, J. M. "Cnidian Peraea and Spartan Coins." *JHS* 81 (1961): 56–72.

Cook, J. M. *The Greeks in Ionia and the East*. London: Thames and Hudson, 1962.

Cook, J. M. "Old Smyrna." *ABSA* 53–54 (1958–59): 1–34.

Cook, J. M. "On the Date of Alyattes' Sack of Smyrna." *ABSA* 80 (1980): 25–28.

Cook, J. M. "The Problem of Classical Ionia." *PCPhS* 187, no. 7 (1961): 9–18.

Cook, J. M. "Review: *Der jüngste Apollotempel von Didyma.*" *JHS* 96 (1976): 243–44.

Cook, R. M. *Clazomenian Sarcophagi.* Mainz: von Zabern, 1981.

Cook, R. M. "The Distribution of Chiot Pottery." *ABSA* 44 (1949): 154–61.

Cooper, C. *Dinarchus, Hyperides, and Lycurgus.* Austin: University of Texas Press, 2001.

Corsten, T. *Lexicon of Greek Personal Names.* Vol. 5A. Oxford: Oxford University Press, 2010.

Coşkun, Altay. "Deconstructing a Myth of Seleucid History: The So-Called 'Elephant Victory.'" *Phoenix* 66, nos. 1–2 (2012): 57–73.

Costa, Eugene A., Jr. "Evagoras I and the Persians, ca. 411 to 391 B.C." *Historia* 23, no. 1 (1974): 40–56.

Coulton, J. J. *Ancient Greek Architects at Work: Problems of Structure and Design.* Ithaca, NY: Cornell University Press, 1982.

Coulton, J. J. "Towards Understanding Greek Temple Design: General Considerations." *ABSA* 70 (1975): 59–99.

Couvenhes, Jean-Christophe. "Les cités grecques d'Asie Mineure et le mercenariat à l'époque hellénistique." In *Les cités grecques en Asie Mineure à l'époque hellénistique*, edited by Jean-Christophe Couvenhes and Henri-Louis Fernoux, 77–113. Tours: Presses universitaires François-Rabelais, 2004.

Crielaard, Jan Paul. "The Ionians in the Archaic Period: Shifting Identities in a Changing World." In *Ethnic Constructs in Antiquity: The Role of Power and Tradition*, edited by Ton Derks and Nico Roymans, 37–84. Amsterdam: Amsterdam University Press, 2009.

Cross, Nicholas. "The Panionia: The Ritual Context for Identity Construction in Archaic Ionia." *Mediterranean Studies* 28, no. 1 (2020): 1–20.

Crowther, C. V. "I.Priene 8 and the History of Priene in the Early Hellenistic Period." *Chiron* 26 (1996): 195–238.

Cuypers, Martine. "Andron of Teos (802)." In *Brill's New Jacoby*, edited by Ian Worthington. Leiden: Brill, 2013.

D'Alessio, Giovan Battista. "Immigrati a Teo e ad Abdera (SEG XXXI 985; Pind. Fr. 52b Sn.-M.)." *ZPE* 92 (1992): 73–80.

D'Angour, Armand. *Socrates in Love: The Making of a Philosopher.* London: Bloomsbury, 2019.

Davies, John K. "Rebuilding a Temple: The Economic Effects of Piety." In *Economies beyond Agriculture in the Classical World*, edited by David J. Mattingly and John Salmon, 209–29. New York: Routledge, 2001.

Davies, John K. "The Well-Balanced *Polis*: Ephesos." In *The Economies of Hellenistic Societies, Third to First Centuries BC*, edited by Vincent Gabrielsen, John K. Davies, and Zosia Archibald, 177–206. Oxford: Oxford University Press, 2011.

Davis, Whitney M. "Egypt, Samos, and the Archaic Style in Greek Sculpture." *JEA* 67 (1981): 61–81.

De Giorgi, Andrea. *Ancient Antioch: From the Seleucid Era to the Islamic Conquest.* Cambridge: Cambridge University Press, 2016.

de Romilly, Jacqueline. "Thucydides and the Cities of the Athenian Empire." *BICS* 13 (1966): 1–12.

de Sanctis, Gaetano. "Aristagora di Mileto." *Rivista di filologia e di istruzione classica* 59 (1931): 48–72.

de Souza, Philip. *Piracy in the Greco-Roman World*. Cambridge: Cambridge University Press, 1999.

de Ste. Croix, G. E. M. "The Character of the Athenian Empire." *Historia* 3, no. 1 (1954): 1–41.

Debord, Pierre. *L'Asie Mineure au IVe siècle (412–323 a.C.)*. Pessac: Ausonius, 1999.

Demand, Nancy. "The Relocation of Priene Reconsidered." *Phoenix* 40, no. 1 (1986): 35–44.

Descat, Raymond. "Les traditions grecques sur les Lélèges." In *Origines Gentium*, edited by Valérie Fromentin and Sophie Gotteland, 169–77. Paris: Ausonius, 2001.

Develin Robert. *Athenian Officials, 684–321 B.C.* Cambridge: Cambridge University Press, 1989.

Devoto, James G. "Agesilaus, Antalcidas, and the Failed Peace of 392/91 B.C." *CPh* 81, no. 3 (1986): 191–202.

Dignas, B. *Economy of the Sacred in Hellenistic and Roman Asia Minor*. Oxford: Oxford University Press, 2002.

Dillery, John. *Xenophon and the History of His Times*. New York: Routledge, 1995.

Dillon, Matthew P. J. "The Ecology of the Greek Sanctuary." *ZPE* 118 (1997): 113–27.

Dmitriev, Sviatoslav. "Alexander's Exiles Decree." *Klio* 86, no. 2 (2004): 348–81.

Dmitriev, Sviatoslav. *The Greek Slogan of Freedom and Early Roman Politics in Greece*. Oxford: Oxford University Press, 2011.

Dougherty, Carol. "Pindar's Second Paean: Civic Identity on Parade." *CPh* 89, no. 3 (1994): 205–18.

Doukellis, Panagiotis N. "Hadrian's *Panhellenion*: A Network of Cities?" *Mediterranean Historical Review* 22, no. 2 (2007): 295–308.

Dover, Kenneth J. "Ion of Chios: His Place in the History of Greek Literature." In *Chios: A Conference at the Homereion in Chios*, edited by J. Boardman and C. E. Vaphopoulou-Richardson, 27–37. Oxford: Oxford University Press, 1986.

Dreher, Martin. *Hegemon und Symmachoi: Untersuchen zum Zweiten Athenischen Seebund*. Berlin: de Gruyter, 1995.

Dreyer, Boris. "Heroes, Cults, and Divinity." In *Alexander the Great: A New History*, edited by Waldemar Heckel and Lawrence A. Tritle, 218–34. Malden, MA: Blackwell, 2009.

Drijvers, Jan Willem. "Strabo 17.1.18 (801C): Inaros, the Milesians and Naucratis." *Mnemosyne^4* 52, no. 1 (1999): 16–22.

Driscoll, Eric W. "The Milesian Eponym List and the Revolt of 412 B.C." *The Journal of Epigraphic Studies* 2 (2019): 11–32.

Dušanić, Slobodan. "The Attic-Chian Alliance ('IG' II² 34) and the 'Troubles in Greece' of the Late 380's BC." *ZPE* 133 (2000): 21–30.

Dušanić, Slobodan. "Isocrates, the Chian Intellectuals, and the Political Context of the Euthydemus." *JHS* 119 (1999): 1–16.

Dusinberre, Elspeth R. M. *Aspects of Empire in Achaemenid Sardis*. Cambridge: Cambridge University Press, 2003.

Dusinberre, Elspeth R. M. *Empire, Authority, and Autonomy in Achaemenid Anatolia*. Cambridge: Cambridge University Press, 2013.

Eddy, Samuel K. "The Cold War between Athens and Persia, ca. 448–412 B.C." *CPh* 68, no. 4 (1973): 241–58.

Eddy, Samuel K. "Some Irregular Amounts of Athenian Tribute." *AJPh* 94, no. 1 (1973): 47–70.

Edmonds, John M. *Fragments of Attic Comedy I*. Leiden: Brill, 1957.

Ehrhardt, Norbert. "Didyma und Milet in archaischer Zeit." *Chiron* 28 (1998): 11–20.

Ellis, J. R. *Philip II and Macedonian Imperialism*. London: Thames and Hudson, 1976.

Ellis-Evans, Aneurin. *The Kingdom of Priam: Lesbos and the Troad*. Oxford: Oxford University Press, 2019.

Ellis-Evans, Aneurin. "Mytilene, Lampsakos, Chios and the Financing of the Spartan Fleet (406–404)." *NC* 176 (2016): 1–19.

Elsner, Jas. "Visual Culture and Ancient History: Issues of Empiricism and Ideology in the Samos Stele at Athens." *CA* 34, no. 1 (2015): 33–73.

Emlyn-Jones, C. J. *The Ionians and Hellenism: A Study of the Cultural Achievement of Early Greek Inhabitants of Asia Minor*. New York: Routledge, 1980.

Engels, Donald W. *Alexander the Great and the Logistics of the Macedonian Army*. Berkeley: University of California Press, 1980.

Engen, Darel Tai. *Honor and Profit: Athenian Trade Policy and the Economy and Society of Greece, 415–307 BCE*. Ann Arbor: University of Michigan Press, 2010.

Eran, Kenan. "Ionian Sanctuaries and the Mediterranean World in the 7th Century B.C." In *SOMA 2011*, vol. 1, edited by Pietro Maria Militello and Hakan Öniz, 321–27. Oxford: Archaeopress, 2015.

Erickson, Kyle. "Seleucus I, Zeus and Alexander." In *Every Inch a King: Comparative Studies on Kings and Kingship in the Ancient and Medieval Worlds*, edited by Lynette G. Mitchell and Charles Melville, 109–27. Leiden: Brill, 2013.

Errington, R. Malcolm. "Diodorus Siculus and the Chronology of the Early Diadochoi, 320–311 B.C." *Hermes* 105, no. 4 (1977): 478–504.

Errington, R. Malcolm. "From Babylon to Triparadeisos: 323–320 B.C." *JHS* 90 (1970): 49–77.

Errington, R. Malcolm. *A History of the Hellenistic World*. Malden, MA: Blackwell, 2008.

Errington, R. Malcolm. "Macedonian Royal Style and Its Historical Significance." *JHS* 94 (1974): 20–37.

Errington, R. Malcolm. "Samos and the Lamian War." *Chiron* 5 (1975): 51–57.

Ersoy, Yasar E. "Pottery Production and Mechanism of Workshops in Archaic Clazomenae." In *Greichische Keramik im kulturellen Kontext*, edited by Bernard Schmaltz and Magdalene Söldner, 254–57. Muenster: Scriptorium, 2003.

Evans, J. A. S. "Herodotus 9.73.3 and the Publication Date of the Histories." *CPh* 82, no. 3 (1987): 226–28.

Evans, J. A. S. "Herodotus' Publication Date." *Athenaeum* 57 (1979): 145–49.

Evans, J. A. S. "Histiaeus and Aristagoras: Notes on the Ionian Revolt." *AJPh* 84, no. 2 (1963): 113–28.

Faraguna, Michele. "Alexander and the Greeks." In *Brill's Companion to Alexander the Great*, edited by Joseph Roisman, 99–130. Leiden: Brill, 2003.

Faraguna, Michele. "Alexander the Great and Asia Minor: Conquest and Strategies of

Legitimation." In *The Legitimation of Conquest*, edited by Kai Trampedach and Alexander Meeus, 243–61. Stuttgart: Franz Steiner Verlag, 2020.

Fauber, C. M. "Was Kerkyra a Member of the Second Athenian League?" *CQ²* 48, no. 1 (1998), 110–16.

Faulkner, Caroline. "Astyochus, Sparta's Incompetent Navarch?" *Phoenix* 53, nos. 3–4 (1999): 206–21.

Federico, Eduardo. "Ioni senza *malakie*: Chio, Erodoto e la rivolta ionica." *Erga-Logoi* 5, no. 2 (2017): 95–112.

Ferla, Kleopatra, ed. *Priene²*. Cambridge, MA: Harvard University Press, 2005.

Ferraioli, Ferdinando. "Tradizioni sull'autoctonia nelle città ioniche d'Asia." *Erga-Logoi* 5, no. 2 (2017): 113–22.

Figueira, Thomas J. "Archaic Naval Warfare." *Historika* 5 (2015): 499–515.

Figueira, Thomas J. *The Power of Money: Coinage and Politics in the Athenian Empire*. Philadelphia: University of Pennsylvania Press, 1998.

Flensted-Jensen, Pernille. "Caria." In *An Inventory of Archaic and Classical Poleis*, edited by Mogens Herman Hansen and Thomas Heine Nielsen, 1108–137. Oxford: Oxford University Press, 2004.

Flower, Michael A. "Agesilaus of Sparta and the Origins of the Ruler Cult." *CQ²* 38, no. 1 (1988): 123–34.

Flower, Michael A. *Theopompus of Chios: History and Rhetoric in the Fourth Century BC*. Oxford: Oxford University Press, 1994.

Fogazza, Giovanni. "Per una storia della lega ionica." *La Parola del Passato* 28 (1973): 157–69.

Fontenrose, Joseph. *Didyma: Apollo's Oracle, Cult, and Companions*. Berkeley: University of California Press, 1988.

Fornara, Charles W. *The Athenian Board of Generals from 501 to 404*. Stuttgart: Franz Steiner, 1971.

Fornara, Charles W. "The Date of the 'Regulations for Miletus.'" *AJPh* 92, no. 3 (1971): 473–75.

Fornara, Charles W. "Evidence for the Date of Herodotus' Publication." *JHS* 91 (1971): 25–34.

Fornara, Charles W. "Herodotus' Knowledge of the Archidamian War." *Hermes* 109, no. 2 (1981): 149–56.

Fornara, Charles W. "*IG* I², 39.52–57 and the 'Popularity' of the Athenian Empire." *CSCA* 10 (1977): 39–55.

Fornara, Charles W. and David M. Lewis. "On the Chronology of the Samian War." *JHS* 99 (1979): 7–19.

Forsdyke, Sara. *Exile, Ostracism, and Democracy: The Politics of Expulsion in Ancient Greece*. Princeton, NJ: Princeton University Press, 2005.

Fredericksen, Rune. *Archaic City Walls of the Archaic Period, 900–480 BCE*. Oxford: Oxford University Press, 2011.

French, A. "Athenian Ambitions and the Delian Alliance." *Phoenix* 33, no. 2 (1979): 134–41.

French, A. *The Athenian Half-Century 478–431 BC*. Sydney: Sydney University Press, 1971.

French, David. "Pre- and Early-Roman Roads of Asia Minor: The Persian Royal Road." *Iran* 36 (1998): 15–43.

Gargola, Daniel J. "Grain Distributions and the Revenue of the Temple of Hera on Samos." *Phoenix* 46, no. 1 (1992): 12–28.

Gehrke, Hans-Joachim. *Stasis: Untersuchungen zu den inneren Kriegen in den grieschen Staaten des 5. und 4. Jahrhunderts v. Chr.* Munich: Hans Beck, 1985.

Georges, Pericles. "Persian Ionia under Darius: The Revolt Reconsidered." *Historia* 49, no. 1 (2000): 1–39.

Gezgin, Ismail. "The Localization Problems of Erythrae's Hinterland." Translated by A. Aykurt. *Arkeoloji Dergisi* 14, no. 2 (2009): 95–108.

Giovannini, Adalberto. "Le Parthenon, le Tresor d'Athena et le tribut des allies." *Historia* 39, no. 2 (1990): 129–48.

Goldman, Tristan A. "Imperializing Hegemony: The Polis and Achaemenid Persia." PhD diss., University of Washington, 2011.

Gomme, A. W., A. Andrewes, and J. K. Dover, *A Historical Commentary on Thucydides.* 5 vols. Oxford: Oxford University Press, 1945–81.

Gonnet, Hatice, J. D. Hawkins, and Jean-Pierre Grélois. "Remarques sur un article recent relative a Telibinu et a Apollon Fondateurs." *Anatolica* 27 (2001): 191–97.

Gorman, Robert J. and Vanessa B. Gorman. *Corrupting Luxury in Ancient Greek Literature.* Ann Arbor: University of Michigan Press, 2014.

Gorman, Vanessa B. *Miletos, the Ornament of Ionia.* Ann Arbor: University of Michigan Press, 2001.

Goukowsky, Paul. *Essai sur les origins du mythe d'Alexandre.* Vol 1, *Les origins politiques.* Nancy: University of Nancy, 1978.

Graf, Fritz. *Nordionische Kulte: Religionsgeschichtliche und epigraphische Untersuchungen zu den Kulten von Chios, Erythrai, Klazomenai und Phokaia.* Rome: Schweizerisches Institut in Rom, 1985.

Graham, A. J. "Abdera and Teos." *JHS* 112 (1992): 44–73.

Graham, A. J. "'Adopted Teians:' A Passage in the New Inscription of Public Imprecations from Teos." *JHS* 111 (1991): 176–78.

Grainger, John D. *Seleukos Nikator: Constructing a Hellenistic Kingdom.* New York: Routledge, 1990.

Gray, Vivienne J. "Two Different Approaches to the Battle of Sardis in 395 B.C." *California Studies in Classical Antiquity* 12 (1979): 183–200.

Greaves, Alan M. "Dionysius of Halicarnassus, *Antiquitates Romane* 2.30 and Herodotus 1.146." *CQ²* 48, no. 2 (1998): 572–74.

Greaves, Alan M. "Divination at Archaic Branchidai-Didyma." *Hesperia* 81, no. 2 (2012): 177–206.

Greaves, Alan M. *The Land of Ionia: Society and Economy in the Archaic Period.* Malden, MA: Wiley-Blackwell, 2010.

Greaves, Alan M. "Milesians in the Black Sea: Trade, Settlement, and Religion." In *The Black Sea in Antiquity*, edited by Vincent Gabrielsen and John Lund, 9–21. Aarhus: Aarhus University Press, 2007.

Greaves, Alan M. *Miletos: A History.* New York: Routledge, 2002.

Greaves, Alan M., John Brendan Knight, and Françoise Rutland. "Milesian élite responses to Persia: The Ionian Revolt in Context." *Hermathena* 204–5 (2020): 68–147.

Green, Peter. *Alexander of Macedon*. Berkeley: University of California Press, 1992.

Green, Peter. *The Greco-Persian Wars*. Reprint ed. Berkeley: University of California Press, 1996.

Green, Peter. "Politics, Philosophy, and Propaganda: Hermias of Atarneus and His Friendship with Aristotle." In *Crossroads of History: The Age of Alexander the Great*, edited by Waldemar Heckel and Lawrence A. Tritle, 29–46. Claremont, CA: Regina Books, 2003.

Griffith, G. T. "Athens in the Fourth Century." In *Imperialism in the Ancient World*, edited by P. D. A. Garnsey and C. R. Whittaker, 127–44. Cambridge: Cambridge University Press, 1978.

Guth, Dina. "The 'Rise and Fall' of Archaic Miletus." *Historia* 66, no. 1 (2017): 2–20.

Habicht, Christian. "Athens, Samos, and Alexander the Great." *PAPS* 140, no. 3 (1996): 397–405.

Habicht, Christian. "Der Beitrag zur Restitution von Samos während des Iamischen Krieges (Ps. Aristoteles, Ökonomik II, 2.9)." *Chiron* 5 (1975): 45–50.

Habicht, Christian. "Hellenistische Inschriften aus dem Heraion von Samos." *MDAI(A)* 87 (1972): 191–228.

Habicht, Christian. "Samische Volksbeschlüsse der hellenistischen Zeit." *MDAI(A)* 72 (1957): 152–274.

Hadji, Athena and Zoe Kontes. "The Athenian Coinage Decree: Inscriptions, Coins and Athenian Politics." In *Proceedings of the XIII Congress of International Numismatics*, edited by Carmen Alfaro Asins, Carmen Marcos Alonso, and Paloma Otero Morán, 263–68. Madrid: Ministerio de Cultura, Secretería General Técnica, 2005.

Hall, Edith. *Inventing the Barbarian: Greek Self-Definition through Tragedy*. Oxford: Oxford University Press, 1989.

Hall, Jonathan. "Ancient Greek Ethnicities: Towards a Reassessment." *BICS* 58, no. 2 (2015): 15–29.

Hall, Jonathan. *Hellenicity: Between Ethnicity and Culture*. Chicago: University of Chicago Press, 2002.

Hallock, Richard T. *Persepolis Fortification Tablets*. Chicago: University of Chicago Press, 1969.

Hamilton, Charles D. *Agesilaus and the Failure of the Spartan Hegemony*. Ithaca, NY: Cornell University Press, 1991.

Hamilton, Charles D. "Spartan Politics and Policy, 405–401 B.C." *AJPh* 91, no. 3 (1970): 294–314.

Hamilton, Charles D. *Sparta's Bitter Victories: Politics and Diplomacy in the Corinthian War*. Ithaca, NY: Cornell University Press, 1979.

Hamilton, J. R. "Alexander and His 'So-Called' Father." *CQ*² 3, nos. 3–4 (1953): 151–57.

Hamilton, J. R. *Plutarch, Alexander: A Commentary*. Oxford: Oxford University Press, 1969.

Hammond, N. G. L. "Alexander's Letter Concerning Samos in Plut. 'Alex.' 28.2." *Historia* 42, no. 3 (1993): 379–82.

Hammond, N. G. L. "The Branchidae at Didyma and in Sogdiana." *CQ*² 48, no. 2 (1998): 339–44.

Hammond, N. G. L. "Inscriptions concerning Philippi and Calindoea in the Reign of Alexander the Great." *ZPE* 92 (1990): 167–75.

Hammond, N. G. L. "The King and the Land in the Macedonian Kingdom." *CQ*² 38, no. 2 (1988): 382–91.

Hammond, N. G. L. "A Note on Badian 'Alexander and Philippi,' *ZPE* 95 (1993) 131–9." *ZPE* 97 (1995): 385–87.

Hammond, N. G. L. *Three Historians of Alexander the Great: The So-Called Vulgate Authors, Diodorus, Justin, and Curtius.* Cambridge: Cambridge University Press, 1983.

Hammond, N. G. L. and G. T. Griffith. *A History of Macedonia.* Vol. 2. Oxford: Oxford University Press, 1979.

Hardwick, N. M. M. "The Coinage of Chios, 6th–4th century BC." In *Proceedings of the XI International Numismatic Congress,* edited by Catherine Courtois, Harry Dewit, and Véronique Van Driessche, 211–22. Louvain: Séminaire de Numismatique Marcel Hoc, 1993.

Hardwick, N. M. M. "The Coinage of Chios from the Sixth to the Fourth Century B.C." PhD diss., Oxford University, 1991.

Hatzopoulos, Miltiades B. "Épigraphie et villages en Grèce du Nord: *Ethnos, polis* et *kome* en Macédoine." In *L'epigrafia del villaggio,* edited by Alda Calbi, Angela Donati, and Gabriella Poma, 151–71. Faenza: Fratelli Lega, 1993.

Hatzopoulos, Miltiades B. "La letter royale d'Olévéne." *Chiron* 25 (1995): 163–85.

Hatzopoulos, Miltiades B. "The Olveni Inscription and the Date of Philip II's Reign." In *Philip II, Alexander the Great and the Macedonian Heritage,* edited by W. Lindsay Adams and Eugene N. Borza, 21–42. Lanham, MD: University Press of America, 1982.

Hatzopoulos, Miltiades B. "Perception of the Self and the Other: The Case of Macedonia." In *Ancient Macedonia,* vol. 7, 51–66. Thessaloniki: Institute for Balkan Studies, 2007.

Hauben, Hans. "The First War of the Successors (321 B.C.): Chronological and Historical Problems." *Anc. Soc.* 8 (1977): 85–119.

Hausoullier, Bernard. *Études sur l'histoire de Milet et du Didymeion.* Paris: Librairie Emile Bouillon, 1902.

Heckel, Waldemar. *The Conquests of Alexander the Great.* Cambridge: Cambridge University Press, 2008.

Heckel, Waldemar. *Marshals of Alexander's Empire.* New York: Routledge, 1992.

Heckel, Waldemar. *Who's Who in the Age of Alexander the Great.* New York: Routledge, 2005.

Heisserer, A. J. *Alexander and the Greeks: The Epigraphic Evidence.* Norman: University of Oklahoma Press, 1980.

Heisserer, A. J. "The Philites Stele (*SIG*³ 284 = *IEK* 503)." *Hesperia* 48, no. 3 (1979): 281–93.

Held, Winifried. "Zur Datierung des klassischen Athenatempels in Milet." *AA,* no. 1 (2004): 123–27.

Henry, Madeleine M. *Prisoner of History: Aspasia of Miletus and Her Biographical Tradition.* Oxford: Oxford University Press, 1995.

Herda, Alexander. "Copy and Paste? Miletos before and after the Persian Wars." In *Reconstruire les villes: Modes, motifs et récits,* edited by Emmanuelle Capet, C. Dogniez, M. Gorea, R. Koch Piettre, F. Mass, and H. Rouillard-Bonraisin, 91–120. Turnhout: Brepols, 2019.

Herda, Alexander. *Der Apollon-Delphinios-Kult in Milet und die Neujahrsprozession nach Didyma*. Darmstadt: Verlag Philipp von Zabern, 2006.

Herda, Alexander. "Greek (and Our) Views on the Karians." In *Luwian Identities: Culture, Language and Religion between Anatolia and the Aegean*, edited by Alice Mouton, Ian Rutherford, and Ilya Yakubovich, 421–505. Leiden: Brill, 2013.

Herda, Alexander. "How to Run a State Cult." In *Current approaches to religion in ancient Greece*, ed. Matthew Haysom and Jenny Wallensten, 57–93. Stockholm: Stockholm Universitet, 2011.

Herda, Alexander, Helmut Brückner, Marc Müllenhoff, and Maria Knipping. "From the Gulf of Latmos to Lake Bafa: On the History, Geoarchaeology, and Palynology of the Lower Maeander Valley at the Foot of the Latmos Mountains." *Hesperia* 88, no. 1 (2019): 1–86.

Higgins, W. E. "Aspects of Alexander's Imperial Administration: Some Modern Methods and Views Reviewed." *Athenaeum* 68 (1980): 129–52.

Hignett, Charles. *Xerxes' Invasion of Greece*. Oxford: Oxford University Press, 1963.

Hill, David. "Conceptualising Interregional Relations in Ionia and Central-West Anatolia from the Archaic to the Hellenistic Period." In *Bordered Places, Bounded Times: Cross-Disciplinary Perspectives on Turkey*, edited by Emma L. Baysal and Leonidas Karakatsanis, 85–96. Ankara: British Institute at Ankara, 2017.

Hoepfner, Wolfram. "Old and New Priene—Pythius and Aristotle." In *Priene²*, edited by Kleopatra Ferla, 29–47. Cambridge, MA: Harvard University Press, 2005.

Holladay, A. J. "The Hellenic Disaster in Egypt." *JHS* 109 (1989), 176–82.

Hollinshead, Mary B. *Shaping Ceremony: Monumental Steps and Greek Architecture*. Madison: University of Wisconsin Press, 2014.

Hornblower, Simon. "Asia Minor." In *Cambridge Ancient History²*, vol. 6, edited by David M. Lewis, John Boardman, Simon Hornblower, and Martin Ostwald, 209–33. Cambridge: Cambridge University Press, 1994.

Hornblower, Simon. *A Commentary on Thucydides*. 3 vols. Oxford: Oxford University Press, 1997–2008.

Hornblower, Simon. "Λιχας καλος Σαμιος." *Chiron* 32 (2002): 237–46.

Hornblower, Simon. *Mausolus*. Oxford: Oxford University Press, 1982.

Hornblower, Simon. "Persia." In *Cambridge Ancient History²*, vol. 6, edited by David M. Lewis, John Boardman, Simon Hornblower, and Martin Ostwald, 45–96. Cambridge: Cambridge University Press, 1994.

Hornblower, Simon. "Thucydides, the Panionian Festival, and the Ephesia (III 104)." *Historia* 31, no. 2 (1982): 241–45.

Horster, Marietta. "Priene: Civic Priests and Koinon-Priesthoods in the Hellenistic Period." In *Cities and Priests in Asia Minor and the Aegean Islands from the Hellenistic to the Imperial Period*, edited by Marietta Horster and Anja Klöckner, 177–208. Berlin: de Gruyter, 2013.

How, W. W. and J. Wells. *A Commentary on Herodotus*. Vol. 1. Oxford: Oxford University Press, 1989.

Howe, Tim. "The Diadochi, Invented Tradition, and Alexander's Expedition to Siwah."

In *After Alexander*, edited by Victor Alonso Tronscoso and Edward M. Anson, 57–70. Oxford: Oxford University Press, 2013.

Howgego Christopher. *Ancient History from Coins*. New York: Routledge, 1995.

Hurwit, Jeffrey M. *The Acropolis in the Age of Pericles*. Cambridge: Cambridge University Press, 2004.

Huxley, George. "Choirilos of Samos." *GRBS* 10, no. 1 (1969): 12–29.

Hyland, John. "The Aftermath of Aegospotamoi and the Decline of Spartan Naval Power." *AHB* 33 (2019): 19–41.

Hyland, John. *Persian Interventions: The Achaemenid Empire, Athens, and Sparta, 450–386 BCE*. Baltimore, MD: Johns Hopkins University Press, 2018.

Hyland, John. "Thucydides' Portrait of Tissaphernes Re-examined." In *Persian Responses*, edited by Christopher Tuplin, 1–25. Swansea: Classical Press of Wales, 2007.

Irwin, Elizabeth. "Herodotus and Samos: Personal or Political." *CW* 102, no. 4 (2009): 395–416.

Isaac, Benjamin H. *The Greek Settlements in Thrace until the Macedonian Conquest*. Leiden: Brill, 1986.

Jackson, A. H. "The Original Purpose of the Delian League." *Historia* 18, no. 1 (1969): 12–16.

Jeffery, L. H. *The Local Scripts of Archaic Greece*. Rev. ed. Oxford: Oxford University Press, 1990.

Jeffrey, L. H. and Paul Cartledge. "Sparta and Samos: A Special Relationship?" *CQ²* 32, no. 2 (1982): 243–65.

Jehne, Martin. *Koine Eirene: Untersuchungen zu den Befriedungs- und Stabilisierungsbemühungen in der griechischen Poliswelt des 4. Jahrhunderts v. Chrs*. Stuttgart: Franz Steiner Verlag, 1994.

Jensen, Erik. *The Greco-Persian Wars: A Short History with Documents*. Indianapolis, IN: Hackett, 2021.

Jensen, Sean R. "Rethinking Athenian Imperialism." PhD diss., Rutgers University, 2010.

Jensen, Sean R. "*Synteleia* and *Apotaxis* on the Athenian Tribute Lists." In *Hegemonic Finances: Funding Athenian Domination in the 5th and 4th Centuries BC*, edited by Thomas J. Figueira and Sean R. Jensen, 55–77. London: Bloomsbury, 2019.

Jensen, Sean R. "Tribute and *Syntely* at Erythrai." *CW* 105, no. 4 (2012): 479–96.

Kagan, Donald. *The Archidamian War*. Ithaca, NY: Cornell University Press, 1990.

Kagan, Donald. *The Fall of the Athenian Empire*. Ithaca, NY: Cornell University Press, 1987.

Kagan, Donald. *The Outbreak of the Peloponnesian War*. Ithaca, NY: Cornell University Press, 1969.

Kahn, Daniel. "Inaros' Rebellion against Artaxerxes I and the Athenian Disaster in Egypt." *CQ²* 58, no. 2 (2008): 424–40.

Kaletsch, Hans. "Zur lydischen Chronologie." *Historia* 7, no. 1 (1958): 1–47.

Kallet, Lisa. "Democracy, Empire and Epigraphy in the Twentieth Century." In *Interpreting the Athenian Empire*, edited by John Ma, Nicholaos Papazarkadas, and Robert Parker, 43–66. London: Duckworth, 2009.

Kallet, Lisa. "Did Tribute Fund the Parthenon?" *CA* 8, no. 2 (1989): 252–66.

Kallet, Lisa. "Epigraphic Geography: The Tribute Quota Fragments Assigned to 421/0–415/4 B.C." *Hesperia* 73, no. 4 (2004): 465–96.

Kallet, Lisa. "Iphikrates, Timotheos, and Athens, 371–360 B.C." *GRBS* 24, no. 3 (1983): 239–52.

Kallet, Lisa. *Money and Corrosion of Power in Thucydides: The Sicilian Expedition and Its Aftermath*. Berkeley: University of California Press, 2001.

Kallet-Marx, Robert Morestein. "Athens, Thebes, and the Foundation of the Second Athenian League." *CA* 4, no. 2 (1985): 127–51.

Kalua, Fetson. "Homi Bhabha's Third Space and African Identity." *Journal of African Cultural Studies* 21, no. 1 (2009): 23–32.

Kaplan, Philip. "Dedications to Greek Sanctuaries by Foreign Kings in the Eighth through Sixth Centuries BCE." *Historia* 55, no. 2 (2006): 129–52.

Karavites, Peter. "Enduring Problems of the Samian Revolt." *RhM* 128, no. 1 (1985): 40–56.

Karkavelias, Nikos. "Phrynichus Stratonidou Deiradiotes and the Ionia Campaign in 412 BC: Thuc. 8.25–27." *AHB* 27 (2013): 149–61.

Karwiese, Stefan. "Lysander as Herakliskos Krakonopnigon: ('Heracles the Snake-Strangler')." *NC* 140 (1980): 1–27.

Kearns, John Michael. "Greek and Lydian Evidence of Diversity, Erasure, and Convergence in Western Asia Minor." *Syllecta Classica* 14 (2003): 23–36.

Keaveney, Arthur. "The Attack on Naxos: A 'Forgotten Cause' of the Ionian Revolt." *CQ²* 38, no. 1 (1988): 76–81.

Kebric, Robert B. "Duris of Samos: Early Ties with Sicily." *AJA* 79, no. 1 (1975): 89.

Kebric, Robert B. *In the Shadow of Macedon, Duris of Samos*. Wiesbaden: Franz Steiner, 1977.

Keen, Antony G. "A 'Confused' Passage of Philochoros (F 149a) and the Peace of 392/1 B.C." *Historia* 44, no. 1 (1995): 1–10.

Keesling, Catherine M. *The Votive Statues on the Athenian Acropolis*. Cambridge: Cambridge University Press, 2003.

Kennedy, Rebecca Futo. "Airs, Waters, Metals, Earth: People and Environment in Archaic and Classical Greek Thought." In *The Routledge Handbook of Identity and the Environment in the Classical and Medieval Worlds*, edited by Rebecca Futo Kennedy and Molly Jones-Lewis, 9–28. New York: Routledge, 2015.

Kennedy, Rebecca Futo. *Immigrant Women in Athens: Gender, Ethnicity, and Citizenship in the Classical City*. New York: Routledge, 2014.

Kennedy, Rebecca Futo. "A Tale of Two Kings: Competing Aspects of Power in Aeschylus' Persians." *Ramus* 42, nos. 1–2 (2013): 64–88.

Kennell, Nigel M. *Ephebeia: A Register of Geek Cities with Citizen Training Systems in the Hellenistic and Roman Periods*. Zurich: Hildesheim, 2006.

Kerschner, Michael. "Die Lyder und das Artemision von Ephesos." In *Die Archäologie der ephischen Artemis: Gestalt und Ritual eines Heiligtums*, edited by Ulrike Muss, 223–33. Vienna: Phoibos, 2008.

Kerschner, Michael. "The Spatial Development of Ephesos from ca. 1000–ca. 670 BC against the Background of Other Early Iron Age Settlements in Ionia." In *Regional Stories: Towards a New Perception of the Early Greek World*, edited by Alexander Marikakis Ainian, Alexandra Alexandridou, and Xenia Charalambidou, 487–503. Volos: University of Thessaly Press, 2017.

Kholod, Maxim M. "Arr. *Ind.* 18.3–8 and the Question of the Enrollment of the Greek Cities of Asia Minor in the Corinthian League." In *Koinon Doron: Studies and Essays in Honour of Valery P. Nikonorov*, edited by Alexander A. Sinitsyn and Maxim M. Kholod, 479–82. St. Petersburg: St. Petersburg University, 2013.

Kholod, Maxim M. "The Financial Administration of Asia Minor under Alexander the Great." In *Ancient Historiography on War and Empire*, edited by Tim Howe, Sabine Müller, and Richard Stoneman, 136–48. Oxford: Oxford University Press, 2017.

Kholod, Maxim M. "The Garrisons of Alexander the Great in the Greek Cities of Asia Minor." *Eos* 97 (2010): 249–58.

Kholod, Maxim M. "Mytilene under Alexander the Great: A Way to a Democracy under the Monarchic Aegis." *Bulletin of St. Petersburg State University*[2] 55, no. 4 (2010): 36–45.

Kholod, Maxim M. "On the Dating of a New Chian Inscription concerning the Property of Returned Exiles." In *Das imperiale Rom und der hellenistische Osten*, edited by Linda-Marie Günther and Volker Grieb, 21–34. Stuttgart: Franz Steiner Verlag, 2012.

Kholod, Maxim M. "On the Financial Relations of Alexander the Great and the Greek Cities in Asia Minor." In *Ruthenia Classica Aetatis Novae*, edited by Andreas Mehr, Alexander V. Makhlayuk, and Oleg Gabelko, 83–92. Stuttgart: Franz Steiner Verlag, 2013.

Kholod, Maxim M. "On the Ionian League in the Fourth Century BC." *Studia Antiqua et Archaeologica* 26, no. 2 (2020): 199–211.

Kim, Hyun Jin. "The Invention of the 'Barbarian' in Late Sixth-Century BC Ionia." In *Ancient Ethnography*, edited by Eran Almagor and Joseph Skinner, 25–48. London: Bloomsbury, 2013.

Kinns, Philip. "The Coinage of Miletus." *NC* 146 (1986): 233–60.

Kinns, Philip. "Ionia: The Pattern of Coinage during the Last Century of the Persian Empire." *REA* 91, nos. 1–2 (1989): 183–93.

Kirbihler, François. "Territoire civique et population d'Éphèse (Ve siècle av. J.-C.-IIIe siècle apr. J.-C.)." In *L'Asie Mineure dans l'Antiquité: Échanges, populations et territoires: Regards actuels sur une péninsule*, edited by Hadrien Bru, François Kirbihler, and Stéphane Lebreton, 301–33. Rennes: Presses Universitaires de Rennes, 2009.

Kirchhoff, A. "Der Delische Bund im Ersten Decennium Seines Bestehens." *Hermes* 11, no. 1 (1876): 1–48.

Knibbe, Dieter. *Ephesos-Ephesus: Geschichte einer bedeutenden antiken Stadt und Portrait einer modern Großgrabung*. Bern: Peter Lang, 1998.

Knibbe, Dieter and Bülent Iplikçioglu. "Neue Inscriften au Ephesos VIII." *JÖAI* 53 (1982): 87–150.

Kõiv, Mait. "Greek Rulers and Imperial Powers in Western Anatolia (8th-6th Centuries BC)." *Studia Antiqua et Archaeologica* 27, no. 2 (2021): 357–73.

Konecny, Andreas L. and Peter Ruggendorfer. "Alinda in Karia: The Fortifications." *Hesperia* 83, no. 4 (2014): 709–46.

Konijnendijk, Roel. "'Neither the Less Valorous nor the Weaker': Persian Military Might and the Battle of Plataia." *Historia* 61, no. 1 (2012): 1–17.

Kosmin, Paul J. *The Land of the Elephant Kings: Space, Territory, and Ideology in the Seleucid Empire*. Cambridge, MA: Harvard University Press, 2014.

Kosmin, Paul J. "A Phenomenology of Democracy: Ostracism as Political Ritual." *CA* 34, no. 1 (2015): 121–62.

Kouka, Ourania and Sergios Menelaou. "Settlement and Society in Early Bronze Age Heraion: Exploring Stratigraphy, Architecture and Ceramic Innovation after Mid-3rd Millennium BC." In *Pottery Technologies and Sociocultural Connections between the Aegean and Anatolia during the 3rd Millennium BC*, edited by Eva Alram-Stern and Barbara Horejs, 119–42. Vienna: Austrian Academy of Sciences Press, 2018.

Kowalzig, Barbara. "Mapping Out *Communitas*: Performances of *Theoria* in Their Sacred and Political Context." In *Pilgrimage in Graeco-Roman and Early Christian Antiquity: Seeing the Gods*, edited by Jas Elsner and Ian Rutherford, 41–72. Oxford: Oxford University Press, 2005.

Krentz, Peter. *Xenophon: Hellenika II.3.11–IV.2.8*. Warminster: Aris & Phillips, 1995.

Kroll, John H. and Alan S. Walker. *The Athenian Agora: Results of Excavations Conducted by the American School of Classical Studies in Athens, vol. 26: The Greek Coins*. Princeton: The American School of Classical Studies at Athens, 1993.

LaBuff, Jeremy. *Polis Expansion and Elite Power in Hellenistic Caria*. Lanham, MD: Lexington Books, 2015.

Ladstätter, Sabine. "Ephesus." In *Spear Won Land: Sardis from the King's Peace to the Peace of Apamea*, edited by Andrea M. Berlin and Paul J. Kosmin, 191–204. Madison: University of Wisconsin Press, 2019.

Lane Fox, Robin. "Theopompus of Chios and the Greek World." In *Chios: A Conference at the Homerion in Chios*, edited by John Boardman and C. E. Vaphopoulou-Richardson, 105–20. Oxford: Oxford University Press, 1986.

Lanfranchi, Giovanni B. "The Ideological and Political Impact of the Assyrian Imperial Expansion on the Greek World in the 8th and 7th Centuries BC." In *The Heirs of Assyria*, edited by Sanna Aro and R. M. Whiting, 7–34. Helsinki: Neo-Assyrian Text Corpus Project, 2000.

Larguinat-Turbatte, Gabrièle. "Les premiers temps d'Arsinoeia-Éphèse: Étude d'une composition urbaine royale (début du IIIᵉ S.)." *REA* 116, no. 2 (2014): 465–91.

Larson, Jennifer. "Review: *The Mysteries of Artemis of Ephesos*." *AHR* 120, no. 2 (2015): 692.

Lateiner, Donald. "The Failure of the Ionian Revolt." *Historia* 31, no. 2 (1982): 129–60.

Lawall, Mark. "Ceramics and Positivism Revisited: Greek Transport Amphoras and History." In *Trade, Traders and the Ancient City*, edited by Helen Parkins and Christopher Smith, 75–101. New York: Routledge, 1998.

Lazenby, John F. *The Defense of Greece, 490–479 B.C.* Warminster: Aris & Phillips, 1993.

Lazenby, John F. *The Peloponnesian War: A Military Study*. New York: Routledge, 2004.

Lecoq, Pierre. *Les Inscriptions de la Perse achéménide*. Paris: Gallimard, 1997.

Lee, John W. I. "Tissaphernes and the Achaemenid Defense of Western Anatolia, 412–395 BC." In *Circum Mare: Themes in Ancient Warfare*, edited by Jeremy Armstrong, 262–81. Leiden: Brill, 2016.

Legon, Ronald P. "Samos in the Delian League." *Historia* 21, no. 2 (1972): 145–58.

Lehmann, Gustav Adolf. *Alexander der Große und die "Freiheit der Hellenen"*. Berlin: de Gruyter, 2015.

Leloux, Kevin. "The Campaign of Croesus against Ephesus: Historical and Archaeological Considerations." *Polemos* 21, no. 2 (2018): 47–63.

Lenfant, Dominique. "Les designations des Grecs d'Asie à l'époque Classique, entre ethnicité et jeux politiques." *Erga-Logoi* 2, no. 2 (2017): 15–33.

Lenschau, Thomas. "Alexander der Grosse und Chios." *Klio* 33 (1940): 201–24.

Leonard, Albert, Jr. "Ancient Naukratis: Excavations at a Greek Emporium in Egypt, Part I: The Excavations at Kom Ge'if." *AASOR* 54 (1997): v–vii + ix–xxi + 1–375 + 377–415.

Lévy, Edmond. "Les trois traités entre Sparte et le roi." *BCH* 107, no. 1 (1983): 221–41.

Lewis, David M. "The Athenian Coinage Decree." In *Coinage and Administration in the Athenian and Persian Empires*, edited by Ian Carradice, 53–63. Oxford: Oxford University Press, 1987.

Lewis, David M. "The Athenian Tribute-Quota Lists, 453–450." *ABSA* 89 (1994): 285–301.

Lewis, David M. *Sparta and Persia*. Leiden: Brill, 1977.

Lewis, David M. "Sparta as Victor." In *Cambridge Ancient History²*, vol. 6, edited by David M. Lewis, John Boardman, Simon Hornblower, and Martin Ostwald, 24–44. Cambridge: Cambridge University Press, 1994.

Lewis, David M. "Temple Inventories in Ancient Greece." In *Pots and Pans*, edited by M. Vickers, 71–81. Oxford: Oxford University Press, 1986.

Lewis, David M. *Greek Slave Systems in Their Eastern Mediterranean Context, c. 800–146 BC*. Oxford: Oxford University Press, 2018.

Lewis, David M. "Near Eastern Slaves in Classical Attica and the Slave Trade with Persian Territories." *CQ²* 61, no. 1 (2011): 91–113.

LiDonnici, Lynn R. "The Images of Artemis Ephesia and Greco-Roman Worship: A Reconsideration." *HThR* 85, no. 4 (1992): 389–415.

Linders, Tulia. "Sacred Finances: Some Observations." In *Economics of Cult in the Ancient World*, edited by Tulia Linders and Brita Alroth, 9–12. Stockholm: Almquist and Wicksell, 1992.

Liuzzo, Pietro Maria. "L'arrivo di Temistocle in Persia e la successione a Serse: Il breve regno di Artabano." *Rivista storica dell'antichità* 40 (2010): 33–50.

Llewellyn-Jones, Lloyd and James Robson. *Ctesias' History of Persia: Tales of the Orient*. New York: Routledge, 2009.

Lohmann, Hans. "The Discovery and Excavation of the Archaic Panionion in the Mycale (Dilek Daglari)." *Kazı Sonuçları Toplantısı* 28 (2007): 575–90.

Lohmann, Hans. "Ionians and Carians in the Mycale: The Discovery of Carian Melia and the Archaic Panionion in the Mycale." In *Landscape, Ethnicity and Identity in the Archaic Mediterranean Area*, edited by Gabriele Cigani and Simon Stoddart, 32–50. Oxford: Oxford University Press, 2011.

Lohmann, Hans. "Miletus after the Disaster of 494 B.C." In *The Destruction of Cities in the Ancient Greek World*, edited by Sylvian Fachard and Edward M. Harris, 50–69. Cambridge: Cambridge University Press, 2021.

Lombardo, Mario. "Osservazioni cronologiche e storiche sul regno di Sadiatte." *ASNP* 10, no. 2 (1980): 307–62.

Loomis, William T. *The Spartan War Fund: IG V 1, 1 and a New Fragment*. Stuttgart: Franz Steiner, 1992.

Low, Polly. "Peace, Common Peace, and War in Mid-Fourth-Century Greece." In *Maintaining Peace and Interstate Stability in Archaic and Classical Greece*, edited by Julia Wilker, 118–34. Mainz: Verlag Antike, 2012.

Lund, Helen S. *Lysimachus: A Study in Early Hellenistic Kingship*. New York: Routledge, 1992.

Lupi, Marcello. "Il duplice massacro dei 'geomoroi.'" In *Da Elea a Samo: Filosofi e politici di fronte all'impero ateniese*, edited by Luisa Breglia and Marcello Lupi, 259–86. Naples: Arte Tipografica Editrice, 2005.

Ma, John. "Afterword: Whither the Athenian Empire?" In *Interpreting the Athenian Empire*, edited by John Ma, Nikolaos Papazarkadas, and Robert Parker, 223–30. London: Duckworth, 2009.

Ma, John. "Empires, Statuses and Realities." In *Interpreting the Athenian Empire*, edited by John Ma, Nikolaos Papazarkadas, and Robert Parker, 125–48. London: Duckworth, 2009.

Ma, John. "Fighting Poleis of the Hellenistic World." In *War and Violence in Ancient Greece*, edited by Hans van Wees, 337–76. London: Duckworth, 2000.

Ma, John. "A Gilt Statue for Konon at Erythrae?" *ZPE* 157 (2006): 124–26.

Ma, John. *Statues and Cities: Honorific Portraits and Civic Identity in the Hellenistic World*. Oxford: Oxford University Press, 2013.

Ma, John. "Une culture militaire en Asie Mineure hellénistique?" In *Les cités grecques en Asie Mineure à l'époque hellénistique*, edited by Jean-Christophe Couvenhes and Henri-Louis Fernoux, 199–220. Tours: Presses universitaires François-Rabelais, 2004.

Mac Sweeney, Naoíse. *Foundation Myths and Politics in Ancient Ionia*. Cambridge: Cambridge University Press, 2013.

Mac Sweeney, Naoíse. "Regional Identities in the Greek World: Myth and *Koinon* in Ionia." *Historia* 70, no. 3 (2021): 268–314.

Mac Sweeney, Naoíse. "Separating Fact from Fiction in the Ionian Migration." *Hesperia* 86, no. 3 (2017): 379–421.

Mac Sweeney, Naoíse. "Violence and the Ionian Migration: Representation and Reality." In *Nostoi: Indigenous Culture, Migration and Integration in the Aegean Islands and Western Anatolia during the Late Bronze Age and Early Iron Age*, edited by Çiğdem Maner and Konstantinos Kopanias, 239–66. Istanbul: Koç University Press, 2013.

MacFarlane, Kelly A. "Choerilus of Samos' Lament (SH 317) and the Revitalization of Epic." *AJPh* 130, no. 2 (2009): 219–34.

Mack, William. "Communal Interests and Polis Identity under Negotiation: Documents Depicting Sympolities between Cities Great and Small." *Topoi* 18, no. 1 (2013): 87–116.

Mack, William. *Proxeny and Polis: Institutional Networks in the Ancient Greek World*. Oxford: Oxford University Press, 2015.

Malachou, Georgia E. "A Second Facsimile of the Erythrai Decree (*IG* I³ 14)." In ΑΘΗΝΑΙΩΝ ΕΠΙΣΚΟΠΟΣ: *Studies in Honour of Harold B. Mattingly*, edited by Angelos P. Matthaiou and Robert K. Pitt, 73–96. Athens: Greek Epigraphical Society, 2014.

Manicas, Peter T. "War, Stasis, and Greek Political Thought." *Comparative Studies in Society and History* 24, no. 4 (1982): 673–88.

Manning, Joseph. *The Open Sea: The Economic Life of the Ancient Mediterranean World from the Iron Age to the Rise of Rome*. Princeton, NJ: Princeton University Press, 2018.

Manville, P. B. "Aristagoras and Histiaios: The Leadership Struggle in the Ionian Revolt." *CQ²* 27, no. 1 (1977): 80–91.

March, Duane A. "Konon and the Great King's Fleet, 396–394." *Historia* 46, no. 3 (1997): 257–69.

Marchese, Ronald T. *The Lower Maeander Flood Plain: A Regional Settlement Study*. Oxford: Oxford University Press, 1986.

Marek, Christian. *In the Land of a Thousand Gods: A History of Asia Minor in the Ancient World*. In collaboration with Peter Frei; translated by Steven Rendall. Princeton, NJ: Princeton University Press, 2016.

Marginesu G. and A. A. Themos. "Ἀνέλοσαν ἐς τὸν πρὸς Σαμίος πόλεμον: A New Fragment of the Samian War Expenses (*IG* I³ 363 + 454)." In ΑΘΗΝΑΙΩΝ ΕΠΙΣΚΟΠΟΣ: *Studies in Honour of Harold B. Mattingly*, edited by Angelos P. Matthaiou and Robert K. Pitt, 171–84. Athens: Greek Epigraphical Society, 2014.

Marksteiner, Thomas. "Bemerkungen zum hellenistischen Stadtmauerring von Ephesos." In *100 Jahre österreichische Forschungen in Ephesos*, edited by Herwig Freisinger and Fritz Krinzinger, 413–20. Vienna: Verlag der Österreichischen Akademie der Wissenschaften, 1999.

Marquand, A. "Reminiscences of Egypt in Doric Architecture." *AJA* 6, nos. 1–2 (1890): 47–58.

Mastrocinque, Attilio. *La Caria e la Ionia méridionale in epoca ellenistica* (Rome: L'Erma di Bretschneider, 1979).

Matthaiou, Angelos P. "Νέες Ἀττικές ἐπιγραφές." *Horos* 17–21 (2004–9): 11–22.

Matthaiou, Angelos P. "The Treaty of Athens with Samos (*IG* I³ 48)." In ΑΘΗΝΑΙΩΝ ΕΠΙΣΚΟΠΟΣ: *Studies in Honour of Harold B. Mattingly*, edited by Angelos P. Matthaiou and Robert K. Pitt 141–70. Athens: Greek Epigraphical Society, 2014.

Matthaiou, Angelos P. and G. A. Pikoulas. "Ἔδον Λακεδαιμονίοις ποττὸν πόλεμον." *Horos* 7 (1988): 77–124.

Matthews, Victor J. *Antimachus of Colophon: Text and Commentary*. Leiden: Brill, 1996.

Mattingly, Harold B. "The Athenian Coinage Decree." In *The Athenian Empire Restored*, 5–52. Ann Arbor: University of Michigan Press, 1996 [= *Historia* 10, no. 2 (1961): 148–88].

Mattingly, Harold M. "The Athenian Decree for Miletos (*IG* I², 22+ = *ATL* II, D 11): A Postscript." In *The Athenian Empire Restored*, 453–60. Ann Arbor: University of Michigan Press, 1996 [= *Historia* 30, no. 1 (1981): 113–17].

Mattingly, Harold B., "Chios and the Athenian Standards Decree." In *The Athenian Empire Restored*, 521. Ann Arbor: University of Michigan Press, 1996.

Mattingly, Harold B. "Coins and Amphoras: Chios, Samos and Thasos in the Fifth Century B.C." In *The Athenian Empire Restored*, 435–52. Ann Arbor: University of Michigan Press, 1996 [= *JHS* 101 (1981), 78–86].

Mattingly, Harold B. "'Epigraphically the Twenties Are Too Late . . .'" In *The Athenian Empire Restored*, 281–314. Ann Arbor: University of Michigan Press, 1996 [= *ABSA* 65 (1970): 129–49].

Mattingly, Harold B. "The Growth of Athenian Imperialism." In *The Athenian Empire Restored*, 87–106. Ann Arbor: University of Michigan Press, 1996 [= *Historia* 12, no. 3 (1963): 257–73].

Mattingly, Harold B. "New Light on the Athenian Standards Decree." in *From Coins to*

History: Selected Numismatic Studies, 24–29. Ann Arbor: University of Michigan Press, 2003 [= *Klio* 75 (1993): 99–102].

Mazoyer, Michel. "Apollon à Troie." In *Homère et l'Anatolie*, edited by Michel Mazoyer, 151–60. Paris: L'Harmattan, 2008.

Mazoyer, Michel. "Télipinu et Apollon fondateurs." *Hethitica* 14 (1999): 55–62.

McGregor, Malcolm F. *The Athenians and Their Empire*. Vancouver: UBC Press, 1987.

McInerney, Jeremy. *The Folds of Parnassos: Land and Ethnicity in Ancient Phocis*. Austin: University of Texas Press, 1999.

McNicoll, Anthony W. *Hellenistic Fortifications from the Aegean to the Euphrates*. Revised by N. P. Milner. Oxford: Oxford University Press, 1997.

Meadows, Andrew R. "A Chian Revolution." In *Nomisma: La circulation monetaire dans le monde grec antique*, edited by Thomas Faucher, Marie-Christine Marcellesi, and Olivier Picard, 273–96. Athens: Ecole française d'Athènes, 2011.

Meeus, Alexander. "Diodorus and the Chronology of the Third Diadoch War." *Phoenix* 66, nos. 1–2 (2012): 74–96.

Meeus, Alexander, "The Power Struggle of the Diadochoi in Babylon, 323 BC." *Anc. Soc.* 38 (2008): 39–83.

Mehl, Andreas. *Seleukos Nikator und sein Reich 1. Teil: Seleukos' Leben und die Entwicklung seiner Machposition*. Leuven: Peeters, 1986.

Meiggs, Russell. *The Athenian Empire*. Oxford: Oxford University Press, 1972.

Meiggs, Russell and David M. Lewis. *A Selection of Greek Historical Inscriptions*. Oxford: Oxford University Press, 1969.

Meister, Klaus. *Die Ungeschichtlichkeit des Kalliasfriedens und deren historische Folgen*. Stuttgart: Franz Steiner, 1982.

Meritt, Benjamin D. "Attic Inscriptions of the Fifth Century." *Hesperia* 14, no. 2 (1945): 61–133.

Meritt, Benjamin D. "Inscriptions of Colophon." *AJPh* 56, no. 4 (1935): 358–97.

Meritt, Benjamin D. "The Samian Revolt from Athens in 440–439 B.C." *PAPhS* 128, no. 2 (1984): 123–33.

Meritt, Benjamin D. and Allen B. West. *The Athenian Assessment of 425 B.C.* Ann Arbor: University of Michigan Press, 1934.

Metcalfe, Michael J. "Reaffirming Regional Identity: Cohesive Institutions and Local Interactions in Ionia 386–129 BC." PhD diss., University College London, 2005.

Meyer, Eyal. "The Athenian Expedition to Egypt and the Value of Ctesias." *Phoenix* 72, nos. 1–2 (2018): 43–61.

Meyer, Eyal. "The Satrap of Western Anatolia and the Greeks." PhD diss., University of Pennsylvania, 2017.

Migeotte, Léopold. "Le pain quotidian dans les cités hellénistiques: À propos des fonds permanents pour l'approvisionnement en grain." *Cahiers du Centre G. Glotz* 2 (1991): 19–41.

Migeotte, Léopold. *Les souscriptions publiques dans les cités grecques*. Paris: Editions du Sphinx, 1992.

Mikalson, Jon D. *Herodotus and Religion in the Persian Wars*. Chapel Hill: University of North Carolina Press, 2003.

Miller, Harvey F. "The Practical and Economic Background to the Greek Mercenary Explosion." *G&R* 31, no. 2 (1984): 153–60.

Miller, Margaret C. "Clothes and Identity: The Case of Greeks in Ionia c.400 BC." In *Culture, Identity and Politics in the Ancient Mediterranean World*, edited by P. J. Burton, 18–38. Canberra: Australasian Society for Classical Studies, 2013.

Mitchell, B. M. "Herodotus and Samos." *JHS* 95 (1975): 75–91.

Mitchell, Lynette G. *Greeks Bearing Gifts: The Public Use of Private Relationships in the Greek World, 435–323 BCE.* Cambridge: Cambridge University Press, 1998.

Mitchell, Lynette G. *Panhellenism and the Barbarian in Archaic and Classical Greece.* Swansea: Classical Press of Wales, 2007.

Mokrišová, Jana. "On the Move: Mobility in Southwest Anatolia and the Southeast Aegean during the Late Bronze to Early Iron Age Transition." PhD diss., University of Michigan, 2017.

Moreno, Alfonso. *Feeding the Democracy: The Athenian Grain Supply in the Fifth and Fourth Centuries BC.* Oxford: Oxford University Press, 2007.

Moretti, Jean-Charles. "Le Temple D'Apollon à Claros: État des recherches en 2007." *RA*[2] 1 (2009): 162–75.

Morgan, C. "Divination and Society at Delphi and Didyma." *Hermathena* 147 (1989): 17–42.

Morison, William S. "Theopompus of Chios (115)." In *Brill's New Jacoby*, edited by Ian Worthington. Leiden: Brill, 2016.

Moritani, K. "*Koine Eirene*: Control, Peace, and *Autonomia* in Fourth-Century Greece." In *Forms of Control and Subordination in Antiquity*, edited by Tōru Yuge and Masaoki Doi, 573–77. Leiden: Brill, 1988.

Moroo, Akiko. "The Erythrai Decrees Reconsidered: *IG* I³ 14, 15 & 16." In ΑΘΗΝΑΙΩΝ ΕΠΙΣΚΟΠΟΣ: *Studies in Honour of Harold B. Mattingly*, edited by Angelos P. Matthaiou and Robert K. Pitt, 97–120. Athens: Greek Epigraphical Society, 2014.

Morris, Sarah P. "Artemis Ephesia: A New Solution to the Enigma of Her 'Breasts'?" In *Das Kosmos der Artemis von Ephesus*, edited by Ulrike Muss, 135–51. Vienna: Österreiches Archäologisches Institut, 2001.

Morris, Sarah P. "The View from East Greece: Miletus, Samos and Ephesus." In *Debating Orientalization*, edited by Corinna Riva and Nicholas C. Vella, 66–84. Sheffield: Equinox, 2006.

Murison, C. L. "The Peace of Callias: Its Historical Context." *Phoenix* 25, no. 1 (1971): 12–31.

Murray, Oswyn. "Ο ΆΡΧΑΙΟΣ ΔΑΣΜΟΣ." *Historia* 15, no. 2 (1966): 142–56.

Murray, Oswyn. "The Ionian Revolt." In *Cambridge Ancient History*², vol. 4, edited by John Boardman, N. G. L. Hammond, David M. Lewis, and Martin Ostwald, 461–90. Cambridge: Cambridge University Press, 1988.

Muss, Ulrike. "Amber from the Artemision from Ephesus and in the Museums of Istanbul and Selçuk Ephesos." *Araştirma Sonuçları Toplantısı* 25 (2008): 13–26.

Nakamura-Moroo, Akiko. "The Attitude of Greeks in Asia Minor to Athens and Persia: The Deceleian War." In *Forms of Control and Subordination in Antiquity*, edited by Tōru Yuge and Masaoki Doi, 576–72. Leiden: Brill, 1988.

Nawotka, Krzysztof. "Apollo, the Tutelary God of the Seleucids, and Demodamas of Miletus." In *The Power of the Individual and Community in Ancient Athens and Beyond*, edited by Zosia. Archibald, 261–84. London: Bloomsbury, 2018.

Nawotka, Krzysztof. "Freedom of Greek Cities in Asia Minor in the Age of Alexander the Great." *Klio* 85, no. 1 (2003): 15–41.

Nawotka, Krzysztof. "Seleukos I and the Origin of the Seleukid Dynastic Ideology." *SCI* 36 (2017): 31–43.

Neville, J. "Was There an Ionian Revolt?" *CQ*[2] 29, no. 2 (1979): 268–75.

Nigel, Kenneth and Anton Powell. "Thibron (581)." In *Brill's New Jacoby*, edited by Ian Worthington. Leiden: Brill, 2014.

Nolte, Ferdinand. *Die historisch-politischen Voraussetzungen des Königsfriedens von 386 v. Chr.* Bamberg: Universität Frankfurt am Main, 1923.

Nudell, Joshua P. "Oracular Politics: Propaganda and Myth in the Restoration of Didyma." *AHB* 32 (2018): 44–60.

Nudell, Joshua P. "Remembering Injustice as the Perpetrator? Athenian Orators, Cultural Memory, and the Athenian Conquest of Samos." In *The Orators and Their Treatment of the Recent Past*, edited by Aggelos Kapellos, 447–63. Berlin: de Gruyter, 2022.

Nudell, Joshua P. "The War between Miletus and Samos περὶ Πριήνης (Thuc. 1.115.2; Diod. 12.27.2; and Plut. Per., 25.1)." *CQ*[2] 66, no. 2 (2016): 772–74.

Nudell, Joshua P. "'Who Cares about the Greeks Living in Asia?': Ionia and Attic Orators in the Fourth Century." *CJ* 114, no. 1 (2018): 163–90.

Nylander, Carl. *Ionians in Pasargadae: Studies in Old Persian Architecture.* Uppsala: Acta Universitatis Upsaliensis, 1970.

Nyvlt, Pavel. "Sparta and Persia between the Second and the Third Treaty in 412/411 BCE: A Chronology." *Eirene* 50, nos. 1–2 (2014): 39–60.

Occhipinti, Egidia. "Political Conflicts in Chios between the End of the 5th and the First Half of the 4th Century B.C." *AHB* 24 (2010): 23–43.

Ogden, Daniel. *The Legend of Seleucus: Kingship, Narrative and Mythmaking in the Ancient World.* Cambridge: Cambridge University Press, 2017.

Ohnesorg, Aenne and Mustafa Büyükkolanci. "Ein ionisches Kapitell mit glatten Voluten in Ephesos." *MDAI(I)* 57 (2007): 209–33.

Oliver, James Henry. "The Athenian Decree concerning Miletus in 450/49 B.C." *TAPhA* 66 (1935): 177–98.

Osborne, Michael J. "Orontes." *Historia* 22, no. 4 (1973): 515–51.

Osborne, Robin. "Archaeology and the Athenian Empire." *TAPhA* 129 (1999): 319–32.

Osborne, Robin. "Cult and Ritual: The Greek World." In *Classical Archaeology*, edited by Susan E. Alcock and Robin Osborne, 246–62. Malden, MA: Blackwell, 2007.

Ostwald, Martin. "Athens and Chalkis: A Study in Imperial Control." *JHS* 122 (2002): 134–43.

Ostwald, Martin. "*Stasis* and *Autonomia* in Samos: A Comment on an Ideological Fallacy." *SCI* 12 (1993): 51–66.

O'Sullivan, Lara. "Asander, Athens, and 'IG' II² 450: A New Interpretation." *ZPE* 119 (1997): 107–16.

O'Sullivan, Lara. *The Regime of Demetrius of Phalerum in Athens, 317–307 BCE.* Leiden: Brill, 2009.

Paarmann, Bjørn. "Aparchai and Phoroi: A New Commented Edition of the Athenian Tribute Lists and Assessment Decrees." PhD diss., University of Fribourg, 2007.

Pafford, Isabelle. "Priestly Portion vs. Cult Fees: The Finances of Greek Sanctuaries." In *Cities and Priests: Cult Personnel in Asia Minor and the Aegean Islands from the Hel-*

lenistic to the Imperial Period, edited by Marietta Horster and Anja Klöckner, 49–64. Berlin: de Gruyter, 2013.

Paganoni, Eloisa. "Priene, il *Panionion* e gli Ecatomnidi." *Aevum* 88 (2014): 37–58.

Papazarkadas, Nicolaos. "Epigraphy and the Athenian Empire: Reshuffling the Chronological Cards." In *Interpreting the Athenian Empire*, edited by John Ma, Nicolaos Papazarkadas, and Robert Parker, 67–88. London: Duckworth, 2009.

Parke, H. W. "Croesus and Delphi." *GRBS* 25, no. 3 (1984): 209–32.

Parke, H. W. "The Development of the Second Spartan Empire (405–371 B.C.)." *JHS* 50, no. 1 (1930): 37–79.

Parke, H. W. "The Massacre of the Branchidae." *JHS* 105 (1985): 59–68.

Parke, H. W. *The Oracles of Apollo in Asia Minor*. New York: Routledge, 1985.

Parker, Victor. "Ephoros (70)." In *Brill's New Jacoby*, edited by Ian Worthington. Leiden: Brill, 2016.

Parker, Victor. "Sphodrias' Raid and the Liberation of Thebes: A Study of Ephorus and Xenophon." *Hermes* 135, no. 1 (2007): 13–33.

Pascual, José. "Conon, the Persian Fleet and a Second Naval Campaign in 393 BC." *Historia* 65, no. 1 (2016): 14–30.

Patronos, Sotiris G. "Public Architecture and Civic Identity in Classical and Hellenistic Ionia." PhD diss., Oxford University, 2002.

Patterson, Cynthia B. *Pericles' Citizenship Law of 451–50 BC*. New York: Arno Press, 1981.

Patterson, Cynthia B. "Those Athenian Bastards." *CA* 9, no. 1 (1990): 40–73.

Patterson, Lee. *Kinship Myth in Ancient Greece*. Austin: University of Texas Press, 2010.

Pearson, Lionel. *The Lost Historians of Alexander the Great*. Oxford: Oxford University Press, 1960.

Pébarthe, Cristophe. "Thasos, l'empire d'Athènes et les emporia de Thrace." *ZPE* 126 (1999): 131–54.

Pedersen, Poul. "The 4th Century BC 'Ionian Renaissance' and Karian Identity." In *4th Century Karia: Defining a Karian Identity under the Hekatomnids*, edited by Olivier Henry, 33–46. Paris: De Boccard, 2013.

Peek, Werner. "Ein Seegefecht aus den Perserkriegen." *Klio* 32 (1939): 289–306.

Perlman, S. "Athenian Democracy and the Revival of Imperialistic Expansion at the Beginning of the Fourth Century B.C." *CPh* 63, no. 4 (1968): 257–67.

Perlman, S. "The Historical Example, Its Use and Importance as Political Propaganda in the Attic Orators." *SH* 7 (1961): 150–66.

Petrakos, Basile Chr. "Dédicae des AEINAYTAI d'Érétrie." *BCH* 87, no. 2 (1963): 545–47.

Piccirilli, Luigi. *Gli arbitrati interstatali Greci: Dalle origini al 338 A.C.* Pisa: Marlin, 1973.

Piejko, Francis. "Decree of the Ionian League in Honor of Antiochus I, CA 267–262 B.C." *Phoenix* 45, no. 2 (1991): 126–47.

Piejko, Francis. "The 'Second Letter' of Alexander the Great to Chios." *Phoenix* 39, no. 3 (1985): 136–47.

Piérart, Marcel. "Chios entre Athènes et Sparte: La contribution des exiles de Chios à l'effort de guerre lacédémonien pendant la guerre du Péloponèse *IG* V 1, 1+*SEG* 39, 370." *BCH* 119, no. 1 (1995): 253–82.

Pleket, H. K. "Thasos and the Popularity of the Athenian Empire." *Historia* 12, no. 1 (1963): 70–77.

Poddighe, Elisabetta. "Alexander and the Greeks." In *Alexander the Great: A New History*, edited by Waldemar Heckel and Lawrence A. Tritle, 99–120. Malden, MA: Blackwell, 2009.

Podlecki, A. J. *Perikles and His Circle*. New York: Routledge, 1998.

Pownall, Frances. "Duris of Samos (76)." In *Brill's New Jacoby*, edited by Ian Worthington. Leiden: Brill, 2016.

Prestiani Giallombardo, Anna Maria. "Philippos o Basileus: Nota a Favorin 'Corinth' 41." *QUCC*² 49 (1985): 19–27.

Pritchett, W. Kendrick. "The Transfer of the Delian Treasury." *Historia* 18, no. 1 (1969): 17–21.

Quinn, T. J. *Athens and Samos, Lesbos and Chios, 478–404 B.C.* Manchester: Manchester University Press, 1981.

Quinn, T. J. "Political Groups at Chios: 412 B.C." *Historia* 18, no. 1 (1969): 22–30.

Quinn, T. J. "Thucydides and the Unpopularity of the Athenian Empire." *Historia* 13, no. 3 (1964): 257–66.

Raccuia, Carmela. "La tradizione sull'intervento Ateniese in Egitto." *Helikon* 18–19 (1978–79): 210–27.

Ragone, Giuseppe. "Pygela/Phygela: Fra Paretimologia e storia." *Athenaeum* 84, no. 1 (1996): 341–79.

Ramage, Andrew. "King Croesus' Gold and the Coinage of Lydia." In *Licia e Lidia Prima dell'Ellenizzazione*, edited by Mauro Giorgieri, 285–90. Rome: Consiglio nazionale Della Richerche, 2003.

Ramsay, Gillian. "The Diplomacy of Seleukid Women: Apama and Stratonike." In *Seleukid Royal Women: Creation, Representation and Distortion of Hellenistic Queenship in the Seleukid Empire*, edited by Altay Coskun and Alex McAuley, 87–105. Stuttgart: Franz Steiner, 2016.

Rathbone, Dominic. "The Grain Trade and Grain Shortages in the Hellenistic East." In *Trade and Famine in Classical Antiquity*, edited by P. D. A. Garnsey and C. R. Whittaker, 45–55. Cambridge: Cambridge University Press, 1983.

Rawlings, Hunter, III. "Thucydides on the Purpose of the Delian League." *Phoenix* 31, no. 1 (1977): 1–8.

Rawlings, Louis. *The Ancient Greeks at War*. Manchester: Manchester University Press, 2007.

Reger, Gary. "The Economy." In *Companion to the Hellenistic World*, edited by Andrew Erskine, 331–53. Malden, MA: Blackwell, 2003.

Rhodes, P. J. "After the Three-Bar 'Sigma' Controversy: The History of Athenian Imperialism Reassessed." *CQ*² 58, no. 2 (2008): 503–4.

Rhodes, P. J. *Commentary on the Aristotelian Athenaion Politeia*. Rev. ed. Oxford: Oxford University Press, 1993.

Rhodes, P. J. "The Delian League to 449 B.C." In *Cambridge Ancient History*², vol. 5, edited by David M. Lewis, John Boardman, J. K. Davies, and Martin Ostwald, 34–61. Cambridge: Cambridge University Press, 1992.

Rhodes, P. J. "Milesian 'Stephanephoroi': Applying Cavaignac Correctly." *ZPE* 157 (2006): 116.

Rhodes, P. J. and Robin Osborne. *Greek Historical Inscriptions, 404–323.* Oxford: Oxford University Press, 2007.

Rhodes P. J. and Robin Osborne. *Greek Historical Inscriptions, 478–404 BC.* Oxford: Oxford University Press, 2017.

Rice, D. G. "Xenophon, Diodorus and the Year 379/8 B.C." *YCS* 24 (1975): 95–130.

Ringwood Arnold, Irene. "Festivals of Ephesus." *AJA* 76, no. 1 (1972): 17–22.

Robert, Louis. "Documents d'Asie Mineure." *BCH* 108, no. 1 (1984): 467–72.

Robert, Louis. "Sur les inscriptions d'Éphèse: Fêtes, athletes, empereurs, épigrammes." *RPh* 41 (1967): 7–84.

Robert, Louis and Jeanne Robert. "Une inscription grecque de Téos en Ionie: L'union de Téos et de Kyrbissos." *JS* (1976): 188–228.

Robertson, Noel. "Government and Society at Miletus, 525–442 B.C." *Phoenix* 41, no. 4 (1987): 356–98.

Robertson, Noel. "The Sequence of Events in the Aegean in 408 and 407 B.C." *Historia* 29, no. 3 (1980): 282–301.

Robertson, Noel. "The True Nature of the 'Delian League.'" *AJAH* 5, no. 1 (1980): 64–96.

Robertson, Noel. "The True Nature of the 'Delian League' II." *AJAH* 5, no. 2 (1980): 110–33.

Robinson, E. S. G. "The Athenian Coinage Decree and the Coinages of the Allies." *Hesperia* suppl. 8 (1949): 324–40.

Robinson, Eric W. "Thucydidean Sieges, Prosopitis, and the Hellenic Disaster in Egypt." *CW* 18, no. 1 (1999): 132–52.

Rockwell, N. *Thebes: A History.* New York: Routledge, 2019.

Roebuck, Carl. "The Economic Development of Ionia." *CPh* 48, no. 1 (1953): 9–16.

Roebuck, Carl. "The Organization of Naukratis." *CPh* 46, no. 4 (1951): 212–20.

Roebuck, Carl. "Tribal Organization in Ionia." *TAPhA* 92 (1961): 495–507.

Rogers, Guy Maclean. *The Mysteries of Artemis of Ephesos: Cult, Polis, and Change in the Graeco-Roman World.* New Haven, CT: Yale University Press, 2012.

Roisman, Joseph. *Alexander's Veterans and the Early Wars of the Successors.* Austin: University of Texas Press, 2012.

Roisman, Joseph and Ian Worthington. *Lives of the Attic Orators: Texts from Pseudo-Plutarch, Photius and the Suda.* Oxford: Oxford University Press, 2015.

Roller, Duane W. "Theokritos of Chios (760)." In *Brill's New Jacoby*, edited by Ian Worthington. Leiden: Brill, 2007.

Roller, Lynn E. "The Legend of Midas." *CA* 2, no. 2 (1983): 299–313.

Romeo, Ilaria. "The Panhellenion and Ethnic Identity in Hadrianic Greece." *CPh* 97, no. 1 (2002): 21–40.

Romm, James. *Ghost on the Throne: The Death of Alexander the Great and the Bloody Fight for His Empire.* New York: Vintage Books, 2011.

Romm, James. *Herodotus.* New Haven, CT: Yale University Press, 1998.

Roosevelt, Christopher H. *The Archaeology of Lydia, from Gyges to Alexander.* Cambridge: Cambridge University Press, 2009.

Root, Margaret Cool. *The King and Kingship in Achaemenid Art: Essays on the Creation of an Iconography of Empire.* Leiden: Brill, 1979.

Rop, Jeffrey. *Greek Military Service in the Ancient Near East, 401–330 BCE.* Cambridge: Cambridge University Press, 2019.

Rosen, Klaus. "Der 'göttliche' Alexander, Athen und Samos." *Historia* 27, no. 1 (1978): 20–25.

Rostovtzeff, Mikhail. *Social and Economic History of the Hellenistic World*. Vol. 1. Oxford: Oxford University Press, 1941.

Rotstein, Andrea. *Literary History in the Parian Marble*. Washington, DC: Center for Hellenic Studies, 2016. http://nrs.harvard.edu/urn-3:hul.ebook:CHS_RotsteinA.Literary_History_in_the_Parian_Marble.2016

Roy, James. "The Son of Pharnabazos and Parapita, a Persian Competing in the Olympic Games: Xenophon *Hellenica* 4.1.39–40." *C&M* 68 (2020): 119–34.

Rubinstein, Lene. "Ionia." In *An Inventory of Archaic and Classical Poleis*, edited by Mogens Herman Hansen and Thomas Heine Nielsen, 1053–107. Oxford: Oxford University Press, 2004.

Ruppe, Uli. "Neue Forschungen an der Stadtmauer von Priene—Erste Ergebnisse." *MDAI(I)* 57 (2007): 271–322.

Rutishauser, Brian. *Athens and the Cyclades: Economic Strategies, 510–314 BC*. Oxford: Oxford University Press, 2012.

Ruzicka, Stephen. "Clazomenae and Persian Foreign Policy, 387/6 B.C." *Phoenix* 37, no. 2 (1983): 104–8.

Ruzicka, Stephen. "Cyrus and Tissaphernes, 407–401 B.C." *CJ* 80, no. 3 (1985): 204–11.

Ruzicka, Stephen. "The Eastern Greek World." In *The Greek World in the Fourth Century*, edited by L. A. Tritle, 107–36. New York: Routledge, 1997.

Ruzicka, Stephen. "Epaminondas and the Genesis of the Social War." *CPh* 93, no. 1 (1998): 60–69.

Ruzicka, Stephen. "Glos, Son of Tamos, and the End of the Cypriot War." *Historia* 48, no. 1 (1999): 23–43.

Ruzicka, Stephen. "The 'Pixodarus Affair' Reconsidered Again." In *Philip II and Alexander the Great: Father and Son, Lives and Afterlives*, edited by Elizabeth Carney and Daniel Ogden, 3–11. Oxford: Oxford University Press, 2010.

Ruzicka, Stephen. *Politics of a Persian Dynasty: The Hecatomnids in the Fourth Century*. Norman: University of Oklahoma Press, 1992.

Ruzicka, Stephen. "War in the Aegean, 333–331 B.C.: A Reconsideration." *Phoenix* 42, no. 2 (1988): 131–51.

Ryder, T. T. B. *Koine Eirene: General Peace and Local Independence in Ancient Greece*. Oxford: Oxford University Press, 1965.

Ryder, T. T. B. "Spartan Relations with Persia after the King's Peace: A Strange Story in Diodorus 15.9." *CQ²* 13, no. 1 (1963): 105–9.

Şahin, Nuran and Pierre Debord. "Découvertes récentes et installation du culte d'Apollon pythien à Claros." *Pallas* 87 (2011): 169–204.

Salmon, John. "Temples the Measures of Men: Public Building in the Greek Economy." In *Economies beyond Agriculture in the Classical World*, edited by David J. Mattingly and John Salmon, 195–208. New York: Routledge, 2001.

Samons, Loren J., II. "Athenian Finance and the Treasury of Athena." *Historia* 42, no. 2 (1993): 129–38.

Samons, Loren J., II *Empire of the Owl: Athenian Imperial Finance*. Stuttgart: Franz Steiner, 2000.

Samons, Loren J., II "Periklean Imperialism and Imperial Finance in Context." In *Hegemonic Finances: Funding Athenian Domination in the 5th and 4th Centuries BC*, edited by Thomas J. Figueira and Sean R. Jensen, 1–23. London: Bloomsbury, 2019.

Sansone, David. "The Date of Herodotus' Publication." *Illinois Classical Studies* 10, no. 1 (1985): 1–9.

Sarikakis, T. C. "Commercial Relations between Chios and Other Greek cities in Antiquity." In *Chios: A Conference at the Homereion in Chios*, edited by John Boardman and C. E. Vaphopoulou-Richardson, 121–32. Oxford: Oxford University Press, 1986.

Sato, Noburo. "Athens, Persia, Clazomenae, Erythrae: An Analysis of International Relationships in Asia Minor at the Beginning of the Fourth Century BCE." *BICS* 49 (2006): 23–37.

Savalli-Lestrade, Ivana. *Les philoi dans l'Asie hellénistique*. Paris: Librairie Droz, 1998.

Scheidel, Walter. "The Greek Demographic Expansion: Models and Comparisons." *JHS* 123 (2003): 120–40.

Schütrumpf, Eckart. *Heraclides of Pontus: Texts and Translations*. New Brunswick, NJ: Rutgers University Press, 2008.

Schweigert, Eugene. "The Athenian Cleruchy on Samos." *AJPh* 61, no. 2 (1940): 194–98.

Scott, Michael. *Delphi: A History of the Center of the Ancient World*. Princeton, NJ: Princeton University Press, 2014.

Seager, Robin. "The Corinthian War." In *Cambridge Ancient History*², vol. 6, edited by David M. Lewis, John Boardman, Simon Hornblower, and Martin Ostwald, 97–119. Cambridge: Cambridge University Press, 1994.

Seager, Robin. "The Freedom of the Greeks of Asia: From Alexander to Antiochus." *CQ*² 31, no. 1 (1981): 106–12.

Seager, Robin. "Thrasybulus, Conon and Athenian Imperialism, 396–386 B.C." *JHS* 87 (1967): 95–115.

Seager, Robin and Christopher Tuplin. "The Freedom of the Greeks of Asia: On the Origins of a Concept and the Creation of a Slogan." *JHS* 100 (1980): 141–54.

Sealey, Raphael. "Athens after the Social War." *JHS* 75 (1955): 74–81.

Sealey, Raphael. *Demosthenes and His Time: A Study in Defeat*. Oxford: Oxford University Press, 1993.

Sealey, Raphael. "*IG* II² 1609 and the Transformation of the Athenian Sea-League." *Phoenix* 11, no. 3 (1957): 95–111.

Sealey, Raphael. "On Lawful Concubinage in Athens." *CA* 3, no. 1 (1984): 111–33.

Sealey, Raphael. "The Origin of the Delian League." In *Ancient Societies and Institutions*, edited by Ernst Badian, 233–55. New York: Barnes and Noble, 1966.

Sears, Matthew A. "Alexander and Ada Reconsidered." *CPh* 109, no. 3 (2014): 211–21.

Segre, Mario. "La Legge Ateniese sull' unificazione della moneta." *Clara Rhodos* 9, no. 4 (1938): 151–78.

Sekunda, Nicholas V. "Iphicrates the Athenian and the Menestheid Family of Miletus." *ABSA* 89 (1994): 303–6.

Shear, T. Leslie, Jr. *Trophies of Victory: Public Building in Periklean Athens*. Princeton, NJ: Princeton University Press, 2016.

Sherk, Robert K. "The Eponymous Officials of Greek Cities: Mainland Greece and the Adjacent Islands." *ZPE* 84 (1990): 231–95.

Sherk, Robert K. "The Eponymous Officials of Greek Cities IV: The Register: Part III: Thrace, Black Sea Area, Asia Minor (Continued)." *ZPE* 93 (1992): 223–72.

Sherwin-White, S. M. "Ancient Archives: The Edict of Alexander to Priene, a Reappraisal." *JHS* 105 (1985): 69–89.

Shipley, Graham. *A History of Samos, 800–188 BC.* Oxford: Oxford University Press, 1987.

Shrimpton, Gordon S. "Horton Hears an Ionian." In *Epigraphy and the Greek Historian*, edited by Craig Cooper, 129–49. Toronto: University of Toronto Press, 2008.

Shrimpton, Gordon S. "Persian Strategy against Egypt and the Date for the Battle of Citium." *Phoenix* 45, no. 1 (1991): 1–20.

Shrimpton, Gordon S. *Theopompus the Historian.* Montreal: McGill University Press, 1991.

Simonton, Matthew. *Classical Greek Oligarchy: A Political History.* Princeton, NJ: Princeton University Press, 2017.

Simonton, Matthew. "The Local History of Hippias of Erythrai: Politics, Place, Memory, and Monumentality." *Hesperia* 87, no. 3 (2018): 497–54.

Simpson, R. H. "Antigonus the One-Eyed and the Greeks." *Historia* 8, no. 4 (1959): 385–409.

Simpson, R. H. "The Historical Circumstances of the Peace of 311." *JHS* 74 (1954): 25–31.

Slawisch, Anja. "Epigraphy versus Archaeology: Conflicting Evidence for Cult Continuity in Ionia during the Fifth Century BC." In *Sacred Landscapes in Anatolia and Neighboring Regions*, edited by Charles Gates, Jacques Morin, and Thomas Zimmermann, 29–34. Oxford: Archaeopress, 2009.

Slawisch, Anja and Toby Christopher Wilkinson. "Processions, Propaganda, and Pixels: Reconstructing the Sacred Way between Miletos and Didyma." *AJA* 122, no. 1 (2018): 101–43.

Snodgrass, Anthony M. "Interaction by Design: The Greek City-State." In *Peer Polity Interaction and Socio-political Change*, edited by Colin Renfrew and John F. Cherry, 47–58. Cambridge: Cambridge University Press, 1986.

Sokolowski, Franciszek. "A New Testimony on the Cult of Artemis of Ephesus." *HThR* 58, no. 4 (1965): 427–31.

Sokolowski, Franciszek. "Fees and Taxes in the Greek Cults." *HThR* 47, no. 3 (1954): 153–64.

Sokolowski, Franciszek. *Lois sacrées des cités grecques.* Paris: De Boccard, 1969.

Sosin, Joshua D. "Endowments and Taxation in the Hellenistic Period." *Anc. Soc.* 44 (2014): 43–89.

Spalinger, Anthony J. "The Date of the Death of Gyges and Its Historical Implications." *JAOS* 98, no. 4 (1978): 400–409.

Spawforth, A. J. and Susan Walker. "The World of the Panhellenion. I. Athens and Eleusis." *JRS* 75 (1985): 78–104.

Stadter, Philip S. *A Commentary on Plutarch's Pericles.* Chapel Hill: University of North Carolina Press, 1989.

Stanley, Phillip V. "The Family Connection of Alcibiades and Axiochus." *GRBS* 27, no. 2 (1986): 173–81.

Stewart, Andrew. *Attika: Studies in Athenian Sculpture of the Hellenistic Age*. London: Society for the Promotion of Hellenic Studies, 1979.

Stock, Friederike, Michael Kerschner, John C. Kraft, Anna Pint, Peter Frenzel, and Helmut Brückner. "The Palaeogeographies of Ephesos (Turkey), Its Harbours, and the Artemision: A Geoarchaeological Reconstruction for the Timespan 1500–300 BC." *Zeitschrift für Geomorphologie* 98, no. 2 (2014): 33–66.

Strang, Jonathan R. "The City of Dionysos: A Social and Historical Study of the Ionian City of Teos." PhD diss., SUNY Buffalo, 2007.

Strauss, Barry S. *The Battle of Salamis: The Naval Encounter That Saved Greece—and Western Civilization*. New York: Simon and Schuster Paperbacks, 2005.

Strauss, Barry S. "Thrasybulus and Conon: A Rivalry in Athens in the 390s B.C." *AJPh* 105, no. 1 (1984): 37–48.

Streets, Heather. *Martial Races: The Military, Race and Masculinity in British Imperial Culture, 1857–1914*. Manchester: Manchester University Press, 2004.

Stylianou, P. J. *Historical Commentary on Diodorus Siculus Book 15*. Oxford: Oxford University Press, 1999.

Stylianou, P. J. "Thucydides, the Panionian Festival, and the Ephesia (III 104), Again." *Historia* 32, no. 2 (1983): 245–49.

Suk Fong Jim, Theodora. *Sharing with the Gods: Aparchai and Dekatai in Ancient Greece*. Oxford: Oxford University Press, 2014.

Tarn, W. W. *Alexander the Great*. 2 vols. Cambridge: Cambridge University Press, 1948.

Tarn, W. W. "The Massacre of the Branchidae." *CR* 36, nos. 3–4 (1922): 63–66.

Tataki, Argyro B. *Macedonians Abroad: A Contribution to the Prosopography of Ancient Macedonia*. Paris: Diffusion de Boccard, 1998.

Tausend, Klaus. *Amphiktyonie und Symmachie: Formen zwischenstaatlicher Beziehungen im archaischen Griechenland*. Stuttgart: Franz Steiner Verlag, 1992.

Teegarden, David A. *Death to Tyrants! Ancient Greek Democracy and the Struggle against Tyranny*. Princeton, NJ: Princeton University Press, 2014.

Thomas, Rosalind. "The Intellectual Milieu of Herodotus." In *The Cambridge Companion to Herodotus*, edited by Carolyn Dewald and John Marincola, 60–75. Cambridge: Cambridge University Press, 2016.

Thomas, Rosalind. *Polis Histories, Collective Memories and the Greek World*. Cambridge: Cambridge University Press, 2019.

Thompson, Wesley E. "The Peace of Callias in the Fourth Century." *Historia* 30, no. 2 (1981): 164–77.

Thonemann, Peter. "Alexander, Priene, and Naulochon." In *Epigraphical Approaches to the Post-Classical Polis*, edited by Paraskevi Martzavou and Nikolaos Papazarkadas, 23–36. Oxford: Oxford University Press, 2013.

Thonemann, Peter. *The Maeander Valley: A Historical Geography*. Cambridge: Cambridge University Press, 2011.

Tober, Daniel. "'Politeiai' and Spartan Local History." *Historia* 59, no. 4 (2010): 412–20.

Tracy, Stephen V. "Hands in Samian Inscriptions of the Hellenistic Period." *Chiron* 20 (1990): 59–96.

Treister, Michail J. and Yuri G. Vinogradov. "Archaeology on the Northern Coast of the Black Sea." *AJA* 97, no. 3 (1993): 521–63.

Tronson, Adrian. "The Hellenic League of 480 B.C.—Fact or Ideological Fiction?" *Acta Classica* 34 (1991): 93–110.

Tuchelt, Klaus. "Die Perserzerstörung von Branchidai-Didyma und ihre Folgen-archäologisch bettrachtet." *AA*, no. 3 (1988): 427–38.

Tuplin, Christopher. "The Treaty of Boiotios." In *Achaemenid History II*, edited by Heleen Sancisi-Weerdenburg and Amelie Kuhrt, 138–42. Leiden: Brill, 1984.

Unz, Ron K. "The Chronology of the Pentekontaetia." *CQ*² 36, no. 1 (1986): 69–73.

Vaessen, Rik. "Cultural Dynamics in Ionia at the End of the Second Millennium BCE: New Archaeological Perspectives and Prospects." PhD diss., University of Sheffield, 2014.

van Alfen, Peter G. "The Coinage of Athens, Sixth to First Centuries B.C." In *The Oxford Handbook of Greek and Roman Coinage*, edited by William E. Metcalf, 88–104. Oxford: Oxford University Press, 2012.

Vanderpool, Eugene. "The Ostracism of the Elder Alkibiades." *Hesperia* 21, no. 1 (1952): 1–8.

van Effenterre, Henri and Françoise Ruzé, *Nomima: Recueil d'inscriptions politiques et juridiques de l'archaisme grec*. Vol. 1. Paris: De Boccard, 1994.

van Wees, Hans, ed. *War and Violence in Ancient Greece*. Swansea: Classical Press of Wales, 2000.

Varınlıoğlu, Ender. "Inscriptions from Erythrae." *ZPE* 44 (1981): 45–50.

Vickers, Michael. "Fifth Century Chronology and the Coinage Decree." *JHS* 116 (1996): 171–74.

Vlassopoulos, Kostas. *Greeks and Barbarians*. Cambridge: Cambridge University Press, 2013.

Vlassopoulos, Kostas. *Unthinking the Greek Polis: Ancient Greek History beyond Euro-centrism*. Cambridge: Cambridge University Press, 2007.

Voigtlander, Walter. *Der jüngste Apollotempel von Didyma: Geschichte seine Baudekors*. Tübingen: Wasmuth, 1975.

von Graeve, Volkmar. "Funde aus Milet XVIII. Fragmente von Bauskulptur aus dem archaischen Aphrodite-Heiligtum." *AA*, no. 2 (2005): 41–48.

von Wilamowitz-Moellendorff, Ulrich. *Panionion*. Berlin: Reichsdruckerei, 1906.

Wade-Gery, H. T. *Essays in Greek History*. Oxford: Oxford University Press, 1958.

Wallace, Robert W. "Redating Croesus: Herodotean Chronologies, and the Dates of the Earliest Coinages." *JHS* 136 (2016): 168–81.

Wallinga, H. T. "The Ancient Persian Navy and Its Predecessors." In *Achaemenid History*, vol. 1, *Sources, Structures, and Synthesis*, edited by Heleen Sancisi-Weerdenburg, 47–77. Leiden: Nederlands Instituut voor het Nabije Oosten, 1987.

Wallinga, H. T. "The Ionian Revolt." *Mnemosyne*⁴ 37, nos. 3–4 (1984): 401–37.

Wallinga, H. T. *Xerxes' Greek Adventure: The Naval Perspective*. Leiden: Brill, 2005.

Walser, Andreas Victor. *Bauern und Zinsnehmer: Politik, Recht und Wirthschaft im früh-hellenistischen Ephesos*. Munich: C.H. Beck, 2008.

Waterfield, Robin. *Dividing the Spoils: The War for Alexander the Great's Empire*. Oxford: Oxford University Press, 2011.

Waters, Matt. *Ancient Persia: A Concise History*. Cambridge: Cambridge University Press, 2013.

Waters, Matt. "Applied Royal Directive: Pissouthnes and Samos." In *The Achaemenid Court*, edited by Bruno Jacobs and Robert Rollinger, 817–28. Wiesbaden: Harrassowitz, 2010.

Weber, Ulf. "Der Altar des Apollon von Didyma." *MDAI(I)* 65 (2015): 5–61.

Webster, T. B. L. "Sophocles and Ion of Chios." *Hermes* 71, no. 3 (1936): 263–74.

Wehrli, Claude. *Antigone et Démétrios*. Geneva: Librairie Droz, 1968.

Weigand, Theodor and Hans Schrader. *Priene: Ergebnisse der Ausgrabungen und Untersuchungen von den Jahren 1895–1898*. Berlin: Reimer, 1904.

Weiskopf, Michael. *The So-Called "Great Satraps' Revolt," 366–360 BC: Concerning Local Instability in the Achaemenid Far West*. Wiesbaden: Franz Steiner, 1989.

Welles, C. Bradford. *Royal Correspondence in the Hellenistic Period*. New Haven, CT: Yale University Press, 1934.

Welsh, M. K. "Honorary Statues in Ancient Greece." *ABSA* 11 (1904–5): 32–49.

Wesenberg, Burkhardt. "Agesilaos im Artemision." *ZPE* 41 (1981): 175–80.

West, M. L. "The Invention of Homer." *CQ²* 49, no. 2 (1999): 364–82.

West, M. L. "Phocylides." *JHS* 98 (1978): 164–67.

Westlake, H. D. "Ionians in the Ionian War." *CQ²* 29, no. 1 (1979): 9–44.

Westlake, H. D. "Spartan Intervention in Asia, 400–397 B.C." *Historia* 35, no. 4 (1986): 405–26.

Westlake, H. D. "Thucydides and the Athenian Disaster in Egypt." *CPh* 45, no. 4 (1950): 209–16.

Westlake, H. D. "Tissaphernes in Thucydides." *CQ²* 35, no. 1 (1985): 43–54.

Wheatley, Pat. "The Chronology of the Third Diadoch War, 315–311 B.C." *Phoenix* 52, nos. 3–4 (1998): 257–81.

Whitehead, David. "Ο ΝΕΟΣ ΔΑΣΜΟΣ: 'Tribute' in Classical Athens." *Hermes* 126, no. 2 (1998): 173–88.

Wickersham, John M. "Spartan Garrisons in Boeotia 382–379/8 B.C." *Historia* 56, no. 2 (2007): 243–46.

Wider, Kathleen. "Women Philosophers in the Ancient Greek World: Donning the Mantle." *Hypatia* 1, no. 1 (1986): 21–62.

Widmer, Marie. "Apamè: Une reine au coer de la construction d'un royaume." In *Femmes influents dans le monde hellénistique et á Rome*, edited by Anne Bielman Sánchez, Isabelle Cogitore, and Anne Kolb, 17–33. Grenoble: UGA Éditions, 2016.

Wilken, Ulrich. *Alexander the Great*. New York: Norton, 1967.

Wilker, Julia. "War and Peace at the Beginning of the Fourth Century: The Emergence of the *Koine Eirene*." In *Maintaining Peace and Interstate Stability in Archaic and Classical Greece*, edited by Julia Wilker, 91–117. Mainz: Verlag Antike, 2012.

Willetts, R. F. "The Neodamodeis." *CPh* 49, no. 1 (1954): 27–32.

Wilson, Emily Sarah. "What's in a Name? Trade, Sanctuaries, Diversity, and Identity in Archaic Ionia." PhD diss., University of Chicago, 2018.

Woodhead, A. G. "Chabrias, Timotheus, and the Aegean Allies, 375–373 B.C." *Phoenix* 16, no. 4 (1962): 258–66.

Woodhead, A. G. "IG II² 43 and Jason of Pherae." *AJA* 61, no. 4 (1957): 367–73.

Worthington, Ian. *By the Spear: Philip II, Alexander the Great, and the Rise and Fall of the Macedonian Empire*. Oxford: Oxford University Press, 2014.

Worthington, Ian. *Demosthenes of Athens and the Fall of Classical Greece.* Oxford: Oxford University Press, 2013.

Worthington, Ian. *A Historical Commentary on Dinarchus: Rhetoric and Conspiracy in Later Fourth-Century Athens.* Ann Arbor: University of Michigan Press, 1992.

Worthington, Ian. *Philip II of Macedonia.* New Haven, CT: Yale University Press, 2008.

Worthington, Ian. *Ptolemy I: King and Pharaoh of Egypt.* Oxford: Oxford University Press, 2016.

Wylie, Graham. "Lysander and the Devil." *AC* 66 (1997): 75–88.

Yates, David. "The Tradition of the Hellenic League against Xerxes." *Historia* 64, no. 1 (2015): 1–25.

Zarghamee, Reza. *Discovering Cyrus: The Persian Conqueror Astride the Ancient World.* Washington, DC: Mage Publishers, 2013.

Zelnick-Abramovitz, R. "Settlers and Dispossessed in the Athenian Empire." *Mnemosyne* 57, no. 3 (2004): 325–45.

Zhou, Vivien Xiaowei and Nick Pilcher. "Revisiting the 'Third Space' in Language and Intercultural Studies." *Language and Intercultural Communication* 19, no. 1 (2019): 1–8.

Zolotarev, Miron I. "A Hellenistic Ceramic Deposit from the North-eastern Sector of the Chersonesos." In *Chronologies of the Black Sea Area, C. 400–100 BC*, edited by Lise Hannestad and Vladimir F. Stolba, 193–216. Aarhus: Aarhus University Press, 2006.

Index

Abdera, 38–39, 39n71

Abydus, 93, 132, 160

Ada, 123, 125, 128, 134, 145n54, 150n73

aesymnetes, 36, 39, 39n72. *See also* Miletus: *aesymnetes* list

Aeolis, 9, 26, 31, 58, 77n30, 92, 93, 95, 132, 153n82, 204

Achaemenid Empire. *See* Persia

Agesilaus, 95–97, 98n31, 102n47, 111n7, 112, 197, 216, 227

Aegospotamoi, battle of, 82, 83

Alcibiades, 49, 69–71, 72–73, 81

Alcidas, 57–60, 61

Alexander III (the Great), 102, 109, 124, 131, 133, 135, 136–142, 144, 145, 146–157, 158–159, 166, 169, 176, 197–200, 202, 205, 208, 216; propaganda, 138

Alyattes, 9n37, 10, 193

Antalcidas, 103n56, 106

Antigonus Monophthalmus, 141, 163–171, 175, 176–178, 179

Antiochus I, 192, 203, 218

Antiochus III: *Megas*, 1–2, 209

aparche, 43, 46, 46n19, 192

arbitration, 16, 36, 49–50, 99n34, 105–106, 151, 154, 179–180, 215

Arginousae, battle of, 80n42, 82

Argos or Argives, 34, 65, 70n10

Ariabignes, 19

Ariobarzanes, 116, 119

Aristagoras of Miletus, 13–14, 15

Aristides, 27, 28, 42

Arsinoeia. *See* Ephesus: refoundation as Arsinoeia

Artaphernes, 14, 16–17, 105

Artaxerxes I, 32, 42, 47

Artaxerxes II, 87–89, 106–107, 112, 119

Artaxerxes III, 119, 129, 226

Artemisia of Caria, 22, 23

Artemisium at Ephesus. *See* Ephesus: Sanctuary of Artemis

Artemisium, battle of, 19–20, 25

Asclepium at Epidaurus, 189–191

Aspasia, 49–50

Assesos, 10

Astyochus, 75–76

Atareneus, 80, 93, 129

Athenian Tribute Lists, 34, 43–44, 61–63, 207

Athens or Athenians, 2, 3, 6, 14, 18, 20, 21–22, 25, 26, 28, 29, 30–32, 33, 40, 41, 42–55, 56–57, 62, 64, 65, 67, 68–69, 70–72, 74–75, 77–78, 79, 80, 81–83, 88, 91, 97, 99–104, 105, 107–108, 110–115, 117, 122, 126–128, 132, 152, 155–157, 158–163, 184, 190, 206–207, 210; occupation of Samos, 115–119, 159–163; propaganda, 21, 30, 104. *See also* Delian League and Second Athenian Naval Confederacy

autonomia, 1–2, 9, 37, 40, 42n6, 87, 90n2, 94, 95, 95n17, 99n35, 104, 106, 107, 107n73, 108, 109, 110, 141, 149, 169–171, 188, 205, 207, 208–210, 226. *See also eleutheria*

Bias of Priene, 9, 10, 26, 213

Black Sea, 8, 54, 69, 103

265

liberation, 24–25, 29, 31, 68–69, 88, 101,
    132n5, 135, 138, 140, 172, 200, 204,
    213. *See also autonomia; eleutheria*
Lichas, 73–74, 79
luxury, 151, 192, 226–227
Lydia or Lydians, 4, 9–11, 34, 60–61, 85,
    167, 184, 193, 194, 196, 207, 224
Lysander, 78–87, 91, 95, 98, 134, 224
Lysandreia, 83, 86
Lysimachus, 167–168, 171, 173–175, 176,
    178–179, 205–206, 217, 222–223

Macedonia or Macedonians, 2, 108, 130,
    132–136, 139–140, 142–146, 149,
    150–155, 156–157, 158–159, 164–
    165, 167, 172, 177
Maeander River, 4, 92, 105, 123
Magnesia on the Maeander, 92, 138, 160,
    173, 223
Mardonius, 17, 19n2, 24n15, 39
Mausolus, 76–77, 116, 119, 120–122,
    124–125, 126, 127–128, 135, 182, 216
medism, 39n72, 60
Megabyxos, 60, 78n34, 195, 195n60, 222
Megara, 68
Melie, 6, 211–212, 219
Melissus of Samos, 51
Melos, 65
Memnon of Rhodes, 132–133, 135, 136,
    143–144, 145–146
mercenaries, 8, 11n42, 48, 50, 52, 57–58,
    70, 76, 91n4, 98n31, 120, 140, 146,
    163n24, 165n30, 171, 203, 203n85
Mermnad Dynasty, 9–11. *See also* Aly-
    attes and Croesus
Miletus, 4, 6, 8, 9, 10, 11, 13–14, 24, 27,
    28, 32, 33, 34–38, 39, 40, 44–46, 47,
    48–53, 57, 62–63, 65–66, 70, 72, 73,
    76–77, 78–79, 80, 82, 84–86, 87–88,
    90, 92, 94, 105, 107, 109, 122–123, 128,
    134, 140–142, 143, 144, 146, 147–148,
    160, 161, 167, 168–169, 171, 174, 177,
    181, 185–186, 187–189, 192, 193–195,
    200, 201–205, 207, 209, 213, 214, 215,
    217, 219, 220–221, 225–226, 227; *ae-*

symnetes list, 38, 86n57, 141, 169–170,
    174, 221; Delphinium, 37, 188, 195,
    20; Lade, 70, 140; Leros, 5, 45; Neleids,
    38; sack, 16; reconstruction, 37; Tei-
    choussa, 45, 187, 189. *See also* Didyma
Mimnermus, 9
Molpoi Decree, 37, 182n1, 188
Mount Mimas, 4, 45
Mount Mycale. *See* Mycale Peninsula
Mycale, battle of, 24–26, 27, 39
Mycale Peninsula, 4, 49, 72, 125, 140, 211,
    214, 216, 223
Mytilene, 51, 53, 57–58, 113, 129, 143,
    145, 154, 179
Myus, 4, 6, 28, 34, 92, 105, 109, 178, 215

nationalism, 15, 15n61
Naucratis, 8, 32–33
Naxos, 13, 14, 30, 34
Nicias, 65
Nile River, 33
Notium, 5n17, 7, 56–57, 83, 204

oligarchy, 38, 48, 48n21, 72, 83, 84–86,
    98, 135, 116n27
Olympia, 83
oracles, 8n30, 147–148, 168–169, 174,
    187–188, 190, 193, 200, 201–203, 207.
    See also Claros; Didyma
Orontobates, 131, 144

Paches, 57–58
Panhellenism, 2, 117, 138–139, 148, 159,
    190
Panionion, 6–7, 15, 105, 125, 161, 177,
    185, 207, 211–218, 219
Paros, 13, 36
Pausanias of Sparta, 26–27
Peace of Antalcidas. *See* King's Peace
Peace of Callias, 41n41
Pedaritus, 76, 76n24
Pedon of Priene, 8
pedieis, 36, 149, 222–223
Peloponnese or Peloponnesian, 6, 34, 58,
    91, 109